International Perspectives on Value Creation and Sustainability Through Social Entrepreneurship

Hesham Magd
Modern College of Business and Science, Oman

Dharmendra Singh
Modern College of Business and Science, Oman

Raihan Taqui Syed
University of Bradford, UK & Modern College of Business and Science, Oman

David Spicer
University of Bradford, UK

IGI Global
PUBLISHER of TIMELY KNOWLEDGE

A volume in the Advances in Logistics, Operations, and Management Science (ALOMS) Book Series

Published in the United States of America by
IGI Global
Business Science Reference (an imprint of IGI Global)
701 E. Chocolate Avenue
Hershey PA, USA 17033
Tel: 717-533-8845
Fax: 717-533-8661
E-mail: cust@igi-global.com
Web site: http://www.igi-global.com

Library of Congress Cataloging-in-Publication Data

Names: Magd, Hesham, 1971- editor.
Title: International perspectives on value creation and sustainability through social entrepreneurship / Hesham Magd, Dharmendra Singh, Syed Raihan Taqui, and David Spicer, editors.
Description: Hershey, PA : Business Science Reference, [2022] | Includes bibliographical references and index. | Summary: "This book explores various issues and ideas about social entrepreneurship through the lens of theoretical, practical, and empirical research, providing an international outlook of social entrepreneurship, focusing primarily on value creation and sustainability"-- Provided by publisher.
Identifiers: LCCN 2022012090 (print) | LCCN 2022012091 (ebook) | ISBN 9781668446669 (hardcover) | ISBN 9781668446676 (paperback) | ISBN 9781668446683 (ebook)
Subjects: LCSH: Social entrepreneurship. | Value. | Sustainable development.
Classification: LCC HD60 .I6645 2022 (print) | LCC HD60 (ebook) | DDC 361.765--dc23/eng/20220318
LC record available at https://lccn.loc.gov/2022012090
LC ebook record available at https://lccn.loc.gov/2022012091

This book is published in the IGI Global book series Advances in Logistics, Operations, and Management Science (ALOMS) (ISSN: 2327-350X; eISSN: 2327-3518)

British Cataloguing in Publication Data
A Cataloguing in Publication record for this book is available from the British Library.

Advances in Logistics, Operations, and Management Science (ALOMS) Book Series

John Wang
Montclair State University, USA

ISSN:2327-350X
EISSN:2327-3518

MISSION

Operations research and management science continue to influence business processes, administration, and management information systems, particularly in covering the application methods for decision-making processes. New case studies and applications on management science, operations management, social sciences, and other behavioral sciences have been incorporated into business and organizations real-world objectives.

The **Advances in Logistics, Operations, and Management Science** (ALOMS) Book Series provides a collection of reference publications on the current trends, applications, theories, and practices in the management science field. Providing relevant and current research, this series and its individual publications would be useful for academics, researchers, scholars, and practitioners interested in improving decision making models and business functions.

COVERAGE

- Operations Management
- Decision analysis and decision support
- Information Management
- Computing and information technologies
- Networks
- Risk Management
- Marketing engineering
- Organizational Behavior
- Production Management
- Political Science

IGI Global is currently accepting manuscripts for publication within this series. To submit a proposal for a volume in this series, please contact our Acquisition Editors at Acquisitions@igi-global.com or visit: http://www.igi-global.com/publish/.

The Advances in Logistics, Operations, and Management Science (ALOMS) Book Series (ISSN 2327-350X) is published by IGI Global, 701 E. Chocolate Avenue, Hershey, PA 17033-1240, USA, www.igi-global.com. This series is composed of titles available for purchase individually; each title is edited to be contextually exclusive from any other title within the series. For pricing and ordering information please visit http://www.igi-global.com/book-series/advances-logistics-operations-management-science/37170. Postmaster: Send all address changes to above address.

Titles in this Series

For a list of additional titles in this series, please visit: http://www.igi-global.com/book-series/

Considerations and Characteristics of the Millennial Leader in Today's Global Society
Tymon M. Graham (TMGraham Consulting, LLC, USA)
Business Science Reference • © 2023 • 300pp • H/C (ISBN: 9781668447116) • US $240.00

Moving From R&D Development to Production and Sales in Start-Up Companies Emerging Research and Opportunities
Amiram Porath (APC, Israel)
Business Science Reference • © 2022 • 300pp • H/C (ISBN: 9781799856856) • US $215.00

Advancing Interpersonal Emotion Regulation and Social Regulation
Donta S. Harper (Argosy University, USA)
Information Science Reference • © 2022 • 384pp • H/C (ISBN: 9781668424780) • US $215.00

Handbook of Research on Activating Middle Executives' Agency to Lead and Manage During Times of Crisis
Ann-Marie Wilmot (The University of the West Indies, Mona, Jamaica) and Canute Sylvester Thompson (The University of the West Indies, Mona, Jamaica)
Business Science Reference • © 2022 • 415pp • H/C (ISBN: 9781668443316) • US $325.00

Business Models to Promote Technology, Culture, and Leadership in Post-COVID-19 Organizations
Joseph Robert Heinzman (Western Governors University, USA) Debbie S. Judge (Western Governors University, USA) Vincent Franklin (Western Governors University, USA) and Jim A. McCleskey (Western Governors University, USA & Houston Community College System, USA)
Business Science Reference • © 2022 • 300pp • H/C (ISBN: 9781668443583) • US $250.00

Global Risk and Contingency Management Research in Times of Crisis
Narasimha Rao Vajjhala (University of New York Tirana, Tirana, Albania) and Kenneth David Strang (W3-Research, USA & RMIT University, Australia)
Business Science Reference • © 2022 • 356pp • H/C (ISBN: 9781668452790) • US $270.00

IGI Global
PUBLISHER of TIMELY KNOWLEDGE

701 East Chocolate Avenue, Hershey, PA 17033, USA
Tel: 717-533-8845 x100 • Fax: 717-533-8661
E-Mail: cust@igi-global.com • www.igi-global.com

This book is a treasure of accumulated knowledge, experiences, and research work across various countries to represent social entrepreneurship. This book is dedicated first and foremost to all individuals who are passionate and committed to social entrepreneurship, sustainable development, and social values. We are blessed with having wonderful families that we treasure the most, and therefore we also would like to dedicate this book to our beloved families for their forbearance, patience and unwavering support and understanding.

Table of Contents

Detailed Table of Contents

This chapter presents an in-depth examination and analysis of published literature indexed in Scopus database on social entrepreneurship, sustainability, and value creation. A descriptive bibliometric analysis coupled with content analysis is presented incorporating citations included in Scopus' multi-disciplinary database over the last 20 years. Two software packages, VOS Viewer and Bibliometrix R, were employed to probe the research questions and create visualizations of the bibliometric networks. The interconnected and multifaceted nature of the research field is demonstrated, thematic evolution is illustrated, and emerging clusters are identified. Findings suggest that the research on social entrepreneurship, sustainability, and value creation has been pioneered by USA followed by India and other countries. Also, further steps need to be undertaken to encourage and enable cross-border international collaboration to draw learning together from different national and regional contexts.

The purpose of this chapter is to analyze the effect of private wealth on the motivation of becoming a social entrepreneur. The authors refer to Maslow's hierarchy and several culture theories to explain core motivations by social entrepreneurs to shed light on the research topic. The applied econometric approach is regression model based on 1,119 observations from the publicly available data set with a U-shape relationship as the main result for the interplay between the amount of private wealth and the probability of becoming a social entrepreneur. Thus, this chapter shows that starting a social venture is a core belief for some social entrepreneurs, which gives their social endeavors a more important role in their life than accumulating or securing any kind of private wealth. The other group of social entrepreneurs, however, needs to first accumulate a certain level of private wealth until they create a social added value for society.

Bhanupriya Khatri, University School of Business, Chandigarh University, India
Shaina Arora, UITHM, Chandigarh University, India
Hesham Magd, Modern College of Business and Science, Oman
Shad Ahmad K. Khan, University of Buraimi, Oman

Social entrepreneurship is a new subject that is gathering researchers' thoughts because of the social data of this kind of business. The chief mark of this chapter is to orchestrate experts in making a theoretical design and to coordinate researchers who are new in cordial business research, so they know which diaries and authors to advise while focusing on this quirk. To do this, this survey uses the Scopus informational index to conclude the investigation districts with the best assessment yield, the countries and lingos responsible for most amicable business research, the journals that disseminate most investigation, the year in which research on agreeable undertaking began, and the most relevant makers with conveyances on well-disposed business.

Hesham Magd, Modern College of Business and Science, Oman
Shad Ahmad Khan, University of Buraimi, Oman

The higher education institutes (HEIs) are playing a key role in imparting entrepreneurship education. Entrepreneurship education is mainly based on experiential education and received a setback due to COVID-19 as all the HEIs in the region were forced to shift to unplanned online teaching. This chapter analyses the situation of COVID-19 from the perspective of economy, entrepreneurship, and HEI roles during the pandemic and post-pandemic scenarios. This chapter proposed an environment model suggesting the need for state intervention in the entrepreneurship education that subsequently influences social entrepreneurship.

In today's business environment, the world faces issues like global warming, climate change, food crisis, poverty, population explosion, etc., and social entrepreneurship is a catalyst to all such problems. Even the governments in various countries try to promote social entrepreneurship. Until the students are oriented towards social entrepreneurship optimally, the dream of having a good presence of social entrepreneurship will remain a distant dream. As the students' demand is correlated to their entrepreneurship intention, this study is proposed to check the same in the business colleges in Oman.

Social entrepreneurship involves groundbreaking and pioneering methodologies to tackle concerns in the domains of education, environment, rational vocation, well-being, and health and human rights and is widely regarded as a building block of the sustainable development of a particular place. Social entrepreneurship is the aptitude an individual has which can transform several economic, environmental, social, and political issues at local and global levels. It is believed that acquaintance of youth to social entrepreneurial practice can impact this change. Social entrepreneurial orientation could be social vision, social attentiveness, innovativeness, and risk-taking. In this chapter, the authors have made an attempt to understand the youth's intention towards the social entrepreneurship. The data is collected from 123 students studying in different institutes and universities, as well as from the individual who are working or have their own startups. The study used partial least squares-based structural equation modelling.

Entrepreneurship is defined as the process of starting or launching a new business with innovative products and services with an intention of not only generating profits but also value to different stakeholders along with its risk. Due to global concerns of climate change and sustainability, consumers have started consuming green products and showing their socially responsible behavior. There is a need to bring change in sustainable production and consumption. This problem can be solved at grass root level by new enterprises that are keen on solving these concerns. So, the transformation of green economy can be entrepreneur-driven by those who have innovative and sustainable ideas which are commercially viable. Hence, the objective of the chapter is to investigate the concept of green entrepreneurship, green innovations in business, and its significance. The chapter also explains the future perspectives and trends of green entrepreneurship paving a way to sustainable development.

This study developed a global sustainable development index (GSDI), economic development index (EDI), social development index (SDI), environmental sustainability index (ESI), science and technological development index (STDI), entrepreneurship ecosystem index (EEI), and green entrepreneurship ecosystem index (GEI) for 34 countries during 2000–2019. Composite Z-score method was used to develop EDI, SDI, ESI, STDI, EEI, and GEI. It also observed the interaction among the estimated indexes using linear regression models.

The environmental problems and employment crises throughout the world have been growing. Economic growth is one of the key parameters for economic policies expected for beneficial effects having good impact on the employment and economic well-being. Changes are required and need to find solutions for the problem instead of creating. These changes affect the environment while facilitating industries/business. To overcome the environmental hazard, green entrepreneurship came to light. The concept of green entrepreneurship came into existence from environmental hazards such as pollution, global warning, depletion of ozone layer, and climatic changes occurring due to disturbance within the ecosystem. This study also aims to analyze the relationship between entrepreneurship, transformation, and green development along with the relation between social, traditional entrepreneurship, and in-between institutions and industries.

The social entrepreneurs consider solving the social problem first rather than minting profits. As the world today is suffering from the problem of rising population, the food demands are destined to rise in the times to come. The shrinking arable land, less availability of fresh water, concentration of population in towns and cities, etc. are becoming a threat to the agriculture sector. Thus, the agriculture sector requires innovative practices that at times comes with cost. Entrepreneurship with an objective of minting profit might escalate the price of the agricultural produce, and being a primary sector, it might further lead to inflation in other sectors as well. To these issues, social entrepreneurship appears to be a potential solution that has been discussed considering literature and reports in this chapter.

The government of India (GoI) launched Swachh Bharat Mission on October 2014 to improve the prevailing sanitation, hygiene, and waste management state in the country. There has been an increased thrust of the authorities in the field of waste collection and management. The main objective of writing this study is to analyze initiatives in India of municipalities or areas with less than 3 Lakhs populations where exemplary solid waste management practices have been deployed through existing government machinery. The study tries to look into the role played by both government and community and smaller municipal corporations which have set an example and benchmarks for larger urban conglomerates to adopt their intervention model/strategy. Also, the chapter tries to bring out the attribute of a decentralized approach in all the cases which has been the basic reason of success in all the projects. Additionally, this study is an attempt to identify and study the best practices across the country to boost the chances of their replication wherever possible.

Preface

Social entrepreneurship is construed as an innovative activity aimed at addressing or mitigating social issues based on self-sufficiency and financial stability. It offers the potential to shift civil society through innovative social ventures that pursue profit and purpose. It is gaining international attention due to the intent of social entrepreneurs to change and to see the world as it can be, not as it is. Social entrepreneurs drive social innovation and transformation in various fields including education, health, the creative arts, the environment, and enterprise development. These changemakers blend lessons from business with the diversity and complexity of social values, and in the process pursue opportunities for change. The 2030 Agenda for Sustainable Development by UNO also advocates that sustainable development is possible with a focus and integration of the three dimensions: *economic, social,* and *environmental*.

The purpose of this edited book is to explore various issues and ideas about social entrepreneurship through the lens of theoretical, practical, and empirical research. The book consists of 12 insightful chapters including concluding remarks. All submissions were accepted based on a double-blind peer review editorial process. The chapters were authored by professionals from across the globe and provide an international outlook of social entrepreneurship - focusing primarily on value creation and sustainability.

Chapter 1 entitled "Social Entrepreneurship, Value Creation, and Sustainability: Systematic Review and Thematic Mapping of the Research" presents an in-depth examination and analysis of published literature, indexed in Scopus database on Social Entrepreneurship, Sustainability, and Value Creation. A descriptive bibliometric analysis coupled with content analysis is presented, incorporating citations included in Scopus' multi-disciplinary database over the last 20 years. Two software packages - VOS viewer and Bibliometrix R were employed to probe the research questions and create visualizations of the bibliometric networks. The interconnected and multifaceted nature of the research field is demonstrated, thematic evolution is illustrated, and emerging clusters are identified. Findings suggest that the research on Social Entrepreneurship, Sustainability, and Value Creation has been pioneered by USA followed by India and other countries. Also, further steps need to be undertaken to encourage and enable cross-border international collaboration, to draw learning together from different national and regional contexts.

Chapter 2 entitled "An Introduction to Social Entrepreneurship and Private Wealth" analyzes the effect of private wealth on the motivation of becoming a social entrepreneur. The authors refer to Maslow's hierarchy and several culture theories to explain core motivations by social entrepreneurs to shed light on the research topic. The applied econometric approach is regression model based on 1,119 observations from the publicly available data set with a U-shape relationship as the main result for the interplay between the amount of private wealth and the probability of becoming a social entrepreneur. Thus, this chapter illustrates that starting a social venture is a core belief for some social entrepreneurs, which gives their social endeavors a more important role in their life than accumulating or securing any kind of private wealth. The other group of social entrepreneurs, however, needs to first accumulate a certain level of private wealth until they create a social added value for society.

Chapter 3 is entitled "Bibliometric Analysis of Social Entrepreneurship." This chapter highlights the nature, expansion, and course of social business research, investigate research hardships, and propose future investigation streets that could furthermore broaden the rich data. The characteristic of social Entrepreneurship has emerged as an ensuing thought of undertaking, as a fundamental issue concerning both improvement and flourishing of social orders. Social Entrepreneurship is a fairly new subject that is gathering researchers' attention and resulting in disintegration of the field due to varied publications in this area. Hence, there is a need to review and consolidate the findings. This study uses the Scopus informational index to conclude the investigation districts with the best assessment yield, the countries, and lingos responsible for most amicable business research, the journals that disseminate most investigation, the year in which research on agreeable undertaking began, and the most relevant makers with conveyances on well-disposed business.

Chapter 4 is entitled "Strategic Framework for Entrepreneurship Education in Promoting Social Entrepreneurship in GCC Countries During and Post COVID-19." This chapter analyses the situation of covid-19 from the perspective of economy, entrepreneurship, and HEIs role during the pandemic and post pandemic scenario. The Gulf Cooperation council (GCC) currently has six rich oil producing nations who are trying to reduce their economic dependency on export of crude oil. One of the areas of development and economic diversification is through entrepreneurship. Entrepreneurship education and training has been considered as a potential tool to promote and nurture entrepreneurship. Social Entrepreneurship emerged as the need of the hour during the pandemic, and the need for promotion of the same was strongly felt. The Higher Education Institutes (HEIs) are playing key role in imparting the entrepreneurship education. entrepreneurship education is mainly based on experiential education received a setback due to covid-19 as all the HEIs in the region were forced to shift to an unplanned online teaching. The chapter proposes an environment model suggesting the need for state intervention in the entrepreneurship education that subsequently influences the social entrepreneurship.

Chapter 5 entitled "Social Entrepreneurship Intentions Among Business Students in Oman" investigates the relationship between social entrepreneurship education, social entrepreneurship self-efficacy and social entrepreneurship intentions. In the arena of Entrepreneurship education, social entrepreneurship focused education is found to be scarce in the academic world. The curriculum structure is designed considering the factors like industry demands, state's vision and the potential market of students willing to pursue that course. In today's business environment, the world faces issues like global warming, climate change, food crisis, poverty, population explosion etc., social entrepreneurship is a catalyst to all such problems. Even of the government in various countries try to promote social entrepreneurship, until the students are oriented towards social entrepreneurship optimally, the dream of having a good presence of social entrepreneurship will remain as a distant dream. The demand of such courses is dependent on the entrepreneurship intention. Thus, this study is proposed to check entrepreneurship intention among the business colleges in Oman. For this purpose, the theories like Theory of planned behavior and theory of reasoned action were investigated and self-efficacy was found to have a major role in the arena of Entrepreneurship Intention with regards to social entrepreneurship. This study highlighted a direct implication on the Higher Education Institutions (HEIs) in Oman and the gulf region who are planning to offer courses on social entrepreneurship or are in the process of reviewing the existing programs on entrepreneurship. This study will also help the government of Oman to device methods to promote social entrepreneurship in the country.

Chapter 6 entitled "Study of Social Entrepreneurship Amongst Youth in Oman" explores youth's intention towards the social entrepreneurship in Oman. Social entrepreneurship involves groundbreaking and pioneering methodologies to tackle concerns in the domains of education, environment, rational vocation, well-being and health and human rights and is widely regarded as a building block of the sustainable development of a particular place. Social entrepreneurship is the aptitude an individual has which can transform several economic, environmental, social and political issues at local and global levels. It is believed that acquaintance of youth to social entrepreneurial practice can impact this change. The entrepreneurial initiatives perform a vital role in developing a country's economic and social wellbeing. Social entrepreneurial orientation could be social vision, social attentiveness, innovativeness, and risk-taking. The data is collected from 123 students studying in different institutes and universities, as well as from the individual who are working, or they have their own startups. The study used partial least squares based structural equation modelling.

Chapter 7 is entitled "Green Entrepreneurship Paving a Way to Sustainable Development: A Bibliometric Review." This chapter demonstrates how scholarly research on Green Entrepreneurship and Innovative practices has progressed in the twenty-first century. There has been a lot of empirical, exploratory, and conceptual work done on green marketing, innovative practices, and sustainable development. However, there have been few attempts to produce a comprehensive scientific mapping of Green Entrepreneurship as a niche topic. As a result, the study's goal is to elicit research trends through knowledge structure synthesis. A Bibliometric Analysis on the topic of green entrepreneurship Practices were undertaken on 146 publications from the Web of Science database for the period 2007-2022. The study was conducted using Biblioshiny. Important journals, countries, authors, and keywords were found using the software's automated workflow, and Thematic Mapping, Citations, and Social Network Analysis were performed. The findings show a relative concentration of more influential work in the said domain amongst a handful of research scholars. Many influential studies have occurred after 2007 and a rally is seen in the studies on green entrepreneurship till 2022. The present research is a Bibliometric analysis that is restricted to science mapping and hence limitations apply to the said studies. Researchers can use Systematic Literature Review (SLR) to build a robust conceptual foundation in the future. It provides future scholars with information on this discipline's issues, contexts, and collaboration opportunities. The current study can give further directions to the researchers for conducting rigorous research on Green Entrepreneurship and sustainable practices and will guide the policymakers to formulate policies in the field of encouraging the start-ups to practice sustainability.

Chapter 8 is entitled "Does Green Entrepreneurship Have an Association with Sustainable Development and Its Components? Evidence From Country-Wise Panel Data Investigation." The study is developed by using data from the global sustainable development index (GSDI), economic development index (EDI), social development index (SDI), environmental sustainability index (ESI), science & technological development index (STDI), entrepreneurship ecosystem index (EEI) and green entrepreneurship ecosystem Index (GEI) for 34 countries during 2000–2019. The composite Z-score method was used to developed EDI, SDI, ESI, STDI, EEI and GEI. It also observed the interaction among the estimated indexes using linear regression models.

Chapter 9 entitled "Green Entrepreneurship and Sustainable Development" investigates the concept of green entrepreneurship, green innovations in business and its significance. Entrepreneurship is defined as process of starting, launching new business with innovative products and services with an intention of not only generating profits but also value to different stakeholders along with its risk. Due to global concerns of climate change and sustainability, consumers have started consuming green products and showing their socially responsible behavior. The authors posit that there is need to bring change in sustainable production and consumption. This problem can be solved at grass root level by new enterprises those are keen is solving these concerns. So, the transformation of green economy can be entrepreneur driven who have innovative and sustainable ideas which are commercially viable. The chapter also explains the future perspectives and trends of Green Entrepreneurship paving a way to sustainable development.

Chapter 10 entitled "Social Entrepreneurship Through Innovations in Agriculture" illustrates the imperative of innovation in agricultural sector. The authors highlight that social entrepreneurs consider solving the social problem first, rather than making profits in a less span of time. As the world today is suffering from the problem of rising population, the food demands are destined to rise in the times to come. The shrinking arable land, less availability of fresh water, concentration of population in towns and cities etc. is becoming a threat to the agriculture sector. Thus, the agriculture sector requires innovative practices, that at times comes with cost. Entrepreneurship with an objective of minting profit might escalate the price of the agricultural produce and being a primary sector, it might further lead to inflation in other sectors as well. Hence, social entrepreneurship appears to be a potential solution that has been discussed in this chapter by reviewing the published literature on these topics.

Chapter 11 entitled "Waste to Wealth Enterprises: A Study on Solid Waste Management Initiatives" analyzes the initiatives in India regarding municipalities / areas where exemplary Solid Waste Management practices have been deployed through existing Government Machinery. Government of India (GoI) launched Swachh Bharat Mission in October 2014 to improve the prevailing sanitation, hygiene and waste management state of affair in the Country. There has been an increased thrust of the authorities in the field of Waste Collection and management. The study tries to investigate the role played by both Government and community and smaller Municipal Corporations which have set an example and benchmarks for larger urban conglomerates to adopt their intervention model/strategy. Also, the chapter tries to bring out the attribute of a decentralized approach in all the cases which has been the basic reason of success in all the projects. Additionally, this study is an attempt to identify and study the best practices across the country to boost the chances of their replication wherever its possible.

Editors' concluding remarks are included at the end, which provide a summary of all the chapters and illuminates on the probable future research directions.

The book aims to improve the understanding on emergence of new models, current trends, benefits, and challenges faced by social entrepreneurs. This book serves as a complete reference resource for both undergraduate and postgraduate students, researchers, academicians, practitioners, and policymakers as it consists of relevant and engaging articles and empirical studies with numerous practical ideas, strategies, and suggestions on emerging markets. We hope that the insightful ideas of this book will receive widespread acceptance in the community.

Hesham Magd
Modern College of Business and Science, Oman

Dharmendra Singh
Modern College of Business and Science, Oman

Raihan Taqui Syed
University of Bradford, UK & Modern College of Business and Science, Oman

David Spicer
University of Bradford, UK

Acknowledgment

We recognize, appreciate, and express sincere gratitude to all authors for the sincere efforts in sharing their valuable thoughts by way of chapters in this edited book. We are thankful to all the reviewers for their constructive feedback which has enhanced the overall quality of this book. Our appreciation and gratitude to the entire team at IGI Global for their assistance, cooperation, and guidance in publishing this book. Lastly, sincere thanks to our respective families for their sacrifices, patience, and support throughout the process. We hope that the insightful ideas of this book will receive widespread acceptance in the community.

Chapter 1
Social Entrepreneurship, Value Creation, and Sustainability:
Systematic Review and Thematic Mapping of the Research

Raihan Taqui Syed
https://orcid.org/0000-0003-2909-7443
University of Bradford, UK & Modern College of Business and Science, Oman

Dharmendra Singh
Modern College of Business and Science, Oman

David Philip Spicer
University of Bradford, UK

ABSTRACT

This chapter presents an in-depth examination and analysis of published literature indexed in Scopus database on social entrepreneurship, sustainability, and value creation. A descriptive bibliometric analysis coupled with content analysis is presented incorporating citations included in Scopus' multi-disciplinary database over the last 20 years. Two software packages, VOS Viewer and Bibliometrix R, were employed to probe the research questions and create visualizations of the bibliometric networks. The interconnected and multifaceted nature of the research field is demonstrated, thematic evolution is illustrated, and emerging clusters are identified. Findings suggest that the research on social entrepreneurship, sustainability, and value creation has been pioneered by USA followed by India and other countries. Also, further steps need to be undertaken to encourage and enable cross-border international collaboration to draw learning together from different national and regional contexts.

DOI: 10.4018/978-1-6684-4666-9.ch001

1. INTRODUCTION

There has been significant growth in academic interest in sustainable development, with researchers trying to approach this through several contexts (Anand *et al.*, 2021). Along this course, a nexus of social entrepreneurship and sustainable development has inevitably been created (Alberti and Varon Garrido, 2017). The nexus indicates that many entrepreneurs strongly recognize themselves as change agents for accomplishing systematic solutions to environmental and social issues (Žalėnienė and Pereira, 2021), whilst not forgoing their own survival and sustainability future (Bansal, Garg and Sharma, 2019). This concept of social entrepreneurship has hence been recognized for its potential to facilitate value creation and economic development (Baima *et al.*, 2020).

Sustainable development through social entrepreneurship has received enormous attention that encompasses economic, environmental, and social concerns (Belz and Binder, 2017), and entrepreneurial knowledge and the innovation capabilities associated with it are instrumental in harnessing opportunities for sustainable development (Belz and Binder, 2017). Social entrepreneurs have, thus, been referred to as 'engines of sustainable development' (Angelidou and Psaltoglou, 2017). There have been a vast number of studies which have determined the goals and boundaries of social entrepreneurship (Monroe-White and Zook, 2018). In addition, the overall understanding of social entrepreneurship, value creation, and sustainability has been improved by integrating previously existing theories (Nasra and Dacin, 2010). However, the various manifestations of social entrepreneurship need to be assessed based on firm theoretical grounds (Choi and Majumdar, 2014). Hence, to ensure that this field does not fragment further and to support an organized generation of further knowledge, it is necessary to understand the structure and extent to which this field has been probed. To address this, an evidence-based roadmap, developed by adopting a bibliometric study method, is pursued, examining current literature and mapping the evolution of this topic is provided here/ This roadmap will facilitate this field's further movement forward. This study, therefore, probes into these research questions:

RQ 1: *How has the publication trend progressed?*
RQ 2: *What structures characterize the literature?*

This study, therefore, seeks to contribute to theory in the following ways. Firstly, systematic insights into the evolution of Social Entrepreneurship, Sustainability, and Value Creation in the last 20 years are illustrated to provide a comprehensive overview of this field. Secondly, the interconnected and multifaceted nature of the research field is demonstrated, and emerging trends and thematic areas are identified, which are used to identify further research directions. Following this introduction, this chapter is structured as follows: Section 2 elucidates the research methodology adopted and the research questions probed. In Section 3, the findings are illustrated and summarized. Section 4 covers this analysis's contributions, limitations, and conclusion.

2. RESEARCH METHODOLOGY

This section explains the process adopted to conduct the bibliometric study of the scientific coverage on Social Entrepreneurship, Sustainability, and Value Creation indexed in the Scopus database. The initial task was to recognize the most appropriate database (Albort-Morant and Ribeiro-Soriano, 2016). We chose the Scopus database for the following reasons: Firstly, the Scopus database possesses greater coverage of journals and articles compared to others – including the Web of Science (Archambault and Campbell, 2013). Secondly, Scopus provides a comprehensive overview of global research output and enables generation of bibliographical interests amongst researchers (Durán-Sánchez *et al.*, 2019)

Figure 1. Research framework of this study

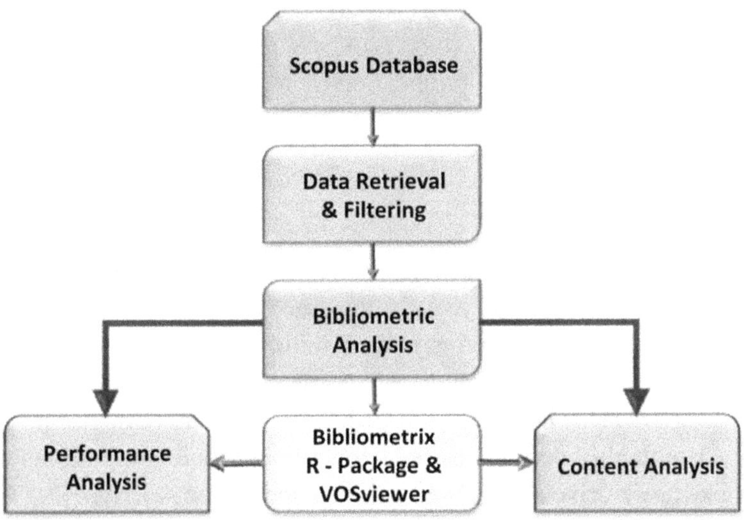

Significantly, and most importantly, no bibliometric work has been carried out on this multi-faceted field, and our study aims to fill this gap. Figure 1 illustrates the research framework of this study. It provides a systematic overview of the work carried out and the thematic structure of this paper: the bibliometric analysis incorporated Performance Analysis and Content Analysis. Two software packages - VOS viewer and Bibliometrix (Aria and Cuccurullo, 2017) were employed to probe the three research questions and create visualizations of the bibliometric networks.

A topic search was conducted in the Scopus database, similar to the works of other authors who have carried out bibliometric analyses. 316 articles published during the last twenty years (2002-2021) were identified through a primary search. The identification process involved the incorporation of targeted topics – "Social Entrepreneurship," "Sustain*" and "Value Creation." During the screening process comprised of a refined search and creation of separate network files for each analysis (keyword co-occurrence and co-citation), 116 articles were filtered out based on type of source and document, language, and relevant fields. Bibliometric analysis was carried out on the remaining 200. Figure 2 illuminates our search strategy and data retrieval process.

3. ANALYSIS AND FINDINGS

3.1 RQ 1: How Has the Publication Trend Progressed?

To probe RQ1, we analyzed the publication trend using total publications by year, country, journal, and authors.

Publication by Year

The number and spread of publications on Social Entrepreneurship, Sustainability, and Value Creation in the last 20 years is illustrated in Figure 3. The beginning of the 2000s witnessed an increased interest in these multiple fields of research. The evident increase in publications in the last decade corresponds to the time during and after the global economic slowdown 2008-10, which has seen practitioners invest more in this field. Also, the last decade has seen governments and corporations worldwide supporting socially driven initiatives (Alberti and Varon Garrido, 2017; Tate and Bals, 2018), aiming to positively impact society, creating value and contributing to a sustainable future. Correspondingly, as evidenced here, there has been an increased interest among researchers to document the progress in this field and probe further into the various other influencing factors.

Figure 2. Search strategy, data retrieval process and statistical summary

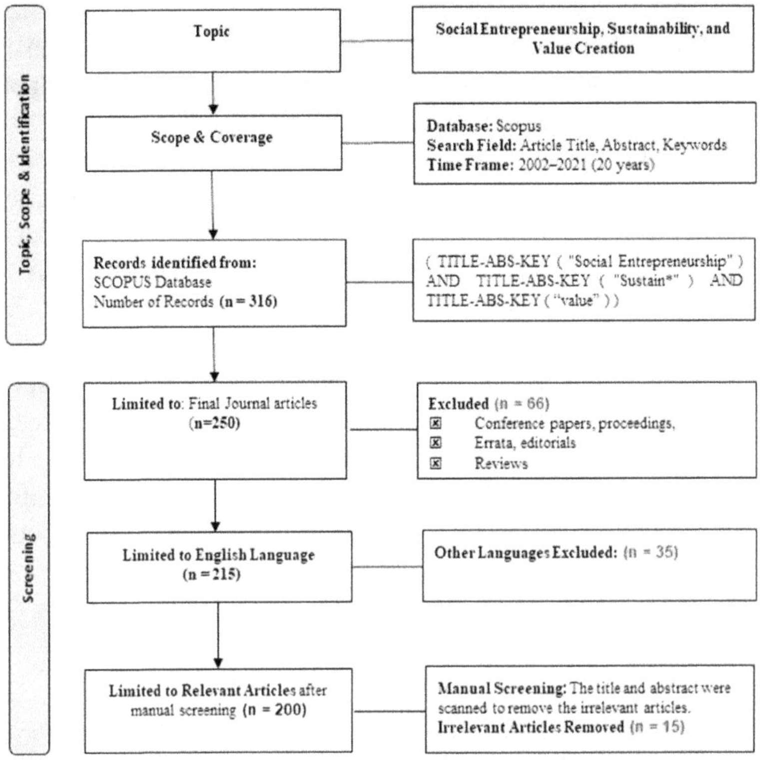

Figure 3. Scopus indexed articles published in the last twenty years, 2002-2021

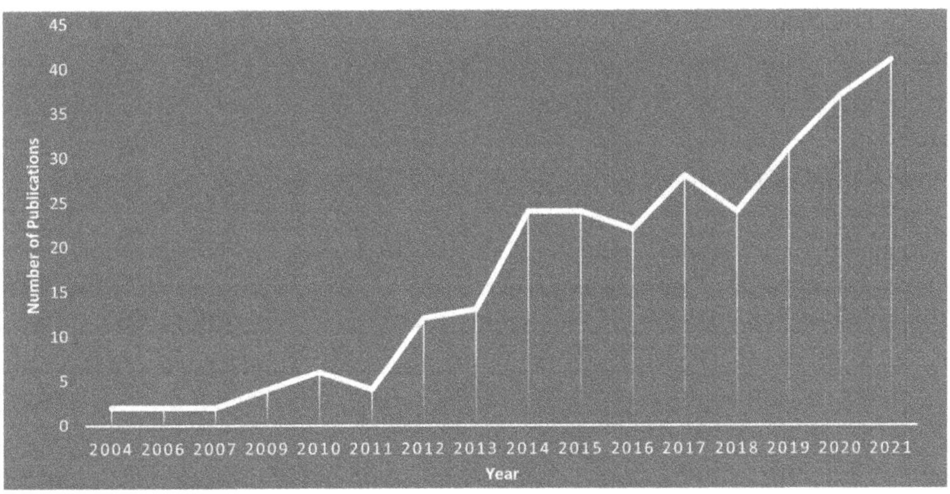

Publication by Country

Social Entrepreneurship, Sustainability, and Value Creation have all drawn substantial attention from academics and researchers, as indicated by the research pursuits of the top 15 countries in Figure 4. The top 5 countries in this list denote the field's geographic reach and impact. The USA pioneered social entrepreneurship to build a sustainable future and create value for society (Tate and Bals, 2018). It is perhaps not surprising that this paved the way for increased research focusing on documenting and proposing empirical frameworks through publications. While the USA dominates the list, other European, Asian, and African countries too have been steadfast in developing and publishing on this topic. India comes second with a substantial contribution to this field. Furthermore, an analysis of total and average citations (Table 1) indicates that the USA leads the group. However, it does not seem true for the rest of the top 4 countries, with fewer citations than it should have been. This indicates that most publications from these countries have not been impactful. France, with the least number of publications (10) on this topic in this list, nonetheless has an impressive citation record, second only to the USA.

Figure 4. Top 15 countries publishing Scopus indexed journal articles

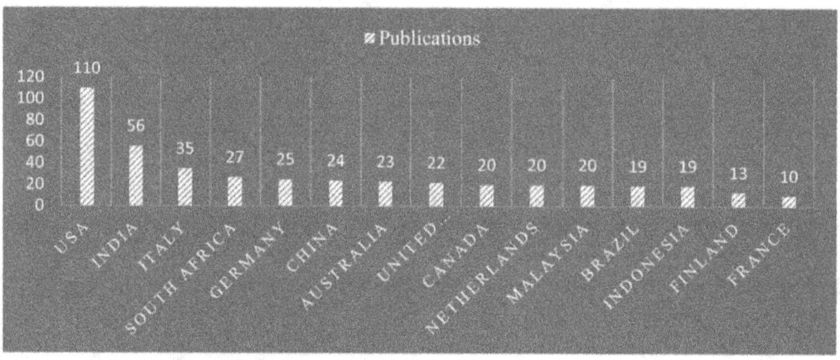

Publication by Author

The quality of researchers' output and its relevance to the academic community is also assessed using other indicators such as the h-index and m-index (Forliano, De Bernardi and Yahiaoui, 2021). These indicators of the top 15 authors are presented in Table 2. The h-index reflects the number of publications and the number of citations per publication (Syed et al., 2022). An author with an h-index of 15 will have 15 papers cited at least 15 times. Furthermore, the authors' country affiliation, the total number of publications (TP), the total number of citations (TC), and the year of their first publication (PY_start) are also shown to provide a comprehensive overview. Mehta leads this table with four publications and 18 citations, followed by Legrand and Sloan with 3 publications and 104 citations. Goyal and Sergi share the third spot with an equal number of publications (3) as that of second-placed authors but lesser citations (77). Regarding the h-index, only Goyal and Sergi have a value of 3, with the rest of the authors in the table having 2 or 1.

Table 1. Top 25 countries based on total citations

Country	Publications	Total Citations
USA	110	775
India	56	98
Italy	35	98
South Africa	27	46
Germany	25	252
China	24	77
Australia	23	332
United Kingdom	22	336
Canada	20	278
Netherlands	20	132
Malaysia	20	321
Brazil	19	48
Indonesia	19	37
Finland	13	36
France	10	656

The m-index of authors was also determined to preclude younger scholars from getting penalized compared to their senior counterparts with longer publication activity timelines. Unlike the h-index, the m-index is limited only to the activity period of the particular author (Forliano, De Bernardi and Yahiaoui, 2021). It is calculated as:

m index = h index / (number of years since first publication)

From this analysis, Ali, who began to publish in 2020, stands out and could already be counted among the influential authors in this field.

Table 2. Top 15 authors ordered by the local number of publications (NP)

Author	NP	h_index	m_index	TC	PY_start
Mehta K	4	2	0.18	18	2012
Legrand W	3	2	0.20	104	2013
Sloan P	3	2	0.20	104	2013
Goyal S	3	3	0.43	77	2016
Sergi BS	3	3	0.43	77	2016
Singh A	3	2	0.29	10	2016
Agrawal A	2	2	0.40	10	2018
Ali M	2	2	0.67	6	2020
Hota PK	2	2	0.40	25	2018
Brennan L	2	2	0.18	25	2012
Ghauri PN	2	2	0.22	62	2014
Carvalho JMS	2	2	0.33	12	2017
Clark C	2	2	0.18	25	2012
Gardetti MA	2	1	0.17	1	2017
Bonnici F	2	1	0.25	1	2019

Publication by Journal

Table 3 demonstrates Top-15 journals to have published articles on Social Entrepreneurship, Sustainability, and Value Creation. The total number of publications (NP), total number of citations (TC), h-index, m-index, and year of their first publication (PY_start) are shown to provide a broad overview.

The foremost journals are *Emerald Emerging Markets Case Studies* and *Sustainability*. These are followed by *Journal of Business Ethics* and *Journal of Enterprising Communities*, with equal number of publications on the topic. Also, few journals in this list are ranked Australian Business Deans Council (ABDC) of B and above and have a Chartered Association of Business Schools (CABS) rating of 2 and above, which suggests that this area has garnered a place among top journals in business, management, and entrepreneurship. On the contrary, many in this list are not included in either of the indexes. This suggests that the multifaceted field still has scope of rigorous, in-depth research to be carried out, which could be publishable in high-ranked journals. Regarding the h-index, Sustainability and Journal of Business Ethics share the highest value, despite lesser publications in this field. *Furthermore*, the m-index value of *Sustainability* is nearly three times that of *Journal of Business Ethics*, due to the shorter time span taken to publish the articles.

Table 3. Top 15 journals with the highest number of publications (NR; Not Ranked)

Source	NP	h Index	m Index	TC	PY Start	CABS	ABDC
Emerald Emerging Markets Case Studies	15	1	0.10	9	2013	1	NR
Sustainability	8	6	1.20	75	2018	NR	NR
Journal of Business Ethics	6	6	0.46	1185	2010	3	A
Journal of Enterprising Communities	6	5	0.42	92	2011	1	C
Academy of Entrepreneurship Journal	5	2	0.18	34	2012	NR	NR
CSR, Sustainability, Ethics and Governance	5	2	0.22	5	2014	NR	NR
Social Enterprise Journal	5	3	0.60	39	2018	1	C
Entrepreneurship: Concepts, Methodologies, Tools, and Applications	4	1	0.17	6	2017	NR	NR
Journal of Social Entrepreneurship	4	4	0.50	70	2015	2	B
Management Decision	4	4	0.50	86	2015	2	B
Emerging Research Directions in Social Entrepreneurship	3	2	0.22	5	2014	NR	NR
Journal of Entrepreneurship and Innovation in Emerging Economies	3	2	0.25	10	2015	NR	NR
Journal of Research in Marketing and Entrepreneurship	3	3	0.21	18	2009	NR	B
Social Responsibility Journal	3	2	0.20	82	2013	1	B
Marketing and Management	2	2	0.5	27	2015	NR	NR

3.2 RQ2: What Structures Characterize the Literature?

3.2.1 Conceptual Structure

This analysis centers around recognizing the most popular themes and understanding the evolution of the research topic. The basis for carrying out co-occurrence and keyword analysis is because of the general observation that the article's content is sufficiently represented by the author's keywords (Comerio and Strozzi, 2019). Keyword co-occurrence indicates when two or more keywords appear together in an article and demonstrate the existence of a relationship between those concepts (Kent Baker *et al.*, 2020). Researchers usually use co-occurrence analysis to distinguish and categorize data (Castriotta *et al.*, 2019). Hence, keyword co-occurrence analyses were conducted. VOSviewer and Biblimetrix R software packages were employed to construct and illustrate bibliometric networks. Figure 5 showcases an overview of the most popular themes around the topic.

Figure 5. Network Visualization of Co-occurrence-Author Keywords

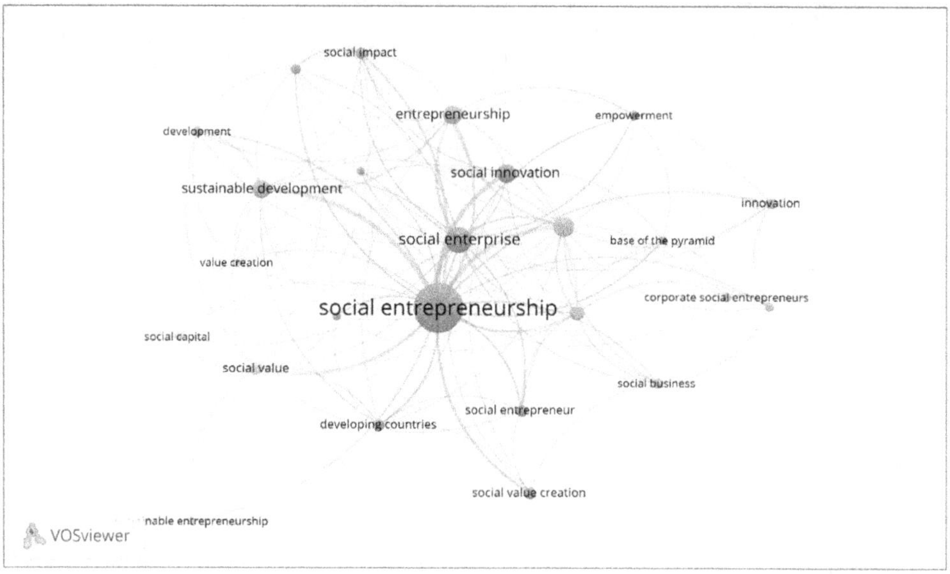

It should be noted that the greater the number of co-occurrences identified, the closer the themes appeared to the center of the network map. Also, the more common the keywords used by authors, the higher their proximity to each other is indicated by thicker links. Furthermore, the size of the bubble is directly proportional to the number of times authors use a particular keyword. The different colors of bubbles and links define separate clusters with related themes grouped into each of them.

The co-occurrence analysis, therefore, shows a field structured around (unsurprisingly) social entrepreneurship (shown in red) and terms often used interchangeably (notably social enterprise and social innovation. Around this theme, three broad clusters are indicated one linking entrepreneurship and sustainable development (in purple), the second a more corporate focus on social business and corporate social entrepreneurs (in green), and the third (in yellow focusing on (social) value creation.

Thematic Mapping

Thematic mapping was carried out to provide an understanding of the various subtopics probed by authors over the years and the evolution of the topic as a whole (Figure 6). The twenty- years timeline was categorized into three slices by identifying two cut-off points based on a similar number of publications in each of the three categories.

The first time slice (2004 – 2014) witnessed articles dedicated mainly to understanding social entrepreneurship and its facets (Eyal, 2008; Acs, Boardman, and McNeely, 2013; Choi and Majumdar, 2014). The concept of 'sustainable development' was central to most research pursuits during this time (Santos, 2012; Lozano *et al.*, 2013). Furthermore, much of the research revolved around 'value creation' in 'developing countries' (Van Praag and Versloot, 2007). This period also saw 'social innovation' gaining prominence in the literature (Etzkowitz, 2003; Hall *et al.*, 2012).

Figure 6. Thematic evolution of the topic

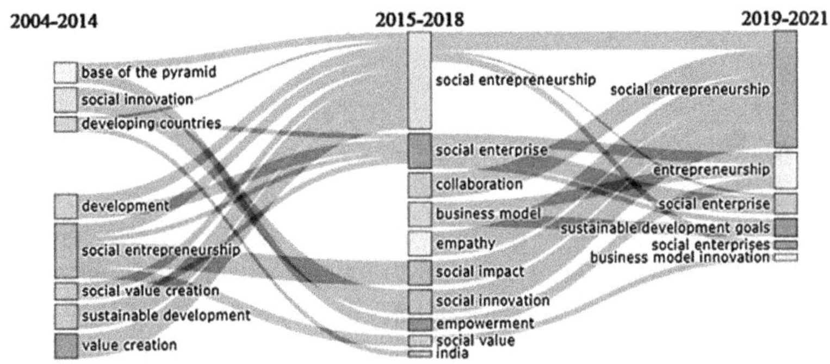

While research areas such as social entrepreneurship and social enterprise still held interest, newer research topics such as social innovation and business models emerged during the second time slice period (2015 – 2018). This was a period of increased emphasis on collaboration between governmental agencies and corporates on initiatives that aimed at creating higher social impact (Alberti and Varon Garrido, 2017; Tate and Bals, 2018). Another interesting aspect of this group is the emergence of 'India' as a geographical research context, primarily because a stronger emphasis was laid on social entrepreneurship development by the government, businesses, and individuals in India at this time (Legrand, Sloan and Chen, 2018). This period also laid the foundation for researchers to probe into aspects enabling social entrepreneurship, such as empathy and empowerment.

The last time slice (2019-2021) witnessed a surge in the number of articles on social entrepreneurship, likely due to increased social entrepreneurship activities across the world, primarily as a result of the growth in social entrepreneurship courses and programs in HEIs across the world (Tuzlukova and Heckadon, 2020). Also, more publications on sustainable development goals were noted during this period (Aubry *et al.*, 2021). This testifies to a comprehensive growth of the research field in the last half a decade, encompassing both broader aspects and niche topics.

Figure 7. Co-authorship across countries (minimum number of citations of a country - 10)

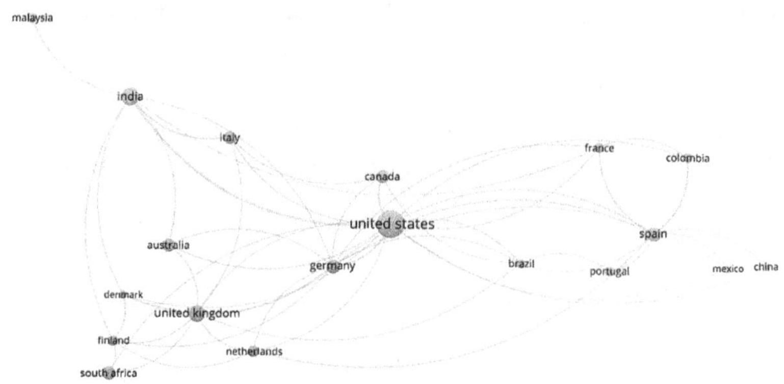

3.2.2 Social Structure

While developed nations usually steer the knowledge creation process, global collaboration links allow other countries to be part of this progression (Palacios-Callender and Roberts, 2018). Collaboration not only results in further development of ideas but also ensures multi-faceted progression due to researchers' contributions from varied backgrounds and disciplines (Tahamtan *et al.*, 2016). This is the pattern demonstrated in Figure 7, with the USA leading the global rankings in research collaboration in this field, followed by India and UK. The evidence from co-authorship analysis exemplifies that the collaboration has extended beyond regional borders, with the involvement of researchers worldwide.

3.2.3 Intellectual Structure

Intellectual structure analysis was developed by authors (Syed et al., 2022) by carrying out Cluster Analysis. Four prominent research clusters (Figure 8) evolved from content analysis incorporating co-occurrence and citation networks. The top 10 papers in each cluster were studied to build a common theme, a conventional approach in bibliometric analysis research (Tian *et al.*, 2018).

Cluster 1: What Is the Impact of Social Entrepreneurship?

This cluster includes articles focusing primarily on the impact of social entrepreneurship. Authors of papers within this cluster largely explore how people at the lower part of the societal pyramid are being affected and empowered (Hall *et al.*, 2012; Ghauri, Tasavori and Zaefarian, 2014). Studies mostly focused on developing countries such as India, China, Malaysia and Brazil (Hall *et al.*, 2012; Ghauri, Tasavori and Zaefarian, 2014).

Figure 8. Development of the four key clusters – content analysis findings

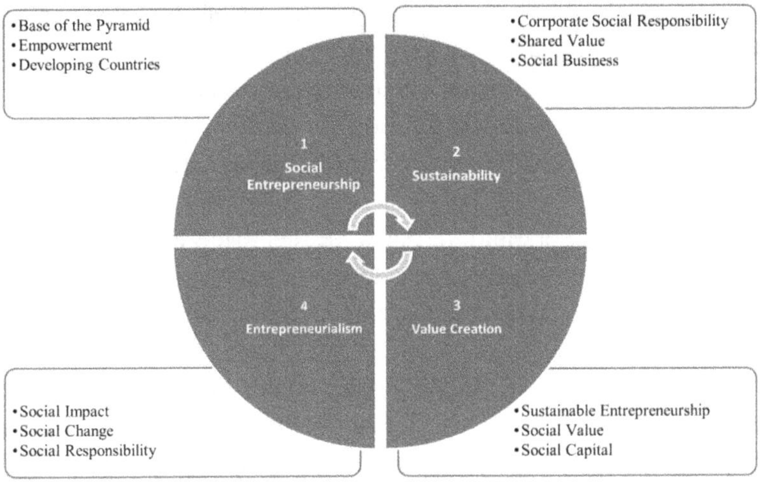

Cluster 2: Pathway to Sustainability

Authors of papers within this cluster have discussed various routes to achieve sustainability such as CSR (Phillips *et al.*, 2015; Alberti and Varon Garrido, 2017), social business (Choi and Majumdar, 2014) and shared value (Pret and Carter, 2017; Tate and Bals, 2018).

Cluster 3: Drivers and Dynamics of Societal Value Creation

This cluster emphasizes the interplay of the various drivers and dynamics of value creation in societies. These include sustainable entrepreneurship (Hermann and Bossle, 2020; Tunio *et al.*, 2021), social value (Weerawardena, McDonald and Mort, 2010; Santos, 2012) and social capital (Mosey and Wright, 2007; Sen and Cowley, 2013).

Cluster 4: Power of Entrepreneurialism

This cluster illustrates the role of entrepreneurialism in a society. Key ideas such as social impact (Weerawardena and Mort, 2012; Maresch *et al.*, 2016), social change (Aubry *et al.*, 2021; García-González and Ramírez-Montoya, 2021) and social responsibility (Glavas and Mish, 2015; Legrand, Sloan and Chen, 2018) have been elucidated through this aspect of the field.

4. CONTRIBUTIONS, LIMITATIONS AND CONCLUSION

This study's findings and analysis suggest that authors from across the world have contributed to this field; however, their relational ties are not heterogeneous and significant impact is confined to a few authors. The most influential works were also identified, which were pivotal in the development of this research field and had a global impact. The keyword and co-occurrence analyses illustrate that the focus of key researchers has been on social enterprise and sustainable development.

This chapter contributes to the field of in several ways. First, the publication patterns spread across the last 20 years were examined by categorizing and analyzing the literature according to the author, journal, institution, and country. Second, the most influential authors and works were identified by carrying out citation analysis. To conclude, this analysis provides a comprehensive overview of Social Entrepreneurship, Sustainability, and Value Creation using bibliometric analysis and structured literature review.

However, two key limitations should be noted, our analysis considers only the Scopus database, and keyword selection is based on our targeted topic; other keywords may be left out or emerge in the future. Further studies based on this paper could be carried out by examining documents indexed in other databases such as the ProQuest, Web of Science, Open Access Journals, etc. Also, comparative, or integrated studies between these databases could be considered.

REFERENCES

Acs, Z. J., Boardman, M. C., & McNeely, C. L. (2013). The social value of productive entrepreneurship. *Small Business Economics*, *40*(3), 785–796. doi:10.100711187-011-9396-6

Alberti, F. G., & Varon Garrido, M. A. (2017). Can profit and sustainability goals co-exist? New business models for hybrid firms. *The Journal of Business Strategy*, *38*(1), 3–13. doi:10.1108/JBS-12-2015-0124

Albort-Morant, G., & Ribeiro-Soriano, D. (2016). A bibliometric analysis of international impact of business incubators. *Journal of Business Research. Elsevier Inc.*, *69*(5), 1775–1779. doi:10.1016/j.jbusres.2015.10.054

Anand, A., Argade, P., Barkemeyer, R., & Salignac, F. (2021). Trends and patterns in sustainable entrepreneurship research: A bibliometric review and research agenda. *Journal of Business Venturing*, *36*(3), 106092. Advance online publication. doi:10.1016/j.jbusvent.2021.106092

Angelidou, M., & Psaltoglou, A. (2017). An empirical investigation of social innovation initiatives for sustainable urban development. Sustainable Cities and Society, 33(December), 113–125. doi:10.1016/j.scs.2017.05.016

Archambault, & Campbell, Y. G., & V. L. (2013). Full-Text Citation Analysis : A New Method to Enhance. *Journal of the American Society for Information Science and Technology*, *64*(July), 1852–1863. doi:10.1002/asi

Aria, M., & Cuccurullo, C. (2017). bibliometrix: An R-tool for comprehensive science mapping analysis. *Journal of Informetrics. Elsevier Ltd*, *11*(4), 959–975. doi:10.1016/j.joi.2017.08.007

Aubry, M. (2021). Higher Education For Sustainability: A Global Perspective. *Journal of Cleaner Production. Elsevier Ltd*, *2*(3), 41–51. doi:10.1002/pmj

Baima, G., Forliano, C., Santoro, G., & Vrontis, D. (2020). Intellectual capital and business model: A systematic literature review to explore their linkages. *Journal of Intellectual Capital*, *22*(3), 653–679. doi:10.1108/JIC-02-2020-0055

Bansal, S., Garg, I., & Sharma, G. D. (2019). Social entrepreneurship as a path for social change and driver of sustainable development: A systematic review and research agenda. *Sustainability (Switzerland)*, *11*(4), 1091. Advance online publication. doi:10.3390u11041091

Belz, F. M., & Binder, J. K. (2017). Sustainable Entrepreneurship: A Convergent Process Model. *Business Strategy and the Environment*, *26*(1), 1–17. doi:10.1002/bse.1887

Castriotta, M. (2019). *What's in a name? Exploring the conceptual structure of emerging organizations, Scientometrics*. Springer International Publishing. doi:10.100711192-018-2977-2

Choi, N., & Majumdar, S. (2014). Social entrepreneurship as an essentially contested concept: Opening a new avenue for systematic future research. *Journal of Business Venturing. Elsevier Inc.*, *29*(3), 363–376. doi:10.1016/j.jbusvent.2013.05.001

Cisneros, L., & .... (2018). *Bibliometric study of family business succession between 1939 and 2017: mapping and analyzing authors' networks, Scientometrics*. Springer International Publishing. doi:10.100711192-018-2889-1

Comerio, N., & Strozzi, F. (2019). Tourism and its economic impact: A literature review using bibliometric tools. *Tourism Economics*, *25*(1), 109–131. doi:10.1177/1354816618793762

Durán-Sánchez, A., Del Río-Rama, M. C., Álvarez-García, J., & García-Vélez, D. F. (2019). Mapping of scientific coverage on education for Entrepreneurship in Higher Education. *Journal of Enterprising Communities*, *13*(1–2), 84–104. doi:10.1108/JEC-10-2018-0072

Etzkowitz, H. (2003). Innovation in innovation: The Triple Helix of university-industry-government relations. *Social Sciences Information. Information Sur les Sciences Sociales*, *42*(3), 293–337. doi:10.1177/05390184030423002

Eyal, O. (2008). When parents choose to start up a school: A social-capital perspective on educational entrepreneurship. *Journal of Educational Administration*, *46*(1), 99–118. doi:10.1108/09578230810849835

Forliano, C., De Bernardi, P., & Yahiaoui, D. (2021). Entrepreneurial universities: A bibliometric analysis within the business and management domains. *Technological Forecasting and Social Change. Elsevier Inc.*, *165*, 120522. doi:10.1016/j.techfore.2020.120522

García-González, A., & Ramírez-Montoya, M. S. (2021). Social entrepreneurship education: Changemaker training at the university. *Higher Education, Skills and Work-based Learning*, *11*(5), 1236–1251. doi:10.1108/HESWBL-01-2021-0009

Ghauri, P. N., Tasavori, M., & Zaefarian, R. (2014). Internationalisation of service firms through corporate social entrepreneurship and networking. *International Marketing Review*, *31*(6), 576–600. doi:10.1108/IMR-09-2013-0196

Glavas, A., & Mish, J. (2015). Resources and Capabilities of Triple Bottom Line Firms: Going Over Old or Breaking New Ground? *Journal of Business Ethics*, *127*(3), 623–642. doi:10.100710551-014-2067-1

Hall, J., Matos, S., Sheehan, L., & Silvestre, B. (2012). Entrepreneurship and innovation at the base of the Pyramid: A recipe for inclusive growth or social exclusion? *Journal of Management Studies*, *49*(4), 785–812. doi:10.1111/j.1467-6486.2012.01044.x

Hermann, R. R., & Bossle, M. B. (2020). Bringing an entrepreneurial focus to sustainability education: A teaching framework based on content analysis. *Journal of Cleaner Production*, *246*. . doi:10.1016/j.jclepro.2019.119038

Kent Baker, H. (2020). A bibliometric analysis of board diversity: Current status, development, and future research directions. *Journal of Business Research*, *108*(August), 232–246. . doi:10.1016/j.jbusres.2019.11.025

Legrand, W., Sloan, P., & Chen, J. S. (2018). Corporate social responsibility and social entrepreneurship. *Sustainability in the Hospitality Industry, 16*(3), 297–334. doi:10.9774/gleaf.9781315690261_13

Lozano, R., Lozano, F. J., Mulder, K., Huisingh, D., & Waas, T. (2013). Advancing Higher Education for Sustainable Development: International insights and critical reflections. *Journal of Cleaner Production, 48*, 3–9. doi:10.1016/j.jclepro.2013.03.034

Maresch, D. (2016). The impact of entrepreneurship education on the entrepreneurial intention of students in science and engineering versus business studies university programs. Technological Forecasting and Social Change, 104, 172–179. doi:10.1016/j.techfore.2015.11.006

Monroe-White, T., & Zook, S. (2018). Social Enterprise Innovation: A Quantitative Analysis of Global Patterns. *Voluntas. Springer US, 29*(3), 496–510. doi:10.100711266-018-9987-9

Mosey, S., & Wright, M. (2007). From Human Capital to Social Capital : A. *Entrepreneurship Theory and Practice, 31*(6), 909–935. doi:10.1111/j.1540-6520.2007.00203.x

Nasra, R., & Dacin, M. T. (2010). Institutional arrangements and international entrepreneurship: The state as institutional entrepreneur. *Entrepreneurship Theory and Practice, 34*(3), 583–609. doi:10.1111/j.1540-6520.2009.00354.x

Palacios-Callender, M., & Roberts, S. A. (2018). Scientific collaboration of Cuban researchers working in Europe: Understanding relations between origin and destination countries. *Scientometrics, 117*(2), 745–769. doi:10.100711192-018-2888-2 PMID:30595611

Phillips, W., Lee, H., Ghobadian, A., O'Regan, N., & James, P. (2015). Social Innovation and Social Entrepreneurship: A Systematic Review. *Group & Organization Management, 40*(3), 428–461. doi:10.1177/1059601114560063

Pret, T., & Carter, S. (2017). The importance of "fitting in": Collaboration and social value creation in response to community norms and expectations. *Entrepreneurship and Regional Development. Routledge, 29*(7–8), 639–667. doi:10.1080/08985626.2017.1328903

Santos, F. M. (2012). A Positive Theory of Social Entrepreneurship. *Journal of Business Ethics, 111*(3), 335–351. doi:10.100710551-012-1413-4

Sen, S., & Cowley, J. (2013). The Relevance of Stakeholder Theory and Social Capital Theory in the Context of CSR in SMEs: An Australian Perspective. *Journal of Business Ethics, 118*(2), 413–427. doi:10.100710551-012-1598-6

Syed, R. T., Singh, D., & Spicer, D. (2022). Entrepreneurial higher education institutions: Development of the research and future directions. *Higher Education Quarterly*, (January), 1–26. doi:10.1111/hequ.12379

Tahamtan, I., Safipour Afshar, A., & Ahamdzadeh, K. (2016). Factors affecting number of citations: A comprehensive review of the literature. *Scientometrics. Springer Netherlands*, *107*(3), 1195–1225. doi:10.100711192-016-1889-2

Tate, W. L., & Bals, L. (2018). Achieving Shared Triple Bottom Line (TBL) Value Creation: Toward a Social Resource-Based View (SRBV) of the Firm. *Journal of Business Ethics. Springer Netherlands*, *152*(3), 803–826. doi:10.100710551-016-3344-y

Tian, X. (2018). *A bibliometric analysis on trends and characters of carbon emissions from transport sector*. doi:10.1016/j.trd.2017.12.009

Tunio, M. N., Chaudhry, I. S., Shaikh, S., Jariko, M. A., & Brahmi, M. (2021). Determinants of the sustainable entrepreneurial engagement of youth in developing country—An empirical evidence from pakistan. *Sustainability (Switzerland)*, *13*(14), 7764. Advance online publication. doi:10.3390u13147764

Tuzlukova, V., & Heckadon, P. (2020). Teaching social entrepreneurship through problem-based learning: Pedagogy and practice in the business english classroom. *Journal of Teaching English for Specific and Academic Purposes*, *8*(2), 71–82. doi:10.22190/JTESAP2002071T

Van Praag, C. M., & Versloot, P. H. (2007). What is the value of entrepreneurship? A review of recent research. *Small Business Economics*, *29*(4), 351–382. doi:10.100711187-007-9074-x

Weerawardena, J., McDonald, R. E., & Mort, G. S. (2010). Sustainability of nonprofit organizations: An empirical investigation. *Journal of World Business. Elsevier Inc.*, *45*(4), 346–356. doi:10.1016/j.jwb.2009.08.004

Weerawardena, J., & Mort, G. S. (2012). Competitive strategy in socially entrepreneurial nonprofit organizations: Innovation and differentiation. *Journal of Public Policy & Marketing*, *31*(1), 91–101. doi:10.1509/jppm.11.034

Žalėnienė, I., & Pereira, P. (2021). Higher Education For Sustainability: A Global Perspective. *Geography and Sustainability*, *2*(2), 99–106. doi:10.1016/j.geosus.2021.05.001

Chapter 2
Private Wealth as a Driving Force for Social Entrepreneurship

Elmar Lins
Heinrich Heine University Düsseldorf, Germany

Anna Michels
University of Cologne, Germany

ABSTRACT

The purpose of this chapter is to analyze the effect of private wealth on the motivation of becoming a social entrepreneur. The authors refer to Maslow's hierarchy and several culture theories to explain core motivations by social entrepreneurs to shed light on the research topic. The applied econometric approach is regression model based on 1,119 observations from the publicly available data set with a U-shape relationship as the main result for the interplay between the amount of private wealth and the probability of becoming a social entrepreneur. Thus, this chapter shows that starting a social venture is a core belief for some social entrepreneurs, which gives their social endeavors a more important role in their life than accumulating or securing any kind of private wealth. The other group of social entrepreneurs, however, needs to first accumulate a certain level of private wealth until they create a social added value for society.

DOI: 10.4018/978-1-6684-4666-9.ch002

1. AN INTRODUCTION TO SOCIAL ENTREPRENEURSHIP AND PRIVATE WEALTH

Governments, non-governmental organizations, and profit-orientated companies are struggling to find solutions for social, ecological, and economic challenges of our time (Verduijn et al., 2014). Solutions developed and implemented by the free market, or the non-profit sector are insufficient (van Dijk, 2019). As a result, new forms of entrepreneurship, corporations and initiatives have emerged, which usually have ecological and socially responsible business models in common. In line with this development, the phenomenon of social entrepreneurship has gained momentum in the scientific literature since the end of the 1990s (e.g. Dees, 1998; Letts et al., 1997; Mair & Marti, 2006). Even though social entrepreneurship is a rather new topic in scientific literature, the concept has received attention in business and academia (Grimes et al., 2013; Shockley & Frank, 2011). A variety of studies have investigated the phenomenon of social entrepreneurship and have helped to gain a detailed understanding. A major topic of interest in entrepreneurship research is the analysis of motivation to explain when and how business ventures occur (e.g. Yamini et al., 2020; Tucker & Croom, 2021; Douglas & Prentice, 2019). However, one topic in the entrepreneurship literature that has received minor attention concerns the questions of how existing private wealth will affect the probability of becoming a social entrepreneur and how related motivations affect the outcome.

Few things have as central a place in our lives as money and our private wealth (Oleson, 2004). It takes an important role, as wealth has more power over our life than any other single commodity (Oleson, 2004). Thereby, it particularly shapes the choices we make and influences our motivation. Furthermore, private wealth is unevenly distributed, which makes this topic difficult to investigate. The following sections will highlight regional and cultural differences for social entrepreneurship and wealth, as the authors have chosen to focus on the USA as a distinct regional research context. Thus, the research goal of this study is to shed light on the motivation stemming from private wealth to become a social entrepreneur.

For this analysis, the Panel Study of Entrepreneurial Dynamics II (PSED II) is applied, which is a large and publicly available data set, and is tackling entrepreneurship topics. The PSED II has been used for scientific research for over a decade and remains relevant in the last years for a variety of studies applying advanced quantitative empirical approaches to verify theoretical concepts and uncover new significant topics in the field of entrepreneurship (e.g. Gartner et al., 2012; Reynolds, 2011; Zettel & Garrett, 2021).

This chapter will contribute to social entrepreneurship research by, first, to explore the relationship between private wealth and the probability of becoming a social entrepreneur. In the literature on entrepreneurial intention and motivation, this relationship can be identified as a substantial research gap. As private wealth is a driving factor for the choices we make, it is rather surprising that there is not a variety of studies about this topic, but the authors trace it back to the lack of data for a comprehensive analysis. Second, this chapter can use the publicly available PSED II data set and isolate social entrepreneurship for the first time, which makes the data applicable and replicable for quantitative empirical analysis. The next sections will explain how the authors use the PSED II and might, thereby, serve as a guideline for future research that aim to follow the way of this study.

This chapter proceeds as follow: In section 2, the authors will briefly give a theoretical background on social entrepreneurship and motivation followed by section 3, which serves as an explanation of why regional and cultural differences are of upmost importance for this research context. Section 4 will then develop the research hypotheses for this study. Section 5 and 6 will explain the methodological approach, the use of the PSED II, and the results of the econometric analysis, respectively. Lastly, in section 7 and 8, the authors will give an in-depth discussion of the results followed by the conclusion.

2. THEORETICAL BACKGROUND OF SOCIAL ENTREPRENEURSHIP

Social entrepreneurship is not a new phenomenon but rather something that always existed. There have always been groups of individuals that had come together to tackle social challenges and drive societal change. However, the term “social entrepreneurship” is rather new and emerged just recently in the last decades (Dacin, Dacin, & Tracey, 2011). The first scientific paper on the activity of social entrepreneurs has only been published in 1991 (Short, Moss, & Lumpkin, 2009), but the topic has gained increasing attention from a wide range of researchers of different backgrounds. Early research on social entrepreneurship established the conceptual framework (Urbano et al., 2017), followed by empirical studies of which an overwhelming majority is based on case studies (Sassmannshausen & Volkmann, 2016; Urbano et al., 2017). Thereby, the necessity for quantitative research has become evident, which is going beyond descriptive statistics (Urbano et al., 2017; Janssen, Fayolle & Wuilaume, 2018).

However, the concept of social entrepreneurship is still fuzzy (Zahra et al., 2009), as even the term “social entrepreneurship” is not defined consistently within the scientific community (Moss et al. 2011). “Entrepreneurship” is usually referring to economic activities, whereas the term “social” can be linked to more altruistic motives (Mair & Martí, 2006; Janssen, Fayolle & Wuilaume, 2018). When considering the terminology of social entrepreneurship, the authors understand that the term itself possesses conflicting elements that are stemming from different origins (Zahra et al., 2009, Bacq & Janssen, 2011). Nevertheless, various definitions for social entrepreneurship share common characteristics (Bacq & Janssen, 2011; Zahra et al., 2009): The core motivation of creating social value (Dacin, Dacin, & Tracey, 2011) based on an innovative process to find a solution to overcome social obstacles (Mair & Martí, 2006; Moss et al., 2011) and to finally increase social wealth (Zahra et al. 2009, Janssen, Fayolle & Wuilaume, 2018).

A social entrepreneur is an individual animated by a social mission (Miller, Wesley, & Curtis, 2010). This mission serves as a catalyst for the underlying business vehicle or organization and defines their goals (Miller, Wesley, & Curtis, 2010). The social entrepreneur generates social value by developing solutions for social challenges or problems (Dacin, Dacin, & Tracey, 2011), which is why economic gains are only a mean to end and for the social entrepreneur (Bacq & Janssen, 2011). At the same time, this does not mean that a social entrepreneur does not understand the necessity of financial gains, as the creation of social value goes hand in hand with certain economic outcomes (Dacin, Dacin, & Tracey, 2011). Similar to the commercial entrepreneur, the social counterpart adopts a visionary approach to be a change agent, but with a strong ethical fiber (Germak & Robinson, 2014; Janssen, Fayolle & Wuilaume, 2018).

External factors, such as social entrepreneurship education, can increase the probability of students to create a social venture in the future. Shahverdi, Ismail & Qureshi (2018) exhibit that social entrepreneurship education at universities can reduce perceived barriers related to a lack of self-confidence or competency to create a social venture. But also, internal factors or personal traits influence the likelihood of becoming a social entrepreneur. Irengün & Arikboga (2015) apply the so-called "Fiver Factor Model" or "Big Five Personality Model" originating from sociology and psychology to assess the motivation of entrepreneurs in their social endeavors. The study revealed that social entrepreneurs are more likely to be agreeable and show a high degree of openness, which can be defined as individuals searching for new experiences (Irengün & Arikboga, 2015). Neuroticism, extraversion and consciousness surprisingly do not have a significant effect on the likelihood of becoming a social entrepreneur.

Research by numerous scientists has also deepened our understanding of social entrepreneurs' motives and entrepreneurial intentions. Table 1 shows a selected overview of relevant literature. Social entrepreneurs do not differ so much from their commercial counterparts as some want to exploit opportunities and be one's own boss (Verduijn et al., 2014). Miller et al. (2012) go a step further and highlight that social entrepreneurs can be characterized as individuals with a high degree of compassion, which can be triggered by various factors. This line of reasoning is based on either a deeply embedded altruistic mindset or a prosocial cost-benefit analysis leading to different starting positions to create a social venture. Similarly, Twari et al. (2020) argue that social entrepreneurs rate higher on altruism and empathy, which can be affected individually and by a manifold of variables.

Table 1. Overview of different sources of social entrepreneurship motivation

Author/s	Key finding on social entrepreneurship motivation
Verduijn et al., 2014	Be one's own boss and independent as strong motivation to create a social business
Shane & Venkataraman, 2000	Desire to exploit an identified entrepreneurial opportunity
Germak & Robinson, 2014	Percieve desirability of their actions because of emotional and cognitive attitudes
Twari et al. 2020	Show higher rate of altruism, empathy, and trust
Miller et al., 2012	Compassion as a major diver for social entrepreneurs
Dickel et al., 2020	Direct or indirect experience of a problem or deficit in childhood
Johnson, 1990	The need for achievement can motivate a to start a business
Lewis et al., 2012	High involvement as public–social sector employees serves as motivation
Hsieh et al., 2011	Productive emotional labor as a result of social entrepreneurship
Campbell et al., 1999	Expect individuals with stronger prosocial motivation to be less desirous of monetary rewards
Phillips et al., 2015	The motivation to innovate
Douglas & Prentice, 2019	High self-confidence to excel in social entrepreneurship

Figure 1. Maslow's hierarchy
(Huitt, 2007)

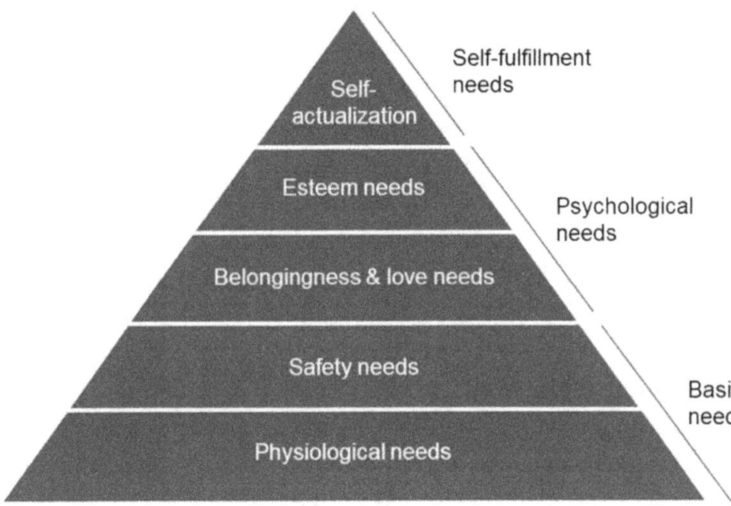

When arguing from the perspective of personal traits, a common model to assess the behavior of individuals is Maslow's hierarchy (Maslow, 1943) as a *theory of need* highlighted on Figure 1. The model suggests that an individual has the basic need to make money to provide for oneself or family members. Particularly, Maslow's self-actualization idea might fundamentally explain why individuals become social or commercial entrepreneurs. Those individuals tend to feel satisfied if they run their own business, which exhibits a high degree of independence and, thereby, actualize their potential as a human being (Germak & Robinson, 2014). This also means that achieving the necessary amount of money to at least secure the life of one's family might be motivation enough to start a social business (Zanakis, Renko, & Bullough, 2012). The goal of extraordinary financial payoffs might play a minor role for individuals with is high degree of self-actualization.

Overall, the lack of a clear definition for the concept of social entrepreneurship shows that this topic is still in a rather early stage and has not achieved a paradigmatic status (Nicholls, 2010). Numerous definitions are currently coexistent (Dacin et al., 2010; Bacq & Janssen, 2011), which is in line with Dees' (1998) recommendation to use both broad and narrow perspectives. Similarly for our research context, those different perspectives help to explain remaining white spots regarding motivations and existing private wealth that influence social entrepreneurship. Much more research is necessary to understand the root causes of the phenomenon social entrepreneurship, as it could particularly help to spur the amount of social entrepreneurship to tackle social, ecological, and economic challenges.

3. CULTURAL AND REGIONAL DIFFERENCES OF SOCIAL ENTREPRENEURSHIP

There have been several studies investigating the relationship between culture and social entrepreneurship activity (SEA) and this chapter wants to present and discuss their results in this section. The problem researchers face analyzing those studies are the following: studies about the influence of culture on SEA are very rare, studies are quite old and use data from the 2010s, data is only available for a few countries worldwide, studies use different definitions of culture and SEA and have therefore different results. Nevertheless, we can build on the early foundations of this topic provided by Hofstede in the 1980s.

Hofstede (1980) shaped the research on organizational behavior and cross-cultural research. His approach is the most widely used concept in entrepreneurship literature (Terjesen et al., 2013). He identified four key dimensions relevant to assess the impact of culture, which are power distance, individualism, masculinity and uncertainty avoidance (Hofstede, 1980). Power distance describes the degree to which people accept that power is distributed unequally among institutions. Individualism refers to a social framework in which individuals are expected to only care for themselves and their immediate families (Puumalainen et al., 2015). The dimension masculinity describes whether the dominant value in a society is assertiveness. Lastly, uncertainty avoidance refers to the degree to which individuals feel uncomfortable with uncertainty (Hofstede, 1983). Those four dimensions vary among different regions and for the context of entrepreneurship activity (Hofstede et al., 2004). This is particularly important for our study as we are focusing on the USA. In line with this, Eroglu & Picak (2011) have shown for a comparison of entrepreneurship activity between the USA and Turkey, that the USA has substantially lower degrees in power distance and higher degrees in individualism, which favor a culture of entrepreneurship. Indeed, entrepreneurship activity is higher in the USA (Eroglu & Picak, 2011), and it lets this research to assume that same holds true for SEA.

When taking a more global perspective, it can be outlined, that SEA is overall a rare phenomenon compared to general entrepreneurial activity with an average rate of 1,9% in the 49 countries clustered in the General Entrepreneurship Monitor (Kedmenec & Strasek, 2017). Kedmenec et al. (2017) grouped these 49 countries into three stages of economic development, based on their GDP per capita and other economic variables. Factor-driven countries export above all primary goods, whereas efficiency-driven economies concentrate on manufacturing standard products and innovation-driven countries focus on the production of knowledge-intensive products and the service sector. They found out that the average SEA rate differs from 1,5% in the factor-driven economies, to 2% in the efficiency-driven and 2,1% in the innovation-driven countries. They further stated that the SEA rates between countries in the same group of economic development can differ widely and resumed that cultural differences might be one reason for that. But by examining this aspect more closely and comparing countries with similar cultural characteristics like the United Arab Emirates and Saudi Arabia, they found out that even if they are culturally similar, they differ extremely in their SEA rates (4,9% and 0,2% SEA respectively). Kedmenec et al. (2017) came to the conclusion that culture was therefore not a sufficient variable to explain the prevalence of SEA.

But nevertheless, other researchers still see culture as one valuable variable to explain different SEA rates. Canestrino et al. (2020) found out that the SEA rate is higher in countries with lower power distance. Other cultural variables like individualism or uncertainty avoidance didn't correlate with the existence of social entrepreneurship activity. They also stated that in innovation-driven countries, higher indulgence, and lower long-term orientation correlate positively with social entrepreneurship, whereas lower masculinity correlates only in some factor-driven economies in a positive way with social entrepreneurship.

As mentioned in the beginning, research about social entrepreneurship might vary in its results, but this chapter can still conclude some central aspects for future policy-making. As general entrepreneurship activity, SEA depends on supply and demand, which is influenced by the economic development (industry, technology, etc.), political structures (institutions, democracy, etc.) and social factors (i.e. demography, gender equality, education) (Kedmenec & Strasek, 2017). The authors are able to shape these factors in a way that they become more favorable towards SEA. Digitalization might for instance empower SEA by creating knowledge networks, the possibility to work remote or to do crowdfunding (Fraczkiewicz-Wronka & Wronka-Pospiech, 2014). Furthermore, policy makers should not rely on social entrepreneurs to solve social problems, because individual and opportunity related processes are as important for social entrepreneurs as for non-social entrepreneurs. Instead, the promotion of entrepreneurship in general and a value-based entrepreneurship education may help to increase the number of SEA (Puumalainen et al., 2015).

4. PRIVATE WEALTH OF SOCIAL ENTREPRENEURS IN THE US

Abraham Maslow introduced human needs theory and his hierarchies, which describe how we develop specific and individual needs. Those needs determine how we respond to our environment. When it comes to an individual's wealth, social science does not agree with typical economic assumptions that decision making is rational (Doyle, 1999). However, rational behavior requires that everyone shares the same set of values and beliefs, as well as towards money and private wealth. Empirical studies have indeed shown that people think and behave differently with regard to money (Jindal, 1990; Wernimont & Fitzpatrick, 1972). Therefore, people also exhibit different attitudes towards private wealth. The major reason for that are different backgrounds and socialization experiences, e.g. cultural or regional differences as shown in the previous chapter. Now, Maslow's hierarchy of needs will help to gain an understanding of the relationship between private wealth and the probability of becoming a social entrepreneur in this context for the US.

Maslow's hierarchy is based on the agreement on the meaning of development as a series of progressive changes that individuals go through in their respective life cycle (Oleson, 2004). *Physiological needs* account for the lowest level in this set of developmental sequences. They include basic requirements, which are perceived as necessary to sustain life. Only of those basic needs are fulfilled, other needs become important, and a person proceeds further to develop higher hierarchies. Thus, once physiological needs are met, *safety and security needs* become the focus of attention, i.e. a life free of danger. The authors argue that generating wealth to be able of taking care of one's life and those of someone's beloved ones belongs at least in this hierarchy and is even linked to enabling someone to fulfill one's physiological needs. This means that generating a certain level of wealth to ensure safely living your life is a basic need in a society, which relies on money or equivalents. Next in line are *belongingness and love needs*. Those refer to the intend to share once life with our immediate circle of family and friends (Oleson, 2004). Those needs are followed by *esteem needs*, which are the desire for status and the respect of others, and *self-actualizations needs*, which is the awareness and desire to achieve one's potential to the greatest extent possible (Oleson, 2004). The authors argue that the intention of starting a social endeavor or to become a social entrepreneur, respectively, will usually be a need for those who want to address their esteem needs or even more their self-actualization needs. Those individuals tend to feel their needs met only if they are able to run their own social business, which exhibits a high degree of independence and, thereby, actualize their potential as human being (Germak & Robinson, 2014).

To shed light on the relationship of private wealth and social entrepreneurship, the authors can conclude that a certain level of wealth has to be accumulated, until a person feels the need for engaging in a social endeavor, leading to the first hypothesis:

H1: The higher one's private wealth, the higher the probability of becoming a social entrepreneur.

Empirical studies have shown that people think differently with regard to wealth (Jindal, 1990; Wernimont & Fitzpatrick, 1972). The major reason might stem from different socialization experiences based upon varying cultural beliefs, as pointed out in the previous chapter. Those might explain that for some individuals social engagement and altruism are deeply embedded in their core habits. Additionally, Hofstede's dimensions power distance and individualism, which are favorable for entrepreneurship activity in the USA, are likely to affect those core values (Eroglu & Picak, 2011). When using Maslow's hierarchy, the authors can transfer those core values into the level of basic needs, which are centered, and refer to safety and security needs, i.e. the bottom of the hierarchy pyramid. This implies for this specific context, that starting a social endeavor is not necessarily linked to a certain safety net based on a specific level of wealth, but rather stands by itself as a basic motivation to live one's life and (Zanakis, Renko & Bullough 2012). It is therefore likely, that for those individuals the need for social engagement has a higher prioritization than accumulating wealth.

H2: For a certain type of individual, the probability of becoming a social entrepreneur is embedded in their core beliefs and therefore not linked to their private level of wealth.

5. DATA

The authors derived this sample from the PSED II. The PSED II is a longitudinal survey of nascent entrepreneurs, which were randomly identified among 30,000 U.S. individuals. The data thereby overcomes potential survivorship and recall bias (Gartner et al., 2004). Furthermore, the PSED II is representative of the U.S. population, as relatively high response rates of 77% and weights used to correct for differences in selection procedures and non-response rates from random data collection (Renko, 2013). Overall, this dataset contains valuable information, which has been used as a publishable source in entrepreneurship literature (e.g. Renko, 2013; Brush, Manolova & Edelman, 2008; Cassar, 2007; Dimov, 2010). For this study, only data is used from "Wave A" of PSED II collected between September 2005 and February 2006, due to the exclusion of not available variables. Even though the data is one and a half decades old and may not generalize across time, it is still used today for groundbreaking science in the field of entrepreneurship (e.g. Cerqueti et al., 2020; Zettel & Garrett, 2021; Lim, 2022). See the PSED data set and publicly available codebooks on the initiative's websites http://www.psed.isr.umich.edu/psed/home.

The PSED II dataset was not initially directed towards the identification and examination of social entrepreneurship, but previous research has conducted an approach to identify potential social entrepreneurs (e.g. Renko, 2013; Gras & Lumpkin, 2012). Identified social entrepreneurs exhibit a certain answer pattern, when responding to the questions AA2 "Why do you want to start a new business?" and AA5 "What are the one or two main opportunities that prompted you to start this new business?". The respondents were given 44 potential answers to the first and 62 for the second question, respectively. The answers "help, others; help community" and "aid in economy; economic development" have both a strong socially oriented focus (Short et al., 2014). Previous studies have argued that respondents who answered either of these options on the first or second question can be reasonably classified as social entrepreneurs or at least significantly more socially oriented than the other respondents (Short et al., 2014). Thus, we add the variable *Social*, which takes the value 1 for a social entrepreneur and 0 otherwise.

In the previous sections, the authors have already highlighted the importance of personal wealth for the decision of becoming a social entrepreneur. To examine this relationship, we use household income as a determinant of an entrepreneur's private wealth. It needs to be acknowledged that wealth has multiple dimensions, which are typically household income, inheritance and pensions or welfare programs (Fessler & Schürz, 2018). In the scientific economics literature, income models have been established in the 1980s and served as the major determinant to analyze a person's wealth (Elliot, 1980). The obvious reason to focus on income is the availability of data, particularly when collecting information via a public survey. Income or salaries are more commonly asked about, compared to inheritance and pensions, which is why there might be a general reluctance of respondents to answer related questions. In line with that, the PSED II has also only asked for the household income to account for a person's wealth. This study follows this suggestion and uses household income as a proxy variable for private wealth, even though acknowledging for the two lacking dimensions, inheritance and pensions. This will be clearly mentioned as a limitation in the last section and as potential for future research. The variable household income contains 10 household income classes in the PSED II, with 0 USD to 14,999 USD as the smallest income class (coded as 1), 15,000 USD to 29,999 USD as the second smallest income class (coded as 2), etc. 100,000 USD or more (coded as 10) is the largest household income class. Thus, the authors add the variable *Income*, which takes on average the value 6, indicating approximately an average household income between 40,000 USD and 54,999 USD. An overview of all variables that we use can be seen on Table 2.

Table 2. Overview of the variables of our economic model

Variables	Description	Obs.	Mean	S.D.	Min	Max
Social	One for social entrepreneurs	1,119	0.08	0.27	0	1
Income	Ranks of household income categories	1,119	6.07	2.91	1	10
EntreExp	One for entrepreneurial experience	1,119	0.82	0.39	0	1
DEduc1	One for incomplete high school degree	1,119	0.06	0.24	0	1
DEduc2	One for complete high school degree	1,119	0.23	0.42	0	1
DEduc3	One for associate's degree	1,119	0.09	0.28	0	1
DEduc4	One for bachelor's degree	1,119	0.24	0.42	0	1
Gender	One for females	1,119	0.37	0.48	0	1
Growth	One for growth oriented entrepreneurs	1,119	0.81	0.39	0	1
Franchise	One for franchise businesses	1,119	0.03	0.17	0	1
Legal	One for legal probelms	1,119	0.10	0.30	0	1
DCat1	One for retail stores	1,119	0.13	0.34	0	1
DCat2	One for gastronomy	1,119	0.04	0.19	0	1
DCat3	One for construction businesses	1,119	0.07	0.25	0	1
DCat4	One for wholesale	1,119	0.04	0.20	0	1

The authors include a wide set of control variables. A topic that has received a lot of attention in previous research is human capital and its effect on entrepreneurship. A viable proxy to control for human capital is the entrepreneurial experience (e.g. Bosma et al., 2004). Previous literature discusses entrepreneurial experience as a major factor of unique human capital, which increases the probability of business organization and success (Fried & Hisrich, 1994). Thus, the authors include the variable *EntrExp*. Additionally, the authors add education dummy variables, since education serves also as a proxy for determining the human capital of an entrepreneur (e.g. Bates, 1990). The variables *DEduc1*, *Deduc2*, *Deduc3* and *Deduc4*, which indicate incomplete high school, complete high school, associate's degree and bachelor's degree, respectively. We refrain from using only one variable covering all educational levels and use dummy variables instead, as it follows established approaches in previous general scientific literature (e.g. Cascavilla et al., 2022; Elert et al., 2015; Leiva et al., 2022) and also in entrepreneurship literature (e.g. Van der Sluis et al., 2008; Wagner & Sternberg, 2004; Seghers et al., 2012). By applying dummy variables, our scientific model can explain more variance as relevant educational levels can clearly be identified and distinguished, compared to a single variable, which is more prone to distortion (Canela et al., 2019; Hardy & Reynolds, 2004). On the downside, dummy variables are occasionally problematic as multicollinearity might occur (Holgersson & Nordström, 2014). In our econometric model, we are controlling for multicollinearity, as shown in the next section and on Table 3.

Another founder-specific characteristic is gender of the entrepreneur. Davis & Shaver (2012) show, based on PSED data, that male and female entrepreneurs differ with regard to their perception of entrepreneurial opportunities. Furthermore, Lins & Lutz (2016) emphasize that there might be gender differences in human capital distribution, which might also affect the decision of becoming a social entrepreneur. Therefore, the authors add the variable *Gender*, which take 1 for female entrepreneurs and 0 for their male counterparts. The authors also control for the business growth intention of entrepreneurs, since Davis & Shaver (2012) find that growth intentions might differ between entrepreneurs. This might be particularly the case for social entrepreneurs, as their primarily goal is to help other or offer economic aid, and are thus less growth oriented compared to traditional businesses aiming to gain as much revenue as possible. Thus, the authors include the dummy variable *Growth*, which takes 1 for growth-oriented entrepreneurs and 0 otherwise.

Furthermore, the authors control for factors that influence the organizational structure of a potential social business venture. Therefore, the variable *Franchise* is added, as an entrepreneur's opportunity to choose social franchising venture might positively affect entrepreneurial behavior. In line with that, Tracey and Jarvis (2007) find that the business format franchising with its distinct characteristics is relevant for an entrepreneur's decision to start a social business venture. Additionally, the variable *Legal* is added, because legal forms usually differ between social enterprises and their non-social counterparts. For instance, Spear (2006) and Vidal (2005) show that social ventures use diverse legal forms, which depends on legal legislation and is bound by certain administrative and organizational requirements. Spear (2006) argues that the choice of a legal form is not always rational and often liked to regulatory or administrative problems. Hence, the variable *Legal* takes the value 1 for new entrepreneurs that experience legal problems and 0 otherwise.

Lastly, the authors take into account the industry in which an entrepreneur is active. As a common approach in entrepreneurship literature, four industry dummies are included, which control for retail stores (*Dcat1*), gastronomy and catering (*Dcat2*), construction (*Dcat3*) and wholesale (*Dcat4*) (e.g. Baptista et al., 2014; Cumming et al., 2021; Grilli et al., 2022). The issue of multicollinearity might arise for dummy variables, as already mentioned for educational levels. Therefore, we control for multicollinearity in the next section to rule out distortion and ensure the validity of the results.

6. ECONOMETRIC APPROACH AND RESULTS

In order to examine the relationship between the household income of individuals and their choice of becoming social or traditional entrepreneurs, the econometric approach is based on a logit regression model analysis, which is a standard econometric model. The logit model relates the variable y_i for an individual i to a linear index of observable characters x_i and unobservable characteristics e_i:

$$y_i = x_i\beta + e_i$$

To ensure that the approach does not suffer from multicollinearity issues, the authors calculate the correlation matrix of the variables. This is particularly important for this regression model, as it relies on dummy variables for industry specificity and educational levels. The correlation matrix is presented on Table 3 and exhibits no evidence for multicollinearity problems.

Table 3. Correlation matrix

	Social	*Income*	*EntreExp*	*DEduc1*	*DEduc2*	*DEduc3*	*DEduc4*	*Gender*	*Growth*	*Franchise*	*Legal*	*DCat1*	*DCat2*	*DCat3*	*DCat4*
Social	1.00														
Income	-0.08	1.00													
EntreExp	0.03	-0.09	1.00												
DEduc1	-0.04	-0.16	-0.02	1.00											
DEduc2	0.01	-0.19	-0.01	-0.14	1.00										
DEduc3	0.04	0.04	0.00	-0.08	-0.17	1.00									
DEduc4	-0.06	0.13	0.02	-0.14	-0.30	-0.17	1.00								
Gender	-0.05	-0.05	0.08	-0.03	-0.08	-0.06	0.08	1.00							
Growth	-0.09	-0.02	-0.06	-0.01	0.03	-0.03	-0.01	0.05	1.00						
Franchise	0.04	0.06	0.00	0.00	-0.02	0.02	0.00	0.00	-0.07	1.00					
Legal	0.01	0.03	0.00	0.03	-0.04	-0.02	0.04	0.06	-0.02	0.01	1.00				
DCat1	-0.06	-0.04	0.05	0.07	0.04	-0.04	0.01	0.10	-0.01	0.07	0.08	1.00			
DCat2	-0.04	-0.10	0.02	-0.01	0.06	0.04	-0.02	-0.02	0.04	0.08	0.00	-0.08	1.00		
DCat3	-0.03	-0.07	-0.05	0.02	0.12	-0.02	-0.05	-0.14	0.07	-0.01	-0.08	-0.11	-0.05	1.00	
DCat4	-0.01	0.05	0.02	0.05	0.03	-0.02	-0.01	-0.05	-0.04	0.04	0.01	-0.08	-0.04	-0.06	1.00

Table 4. Logistic regression analysis

Variables	Model 1 *Social*	Model 2 *Social*	Model 3 *Social*
Income		-0.0850***	-0.207***
		(0.0324)	(0.0689)
IncomeSquared			0.00680**
			(0.00328)
EntreExp	0.394	0.329	0.287
	(0.326)	(0.328)	(0.329)
DEduc1	-0.744	-0.952	-1.039*
	(0.620)	(0.626)	(0.629)
DEduc2	0.0461	-0.0599	-0.105
	(0.286)	(0.290)	(0.292)
DEduc3	0.204	0.274	0.265
	(0.367)	(0.369)	(0.371)
DEduc4	-0.648*	-0.632*	-0.623*
	(0.334)	(0.336)	(0.337)
Gender	-0.324	-0.336	-0.359
	(0.250)	(0.252)	(0.253)
Growth	-0.610**	-0.634**	-0.633**
	(0.252)	(0.254)	(0.255)
Franchise	0.822	0.890*	0.973*
	(0.518)	(0.522)	(0.526)
Legal	0.156	0.212	0.219
	(0.376)	(0.377)	(0.378)
DCat1	-0.903**	-0.946**	-0.977**
	(0.443)	(0.445)	(0.448)
DCat2	-1.455	-1.642	-1.705*
	(1.029)	(1.033)	(1.035)
DCat3	-0.635	-0.721	-0.754
	(0.540)	(0.543)	(0.545)
DCat4	-0.561	-0.492	-0.451
	(0.621)	(0.625)	(0.626)
Constant	-1.959***	-1.317***	-0.887*
	(0.387)	(0.455)	(0.496)
Observations	1,119	1,119	1,119

Table 3 shows the results of three logisitc regression models to examine the effect of household income on the probability of becoming a social entrepreneur. First, we conduct the first model only with control variables. In Model 2, we include the variable *Income* The results show a negative and significant effect for the relation of *Income* on *Social*. In Model 3, we also add the squared value of *Income* in order to examine the curvilinear relationship between *Income* and *Social*. The symbols *, **, *** denote statisticsal significance at the 10%, 5% and 1% level respectively.

The main analysis consists of three logistic regression models, which can be seen on Table 4. In the first model, the authors include the control variables. The authors find significant results on the 5% level for the variable *Growth*. This is in line with the expectations, as the main goal of social entrepreneurs is to support others or offer economic aid and are thus less growth oriented compared to traditional entrepreneurs. Furthermore, the authors find a significant result for the industry dummy variable *Dcat1*, indicating that there are indeed industry differences for social and traditional entrepreneurs.

Now, the authors want to consider the household income and thus add the variable *Income* in Model 2. The authors find evidence on the 1% level that an increase of household income negatively affects the probability of becoming a social entrepreneur. To gain more detailed insights in the connection between both variables, the authors include the squared value of *Income* in the third model. As the authors expected, the estimate is positive and significant on the 5% level. This result indicates that low levels of household income negatively influence the probability of becoming a social entrepreneur, while at a turning point of approximately 150,000 USD the authors find the contrary effect. The authors have plotted this result in Figure 2 to visualize this result.

Figure 2. Plot of the relationship between household income and social entrepreneurship

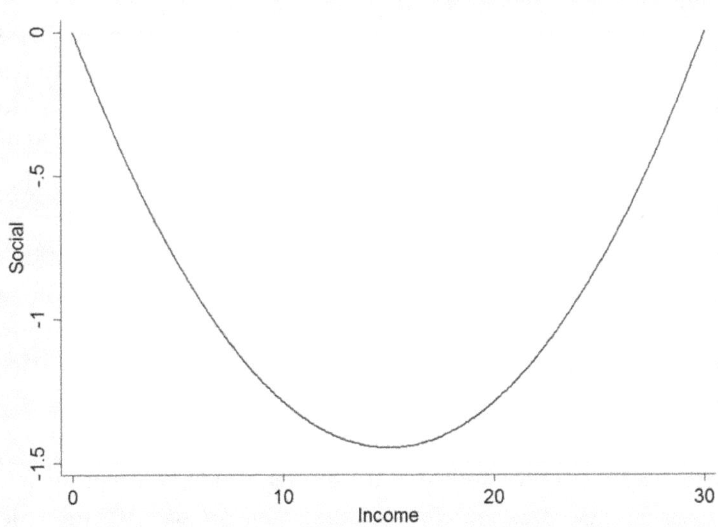

Furthermore, all highly significant estimates stay significant in all three regression models. Hence, the authors suggest that the stepwise approach of using three logistic regression model serves also as a valid robustness check for the results. However, since the econometric approach is based on the use of the squared value of the variable *Income*, multicollinearity might be indeed present between *Income* and the squared value. Nevertheless, the results remained quite stable across all models, and this fact, coupled with the low correlations among the other variables highlighted on Table 2, let us conclude that multicollinearity is not an issue in this study (McFayden & Cannella, 2004).

7. DISCUSSION

The results show that the hypotheses of this study hold true. Starting a social venture is not necessarily linked to a specific level of private wealth, but rather a core belief rooting from social or even altruistic needs (Zanakis, Renko, & Bullough, 2012). This why those individuals exhibit a high probability of becoming social entrepreneurs without having much already existing private wealth in terms of income. The accumulation of private wealth has a lower prioritization, when arguing from Maslow's hierarchy, and will therefore be accumulated after becoming socially engaged. The authors also interpret that with increasing wealth people are also likely to constantly move up Maslow's hierarchy of needs. At first, to cover one's basic needs and in later stages to achieve a certain status or reputation. Once this happens, the likelihood for those individuals to become social entrepreneurs will increase. According to Maslow hierarchy, those people want to address their esteem needs or even more their self-actualization needs. They tend to feel their purpose met only if they are able to run their own social endeavor, which exhibits a high degree of independence and, thereby, actualize their potential as human being (Germak & Robinson, 2014). This line of reasoning also implies that people in the middle stages of Maslow hierarchy, in the stage of accumulating wealth, are far less likely to become socially engaged via a social entrepreneurship. The authors can identify a turning point of 150kUSD accumulated private wealth from which the probability of becoming a social entrepreneur constantly increases. Therefore, the authors verify both hypotheses H1 and H2.

When considering the control variables, it can be found that a college degree has a negative impact on the probability of becoming a social entrepreneur. This result comes as a surprise because previous studies have shown that for at least profit-oriented entrepreneurs the probability of creating your own venture is positively affected by the years of receiving formal education (Robinson & Sexton, 1994). The authors suggest making a distinct differentiation between different types of entrepreneurs and motives, such as more socially oriented entrepreneurs. For instance, profit-oriented entrepreneurs might be more focused on creating their own wealth as they have achieved an educational degree, which makes them particularly valuable for the labor market. Furthermore, they are likely to repay student loans as a high debt burden for students is common in the specific US-cultural context (Webber & Burns, 2021), which might lead to a path of chasing high-paying jobs. Social entrepreneurs on the other hand see the creation of social value as a basic need, which might not be linked to achieving a higher educational degree, as a college degree might be more perceived as a status symbol or as an entry ticket for high-paying jobs. Nevertheless, those findings and the suggestions leave room for future research to shed more light on this relationship.

The results for the control variables show that growth intention has a negative effect on the probability of starting a social venture. This is what the authors have expected, as Davis and Shaver (2012) have pointed to different degrees of growth intentions for entrepreneurs. In that sense, social entrepreneurs appear to don't have the overarching goal of growing the business, but rather to offer aid and social purpose. But this might only be the half of the truth. Simms and Robinson (2009) have for instance investigated for-profit social ventures, which shows that there is not only are growth-oriented business and a non-growth-oriented counterpart but variations in between. However, the research setting is using a dummy variable for controlling growth intention, so that an in-depth examination of this variable with more variances might serve as a fruitful way for further research to add context to this research topic.

Another significant result of the analysis refers to the concept of social franchising. One of the major challengers of social entrepreneurs is to scale up their business idea (Volery & Hackl, 2010). Franchising can represent an effective way to overcome many organizational obstacles by replicating a proven and successful concept (Volery & Hackl, 2010). The franchising concept does not only provide concrete guidelines to set up a new business structure from scratch, but also serves to provide a network and support for a risky endeavor, such as creating a business. Thereby, this concept can mitigate the challenge of a scarcity of resource, which entrepreneurs must deal with. Furthermore, this is to the first quantitative-empirical investigation to verify the important role of the franchising concept for social entrepreneurship, which again emphasizes the potential of the publicly available data for future research on that research field.

Lastly, the authors also show that certain industry sectors are less prone for social entrepreneurship, such as the retail sector. The retail sector is per definition less attractive for social ventures as businesses usually sell goods through stores. But when also considering the existence of for-profit social ventures as mentioned before, it cannot be completely ruled out that social endeavors will be started in the retail sector, but according to our results with a lower probability compared to all other sectors. Again, a more focused quantitative-empirical investigation of the social entrepreneurship approach for different industries might be worthwhile to pursue for future research.

8. CONCLUSION

Research on social entrepreneurship vastly agrees on entrepreneurs with a social agenda to be a solution to a public goods problem that is caused by a combination of market failure and government failure (McMullen & Bergman, 2017). Because of their motivation to create a social added-value, social entrepreneurs can introduce solutions, which enable institutional, social and economic improvements that would not occur by financial incentives through profit-oriented entrepreneurship alone (McMullen & Bergman, 2017). Due to their important role for a society, research on social entrepreneurs wants to shed light on their motivation. This chapter identified the research gap of how private wealth of an individual might affect the probability to become a social entrepreneur to explain how the basic need of having or securing enough financial resources to live a safe life compares to the wish of also creating a social benefit for others. Will individuals decide to turn to create a social venture once they have secured a certain amount of private wealth or is the wish of becoming a social entrepreneur more deeply embedded and can be considered a basic need?

This study can in fact find evidence to affirm both parts of the research questions. A certain group of individuals that will become entrepreneurs don't care about amassing financial resources before becoming self-employed. They rather become entrepreneurs and start a social venture solely based on their altruistic and compassionate motives. The second group on the other hand starts a social venture only if they have reached a certain amount of private wealth and then starts to engage in more social endeavors, as they consider this a personal fulfillment activity and less important than a basic need.

This result could not only be theoretically verified but also quantitative-empirically, as the authors applied the publicly available PSED II data set and found an approach so isolate social entrepreneurs for the first time for further investigation. This leaves room for future research to build upon the results, verify or even expand on quantitative social entrepreneurship studies. The results offer promising ways for research, as they cannot explain who the people are, who either consider social entrepreneurship as a basic need or a self-fulfillment wish. Both groups should be compared to gain a better understanding who those individuals are, how the strength of their motivation differs and the probability of being successful with their ventures. Other fruitful ways of applying the PSED II for research might expand on ethnicity, industry specificity, educational background, and innovation, as the data covers all those topics.

However, the authors have also to highlight limitations of this study. First, this chapter has a regional focus as the data is US-rated. Therefore, the results can only be considered as valid for this region, as implied in section 3. Second, the authors conceptualized social entrepreneurship and profit-oriented entrepreneurship as diametral based on how this data is structured. However, the study cannot differentiate between different ranges of social entrepreneurship as there are, for instance, profit-oriented social entrepreneurs in between. Third, the PSED II data was collected in 2005 and 2006, which is why the actuality of the results must be considered with caution. While this data set is arguably the richest available source for information on entrepreneurship in the United States, the fact that it is older than one and a half decades might reduce the generalizability of our results. Hence, we ask scholars interested in this field of research to accept our results and consider collecting new data on social entrepreneurship. And fourth, household income has been used as a proxy variable for wealth. However, wealth has two more determinants besides income, which are inheritance and pensions. Even if income is the dominating determinant in the scientific literature for a long time (Elliot, 1980), a complete picture would comprise of a full analysis of one person's private wealth. The collection of data might face a significant obstacle, but this route might shed more light on this research topic and would help to gain a better understanding of private wealth, even going beyond this context of social entrepreneurship.

In conclusion, the authors add to social entrepreneurship research by uncovering the relationship between private wealth as either a basic or a personal fulfillment need and the effect on starting a social endeavor. Furthermore, this study serves as a blueprint to finally have a publicly available data set to verify and expand on social entrepreneurship research. Thus, it is hope of the authors that their investigation will help the research community on social entrepreneurship to uncover new challenges and make new discoveries.

REFERENCES

Bacq, S., & Janssen, F. (2011). The multiple faces of social entrepreneurship: A review of definitional issues based on geographical and thematic criteria. *Entrepreneurship and Regional Development*, *23*(5-6), 373–403. doi:10.1080/08985626.2011.577242

Baptista, R., Karaöz, M., & Mendonça, J. (2014). The impact of human capital on the early success of necessity versus opportunity-based entrepreneurs. *Small Business Economics*, *42*(4), 831–847. doi:10.100711187-013-9502-z

Bates, T. (1990). Entrepreneur human capital inputs and small business longevity. *The Review of Economics and Statistics, 72*(4), 551–559. doi:10.2307/2109594

Bosma, N., Van Praag, M., Thurik, R., & De Wit, G. (2004). The value of human and social capital investments for the business performance of startups. *Small Business Economics, 23*(3), 227–236. doi:10.1023/B:SBEJ.0000032032.21192.72

Brush, C. G., Manolova, T. S., & Edelman, L. F. (2008). Properties of emerging organizations: An empirical test. *Journal of Business Venturing, 23*(5), 547–566. doi:10.1016/j.jbusvent.2007.09.002

Campbell, L., Gulas, C. S., & Gruca, T. S. (1999). Corporate giving behavior and decision-maker social consciousness. *Journal of Business Ethics, 19*(4), 375–383. doi:10.1023/A:1006080417909

Canela, M. Á., Alegre, I., & Ibarra, A. (2019). Dummy variables. In *Quantitative methods for management* (pp. 57–63). Springer. doi:10.1007/978-3-030-17554-2_6

Canestrino, R., Ćwiklicki, M., Magliocca, P., & Pawełek, B. (2020). Understanding social entrepreneurship: A cultural perspective in business research. *Journal of Business Research, 110*, 132–143. doi:10.1016/j.jbusres.2020.01.006

Cascavilla, I., Hahn, D., & Minola, T. (2022). How You Teach Matters! An Exploratory Study on the Relationship between Teaching Models and Learning Outcomes in Entrepreneurship Education. *Administrative Sciences, 12*(1), 12. doi:10.3390/admsci12010012

Cassar, G. (2007). Money, money, money? A longitudinal investigation of entrepreneur career reasons, growth preferences and achieved growth. *Entrepreneurship and Regional Development, 19*(1), 89–107. doi:10.1080/08985620601002246

Cerqueti, R., Lucarelli, C., Marinelli, N., & Micozzi, A. (2020). Teams in new ventures: Gender, human capital and motivation. *International Journal of Gender and Entrepreneurship, 12*(2), 145–171. doi:10.1108/IJGE-07-2019-0115

Cumming, D., Meoli, M., & Vismara, S. (2021). Does equity crowdfunding democratize entrepreneurial finance? *Small Business Economics, 56*(2), 533–552. doi:10.100711187-019-00188-z

Dacin, M. T., Dacin, P. A., & Tracey, P. (2011). Social entrepreneurship: A critique and future directions. *Organization Science, 22*(5), 1203–1213. doi:10.1287/orsc.1100.0620

Dacin, P. A., Dacin, M. T., & Matear, M. (2010). Social entrepreneurship: Why we don't need a new theory and how we move forward from here. *The Academy of Management Perspectives*, *24*(3), 37–57.

Davis, A. E., & Shaver, K. G. (2012). Understanding gendered variations in business growth intentions across the life course. *Entrepreneurship Theory and Practice*, *36*(3), 495–512. doi:10.1111/j.1540-6520.2012.00508.x

Dees, J. G. (1998). Enterprising Nonprofits. *Harvard Business Review*, (January-February), 55–67. PMID:10176919

Dickel, P., Sienknecht, M., & Hörisch, J. (2021). The early bird catches the worm: An empirical analysis of imprinting in social entrepreneurship. *Journal of Business Economics*, *91*(2), 127–150. doi:10.100711573-020-00969-z

Dimov, D. (2010). Nascent entrepreneurs and venture emergence: Opportunity confidence, human capital, and early planning. *Journal of Management Studies*, *47*(6), 1123–1153. doi:10.1111/j.1467-6486.2009.00874.x

Douglas, E., & Prentice, C. (2019). Innovation and profit motivations for social entrepreneurship: A fuzzy-set analysis. *Journal of Business Research*, *99*, 69–79. doi:10.1016/j.jbusres.2019.02.031

Doyle, K. O. (1999). *The Social Meanings of Money and Property in Search of a Talisman*. Sage. doi:10.4135/9781483328324

Elert, N., Andersson, F. W., & Wennberg, K. (2015). The impact of entrepreneurship education in high school on long-term entrepreneurial performance. *Journal of Economic Behavior & Organization*, *111*, 209–223. doi:10.1016/j.jebo.2014.12.020

Elliott, J. W. (1980). Wealth and wealth proxies in a permanent income model. *The Quarterly Journal of Economics*, *95*(3), 509–535. doi:10.2307/1885091

Eroglu, O., & Piçak, M. (2011). Entrepreneurship, national culture and Turkey. *International Journal of Business and Social Science*, *2*(16).

Fessler, P., & Schürz, M. (2018). Private wealth across European countries: The role of income, inheritance and the welfare state. *Journal of Human Development and Capabilities*, *19*(4), 521–549. doi:10.1080/19452829.2018.1507422

Frączkiewicz-Wronka, A., & Wronka-Pośpiech, M. (2014). The use of ICT for achieving the objectives of the business model: Social enterprise perspective. *Polish Journal of Management Studies, 10*.

Fried, V. H., & Hisrich, R. D. (1994). Toward a model of venture capital investment decision making. *Financial Management, 23*(3), 28–37. doi:10.2307/3665619

Gartner, W. B., Frid, C. J., & Alexander, J. C. (2012). Financing the emerging firm. *Small Business Economics, 39*(3), 745–761. doi:10.100711187-011-9359-y

Gartner, W. B., Gartner, W. C., Shaver, K. G., Carter, N. M., & Reynolds, P. D. (Eds.). (2004). *Handbook of entrepreneurial dynamics: The process of business creation*. Sage. doi:10.4135/9781452204543

Germak, A. J., & Robinson, J. A. (2014). Exploring the motivation of nascent social entrepreneurs. *Journal of Social Entrepreneurship, 5*(1), 5–21. doi:10.1080/19420676.2013.820781

Gras, D., & Lumpkin, G. T. (2012). Strategic foci in social and commercial entrepreneurship: A comparative analysis. *Journal of Social Entrepreneurship, 3*(1), 6–23. doi:10.1080/19420676.2012.660888

Grilli, L., Mrkajic, B., & Giraudo, E. (2022). Industrial policy, innovative entrepreneurship, and the human capital of founders. *Small Business Economics*, 1–22. doi:10.100711187-022-00611-y

Grimes, M. G., McMullen, J. S., Vogus, T. J., & Miller, T. L. (2013). Studying the origins of social entrepreneurship: Compassion and the role of embedded agency. *Academy of Management Review, 38*(3), 460–463. doi:10.5465/amr.2012.0429

Hardy, M., & Reynolds, J. (2004). Incorporating categorical information into regression models: The utility of dummy variables. Handbook of Data Analysis, 229-55.

Hofstede, G. (1980). *Culture's consequences: International differences in work-related values*. Sage.

Hofstede, G. (1983). National cultures revisited. *Behavior Science Research, 18*(4), 285–305. doi:10.1177/106939718301800403

Hofstede, G., Noorderhaven, N. G., Roy, A., Thurik, L. M. U., & Alexander, R. M. (2004). 8. Culture's role in entrepreneurship: self-employment out of. *Innovation, entrepreneurship and culture: The interaction between technology, progress and economic growth*, 162.

Holgersson, H. E. T., Nordström, L., & Öner, Ö. (2014). Dummy variables vs. category-wise models. *Journal of Applied Statistics, 41*(2), 233–241. doi:10.1080/02664763.2013.838665

Hsieh, C. W., Yang, K., & Fu, K. J. (2012). Motivational bases and emotional labor: Assessing the impact of public service motivation. *Public Administration Review, 72*(2), 241–251. doi:10.1111/j.1540-6210.2011.02499.x

Huitt, W. (2007). Maslow's hierarchy of needs. *Educational Psychology Interactive, 23*.

İrengün, O., & Arıkboğa, Ş. (2015). The effect of personality traits on social entrepreneurship intentions: A field research. *Procedia: Social and Behavioral Sciences, 195*, 1186–1195. doi:10.1016/j.sbspro.2015.06.172

Janssen, F., Fayolle, A., & Wuilaume, A. (2018). Researching bricolage in social entrepreneurship. *Entrepreneurship and Regional Development, 30*(3-4), 450–470. doi:10.1080/08985626.2017.1413769

Jindal, S. K. (1990). Money usage: A psychological analysis. *Indian Journal of Applied Psychology.*

Johnson, B. R. (1990). Toward a multidimensional model of entrepreneurship: The case of achievement motivation and the entrepreneur. *Entrepreneurship Theory and Practice, 14*(3), 39–54. doi:10.1177/104225879001400306

Kedmenec, I., & Strašek, S. (2017). Are some cultures more favourable for social entrepreneurship than others? *Economic research-. Ekonomska Istrazivanja, 30*(1), 1461–1476. doi:10.1080/1331677X.2017.1355251

Leiva, J. C., & Mora-Esquivel, R. (2022). The entrepreneurial activity of university students in Costa Rica: The role of the university ecosystem. *International Journal of Intellectual Property Management, 12*(1), 109–128. doi:10.1504/IJIPM.2022.120986

Letts, C. W., Ryan, W., & Grossman, A. (1997). Virtuous capital: What foundations can learn from venture capitalists. *Harvard Business Review, 75*, 36–50. PMID:10165448

Lewis, J. A., Packard, T. R., & Lewis, M. D. (2011). *Management of Human Service Programs*. Cengage Learning.

Lim, Y. (2022). Relational composition and member turnover of entrepreneurial founder teams at the nascent stage: A typology and empirical evidence. *Journal of Small Business and Entrepreneurship*, 1–24. doi:10.1080/08276331.2022.2045543

Lins, E., & Lutz, E. (2016). Bridging the gender funding gap: Do female entrepreneurs have equal access to venture capital? *International Journal of Entrepreneurship and Small Business, 27*(2-3), 347–365. doi:10.1504/IJESB.2016.073993

Mair, J., & Marti, I. (2006). Social entrepreneurship research: A source of explanation, prediction, and delight. *Journal of World Business, 41*(1), 36–44. doi:10.1016/j.jwb.2005.09.002

Maslow, A. H. (1943). A theory of human motivation. *Psychological Review, 50*(4), 370–396. doi:10.1037/h0054346

McFadyen, M. A., & Cannella, A. A. Jr. (2004). Social capital and knowledge creation: Diminishing returns of the number and strength of exchange relationships. *Academy of Management Journal, 47*(5), 735–746.

McMullen, J. S., & Bergman, B. J. Jr. (2017). Social entrepreneurship and the development paradox of prosocial motivation: A cautionary tale. *Strategic Entrepreneurship Journal, 11*(3), 243–270. doi:10.1002ej.1263

Miller, T. L., Grimes, M. G., McMullen, J. S., & Vogus, T. J. (2012). Venturing for others with heart and head: How compassion encourages social entrepreneurship. *Academy of Management Review, 37*(4), 616–640. doi:10.5465/amr.2010.0456

Moss, T. W., Short, J. C., Payne, G. T., & Lumpkin, G. T. (2011). Dual identities in social ventures: An exploratory study. *Entrepreneurship Theory and Practice, 35*(4), 805–830. doi:10.1111/j.1540-6520.2010.00372.x

Nicholls, A. (2010). The legitimacy of social entrepreneurship: Reflexive isomorphism in a pre–paradigmatic field. *Entrepreneurship Theory and Practice, 34*(4), 611–633. doi:10.1111/j.1540-6520.2010.00397.x

Oleson, M. (2004). Exploring the relationship between money attitudes and Maslow's hierarchy of needs. *International Journal of Consumer Studies, 28*(1), 83–92. doi:10.1111/j.1470-6431.2004.00338.x

Phillips, W., Lee, H., Ghobadian, A., O'regan, N., & James, P. (2015). Social innovation and social entrepreneurship: A systematic review. *Group & Organization Management, 40*(3), 428–461. doi:10.1177/1059601114560063

Puumalainen, K., Sjögrén, H., Syrjä, P., & Barraket, J. (2015). Comparing social entrepreneurship across nations: An exploratory study of institutional effects. *Canadian Journal of Administrative Sciences/Revue Canadienne des Sciences de l'Administration, 32*(4), 276-287.

Renko, M. (2013). Early challenges of nascent social entrepreneurs. *Entrepreneurship Theory and Practice, 37*(5), 1045–1069. doi:10.1111/j.1540-6520.2012.00522.x

Reynolds, P. D. (2011). Informal and early formal financial support in the business creation process: Exploration with PSED II data set. *Journal of Small Business Management*, *49*(1), 27–54. doi:10.1111/j.1540-627X.2010.00313.x

Robinson, P. B., & Sexton, E. A. (1994). The effect of education and experience on self-employment success. *Journal of Business Venturing*, *9*(2), 141–156. doi:10.1016/0883-9026(94)90006-X

Sassmannshausen, S. P., & Volkmann, C. (2018). The scientometrics of social entrepreneurship and its establishment as an academic field. *Journal of Small Business Management*, *56*(2), 251–273. doi:10.1111/jsbm.12254

Seghers, A., Manigart, S., & Vanacker, T. (2012). The impact of human and social capital on entrepreneurs' knowledge of finance alternatives. *Journal of Small Business Management*, *50*(1), 63–86. doi:10.1111/j.1540-627X.2011.00344.x

Shahverdi, M., Ismail, K., & Qureshi, M. (2018). The effect of perceived barriers on social entrepreneurship intention in Malaysian universities: The moderating role of education. *Management Science Letters*, *8*(5), 341–352. doi:10.5267/j.msl.2018.4.014

Shane, S., & Venkataraman, S. (2000). The promise of entrepreneurship as a field of research. *Academy of Management Review*, *25*(1), 217–226. doi:10.5465/amr.2000.2791611

Shockley, G. E., & Frank, P. M. (2011). The functions of government in social entrepreneurship: Theory and preliminary evidence. *Regional Science Policy & Practice*, *3*(3), 181–198. doi:10.1111/j.1757-7802.2011.01036.x

Short, J., Ketchen, D. J. Jr, & Bergh, D. D. (Eds.). (2014). *Social entrepreneurship and research methods*. Emerald Group Publishing. doi:10.1108/S1479-838720149

Short, J. C., Moss, T. W., & Lumpkin, G. T. (2009). Research in social entrepreneurship: Past contributions and future opportunities. *Strategic Entrepreneurship Journal*, *3*(2), 161–194. doi:10.1002ej.69

Spear, R. (2006). Social entrepreneurship: A different model? *International Journal of Social Economics*, *33*(5 & 6), 399–410. doi:10.1108/03068290610660670

Terjesen, S., Hessels, J., & Li, D. (2016). Comparative international entrepreneurship: A review and research agenda. *Journal of Management*, *42*(1), 299–344. doi:10.1177/0149206313486259

Tiwari, P., Bhat, A. K., & Tikoria, J. (2022). Mediating role of prosocial motivation in predicting social entrepreneurial intentions. *Journal of Social Entrepreneurship*, *13*(1), 118–141. doi:10.1080/19420676.2020.1755993

Tracey, P., & Jarvis, O. (2007). Toward a theory of social venture franchising. *Entrepreneurship Theory and Practice*, *31*(5), 667–685. doi:10.1111/j.1540-6520.2007.00194.x

Tucker, R., & Croom, R. M. (2021). A xenophilic perspective of social entrepreneurship. *Journal of Business Venturing Insights, 15*.

Urbano, D., Ferri, E., Alvarez, C., & Noguera, M. (2017). Social entrepreneurship and institutional conditions: An empirical analysis in Spain. In *Social entrepreneurship in non-profit and profit sectors* (pp. 53–64). Springer. doi:10.1007/978-3-319-50850-4_4

Van der Sluis, J., Van Praag, M., & Vijverberg, W. (2008). Education and entrepreneurship selection and performance: A review of the empirical literature. *Journal of Economic Surveys*, *22*(5), 795–841. doi:10.1111/j.1467-6419.2008.00550.x

Van Dijk, G., Sergaki, P., & Baourakis, G. (2019). *The Cooperative Enterprise – Practical Evidence for a Theory of Cooperative Entrepreneurship*. Springer Nature Switzerland AG. doi:10.1007/978-3-030-16279-5

Verduijn, K., Dey, P., Tedmanson, D., & Essers, C. (2014). Emancipation and/or oppression? Conceptualizing dimensions of criticality in entrepreneurship studies. *International Journal of Entrepreneurial Behaviour & Research*, *20*(2), 98–107. doi:10.1108/IJEBR-02-2014-0031

Vidal, I. (2005). Social enterprise and social inclusion: Social enterprises in the sphere of work integration. *International Journal of Public Administration*, *28*(9-10), 807–825. doi:10.1081/PAD-200067347

Volery, T., & Hackl, V. (2010). The promise of social franchising as a model to achieve social goals. In *Handbook of Research on Social Entrepreneurship*. Edward Elgar Publishing. doi:10.4337/9781849804684.00015

Wagner, J., & Sternberg, R. (2004). Start-up activities, individual characteristics, and the regional milieu: Lessons for entrepreneurship support policies from German micro data. *The Annals of Regional Science*, *38*(2), 219–240. doi:10.100700168-004-0193-x

Webber, K. L., & Burns, R. (2021). Increases in graduate student debt in the US: 2000 to 2016. *Research in Higher Education*, *62*(5), 709–732. doi:10.100711162-020-09611-x

Wernimont, P. F., & Fitzpatrick, S. (1972). The meaning of money. *The Journal of Applied Psychology*, *56*(3), 218–226. doi:10.1037/h0033107

Yamini, R., Soloveva, D., & Peng, X. (2020). What inspires social entrepreneurship? The role of prosocial motivation, intrinsic motivation, and gender in forming social entrepreneurial intention. *Entrepreneurship Research Journal*.

Zahra, S. A., Gedajlovic, E., Neubaum, D. O., & Shulman, J. M. (2009). A typology of social entrepreneurs: Motives, search processes and ethical challenges. *Journal of Business Venturing*, *24*(5), 519–532. doi:10.1016/j.jbusvent.2008.04.007

Zanakis, S. H., Renko, M., & Bullough, A. (2012). Nascent entrepreneurs and the transition to entrepreneurship: Why do people start new businesses? *Journal of Developmental Entrepreneurship*, *17*(01), 1–25. doi:10.1142/S108494671250001X

Zettel, L. A., & Garrett, R. P. (2021). Venture-level outcomes of juggling and struggling. *Journal of Business Venturing Insights*, *15*, e00225. doi:10.1016/j.jbvi.2021.e00225

Chapter 3
Bibliometric Analysis of Social Entrepreneurship

Bhanupriya Khatri
University School of Business, Chandigarh University, India

Shaina Arora
UITHM, Chandigarh University, India

Hesham Magd
Modern College of Business and Science, Oman

Shad Ahmad K. Khan
https://orcid.org/0000-0001-7593-3487
University of Buraimi, Oman

ABSTRACT

Social entrepreneurship is a new subject that is gathering researchers' thoughts because of the social data of this kind of business. The chief mark of this chapter is to orchestrate experts in making a theoretical design and to coordinate researchers who are new in cordial business research, so they know which diaries and authors to advise while focusing on this quirk. To do this, this survey uses the Scopus informational index to conclude the investigation districts with the best assessment yield, the countries and lingos responsible for most amicable business research, the journals that disseminate most investigation, the year in which research on agreeable undertaking began, and the most relevant makers with conveyances on well-disposed business.

DOI: 10.4018/978-1-6684-4666-9.ch003

INTRODUCTION

Recently, social enterprises have become more recognizable and have increased income and rewards from funders, customers, academia, media, and policymakers. Social entrepreneurs mainly try to characterize, given that ideas have evolved rapidly in recent years, increasingly blurring the boundaries between normal business, government, and non-use areas. The central purpose of people in social business is to make a significant contribution to society by looking for important goals and points. To accomplish their objectives, social business visionaries decide social issues and collect resources for meet essential human necessities. social business gas pedals like Satisfaction draw in and maintain different new social enterprises and help with changing thought into a new social business. Accordingly, it is crucial that productive occurrences of social entrepreneurship are progress from one side of the country to the next (Erpf et al., 2022).

The social business focuses on one mission that is to make changes towards the society usually by addressing a social issue. This arises out of the societal obligations that a person owns (Rey-Martí et al., 2016). Some extra exploration on the objectives and inspiration of social ventures would not only help to get a profound understanding of the subject but also would help to gain functional applications. Second, the incorporation of social capital into Social Entrepreneurship writing would work with a more far-reaching comprehension of the presentation of social endeavours. At last, the inspiration for the formation of social undertakings is without question a theme that should be the focal point of future examination (Kraus et al., 2014). It is critical to remember that the examination introduced in this study covers a variety of studies and in this manner a variety of strategies for dissecting scholarly constructions. Furthermore, it unearths the research patterns connecting with the business venture peculiarity (Ferreira et al., 2019). Social inventive activities are extraordinarily affected by pertinent settings and thus, we propose future researchers consider different focused settings while conveying their theoretical central focuses (Gupta et al., 2020). Works with an investigation into social business in the UK by defeating the debilitations brought about by the absence of a standard and generally adequate meanings of the social undertaking, social business person, and social business as well as the shortfall of a public register of social ventures (Haugh, 2005).

This study concentrates on subsequently expecting to arrange specialists who are new in friendly business venture research so they know which diaries and creators to counsel while concentrating on this peculiarity. And also presents a bibliometric examination using the Scopus database to conclude the investigation locales with the best assessment yield, the countries and vernaculars liable for most cordial undertaking research, the year in which research on amicable business began, the journals that appropriate most assessment, and the main makers with circulations on well-disposed business.

FACETS OF SOCIAL ENTREPRENEURSHIP

Definitions and conceptualizations exist in this field of study, which ranges from broad to narrow. The term social entrepreneurship portrays reasonable undertakings that join "business norms eagerly for social impact". Now there is no single, extensively settled after the importance of SE, regardless of the way that it is generally recognized that it will most likely change the social equilibrium to a more needed state (A. & D., 2012). The business has been the engine pushing a huge piece of the improvement of the business region as well as a primary purpose behind the quick expansion of the social region (Austin et al., 2012). The business has been pondered by the perspective of monetary issues, mind research, sociology, and human examinations. Right away, monetary issues scientists focused on business, searching for a relationship with the financial turn of events and keeping an eye on business as per a straightforward monetary viewpoint (Guzman & Trujillo, 2008). As needs are, cerebrum examination, humanism, and humanities made responsibilities in the examination of business as indicated by a social point of view. Social business, spearheading social activity, or social undertakings could convey comparative importance at the first look. Regardless, portraying social undertaking and making qualification among it and other related areas, is everything except a basic endeavour (Salamzadeh et al., 2011).

METHODOLOGY

A bibliometric assessment includes applying real procedures to conclude emotional and quantitative changes in a given intelligent investigation subject, spread out the profile of appropriations on the point, and distinguish tendencies inside a discipline. This review uses the Scopus database collection across all disciplines. The way that the Scopus gives data on consistent investigation yield engages the bibliometric assessment considering the way that the Scopus offers data on yield, dispersal, facilitated endeavors, and impact. Furthermore, this kind of investigation gives helpful data to specialists looking to assess the logical action (Jair Duque Oliva et al., n.d.).

ANALYSIS INDICATORS

The evaluation of the Scopus database centring on social entrepreneurship was performed. To do so, this study analyses all documents on this subject found in the Scopus database. The resulting sample comprises 4040 search items. Table 1 shows precise article determination standards that is perceived as a fundamental part of the bibliometric survey process. This incorporates a deliberate pursuit of studies and is planned to accomplish a straightforward report on the ID of concentrates so the researcher can comprehend the work done to characterize the examination and its outcomes. How the aftereffects of the audit connect with pertinent proof. From the area of Subjects ''Business, management and accounting'', ''Social sciences'', and ''Arts and humanities'' 518 articles were dismissed and 3522 were acknowledged and then again of ''Articles'', ''Conference papers'', and ''Reviews'' 715 were dismissed and 2807 were acknowledged. 2667 articles were screened with Language Selection: Includes English-just reports.

Table 1. Article selection and search criteria

Filtering Criteria	Reject	Accept
Search Criteria		
Search Engine: Scopus		
Search Date: 20 Dec 2021		
Search term: ("Social entrepreneurship" OR "Social entrepreneur" OR "Social entrepreneurial")		4040
Subject Area: ''Business, management and accounting'', ''Social sciences'', and ''Arts and humanities''	518	3522
Document Type: ''Articles'', ''Conference papers'', and ''Reviews''	715	2807
Article selection		
Language screening: Include documents in English only	140	2667
Year (2022 to 2017)	1752	942
content screening: Include articles if ''Titles, abstracts, and keywords'' indicate relevance to scope of study only	0	942

The bibliometric indicators used in this research are as follows:

1. What are the current trends in the area of social entrepreneurship?
2. Which are the leading, influential authors and most cited articles in the area of social entrepreneurship?

3. Which are the leading, influential and impactful Co-Authorship based on organizations to Extend the Literature extend the literature?
4. What are the leading countries where most of the research domain is carried out?

Figure 1. Current trends in the area of social entrepreneurship
Source: *Authors' Calculation through Vos viewer on the data retrieved from scopus.com*

Year of publication	No. of Research Papers
2017	140
2018	145
2019	159
2020	238
2021	245
2022	15

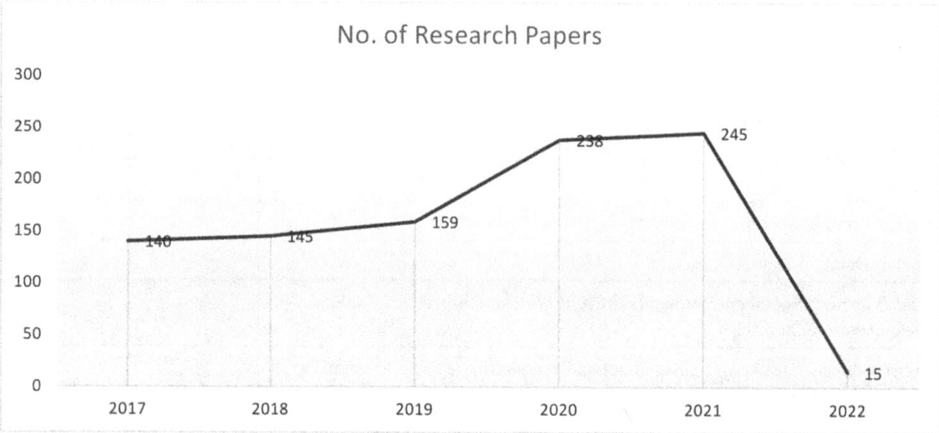

The performance in Figure 1 gets from the penchant to unveil the idea of social entrepreneurship. The latest things in the space of social business have been dissected by thinking about the number of exploration papers and long periods of distribution. Therefore, it can be clearly seen from table 2 and the graph above that trend has increased till the year 2021. In the current year, Trends to study social entrepreneurship areas are still in process. Reasonable undertaking seeks after a triple essential concern approach of financial, social, and organic goals. Conservative undertaking is an early stream of assessment at the intersection point of sensible organization and business (Belz & Binder, 2017).

Table 2 reveals the top 20 Articles on Social Entrepreneurship (SE). The top most article revealed that SE research at basically one level twists the eccentricity as well as risks earlier the entryways for impelling data by thinking about more levels. Moreover, even the farewell of a social undertaking is only a phase toward accomplishing the objective of SE: social worth creation (Saebi et al., 2019). Compassion is a key quality distinctive social business people from conventional business people, and a significant forerunner of social enterprising (SE) goals (Bacq & Alt, 2018). Numerous business people are battling with the subject of how to convey a fruitful raising support pitch on crowdfunding stages (Parhankangas & Renko, 2017). Making one more present-day climate harmless to the ecosystem power included the improvement of a new institutional system. In addition, social business affiliations introduced new cycles in the organic framework (Surie, 2017). Passion in assists coordinating wisdom and direction of the business with peopling, giving the fire that stimulates advancement, innovation, and outrageous accomplishment. In any case, our insight into the wellsprings of energy is restricted and dependent fundamentally upon rehearses destined by researchers, rather than those made by business visionaries themselves (Cardon et al., 2017). Social business visionaries use delegitimization of existing social impact methods of reasoning to account for their bricolage accounts (Molecke & Pinkse, 2017).

Table 2. Leading, influential authors and most cited articles in the area of social entrepreneurship

S.N	Authors	Title	Year	Cited by
1	Saebi T., Foss N.J., Linder S.	Social Entrepreneurship Research: Past Achievements and Future Promises	2019	207
2	Parhankangas A., Renko M.	Linguistic style and crowdfunding success among social and commercial entrepreneurs	2017	200
3	Belz F.M., Binder J.K.	Sustainable Entrepreneurship: A Convergent Process Model	2017	163
4	Popkova E.G., Sergi B.S.	Human capital and AI in industry 4.0. Convergence and divergence in social entrepreneurship in Russia	2020	123
5	Bacq S., Alt E.	Feeling capable and valued: A prosocial perspective on the link between empathy and social entrepreneurial intentions	2018	98
6	Rawhouser H., Cummings M., Newbert S.L.	Social Impact Measurement: Current Approaches and Future Directions for Social Entrepreneurship Research	2019	95
7	Littlewood D., Holt D.	Social Entrepreneurship in South Africa: Exploring the Influence of Environment	2018	94

continues on following page

Table 2. Continued

S.N	Authors	Title	Year	Cited by
8	Urban B., Kujinga L.	The institutional environment and social entrepreneurship intentions	2017	88
9	Hechavarría D.M., Terjesen S.A., Ingram A.E., Renko M., Justo R., Elam A.	Taking care of business: the impact of culture and gender on entrepreneurs' blended value creation goals	2017	84
10	Thompson T.A., Purdy J.M., Ventresca M.J.	How entrepreneurial ecosystems take form: Evidence from social impact initiatives in Seattle	2018	77
11	Fraser A., Tan S., Lagarde M., Mays N.	Narratives of Promise, Narratives of Caution: A Review of the Literature on Social Impact Bonds	2018	77
12	Tracey P., Stott N.	Social innovation: a window on alternative ways of organizing and innovating	2017	76
13	Gupta P., Chauhan S., Paul J., Jaiswal M.P.	Social entrepreneurship research: A review and future research agenda	2020	74
14	Becker S., Kunze C., Vancea M.	Community energy and social entrepreneurship: Addressing purpose, organisation and embeddedness of renewable energy projects	2017	71
15	Rao-Nicholson R., Vorley T., Khan Z.	Social innovation in emerging economies: A national systems of innovation based approach	2017	69
16	Tate W.L., Bals L.	Achieving Shared Triple Bottom Line (TBL) Value Creation: Toward a Social Resource-Based View (SRBV) of the Firm	2018	68
17	Brown T.E., Boon E., Pitt L.F.	Seeking funding in order to sell: Crowdfunding as a marketing tool	2017	67
18	Surie G.	Creating the innovation ecosystem for renewable energy via social entrepreneurship: Insights from India	2017	64
19	Cardon M.S., Glauser M., Murnieks C.Y.	Passion for what? Expanding the domains of entrepreneurial passion	2017	63
20	Molecke G., Pinkse J.	Accountability for social impact: A bricolage perspective on impact measurement in social enterprises	2017	60

Source: Authors' Calculation through the data retrieved from scopus.com

Table 3 describes Leading, Influential, and Impactful Co-Authorship based on organizations to Extend the Literature. We can investigate this from the actual table that Altai State University, Russian Federation and Pekhanov Russian University of Economics, Russian Federation has 76 references with great connection strength. Then again Universities like Harvard University, Cambridge, and Norweigian school of Economics, Bergen, Norway has the most elevated references with zero connection strength.

Table 3. Leading, influential, and impactful co-authorship based on organizations to extend the literature

ID	Organization	Documents	Citations	Total Link Strength
1	Altai State University, Russian Federation	3	76	4
2	College of Business Administration, Kansas State University, Manhattan, United States	3	74	0
3	Faculty of Business Management, Universiti Teknologi Mara Sarawak, ota samarahan, sarawak, 94300, malaysia	3	3	6
4	faculty of economics and management sciences, Universiti Sultan Sainal Abidin, Kuala Terengganu, terengganu, Malaysia	3	3	6
5	Faculty of Entrepreneurship and Business, Universiti Malaysia Kelantan, Kota Bharu, Kelantan, Malaysia	3	3	6
6	Harvard University, Cambridge, United States	3	132	0
7	Latvia University of Life Sciences and Technologies, Latvia	4	3	0
8	Norwegian School of Economics, Bergen, Norway	3	107	0
9	Pekhanov Russian University of Economics, Russian Federation	3	76	4
10	Universidad de Monterrey, Mexico	3	35	0
11	Yugra State University, Russian Federation	3	4	2

Source: Authors' Calculation through Vos viewer on the data retrieved from scopus.com

Citation investigation has been done in Table 5 based on nations where the United States represents the most extreme number of references that is 2540 with 190 exploration papers and then again Chile is having the most un-number of references that is 177 with 12 reports. Different Countries like Italy, France, Spain, Canada, India, Netherlands has a normal number of references in the space of social entrepreneurship.

Co-Citation Analysis

Figure 2 describes one methodology was utilized to rate journals. Assuming many papers are referred to after a journal, the diary is powerful and does awesome work. The number of diaries was to actually look at their realness. One renowned bibliographic marker, the Journal Impact Factor (JIF), is essentially the number of follow-up references got from the typical article. It will presumably help experts with understanding the value of content circulated in one journal that appeared differently in relation to others in a particular field. The higher the score, the more unmistakable the effect of the journal. On the off chance that a diary frequently distributes review articles, the diary works effectively by choosing and distributing unique articles. Consequently, we played out a bibliographic examination in light of sources and observed that diaries of applied brain research were generally pertinent to other unmistakable journals.

Table 4. Leading countries where most of the research domain is carried out

S.N.	Country	Research Papers	Citations
1	United States	190	2540
2	United Kingdom	102	1551
3	Spain	68	690
4	Germany	62	843
5	India	53	480
6	Italy	46	712
7	France	41	691
8	Russian Federation	39	304
9	Canada	38	523
10	Malaysia	36	76
11	Netherlands	36	429
12	South Africa	33	187
13	Australia	31	367
14	Portugal	30	263
15	Mexico	26	150
16	Indonesia	24	52
17	Brazil	21	126
18	Denmark	21	304
19	New Zealand	20	130
20	China	18	129

Source: Authors' Calculation through Vos viewer on the data retrieved from scopus.com

Here, bibliographic examination based on countries as shown in Figure 3 is incredible for finding and dissecting huge volumes of logical information. This permits us to uncover the advancing subtleties of specific countries, while likewise featuring arising regions inside that area. In any case, its application in business research is generally new and as a rule, it is immature. Consequently, we endeavor to introduce an outline of the bibliometric strategy, with specific accentuation on its various methods, and to examine the relationship with various countries. As displayed in the United States has joined with numerous different countries for this specific area of study.

Figure 2. On the basis of sources

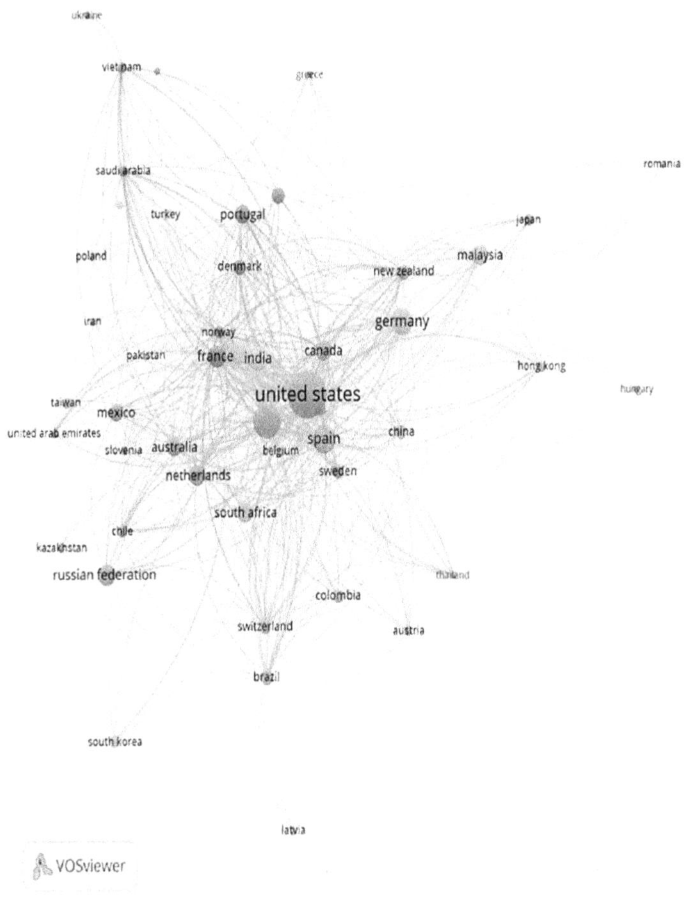

Co-occurrence of keywords was the bibliometric strategy used to plan the exploration field. The most common way of making watchwords organizations and grouping catchphrases was upheld with the utilization of the co-occurrence analysis and bunching of high-recurrence keywords are conducted with the help of the VOSviewer application. With the utilization of the technique for co-event examination, distinguished high-recurrence catchphrases can be classified into different bunches compared with the areas of exploration interest in the field.

Figure 3. Top countries based on citations

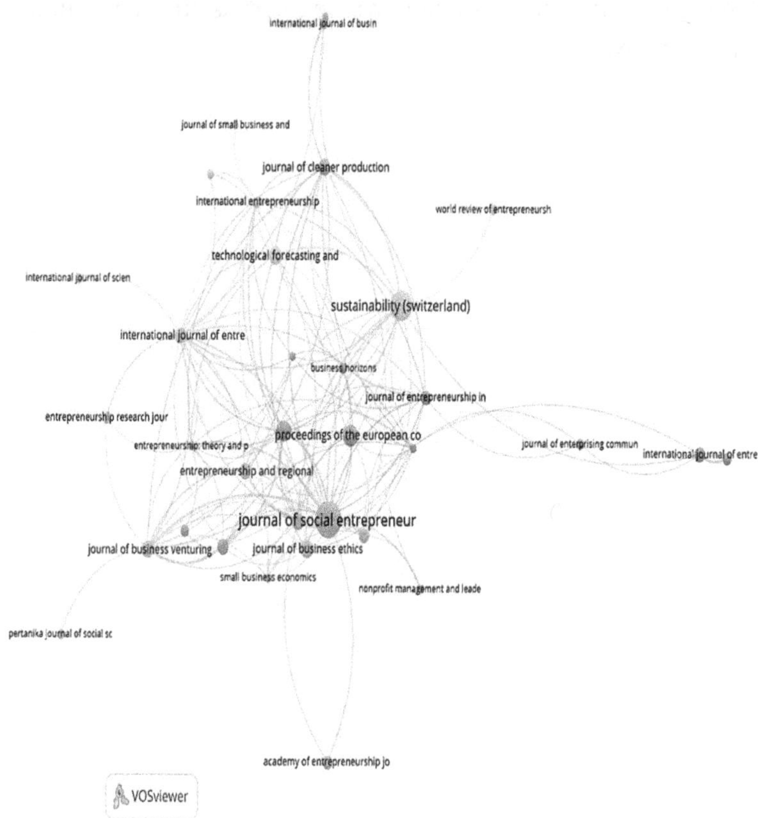

DISCUSSION

As a bibliometric study, the paper produces the additional worth principally according to the perspective of the hypothesis improvement. Its creativity gets from an exceptionally predetermined number of studies that utilize the approach of catchphrases examination to plan the exploration field and recognize driving subjects inside it. The social monetary experts in the cases had titanic social capital, were to some degree especially organized monetarily to begin their endeavors, and had material information, limits, and experience to draw upon (Littlewood & Holt, 2018). Another particular nature of the improvement of SEs in a post-Socialist society which can be tended to by a genuine setting is a confused control of progress in managing social worries. Low end concerning improvement in the nation and all things considered late interests into R&D framework sway the field of social business (Erpf et al., 2022)

Figure 4. Co-occurrence of keywords

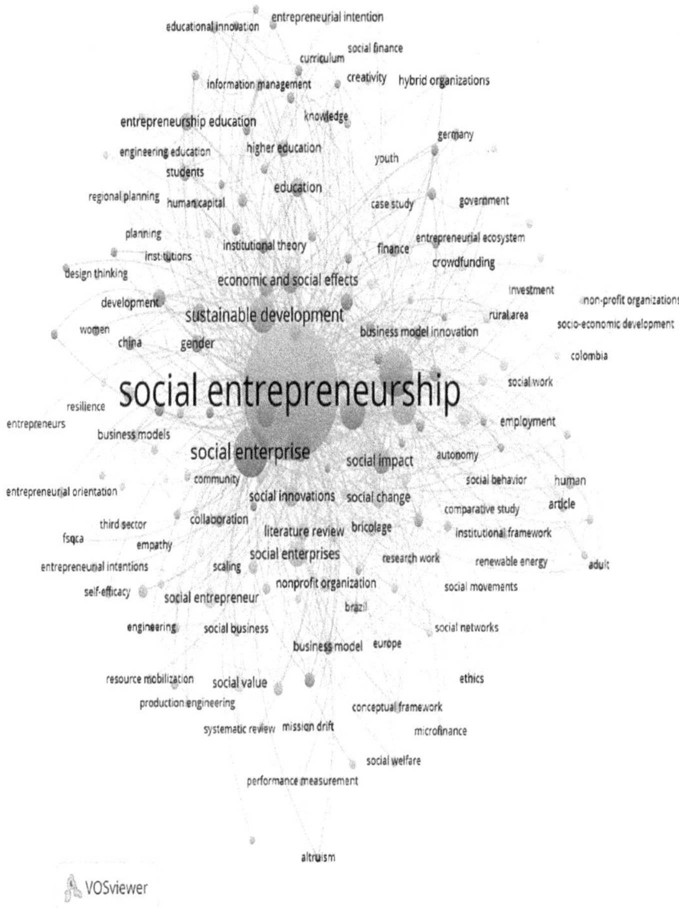

Bibliometric Analysis is used to plan the exploration field. The technique of methodical writing survey is applied to direct the examination of exploration status in the recognized driving topical regions inside the examination field. Planning of the examination field and recognizing arising points gives rules to additional investigations, which can be considered as an important commitment to the hypothesis and exploration advancement. Nonetheless, because of the hypothetical person of the review, its down-to-earth suggestions are fairly restricted. Social business visionaries are vigorous, industrious, and normally certain, with a capacity to motivate others to go along with them in their work. Ordinarily, they feel answerable for a purpose or a mission. Social business visionaries are typically very commonsense, ready to portray their marketable strategies down to the little subtleties (Barendsen Lynn & Gardner Howard, 2004)

CONCLUSION

These days, business, explicitly friendly business venture, is drawing the consideration of so many scholars, specialists, and strategy producers. Social entrepreneurship people assume a basic and critical part in any economy. They are known as friendly change specialists, which can make major commitments to monetary and social advancement. To do as such, the paper reviews the existing writing on SE and proposes a model to assemble the ideas and thoughts and give a comprehensive and normal view to the recipients of this peculiarity. In any case, there is absolutely not an ordinary view with respect to the subject, especially in the field of social business. This paper hopes to elucidate the possibility of SE, as a phenomenal and unquestionable thought. This paper reproduced the current perspective on friendly business as the most recent pattern in undertakings.

This study reveals several disclosures that can assist with planning inspectors in the field of social business. Since they have no effect factor, spread out investigators don't consider these articles as huge, yet they would in any case overhaul the information utilized in the current review with more data about the sincere business. Additionally, following bibliometric studies could keep the bibliometric appraisal by zeroing in on genial business articles inside the Scopus and despite any report that isn't an article, similar to audits, procedures, book surveys, etc.

REFERENCES

A., L., & D., D. (2012). *Social Entrepreneurship. In Entrepreneurship - Gender, Geographies and Social Context*. InTech. doi:10.5772/36056

Austin, J., Stevenson, H., & Wei-Skillern, J. (2012). Social and commercial entrepreneurship: Same, different, or both? *Revista ADM*, *47*(3), 370–384.

Bacq, S., & Alt, E. (2018). Feeling capable and valued: A prosocial perspective on the link between empathy and social entrepreneurial intentions. *Journal of Business Venturing*, *33*(3), 333–350. doi:10.1016/j.jbusvent.2018.01.004

Belz, F. M., & Binder, J. K. (2017). Sustainable Entrepreneurship: A Convergent Process Model. *Business Strategy and the Environment*, *26*(1), 1–17. doi:10.1002/bse.1887

Cardon, M. S., Glauser, M., & Murnieks, C. Y. (2017). Passion for what? Expanding the domains of entrepreneurial passion. *Journal of Business Venturing Insights*, *8*, 24–32. doi:10.1016/j.jbvi.2017.05.004

Erpf, P., Butkevičienė, E., & Pučėtaitė, R. (2022). Between *de Jure* and *de Facto* : Embedding Western Concepts of Social Entrepreneurship in Post-Socialist Reality. *Journal of Social Entrepreneurship, 13*(1), 1–28. doi:10.1080/19420676.2020.1751245

Ferreira, J. J. M., Fernandes, C. I., & Kraus, S. (2019). Entrepreneurship research: Mapping intellectual structures and research trends. *Review of Managerial Science, 13*(1), 181–205. doi:10.100711846-017-0242-3

Gupta, P., Chauhan, S., Paul, J., & Jaiswal, M. P. (2020). Social entrepreneurship research: A review and future research agenda. *Journal of Business Research, 113*, 209–229. doi:10.1016/j.jbusres.2020.03.032

Guzman, A., & Trujillo, M. (2008). Social Entrepreneurship – Literature Review. *Estudios Gerenciales, 24*.

Haugh, H. (2005). A research agenda for social entrepreneurship. *Social Enterprise Journal, 1*(1), 1–12. doi:10.1108/17508610580000703

Jair Duque Oliva, E., Cervera Taulet, A., Rodríguez Romero, C., Mba Dea, M., & de la, Profesor. (n.d.). *Estudio bibliométrico de los modelos de medición del concepto de calidad percibida del servicio en Internet.*

Kraus, S., Filser, M., O'Dwyer, M., & Shaw, E. (2014). Social Entrepreneurship: An exploratory citation analysis. *Review of Managerial Science, 8*(2), 275–292. doi:10.100711846-013-0104-6

Littlewood, D., & Holt, D. (2018). Social Entrepreneurship in South Africa: Exploring the Influence of Environment. *Business & Society, 57*(3), 525–561. doi:10.1177/0007650315613293

Lynn & Howard. (2004). *Is the social entrepreneur a new type of leader?* Academic Press.

Molecke, G., & Pinkse, J. (2017). Accountability for social impact: A bricolage perspective on impact measurement in social enterprises. *Journal of Business Venturing, 32*(5), 550–568. doi:10.1016/j.jbusvent.2017.05.003

Parhankangas, A., & Renko, M. (2017). Linguistic style and crowdfunding success among social and commercial entrepreneurs. *Journal of Business Venturing, 32*(2), 215–236. doi:10.1016/j.jbusvent.2016.11.001

Rey-Martí, A., Ribeiro-Soriano, D., & Palacios-Marqués, D. (2016). A bibliometric analysis of social entrepreneurship. *Journal of Business Research, 69*(5), 1651–1655. doi:10.1016/j.jbusres.2015.10.033

Saebi, T., Foss, N. J., & Linder, S. (2019). Social Entrepreneurship Research: Past Achievements and Future Promises. *Journal of Management*, *45*(1), 70–95. doi:10.1177/0149206318793196

Salamzadeh, A., Salamzadeh, Y., & Nejati, M. (2011). *Social entrepreneurship: Analyzing literature and proposing a comprehensive model*. Academic Press.

Surie, G. (2017). Creating the innovation ecosystem for renewable energy via social entrepreneurship: Insights from India. *Technological Forecasting and Social Change*, *121*, 184–195. doi:10.1016/j.techfore.2017.03.006

Chapter 4
Strategic Framework for Entrepreneurship Education in Promoting Social Entrepreneurship in GCC Countries During and Post COVID-19

Hesham Magd
Modern College of Business and Science, Oman

Shad Ahmad Khan
https://orcid.org/0000-0001-7593-3487
University of Buraimi, Oman

ABSTRACT

The higher education institutes (HEIs) are playing a key role in imparting entrepreneurship education. Entrepreneurship education is mainly based on experiential education and received a setback due to COVID-19 as all the HEIs in the region were forced to shift to unplanned online teaching. This chapter analyses the situation of COVID-19 from the perspective of economy, entrepreneurship, and HEI roles during the pandemic and post-pandemic scenarios. This chapter proposed an environment model suggesting the need for state intervention in the entrepreneurship education that subsequently influences social entrepreneurship.

DOI: 10.4018/978-1-6684-4666-9.ch004

INTRODUCTION

Gulf Cooperation council is constellation of six member countries namely, Saudi Arabia, Oman, Qatar, Bahrain, United Arab Emirates (UAE), & Kuwait. The six member counties being rich in natural oil and gases, have harnessed the oil and gas sector for almost five to eight decades. The revenues generated from Oil & gas exports led the GCC countries to achieve the development goals comfortably. These nations are also members to the Paris agreement (singed in 2015) that requires the member states to come up with measures to combat the issues of global warming and reduction of carbon footprints that directly has an effect on the reduction of fossil fuel usage. To comply with the agreement, and taking the learnings from failed oil producing nations like Venezuela, the GCC countries are preparing themselves for the future by envisioning vision documents for each GCC nation. One of the areas of development and economic diversification is through entrepreneurship. For this, Geo-Political stability, world class infrastructure, strategic location on the global map & surplus of foreign exchange has been an advantage for the GCC nations.

Entrepreneurship education and training has been considered as a potential tool to promote and nurture entrepreneurship (Khan et al., 2019). The innovation in the entrepreneurship are other domains to consider be it agripreneurship or the concepts like self-help groups (Gangwar & Khan, 2022). When it comes to social entrepreneurship (SE), the role of education becomes even more relevant, as education is directly correlated with moral trainings, ethics and civil society, the essential pillars of any social activity including social SE. The social entrepreneurs do not believe in getting direct monetary profit from their enterprise; thus, SE works like a catalyst for social change (Barberá-Tomás et al. 2019). The present study analyses the entrepreneurship education in general and social entrepreneurship in particular, and attempts to provide a strategic framework for promotion of the same.

BACKGROUND OF THE STUDY

The Higher Education Institutes (HEIs) in the GCC countries are also promoting entrepreneurship education by running specialized courses on entrepreneurship (Gangi,2017; Faisal et.al., 2017). These courses touch the element of social entrepreneurship as well. The delivery method of the classes was mainly face to face till the time the outbreak of Covid-19 pandemic happened. This pandemic was a surprise for the world as it quickly spread over the other parts of the world (Ratten,2020; Cortez and Johnston, 2020). This pandemic lead to disruption to global interactions as the countries were forced to close their border, and impose lockdowns/shutdowns (Alon et al., 2020). The Universities too had to close their routine activities and had to conduct their teaching and learning process, through online platform (Ratten,2020; Liguori and Winkler, 2020).

The higher education institutes are equipped to handle the natural disasters like earth quake, tornados etc but are not ready do deal with the health crisis like covid 19 (Ratten,2020). Thus, the universities were not prepared to handle such crisis. Another, aspect to consider was the uncertainty of the duration of this crisis, that again led to miscalculations in terms of strategic formulations on many levels. The Higher Education Institutes were majorly found dependent on the government directives and many universities found limited scope in terms of innovation and out of the box thinking. In other words, education innovation received negligible attention during the current pandemic (Ferreira et al., 2018).

The current Covid-19 crisis has had significant health and workplace implications particularly for educators (Bacq et al., 2020; Bocar et al., 2022). Working and learning from home that used to be considered as a luxury and was optional before the crisis, became a necessity (Ratten,2020). The students were asked to attend the classes online on the other hand the teachers involved in online teaching didn't have the experience of using the digital platform. The availability of the appropriate devices is another issue that needs to be taken care of while implementing the work from home/ learn from home (Scott, 2020; Bocar et al., 2022). All together the current Covid-19 crisis is complex as it changed the way individuals conduct their daily life and for the universities and HEIs it changed the way their services are offered. Ratten, (2020, p 754) states, "The impact of Covid-19 on the global education system has been profound and impacted all areas of teaching, research and service."

Social entrepreneurship, as the name suggests, emerged as the need of the hour, as many non-profit centric activities were found to be doing well during the time of pandemic (Nuringsih, et al., 2020). The social entrepreneurs were involved in the activities like awareness, health volunteer, opening of low cost or free quarantine/ isolation centres, fund raising, helping the needy etc. Covid-19 revealed breaches in the established practices such as healthcare, housing, finance etc, that warrants the need for SE than ever, as SE offers coordinated response that is crucial for cross sector solutions (Bacq and Lumpkin (2020).

The crisis has also brought unique opportunities for the entrepreneurship and entrepreneurship education. There is a need to repurpose the exiting teaching pedagogy with more incorporation of digital technology. The way global community is rapidly responding to the change in teaching and learning methods, the HEIs also need to help their educators to quickly strategize the entrepreneurship education so that better teaching pedagogy can be developed for the ongoing pandemic along with the post covid planning. The researchers, feel that considering the system and practices in the GCC countries, special interventions will be required from the policy makers and the HEIs top management. Although the digital based education needs to be examined more closely to derive on more conclusive practices (Ferreira et al., 2018).

The entrepreneurial opportunities that have emerged in the arena of food security, health care sector, hygiene and sanitation, agriculture, and education needs to be immediately harnessed, thus, requires special attention of the entrepreneurial universities and educators, as entering these sectors will also provide an opportunity for the GCC nations to diversify their economy as envisioned in their vision documents. The HEIs thus, need to have a focused efforts to change their behaviour and take advantage of the change to the digital learning environment. This requires coordinated efforts to be put in by different stakeholders of the HEIs. The universities need an entrepreneurial spirit to cope with the current crisis (Bacq et al., 2020). The educators also have to be innovative in their approach to bring about the change in the present scenario. A more creative and innovative approach is needed to handle the present crisis (Ansell and Boin, 2019). This article aims to provides practical guidance to the policy makers, HEIs management, educators, students and researchers to develop strategies in responding quickly to the ongoing crisis by way on finding the ways of imparting the entrepreneurship education effectively. This article also attempts to analyse the way entrepreneurship education has been affected due Covid-19 in the GCC nations.

ENTREPRENEURSHIP EDUCATION

The entrepreneurship education requires a different approach that often requires it to look beyond classroom teaching to develop entrepreneurial talent. (Ribeiro et al., 2018; Fayolle & Gailly, 2008). The creative thinking, team building, group activities, case studies, action-based learnings are some of the prescribed activities to give a practical experience to the entrepreneurship students (Mahmood et al., 2020; Rae et al., 2009). Field trips to companies, business simulation related activities, business games and related activities are also part of the effective entrepreneurship education (Ruskovaara & Pihkala, 2013; Honig,2004; Pittaway & Cope,2007). In the recent year, idea pitching, start-up exercises, business plan development and presentations have also pitched popularity in the entrepreneurship education (Ribeiro,2018: Singh et al., 2020). In short, experiential learning is the gist of entrepreneurial education, imparting which through online teaching is a point of concern.

The Entrepreneurship educators have been facing the challenge of reducing gap experiential learning and online teaching (He & Harris,2020; Ratten,2020). Even if the entrepreneurship educators propose the use of experiential learnings, but due to the current Covid-19 restrictions, they will not be able to do so. Experiential learning being a widely advocated style of teaching entrepreneurship enables the students to deal directly with reality. They are also encouraged to reflect on their experiences gained thereof (Anggadwita et al., 2017a, 2017b). Increasing the student's ability to connect with the real-life business situation and business community is the primary goal of the entrepreneurship programme. The development of hard as well as soft skills are to be development in a student (Dana,1992). It is worth mentioning that the modern digital platform users are liberated audience as they can respond, react, and contribute to the content shared with them (Verma,2020). The availability of technology and infrastructure to support online education is another aspect to be considered (Ahmad Khan & Magd, 2021).

This challenge cannot be worked out by the educators in isolation and thus, requires the role of all the stakeholder i.e., government, students, industry, community and professionals. The entrepreneurship program needs to get refreshed in order to stay relevant during and post covid-19. Expecting that the world will get back to face to face teaching and old days practice would be back in trade appears to be a miscalculation as legacy of online teaching is expected to stay even after the end of pandemic (Kirk and Rifkin, 2020). It is worth noting that teaching entrepreneurship is not a new idea, but history tells us that it has failed to gain popularity as entrepreneurship education needs real-world immersion and experiential approaches (Ligouri & Winkler,2020; Kassean et al., 2015; Neck et al., 2014).

The online education should not be considered as a replacement to traditional method. Rather online teaching should be considered as a means to elevate the entrepreneurship education (Ligouri & Winkler,2020). The involvement of technology is going to stay in the entrepreneurship education, a balance between traditional learning and online learning has to be created to justify the essence of entrepreneurship education. The education sector in general view Covid19 as a highly problematic event, with serious consequences, however, it should be noted that it has opened the potential for innovation in curriculum development and pedagogy. It has opened up the previously restrictive learning environment to new waves of innovative practices in the arena of entrepreneurship education (Maritz, et al.,2020; Liguori & Winkler,2020). Never in the history of education this kind of shift has happened, thus this requires the entrepreneurship educators to analyse this change in their pedagogy and suggest improvements in entrepreneurship education (Liguori & Winkler,2020).

IMPACT OF COVID-19 ON ECONOMY AND ENTREPRENEURSHIP

Since the initial days of pandemic, a global slowdown in the economy was observed as the economic activities with few exceptions suffered lockdowns as part of Standard

Operating Procedure for Covid-19 protocols. "The pandemic of COVID19 has disrupted every aspect of life. From groceries to medicines, travel to events, sports to funerals, economics to politics and religion to social rights all domains of life have been shaken up by this infectious virus. The impact is deep and will have a lasting effect" (Hasnan, 2020, p. 177). For GCC countries year 2020 was not favourable on the economic front (Al-Kharusi & Murti,2020). The GCC countries that usually backs on Oil exports and tourism suffered the most, as both sectors faced a setback.

The financial and hospitality industry suffered a substantial negative impact globally (Hasnan, 2020). Along with hospitality industry, the banks in the GCC nations have become vulnerable to financial instability due to negative profitability, unacceptably low capital ratios and credit losses during the pandemic (Al-Kharusi & Murti,2020). The stock market in the GCC countries also faced turbulence as the daily returns of the major stock market indices declined following the increase in covid-19 related deaths (Bahrini & Filfilan,2020). Crude Oil prices during the pandemic affected the GCC countries to the maximum, as the GCC stock markets were positively impacted by the crude oil prices and negatively by the variation of implied volatility in global oil market (Bahrini & Filfilan,2020). The largest country in GCC by area and population, Saudi Arabia experienced significantly high exposure to oil risk in the first phase of Covid-19. In second phase of Covid-19, UAE and Saudi Arabia appeared to be more vulnerable to oil extreme risks as compared to other countries (Abu Zayed & Al-Fayomi,2021). The slow-down in the economy and the pressure of reducing the covid-19 cases lead to the problems lower profitability, reduction in demand and job losses.

Entrepreneurship, emerged as an unsung hero during the pandemic (Maritz, et. al., 2020). The GCC entrepreneurs were found to influence the process of procuring resources and improving SMEs performance during the time of pandemic as they possess specific traits to do so (Khan, et.al., 2021). Globally entrepreneurs were found offering their products and services through different channels. Harnessing different infrastructures and embracing diversification by changing their products and services to meet new demands (Maritz, et.al.,2020). The enterprises age & entrepreneur education level were also found to be a key influencer in the performance of Small and Medium Enterprises in the GCC during the COVID-19 (Khan, et.al., 2021). The suddenness of covid-19 pandemic required an immediate attention to the emerging business and economic scenarios. Entrepreneurs being innovative in their approach were able to cope up with it faster (Ratten,2020). In the event of crisis an organisation needs to think in new ways to maintain their competitiveness (Ratten et al., 2017).

Thus, it can be seen that the nation needs to produce and nurture entrepreneurship for which entrepreneurship education is the key. The creation of new businesses is potential solution to create employment, increase productivity, and provide diversification that GCC nations are envisioning through their vision document. As the future generation of entrepreneurs would require additional skills and capabilities to survive and thrive (Maritz, et.al.,2020). The current challenge would be the change in the shifting of traditional face to face teaching method into online platforms that equally creates many opportunities for curriculum innovation (Maritz, et.al.,2020; Liguori and Winkler, 2020).

IMPACT ON HIGHER EDUCATION INSTITUTES (HEIS)

A good higher education system is defined as, "one that maximises its returns (however defined) by creating knowledge and ensuring society, in its intrinsic delivery, is served by a populace with a variety of skills, educated at different yet complementary levels" (Cremonini et al., 2014, p. 343).

Universities & Higher education providers play a significant role in supporting economies and promoting societal well-being (Ratten, 2017). Universities and colleges have always been a point of community building and socialising. The covid-19 led to implementation of serious restrictions. As the remedial measures of covid-19, the borders were closed and lock down were imposed. The HEIs were mandated to have work from home policy that is expected to bring extraordinary changes to the students-teacher relationship and behaviour (Ratten,2020). The shift to online platforms led to reduction in physical contact and dramatically affected the socialisation strategies used in the classrooms (Ratten,2020). Working/Learning from home also requires availability of proper devices and infrastructure (Scott, 2020). The pandemic came as a surprise for world including HEIs who were not prepared with strategies to handle the activities during the covid outbreak.

It cannot be ignored that many innovations happened to complement the social behaviours in the online format. In the technological world, the HEIs are trying to engage more in the community. For this, the characteristics of online learning that it can happen anywhere and anytime is to be properly take advantage of. In view of present pandemic, the universities need to become prepared to the financial threats but at the same time should utilise the innovation to flourish. It would require them to think differently, design new pedagogy and engagement practices considering the social distancing norms. Adoption of the new digital world with proper approach would be the need for the hour (Ratten, 2017; Ratten, 2020).

Universities need to keep imparting their roles to contribute and keep intact the social fabric of the community (Scott et al., 2019). This would require the universities to develop their knowledge capabilities that can influence innovation and creative thinking. This would require proper alignment and coordination between different stakeholders of the universities. Although the world was able to shift to online teaching quickly but an undeniable fact is that this rapid shift was unplanned and might show its adverse outcomes in the times to come. As the students as well as teachers did not have much time to shift digitally. In absence of face-to-face teaching and while engaging in online teaching. Ensuring the students engagement in online teaching same as face-to-face teaching is a dilemma that an educator is expected to suffer (Weick and Sutcliffe, 2011).

Practical and real-life environment are important considerations for an educator. Learning in team through collaboration, experiential learning, and learning by doing have been considered to be very effective (Palalic et al., 2017). Further, training on using online platform is another issue, as the students and teachers were not trained to use the online platform and have to suffer this struggle. Although, some level of knowledge has been grasped by the teachers and students, but lack of formal training would be a consideration (Oyedotun,2020). On the other hand, the government policies and the accreditation requirements are other considerations for the universities. The business schools need to follow the norms set by their regional accreditation bodies, Association to Advance Collegiate Schools of Business (AACSB), the Accreditation Council for Business Schools and Programs (ACBSP), and the International Accreditation Council for Business Education (IACBE) are influencing the educational policy (Ratten,2020). The situation is applicable on all the GCC nations' HEIs as they have been aspiring to get global recognition and attracting international students.

MANAGERIAL IMPLICATIONS

Entrepreneurship is an area that has huge potential specially in the context of GCC. The limitations of finances, infrastructure, complex policies and rules, and unstable geo-political circumstances are not found in the GCC countries. The six oil rich economies have Geo-Political stability, world class infrastructure, strategic location on the global map & surplus of foreign exchange, that multiplies the opportunities for the entrepreneurship in these nations. Entrepreneurship appears to a potential tool in helping the economy of these nations to shift from oil dependency. The living example of entrepreneurship excellence in the region is already available in the form of Dubai. The strategy if Dubai, however was to attract entrepreneurs from the world rather creating its own. Along with attracting entrepreneurs, much of the efforts are to be made in creating entrepreneurs from the region or within the country, that can be only achieved by strengthening the education sector. The type of diversification required by these nations can only be ensured through proper nurturing of future entrepreneurs for which entrepreneurship education and training is essential.

Entrepreneurship education that was already in an embryonic stage in most of the HEIs in the region, has suffered a sudden shock in the name of Covid-19, because of which the way to offer entrepreneurship program in a traditional manner is no longer feasible. Social Entrepreneurship, that was underestimated in many countries emerged as a potential solution during the times of crisis like Covid-19, as it offers sustainability and better coordination among different sectors. The responsibility of promoting entrepreneurship in general and social entrepreneurship in particular lies greatly on the shoulders of the HEIs. As bringing about a change, or implement innovative or creative thinking is not completely under control of the entrepreneurship educators, thus, Entrepreneurship education needs a strategic intervention in the GCC countries, as entrepreneurship is the need for these nations in order to stay abreast with the changing global requirements and their own vision targets. Online education is no longer a passive, and comes with variety of tools and addons to ensure active learning for the learners. Online education also makes the learning process flexible and brings a flair of efficiency in to the learning process. Thus, in the post covid scenario going back completely to traditional method of face to face would not be advisable.

On the other hand, the educators involved in entrepreneurship education need to adapt to the online learning and teaching, this means that the educators need to invest time, energy and money in learning the new digital platforms so that they can improve their online teaching experience for the students. Even if, the situation normalises, the relevance of online teaching and platform will stay because of its undeniable benefits and learning capabilities. The teaching strategies for the GCC countries are expected to revolve around the process adopted from Ratten (2020) as given in Figure 1.

Figure 1. Pre- and post-Covid 19 changes in entrepreneurship education (adopted from Ratten (2020)

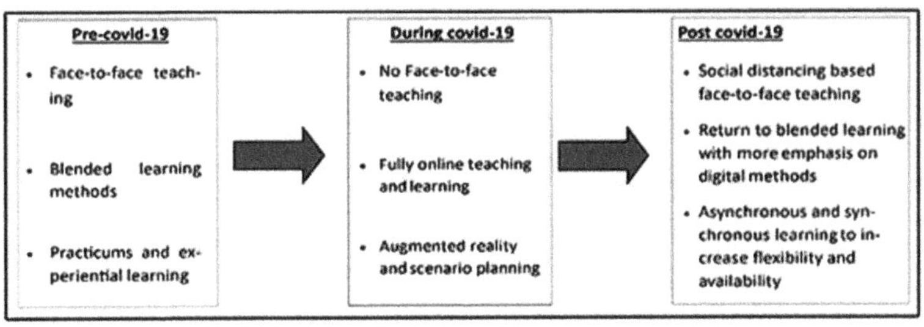

Given the type of society and government in GCC countries the policymakers will have to make policies for the universities in creating avenues for training and development of their teachers and students in learning about the online platforms relevant for the entrepreneurship education. Further, the policies should also cover the availability and affordability of proper devices facilitating effective online and blended learning, strengthening of digital infrastructure along with measures to reduce its cost and implementing a national code for online teaching. This would not be possible if the government of the GCC nations do not intervene and take strategic decisions to ensure effective entrepreneurship education. Thus, the entrepreneurship environment for the GCC nations would have an inclusion of the government policies and intellectual capacities available within the region. The intellectual capacity would include the elements of Resilience, innovation, interactive learning based on a virtual setting, crisis management, that is essential for the entrepreneurship educator as well as the learners to possess. This set requires a good digital and physical capacity in terms of facilities and infrastructure. Further, the Government's vision, approach and policies would supersede all the given platform, the environment of Government's vision, approach and policies would be a super set, under which all the elements would be functioning. This has been illustrated by Figure 2. Modified Environmental changes in pre and post entrepreneurship education.

Figure 2. Modified Environmental changes in pre and post entrepreneurship education

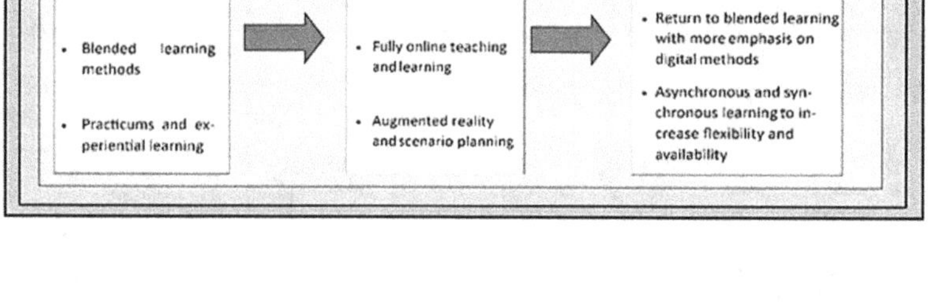

The environmental mapping as done under Fig.2., appears to be a logical environmental analysis for the education in general and entrepreneurship education. This clearly indicates the role that the government has to take with regards to promotion and development of entrepreneurship in the country. If the government doesn't have a will power and vision to promote entrepreneurship, the educators cannot do wonders in isolation, as upon graduation from the HEIs the potential entrepreneurs need further support in terms of finance, ease of doing business, flexibility to apply innovative ideas and take calculated risk. That even makes the role of the government more intense with regards to entrepreneurship education and promote specialised courses on social entrepreneurship.

CONCLUSION

This commentary article has provided an overview of the effect of Covid-19 on HEIs & Entrepreneurship education in the GCC countries. The article has evaluated the aspects of online and offline teaching in light of different available literatures and made an attempt to contextualise the same with the GCC scenario. It made a clear point that the aspirations from the entrepreneurship education cannot be fulfilled without the coordination of different stakeholders, the strategic intervention of the policy makers and the HEIs management is needed in an aligned manner. This article will help the universities to come out of the dilemma of waiting for the traditional ways of teaching rather looking forward and strengthening the online teaching with a blend of face to face once the situation becomes normal.

Limitation of the Study and Direction for Future Research

This paper is based on the literatures published in the arena of entrepreneurship education in context of covid-19 lacks empirical evidence from the GCC countries. The researcher could only estimate the outcomes and results for entrepreneurship as the real impact can only be calculated once the pandemic is over and the real data is computed. Same is applicable on social entrepreneurship being a sub part of entrepreneurship. As the GCC nations are still observing pandemic, the entire education is based on online learning and talking anything about post covid would be anticipatory. The researchers in the arena of entrepreneurship education are gaining interest to understand the changes that the sudden change in teaching pedagogy has been brought in by the covid-19 from the real-life experiences of teachers and students. The strategic intervention too needs to be observed closely, as currently the first focus of every nation is to control the spread of the virus and vaccinate the population, the interventions in the arena of entrepreneurship would be interesting to analyse on a quantitative scale. The way entrepreneurship education has undergone a paradigm shift in terms of teaching and learning methods, the scope for future researches have been widened and multidisciplinary.

REFERENCES

Abuzayed, B., & Al-Fayomi, N. (2021). Risk spill over from crude oil prices to GCC stock market returns: New evidence during the COVID-19 outbreak. *The North American Journal of Economics and Finance*, *58*, 101476. doi:10.1016/j.najef.2021.101476

Ahmad Khan, S., & Magd, H. (2021). Empirical examination of MS Teams in conducting webinar: Evidence from international online program conducted in Oman. *Journal of Content Community and Communication*, *14*(8), 159–175. doi:10.31620/JCCC.12.21/13

Al-Kharusi, S., & Murthy, S. R. (2020, December). Financial Stability of GCC Banks in the COVID-19 Crisis: A Simulation Approach. *The Journal of Asian Finance, Economics and Business*, *7*(12), 337–344. doi:10.13106/jafeb.2020.vol7.no12.337

Alon, I., Farrell, M., & Li, S. (2020). *Regime type and COVID-19 response*. FIIB Business Review. doi:10.1177/2319714520928884

Anggadwita, G., Luturlean, B., Ramadani, V., & Ratten, V. (2017a). Socio-cultural environments and emerging economy entrepreneurship: Women entrepreneurs in Indonesia. *Journal of Entrepreneurship in Emerging Economies*, *9*(1), 85–96. doi:10.1108/JEEE-03-2016-0011

Anggadwita, G., Ramadani, V., Alamanda, D. T., Ratten, V., & Hashani, M. (2017b). Entrepreneurial intentions from an Islamic perspective: A study of Muslim entrepreneurs in Indonesia. *International Journal of Entrepreneurship and Small Business*, *31*(2), 165–179. doi:10.1504/IJESB.2017.10004845

Bacq, S., Geoghegan, W., Josefy, M., Stevenson, R., & Williams, T. (2020). The COVID-19 virtual idea blitz: Marshalling social entrepreneurship to rapidly respond to urgent grand challenges. *Business Horizons*, *63*(6), 705–723. doi:10.1016/j.bushor.2020.05.002 PMID:32398883

Bacq, S., & Lumpkin, G. T. (2020). Social entrepreneurship and COVID-19. *Journal of Management Studies*. Advance online publication. doi:10.1111/joms.12641 PMID:32398883

Bahrini, R., & Filfilan, A. (2020). Impact of the novel coronavirus on stock market returns: Evidence from GCC countries. *Quantitative Finance and Economics.*, *4*(4), 640–652. doi:10.3934/QFE.2020029

Barberá-Tomás, D., Castelló, I., de Bakker, F. G., & Zietsma, C. (2019). Energizing through visuals: How social entrepreneurs use emotion-symbolic work for social change. *Academy of Management Journal*, *62*(6), 1789–1817. doi:10.5465/amj.2017.1488

Bocar, A. C., Khan, S. A., & Epoc, F. (2022). (in press). COVID-19 Work from Home Stressors and the Degree of its Impact: Employers and Employees Actions. *International Journal of Technology Transfer and Commercialisation. Inderscience*.

Cortez, R., & Johnston, W. (2020). The coronavirus crisis in B2B settings: Crisis uniqueness and managerial implications based on social exchange theory. *Industrial Marketing Management*, *88*, 125–135. doi:10.1016/j.indmarman.2020.05.004

Dana, L. P. (1992). Entrepreneurial education in Europe. *Journal of Education for Business*, *68*(2), 74–78. doi:10.1080/08832323.1992.10117590

Faisal, M.N., Jabeen, F., & Katsioloudes, M. (2017). Strategic interventions to improve women entrepreneurship in GCC countries: A relationship modeling approach. *Journal of Entrepreneurship in Emerging Economies*, *9*(2), 161–180. doi:10.1108/JEEE-07-2016-0026

Fayolle, A., & Gailly, B. (2008). From craft to science: Teaching models and learning processes in entrepreneurship education. *Journal of European Industrial Training*, *32*(7), 569–593. doi:10.1108/03090590810899838

Ferreira, J. J., Fayolle, A., Ratten, V., & Raposo, M. (Eds.). (2018). *Entrepreneurial Universities*. Edward Elgar Publishing. doi:10.4337/9781786432469

Gangi, Y. A. (2017). The role of entrepreneurship education and training on creation of the knowledge economy: Qatar leap to the future. *World Journal of Entrepreneurship, Management and Sustainable Development*, *13*(4), 375–388. doi:10.1108/WJEMSD-06-2017-0032

Gangwar, V. P., & Khan, S. A. (2022). Analyzing the Role of Micro-Entrepreneurship and Self-Help Groups (SHGs) in Women Empowerment and Development. In M. Arafat (Ed.), Driving Factors for Venture Creation and Success in Agricultural Entrepreneurship (pp. 213–226). IGI Global. doi:10.4018/978-1-6684-2349-3.ch011

Hasnan, B. (2020). Spillover effect of COVID19 on the Global Economy. *Transnational Marketing Journal.*, *8*(2), 177–196. doi:10.33182/tmj.v8i2.1067

He, H., & Harris, L. (2020). The impact of covid-19 pandemic on corporate social responsibility and marketing philosophy. *Journal of Business Research*, *116*, 176–182. doi:10.1016/j.jbusres.2020.05.030 PMID:32457556

Kassean, H., Vanevenhoven, J., Liguori, E., & Winkel, D. E. (2015). Entrepreneurship education: A need for reflection, real-world experience and action. *International Journal of Entrepreneurial Behaviour & Research, 21*(5), 690–708. doi:10.1108/IJEBR-07-2014-0123

Khan, M. A. I., Azharuddin, S., Khan, S. S., & Ali, M. M. (2021). Influence of Entrepreneur Traits on SME's Financial Performance: Case Study of GCC Entrepreneurs Who Survived during COVID-19. *International Journal of Advance Research and Innovative Ideas in Education, 7*(1).

Khan, S. A., Sharma, P. P., & Thoudam, P. (2019). Role of Attitude and Entrepreneurship Education towards Entrepreneurial Orientation among Business Students of Bhutan. *International Journal of Recent Technology and Engineering, 8*(3S), 335–345. doi:10.35940/ijrte.C1072.1083S19

Kirk, C. P., & Rifkin, L. S. (2020). I'll trade you diamonds for toilet paper: Consumer reacting, coping and adapting behaviors in the COVID-19 pandemic. *Journal of Business Research, 117*, 124–131. doi:10.1016/j.jbusres.2020.05.028 PMID:32834208

Ligouri, E., & Winkler, C. (2020). From Offline to Online: Challenges and Opportunities for Entrepreneurship Education Following the COVID-19 Pandemic. *Entrepreneurship Education and Pedagogy, 3*(4), 1–6. doi:10.1177/2515127420916738

Mahmood, N., Elahi, R. M., Mukhtar, B., Khan, M. M., Javaid, O., & Hyder, I. (2020). Bottom-up framework for experiential & project-based 4-year BS entrepreneurship program: An intrapreneurial conceptualization at institute of business management (IOBM). *Journal of Entrepreneurship Education, 23*(5).

Maritz, A., Perenyi, A., Waal, G., & Buck, C. (2020). Entrepreneurship as the Unsung Hero during the Current COVID-19 Economic Crisis: Australian Perspectives. *Sustainability, 12*(11), 4612. doi:10.3390u12114612

Neck, H. M., Greene, P. G., & Brush, C. G. (Eds.). (2014). *Teaching entrepreneurship: A practice-based approach.* Edward Elgar Publishing.

Nuringsih, K., Nuryasman, M. N., & Amelinda, R. (2020). The propensity for social entrepreneurship during the coronavirus outbreak. *J. Manaj, 24*(2), 174–193.

Oyedotun, T. D. (2020). Sudden change of pedagogy in education driven by COVID-19: Perspectives and evaluation from a developing country. *Research in Globalization, 2*, 1–5. doi:10.1016/j.resglo.2020.100029

Palali´c, R., Ramadani, V., Đilovi´c, A., Dizdarevi´c, A., & Ratten, V. (2017). Entrepreneurial intentions of university students: A case-based study. *Journal of Enterprising Communities: People and Places in the Global Economy, 11*(3), 393–413. doi:10.1108/JEC-12-2016-0046

Pittaway, L., & Cope, J. (2007). Simulating entrepreneurial learning: Integrating experiential and collaborative approaches to learning. *Management Learning, 38*(2), 211–233. doi:10.1177/1350507607075776

Rae, D., Gee, S., & Moon, R. (2009). Creating an enterprise culture in a university: The role of an entrepreneurial learning team. *Industry and Higher Education, 23*(3), 183–197. doi:10.5367/000000009788640279

Ratten, V. (2017). Entrepreneurial universities: The role of communities, people and places. *Journal of Enterprising Communities: People and Places in the Global Economy, 11*(3), 310–315. doi:10.1108/JEC-03-2017-0021

Ratten, V. (2020). Coronavirus (Covid-19) and the entrepreneurship education community. *Journal of Enterprising Communities: People and Places in the Global Economy, 14*(5), 753–764. doi:10.1108/JEC-06-2020-0121

Ribeiro, A. T. V. B., Uechi, J. N., & Plonski, G. A. (2018). Building builders: Entrepreneurship education from an ecosystem perspective at MIT. *Triple Helix (Heidelberg), 5*(1), 1–20. doi:10.118640604-018-0051-y

Ruskovaara, E., & Pihkala, T. (2013). Teachers implementing entrepreneurship education: Classroom practices. *Education + Training, 55*(2), 204–216. doi:10.1108/00400911311304832

Scott, E. (2020). *How to Handle the Stress of Working from Home*. Available from: https://www.verywellmind.com/the-stress-of-working-from-home-4141174

Scott, S., Hughes, M., & Kraus, S. (2019). Developing relationships in innovation clusters. *Entrepreneurship and Regional Development, 31*(1/2), 22–45. doi:10.1080/08985626.2018.1537145

Singh, E. H., Wangda, S., Khan, S., & Khan, S. A. (2020). Exploring the obstacles for start-ups in Bhutan: From a prevented entrepreneurs perspective. *International Journal of Innovation, Creativity and Change, 4.*

Verma, M. (2020). Editorial: Digital Media and the Academic World. *Journal of Content, Community & Communication, 13*(1), 2.

Weick, K. E., & Sutcliffe, K. M. (2011). *Managing the Unexpected: Resilient Performance in an Age of Uncertainty* (Vol. 8). John Wiley and Sons.

Chapter 5
Social Entrepreneurship Intentions Among Business Students in Oman

Hesham Magd
Modern College of Business and Science, Oman

Shad Ahmad K. Khan
https://orcid.org/0000-0001-7593-3487
University of Buraimi, Oman

Ujjal Bhuyan
Jagannath Barooah College (Autonomous), India

ABSTRACT

In today's business environment, the world faces issues like global warming, climate change, food crisis, poverty, population explosion, etc., and social entrepreneurship is a catalyst to all such problems. Even the governments in various countries try to promote social entrepreneurship. Until the students are oriented towards social entrepreneurship optimally, the dream of having a good presence of social entrepreneurship will remain a distant dream. As the students' demand is correlated to their entrepreneurship intention, this study is proposed to check the same in the business colleges in Oman.

DOI: 10.4018/978-1-6684-4666-9.ch005

INTRODUCTION AND BACKGROUND OF THE STUDY

Entrepreneurship has always remained a subject of discussion and a major thrust area among policymakers around the globe. Concern over entrepreneurship has grown over the past few decades, owing to its immense potential in lifting the socio-economic facet of an economy. However, with global focus shifting towards sustainable development and inclusive growth, social entrepreneurship, as a subset of the domain of entrepreneurship has gained paramount importance. To address the various persistent social problems, crippling most economies around the globe, such as poverty, hunger, unemployment, lack of housing, racial discrimination, denial of basic education and many more to this never-ending list, role of social entrepreneurship is of predominant (Hamirul, 2020). A social problem arises when there is a significant gap between what is expected in a society (ideals) and what is achieved. For instance, racial prejudice can be considered a social issue (problem), as even though fair and equitable treatment for all is well accepted in any society, a sizable part of the society is deprived of such treatment. An attempt to narrow down such gap would demand a positive social orientation, which is ultimately the 'set in motion' factor for any social entrepreneur (Kerbo and Coleman, 2006).

To gain a better understanding on the concept of social entrepreneurship, differentiating it with 'traditional' or 'conventional' or 'commercial' entrepreneurship is important. In both types of entrepreneurships, the process of identifying, analyzing, and exploiting of opportunities is involved. However, in conventional entrepreneurship, the process results in profit generation and in case of social entrepreneurship, the resultant output is social values. In order words, the former caters to the entrepreneur's need to create personal wealth, while the latter intent to deliver social value or welfare (Austin et al., 2006). To benefit diverse individuals and society, social businesses and social entrepreneurs establish creative solutions to resolve societal problems, placing social value creation at the center of their goal (Dobele, L, 2016). The concept of Self-Help Groups (SHGs) and micro enterprises too has emerged as a point of study in the recent years as it too aims to overcome the societal problems (Gangwar & Khan, 2022). On the hand entrepreneurship education although is intended to generate entrepreneurship intention, but doesn't guarantee the same (Khan et al., 2019). The same goes with start-ups that may suffer obstacles and often lead to discouragement amongst the potential entrepreneurs (Singh et al., 2020).

SOCIAL ENTREPRENEURSHIP EDUCATION

Dees (1998), recognized a social entrepreneur as change agents who relentlessly strive at creating and sustaining social value. Austin et al., (2006) defined social entrepreneurship as "social entrepreneurship as innovative, social value creating activity that can occur within or across the nonprofit, business, or government sectors". The identification, appraisal, and exploitation of possibilities that contribute to social value, rather than private or stockholder gain, is what social entrepreneurship is all about (Certo & Miller, 2008). A social entrepreneur is thus a person who intends to generate profit by way of risk taking and innovation for the society as a whole or a particular segment of it. Altruism is at the heart of a social entrepreneur (Tan et al., 2015).

Integrating courses related to social entrepreneurship into the present curriculum of colleges and universities is of utmost importance. Introducing social entrepreneurship in higher education would go a long way in creating awareness among student fraternity about various social issues that demands immediate attention, make them more responsive to the problems faced by community members by bringing out creative solutions to such problems, in addition to them becoming more knowledgeable in expressing their opinions to already available solutions in hand (Roslan et al., 2020).

Orientation towards social entrepreneurship would not only promote creative thinking among the students, but also help in revitalizing student's social morality in the modern times and make them more conscious towards sustainable development, which dire need of the hour (Li and Yuan, 2019). Moreover, it would also allow students to leverage the institutional platform in establishing networks or connections with promising social entrepreneurs. Thus, education in or exposure to social entrepreneurship domain would play a significant role in boosting motivation of the younger generation to address pressing social problems. It would help in cultivating a sense of responsibility towards the society and instill a sense of personal accountability (Roshan et al., 2020). However, various challenges may be encountered by the concerned authorities while introducing social entrepreneurship in higher education. Four major challenges in contextualizing social entrepreneurship in higher education: firstly, difficulty faced in designing Social entrepreneurship curriculum, owing to the unawareness and ambiguity surrounding the term 'social entrepreneur', Secondly, lack of proper funding to finance social entrepreneurial initiatives, thirdly, lack of trained professionals in the field of social entrepreneurship and lastly, restrictive institutional environment to foster social entrepreneurial activities (Roshan et al., 2020).

SOCIAL ENTREPRENEURIAL EDUCATION AND INTENTION

Previous literatures on entrepreneurship have placed major thrust on the concept of entrepreneurial intent, as it forms the inception point for any form of entrepreneurship. Thompson (2009) defined entrepreneurial intent as "a self-acknowledged conviction by a person that they will set up a new business venture and consciously plan to do so at some point in the future. Intent is used in the sense of a conscious and planned resolve that drives actions necessary to launch a business". Intention, hence, implies the amount of effort and time one would be willing to devote for a particular behavior. Likelihood of performing such behavior increases with the stronger intentions to perform the same. The precursor role of entrepreneurial intent in driving behavior towards entrepreneurship is endorsed by prominent entrepreneurial theories such as Theory of Planned Behavior and Theory of Reasoned Action. Icek Ajzen in 1985 developed the theory of planned behavior, which is an extension of the theory of Reasoned Action. The theory advocates the significant positive influence of entrepreneurial intention on an individual's likelihood to engage in entrepreneurial activity.

According to the theory, there are three antecedents to behavioral intention: attitude towards the behavior, perceived social norms and perceived behavioral control. All these three variables shaping one's behavioral intention could be positively influenced by entrepreneurial education (Heuer and Kolvereid, 2014; Badr et al., 2018). The theory posits that propensity to execute a particular behavior would likely to increase with the increase in perceived control of such behavioral. Education in this domain of entrepreneurship would motivate individuals to launch new enterprise, if they are confident in their capability to do so (Kirby and Ibrahim, 2011). Hence, entrepreneurial education has a pivotal role to play in boosting one's inclination towards entrepreneurship and his propensity to engage in entrepreneurial activities as it equips one with the desired traits (behavior), skills and knowledge related to entrepreneurship (Paco, et al. 2013).

Such teachings should not only focus on bringing clarity among students regarding the concept of a social entrepreneur and its significance in the current era, but also equip them with skills and competencies necessary for setting up a social enterprise (Kirby and Ibrahim, 2011). Courses on social entrepreneurship in educational institutes would increase the likelihood of students to engage in the process of creation of social enterprise as it has a positive impact on their self-efficacy and on their inclination towards social entrepreneurship (Hockerts, 2018). Considerable amount of research in the past shed light on the influence of personality traits such as propensity to take risk, need for achievement, locus of control etc. on entrepreneurial intention. Such traits become a driving force behind individuals' entrepreneurial intention (Karabulut, 2016). Entrepreneurship education has been found to have significant positive association with such personality traits that induces a person towards entrepreneurial activities (Ndofirepi, 2020).

Educating students on this domain would also help in cultivating a sense of social responsibility and gain desired entrepreneurial competencies and skill set to effectively leverage the available resource pool and provide ingenious solutions to societal problems (Naveed and Zia, 2021). Hasan (2020) also reinforces the influence of education on social entrepreneurship, along with entrepreneurial self-efficacy, in boosting one's intention towards social entrepreneurship. Shahverdi et al., (2018) in their study posits three perceived barriers among students to boosts their social entrepreneurial intention: absence of required competency and skill, lack of self-self-belief and paucity of resources. The findings of the study show that education on social entrepreneurship would significantly help to overcome such barriers and enhance students' inclination towards social entrepreneurship. Moreover, entrepreneurial education also has a significant role to play in building entrepreneurial self-efficacy among students. Kilenthong et al., (2008) in their study found that entrepreneurial education to have significant positive impact on enhancing the level of self confidence among students in performing various entrepreneurial tasks. Studdard et al., (2017) also their study highlighted the importance of teaching students on social entrepreneurship, as it has significant influence on their self-efficacy.

Based on the above reviews, the researchers have postulated the following alternate hypothesis.

H1: Social entrepreneurial education has a significant effect on social entrepreneurial intention

H2: Social entrepreneurial education has a significant effect on social entrepreneurial self-efficacy

SOCIAL ENTREPRENEURIAL SELF EFFICACY AND ENTREPRENEURIAL INTENTION

Entrepreneurial self-efficacy has been found to have positive significant effect on individuals' inclination towards entrepreneurship (Wung and Huang, 2019). Entrepreneurial self-efficacy can be defined "an individual's belief in his or her ability to achieve various entrepreneurial tasks" (Miao, Qian & Ma, 2017; Chen et al., 1998). Individuals with high entrepreneurial self-efficacy tend to perceive consequences differently when compared to those with scoring low on self-efficacy. One with high self-efficacy view the same business environment filled with new opportunities to exploit, while those having low level of entrepreneurial self-efficacy view the same loaded with uncertainties and costs. In a way, individuals with higher level of entrepreneurial self-efficacy exhibit more confidence in dealing with situations filled with risks and obstacles, than those who exhibit lower level of self-efficacy (Chen, et al, 1998). Students' confidence in their ability to manage entrepreneurial activities proves to have significant impact on their motivation to become an entrepreneur (Zhao et al., 2005). Konakli (2015) in her study found that dimensions of self-efficacy: effort and persistence successfully predicted the tenets of social entrepreneurship. Hossain et al., (2021) in their study also supported the role of social self-efficacy on social entrepreneurial intentions.

Based on such review of literature, the researchers propose the following alternate hypothesis:

H3: Social entrepreneurial self-efficacy has a significant effect on social entrepreneurial intention

MEDIATING ROLE OF ENTREPRENEURIAL SELF EFFICACY

Individuals' confidence in their ability to deal or manage entrepreneurial activities (entrepreneurial self-efficacy) has been found to mediate the relationship between entrepreneurial education and their inclination towards entrepreneurship (Nowinski, et al., 2017). Setiwan and Lestari (2021) also confirms the partial mediation effect of entrepreneurial self-efficacy on association between the two variables: entrepreneurial education and entrepreneurial intention. Hoang, et al., (2020) conducted a study on 1,021 students in Vietnam and found that entrepreneurial teaching has a significantly positive impact on the students' entrepreneurial intention. Moreover, the study highlighted the mediation effect of students' self-efficacy and their learning orientation on the above stated relationship. This shows that self-confidence gained from entrepreneurial education plays an important role in shaping one's orientation towards entrepreneurship. Based on the reviews, the researchers propose the following alternate hypothesis:

H4: Social Entrepreneurial self-efficacy mediates the relationship between social entrepreneurial education and social entrepreneurial intention.

METHODOLOGY AND RESEARCH FRAMEWORK

This section intends to explain the research methods and the proposed research framework that is been utilized in the current study. The literatures reviewed as background of the study and hypotheses established, the research framework (Figure

1) is proposed that shows a structural relationship between the constructs. This model warrants to use Structural equation modelling (SEM) as it intends to check the relationship between constructs. As per Hair et al., (2017), SEM analysis helps to identify the causal effect relationship among the constructs by harnessing the combination of factor analysis and multiple linear regressions.

Figure 1. Proposed conceptual framework

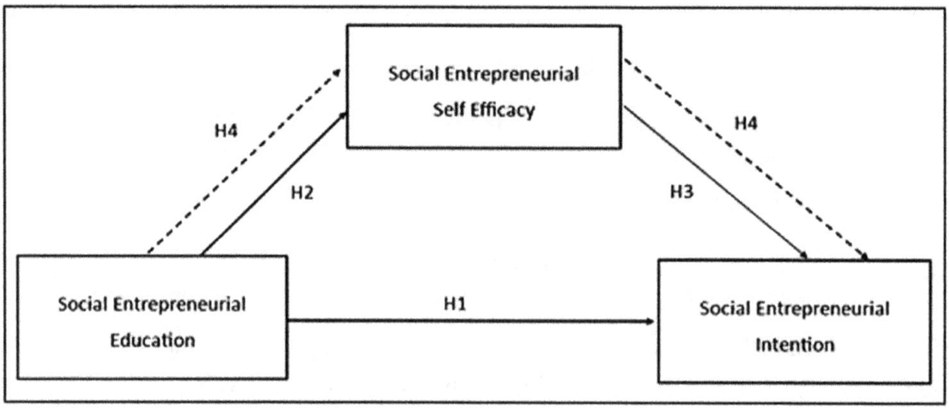

A questionnaire containing 38 items based on 7-point Likert scale and representing three variables was administered through google forms, since the data administration was performed during the time when the face-to-face classes didn't resume in the sultanate, the response rate was poor. The sampled population were mainly from the two prominent HEIs of the sultanate i.e., University of Buraimi and Modern College of Business and Science. The overview of the demographic information segregated in terms of gender is given in Table 1.

To calculate the minimum sample size required for the purpose of this study G*Power (version 3.1.9.7) was utilised (Faul et al., 2007; 2009) that determined the minimum sample size as 59 (Figure 2). That was lower than the actual samples collected i.e., 71. The processed data was analyzed through smart PLS 3.3.6 one of the most recommended software to perform these kinds of studies with wider acceptance of the results (Hair et al., 2019).

Table 1. Demographic statistics of the sample covered for the present study

Row Labels	Frequency Count
Female	**58**
Advanced Diploma	**8**
Non Omani	1
Omani	7
Bachelors	**27**
Omani	27
Diploma	**9**
Non Omani	1
Omani	8
High School	**13**
Non Omani	3
Omani	10
Senior Secondary School	**1**
Omani	1
Male	**13**
Bachelors	**3**
Omani	3
Diploma	**3**
Omani	3
High School	**5**
Non Omani	2
Omani	3
Senior Secondary School	**2**
Non Omani	2
Grand Total	**71**

RESULTS AND DISCUSSION

The model assessment including the considerations like factor load, reliability, and validity of the constructs was performed through the PLS-SEM in SmartPLS. This platform was chosen considering the flexibility and dynamism of this platform for multivariate analytical method. (Ringle et al., 2015; Ahmad Khan & Magd, 2021; Hair et al., 2022; Hair et al., 2019; Richter et al.,2016; Rigdon, 2016; Hair et al., 2020).

*Figure 2. G*power analysis*

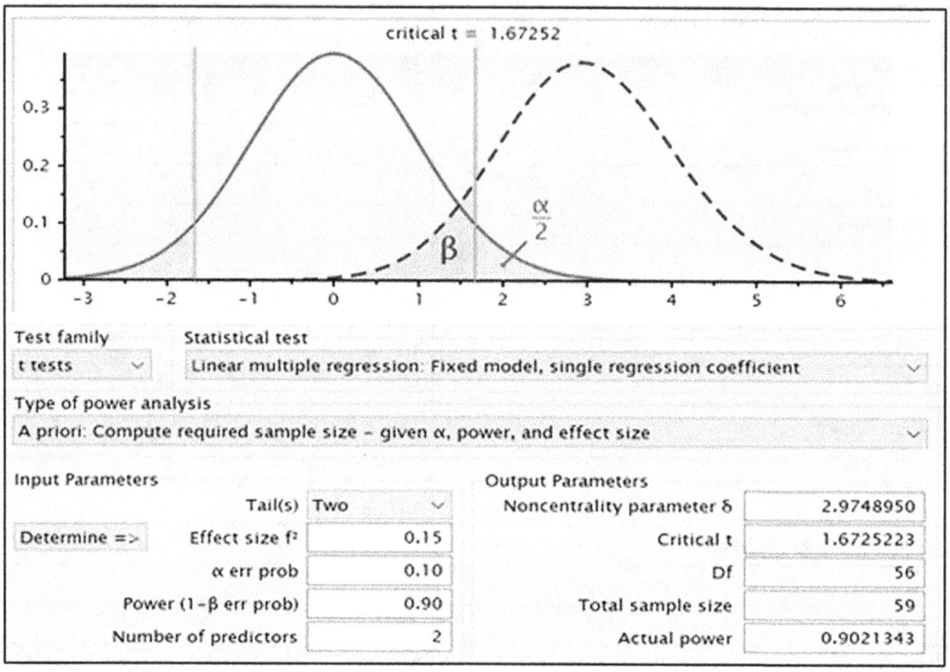

MEASUREMENT MODEL ASSESSMENT

To ensure that efficiency of model assessment, the certain thresholds were adopted i.e., Cronbach's Alpha; rho A; and Composite Reliability (CR) were utilized to check reliability and convergent validity of the constructs, all the values were found to be above the threshold of 0.7 signifying that the data is reliable (Hair et al., 2017; 2020). AVE (Average Variance Extracted) is used to check the convergent validity that was also found greater than 0.50 for the constructs (Hair et al., 2022; Hair et al., 2019). All these values are explained in detail under table 2 and qualify the required threshold. Fornell and Larcker Criterion is utilised to check discriminant validity which under the root of AVE was diagonally higher than the inter-item correlation values (Fornell and Larcker, 1981). The type of the model is reflective where every construct is distinct from each other and therefore the study is best suited for conducting final analysis as explained in Table 3.

An improved tool to check discriminant validity is HTMT method (Henseler et al.,2015), HTMT values need to be less than 0.85 on a conservative side (Henseler et al.,2015; Voorhees et al.,2016; Khan et al., 2021) that was achieved as presented in table 4.

Table 2. Reflective model assessments-quality criteria

	Load	Cronbach's Alpha	rho_A	Composite Reliability	AVE
EE		0.828	0.833	0.874	0.537
EE2	0.691				
EE3	0.786				
EE4	0.750				
EE5	0.692				
EE6	0.723				
EE7	0.752				
EINT		0.918	0.922	0.931	0.55
EINT1	0.703				
EINT11	0.687				
EINT12	0.802				
EINT2	0.735				
EINT3	0.713				
EINT4	0.790				
EINT5	0.730				
EINT6	0.772				
EINT7	0.817				
EINT8	0.679				
EINT9	0.715				
ESE		0.919	0.923	0.931	0.51
ESE01	0.799				
ESE10	0.799				
ESE14	0.733				
ESE15	0.650				
ESE16	0.696				
ESE19	0.615				
ESE2	0.787				
ESE4	0.680				
ESE5	0.650				
ESE6	0.640				
ESE7	0.623				
ESE8	0.778				
ESE9	0.790				

Note: ESE3; ESE11; ESE12; ESE13; ESE17; ESE18; EINT10; and EE1 were dropped from analysis due to low factor load.

Source: Authors' Calculations

Table 3. Discriminant validity- fornel-larckel criterion

	EE	EINT	ESE
EE	0.733		
EINT	0.612	0.775	
ESE	0.731	0.742	0.714

Source: Authors' Calculations

Table 4. Discriminant validity- HTMT ratio

	EE	EINT	ESE
EE			
EINT	0.677		
ESE	0.826	0.824	

Source: Authors' Calculations

STRUCTURAL MODEL ASSESSMENT

The predictive relevance and relationship between constructs can be assessed through structural model assessment (Hair et al., 2017). Once the reliability and the vvalidity are established, it becomes essential to check the multi-collinearity issues, for this VIF (Variance Inflation Factor) is utilized that should be less than 3.33 on a conservative side (Diamantopoulous et al., 2008), however, VIF value less than 5 conforms that there is no collinearity issue among predictor variables (Kock and Lynn, 2012). All outer VIF values for the present model was found to be less than 3.33, that meets with the conservative criteria as per Diamantopoulous et al., (2008). Once the collinearity issue is addressed the significance and relevance of the path coefficient is checked (Shiva et al., 2020). The regression coefficient for the tested model is given in Figure 3.

The coefficient of determination is reported through R^2 which is used to measure the variance in each of the endogenous construct and represents the model's explanatory power (Hair et al., 2017), higher the R^2 signifies higher explanatory power of a construct however, to have a valid threshold, Rasoolimanesh et al., (2017) recommendation i.e., a R^2 value equal to or greater than 0.20 is inferred as high in behavioral and social sciences. As presented in table 6., the R^2 values ranged between 0.53 to 0.60 signifying the explaining ability of the EINT and EE in the proposed model. The hypotheses testing as presented in Table 5, was done through bootstrapping with subsamples as 5000 as per the recommendation of (Hair et al., 2020).

Figure 3. Structural equation model

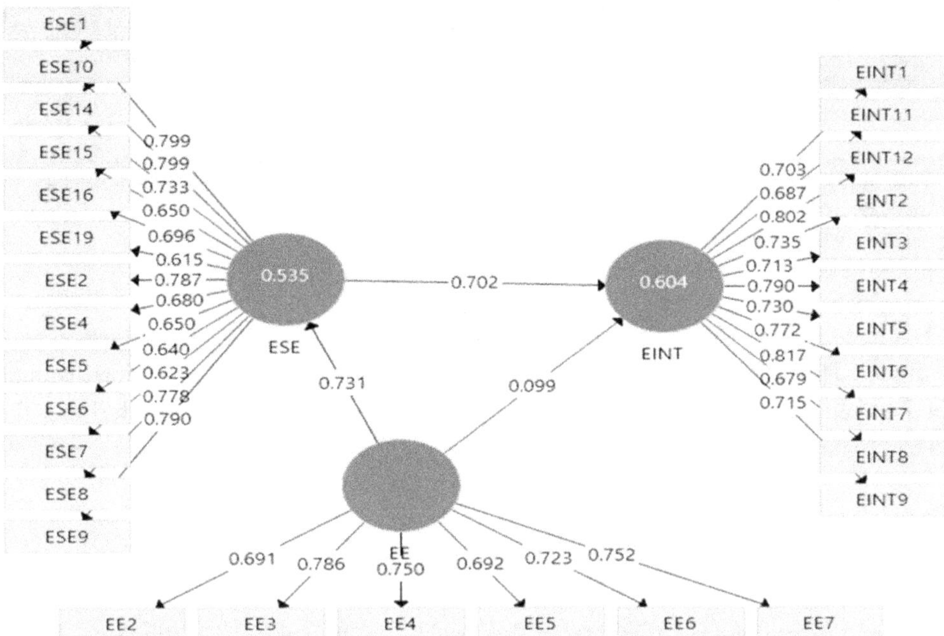

Table 5 discusses that SEM analysis and hypotheses, that suggests that EE (β=0.731, p<0.000) has a significant influence on ESE; ESE (β=0.702, p<0.000) has a significant impact on EINT, thus, on this premise, the hypothesis H2 & H3 are supported in the empirical assessment. The EE (β=0.099) was not found to have a significant impact on EINT. The mediation analysis suggests that ESE is a mediator between EE and EINT, that otherwise has an insignificant relationship, in other words the type of mediation identified was full mediation, and acceptance of H4.

Table 5. Hypotheses testing using PLS structural model for the proposed model

Hypothesis	Beta (β)	Mean	T Statistics	CI (2.5%)	CI (97.5%)	Decision
H_1: EE -> EINT	0.099	0.101	0.700	-0.153	0.399	Not Supported
H_2: EE -> ESE	0.731	0.741	10.699***	0.561	0.838	Supported
H_3: ESE -> EINT	0.702	0.706	5.554***	0.408	0.911	Supported
H_4: EE -> ESE -> EINT	0.514	0.521	5.231***	0.318	0.704	Supported

Note: ***significant at 0.000

Source: Authors' Calculations

Table 6. Predictive power of the model

	R Square	R Square Adjusted	Q Square
EE	-	-	0.341
EINT	0.604	0.593	0.449
ESE	0.535	0.528	0.423

Note: AU: Actual Use; AT: Attitude towards E-Learning; BI: Behavioural Intention; NT: New technology anxiety; PE: Perceived ease of use; PU: Perceived usefulness
Source: Authors' Calculations

Stone-Geisser's Q^2 cross- validated redundancy highlights the predictive power of a model. Through blindfolding method, the Q^2 was obtained with omission distance of 7 as recommended by by Chin (2010) & Hair et al., (2016) suggested that the predictive power is strong i.e., the model has higher generalizability.

CONCLUSION AND RECOMMENDATIONS

One of the evident facts that has emerged in the analysis is that the social entrepreneurship education is inefficient in stimulating the social entrepreneurship intentions among students in Oman. Unless those students have a social entrepreneurship self-efficacy, they will not take up social entrepreneurship as a career option. Individuals' confidence in their ability to deal or manage entrepreneurial activities known as entrepreneurial self-efficacy has been found to have a mediating role in the present study as well supporting the findings of Nowinski et al., (2017); Setiwan and Lestari (2021); and Hoang et al., (2020). This means that the HEIs in Oman needs to put in extra efforts in building confidence, along with the zeal to contribute something towards the society without bothering much about the profits. One of the inevitable threats to social entrepreneurship is the conventional entrepreneurship, that talks about profit maximization and lowering of risk. The social entrepreneurs earn profits without aiming for it, with a prime objective of solving a social problem. This required universities to come up with strategies and living examples of social entrepreneurs. As increased interface with government programs, access to CSR funds, corporate governance and civic responsibility needs to be developed among the youngsters. The key element of the social entrepreneurship i.e., social value creation, can only happen through realizations and prioritization of societal values over the profit motives.

Limitations and Direction for Future Studies

Small sample size was one of the major concerns for this study. As the study focuses on only three constructs the other elements like competence, Social Norm, Personal Attitude, Entrepreneurial Opportunity Recognition, Social Capital, Innovativeness, Locus of control, Risk Taking Propensity etc. are not covered in this study, for which a future study would be recommended to be a more comprehensive and detailed in the arena of social entrepreneurship with relatively higher sample size.

REFERENCES

Ahmad Khan, S., & Magd, H. (2021). Empirical Examination of MS Teams In Conducting Webinar: Evidence from International Online Program Conducted In Oman. *Journal Of Content Community and Communication*, *14*(8), 159–175. doi:10.31620/JCCC.12.21/13

Austin, J., Stevenson, H., & Wei–Skillern, J. (2006). Social and Commercial Entrepreneurship: Same, Different, or Both? *Entrepreneurship Theory and Practice*, *30*(1), 1–22. doi:10.1111/j.1540-6520.2006.00107.x

Badr, N., El-Gharbawy, A., Wahba, M., & Bary, A. A. (2018). The impact of entrepreneurship education on planned behavior. *The Business and Management Review*, *9*(4), 213–222.

Certo, T., & Miller, T. (2008). Social Entrepreneurship: Key Issues and Concepts. *Business Horizons*, *51*(4), 267–271. doi:10.1016/j.bushor.2008.02.009

Chao, C. C., Patricia, G. G., & Ann, C. (1998). Does entrepreneurial self-efficacy distinguish entrepreneurs from managers? *Journal of Business Venturing*, *13*(4), 295–316. doi:10.1016/S0883-9026(97)00029-3

Dees, J. G. (1998). *The Meaning of "Social Entrepreneurship"*. The Kauffman Center for Entrepreneurial Leadership.

Diamantopoulos, A. (2008). Formative indicators: Introduction to the special issue. *Journal of Business Research*, *61*(12), 1201–1202. doi:10.1016/j.jbusres.2008.01.008

do Paço, A., Ferreira, J. M., Raposo, M., Rodrigues, R. G., & Dinis, A. (2015). Entrepreneurial intentions: Is education enough? *The International Entrepreneurship and Management Journal*, *11*(1), 57–75. doi:10.100711365-013-0280-5

Dobele, L. (2016). A New Approach in Higher Education: Social Entrepreneurship Education. In *Proceedings- 11th International Conference on Management, Enterprise and Benchmarking (MEB 2016)*. Óbuda University, Keleti Faculty of Business and Management.

Faul, F., Erdfelder, E., Buchner, A., & Lang, A.-G. (2009). Statistical power analyses using G*Power 3.1: Tests for correlation and regression analyses. *Behavior Research Methods*, *41*(4), 1149–1160. doi:10.3758/BRM.41.4.1149 PMID:19897823

Faul, F., Erdfelder, E., Lang, A.-G., & Buchner, A. (2007). G*Power 3: A flexible statistical power analysis program for the social, behavioral, and biomedical sciences. *Behavior Research Methods*, *39*(2), 175–191. doi:10.3758/BF03193146 PMID:17695343

Fornell, C. G., & Larcker, D. F. (1981). Evaluating Structural Equation Models with Unobservable Variables and Measurement Error. *JMR, Journal of Marketing Research*, *18*(1), 39–50. doi:10.1177/002224378101800104

Gangwar, V. P., & Khan, S. A. (2022). Analyzing the Role of Micro-Entrepreneurship and Self-Help Groups (SHGs) in Women Empowerment and Development. In M. Arafat (Ed.), Driving Factors for Venture Creation and Success in Agricultural Entrepreneurship (pp. 213–226). IGI Global. doi:10.4018/978-1-6684-2349-3.ch011

Gold, A. H., Malhotra, A., & Segars, A. H. (2001). Knowledge management: An organizational capabilities perspective. *Journal of Management Information Systems*, *18*(1), 185–214. doi:10.1080/07421222.2001.11045669

Hair, J. F. Jr, Howard, M., & Nitzl, C. (2020). Assessing measurement model quality in PLS-SEM using confirmatory composite analysis. *Journal of Business Research*, *109*, 101–110. doi:10.1016/j.jbusres.2019.11.069

Hair, J. F., Hult, G. T. M., Ringle, C., & Sarstedt, M. (2017). *A primer on partial least squares structural equation modeling (PLS-SEM)* (2nd ed.). SAGE Publications.

Hair, J. F., Hult, G. T. M., Ringle, C. M., & Sarstedt, M. (2022 in press). *A Primer on Partial Least Squares Structural Equation Modeling (PLS-SEM)* (3rd ed.). Sage.

Hair, J. F., Sarstedt, M., & Ringle, C. M. (2019). Rethinking some of the rethinking of partial least squares. *European Journal of Marketing*, *53*(4), 566–584. doi:10.1108/EJM-10-2018-0665

Hassan, H. M. K. (2020). Intention towards social entrepreneurship of university students in an emerging economy: The influence of entrepreneurial self-efficacy and entrepreneurship education. *On the Horizon*, *28*(3), 133–151. doi:10.1108/OTH-04-2020-0012

Heuer, A., & Kolvereid, L. (2014). Education in entrepreneurship and the Theory of Planned Behaviour. *European Journal of Training and Development, 38*(6), 506–523. doi:10.1108/EJTD-02-2013-0019

Hockerts, K. (2018). The Effect of Experiential Social Entrepreneurship Education on Intention Formation in Students. *Journal of Social Entrepreneurship, 9*(3), 234–256. doi:10.1080/19420676.2018.1498377

Hossain, M. U., Arefin, M. S., & Yukongdi, V. (2021). Personality Traits, Social Self-Efficacy, Social Support, and Social Entrepreneurial Intention: The Moderating Role of Gender. *Journal of Social Entrepreneurship*, 1–21. doi:10.1080/19420676.2021.1936614

Karabulut, A. T. (2016). Personality Traits on Entrepreneurial Intention. *Procedia: Social and Behavioral Sciences, 229*, 12–21. doi:10.1016/j.sbspro.2016.07.109

Kerbo, H. R., & Coleman, J. W. (2006). *Social Problems: A brief introduction* (2nd ed.). Pearson.

Khan, S. A., Epoc, F., Gangwar, V. P., Ligori, T. A. A., & Ansari, Z. A. (2021). Will Online Banking Sustain in Bhutan Post Covid-19? A Quantitative Analysis of The Customer E-Satisfaction and E-Loyalty in The Kingdom of Bhutan. *Transnational Marketing Journal, 9*(3). Advance online publication. doi:10.33182/tmj.v9i3.1288

Khan, S. A., Sharma, P. P., & Thoudam, P. (2019). Role of Attitude and Entrepreneurship Education towards Entrepreneurial Orientation among Business Students of Bhutan. *International Journal of Recent Technology and Engineering, 8*(3S), 335–345. doi:10.35940/ijrte.C1072.1083S19

Kilenthong, P., Hills, G., & Monllor, J. (2008). Impact Of Entrepreneurship Education on Entrepreneurial Self-Efficacy and Intention (Summary). *Frontiers of Entrepreneurship Research., 28*(4), 11.

Kirby, D. A., & Ibrahim, N. (2011). The case for (social) entrepreneurship education in Egyptian universities. *Education + Training, 53*(5), 403–415. doi:10.1108/00400911111147712

Konakli, T. (2015). Effects of Self-Efficacy on Social Entrepreneurship in Education: A Correlational Research. *Research in Education, 94*(1), 30–43. doi:10.7227/RIE.0019

Li, L., & Yuan, F. (2019). Integrating Social Entrepreneurship into Higher Education in the New Era. *Proceedings of the 2019 3rd International Conference on Education, Economics and Management Research.* 10.2991/assehr.k.191221.039

Miao, C., Qian, S., & Ma, D. (2017). The relationship between entrepreneurial self-efficacy and firm performance: A meta-analysis of main and moderator effects. *Journal of Small Business Management*, *55*(1), 87–107. doi:10.1111/jsbm.12240

Naveed, M., Zia, M. Q., Younis, S., & Shah, Z. A. (2021). Relationship of individual social entrepreneurial orientations and intentions: Role of social entrepreneurship education. *Asia Pacific Journal of Innovation and Entrepreneurship*, *15*(1), 39–50. doi:10.1108/APJIE-07-2020-0118

Ndofirepi, T. M. (2020). Relationship between entrepreneurship education and entrepreneurial goal intentions: Psychological traits as mediators. *Journal of Innovation and Entrepreneurship*, *9*(2), 1–20. doi:10.118613731-020-0115-x

Nitzl, C., Roldan, J. L., & Cepeda, G. (2016). Mediation analysis in partial least squares path modeling: Helping researchers discuss more sophisticated models. *Industrial Management & Data Systems*, *116*(9), 1849–1864. doi:10.1108/IMDS-07-2015-0302

Nowiński, W., Haddoud, M., Lančarič, D., Egerová, D., & Czeglédi, C. (2017). The impact of entrepreneurship education, entrepreneurial self-efficacy and gender on entrepreneurial intentions of university students in the Visegrad countries. *Studies in Higher Education*, *44*, 1–19.

Rasoolimanesh, S. M., Jaafar, M., Kock, N., & Ahmad, A. G. (2017). The effects of community factors on residents' perceptions toward World Heritage site inscription and sustainable tourism development. *Journal of Sustainable Tourism*, *25*(2), 198–216. . 1195836 doi:10.1080/09669582.2016

Richter, N. F., Cepeda, G., Roldán, J. L., & Ringle, C. M. (2016). European Management Research Using Partial Least Squares Structural Equation Modeling (PLSSEM). *European Management Journal*, *34*(6), 589–597. doi:10.1016/j.emj.2016.08.001

Rigdon, E. E. (2016). Choosing PLS Path Modeling as Analytical Method in European Management Research: A Realist Perspective. *European Management Journal*, *34*(6), 598–605. doi:10.1016/j.emj.2016.05.006

Ringle, C. M., Wende, S., & Becker, J.-M. (2015). *SmartPLS 3*. Bönningstedt: SmartPLS. Retrieved from http://www.smartpls.com

Roslan, M. H. H., Hamid, S., Ijab, M. T., Yusop, F. D., & Norman, A. A. (2020). Social entrepreneurship in higher education: Challenges and opportunities. *Asia Pacific Journal of Education*, 1–16. doi:10.1080/02188791.2020.1859354

Setiawan, G., & Lestari, E. (2021). The Effect of Entrepreneurship Education to Student's Entrepreneurial Intention With Self-Efficacy As Mediating Variable. *DeReMa (Development Research of Management) Jurnal Manajemen, 16*, 158–178.

Shahverdi, M., Ismail, K., & Qureshi, M. I. (2018). The effect of perceived barriers on social entrepreneurship intention in Malaysian universities: The moderating role of education. *Management Science Letters, 8*, 341–352. doi:10.5267/j.msl.2018.4.014

Singh, E. H., Wangda, S., Khan, S., & Khan, S. A. (2020). Exploring the obstacles for start-ups in Bhutan: From a prevented entrepreneurs perspective. *International Journal of Innovation, Creativity and Change, 4.*

Studdard, N., Dawson, M., Burton, S.L., Leonard, B., and Quisenberry, W. (2017). *Nurturing Social Entrepreneurship and Building Social Entrepreneurial Self-Efficacy: Focusing on Primary and Secondary Schooling to Develop Future Social Entrepreneurs.* Information Resources Management Association. doi:10.4018/978-1-5225-1923-2.ch011

Tan, W., Williams, J., & Tan, T. (2005). Defining the 'Social' in 'Social Entrepreneurship': Altruism and Entrepreneurship. *The International Entrepreneurship and Management Journal, 1*(3), 353–365. doi:10.100711365-005-2600-x

Thompson, E. R. (2009). Individual Entrepreneurial Intent: Construct Clarification and Development of an Internationally Reliable Metric. *Entrepreneurship Theory and Practice, 33*(3), 669–694. doi:10.1111/j.1540-6520.2009.00321.x

Voorhees, C. M., Brady, M. K., Calantone, R., & Ramirez, E. (2016). Discriminant Validity Testing in Marketing: An Analysis, Causes for Concern, and Proposed Remedies. *Journal of the Academy of Marketing Science, 44*(1), 119–134. doi:10.100711747-015-0455-4

Wung, L., & Huang, J. (2019). Effect of Entrepreneurial Self-Efficacy on the Entrepreneurial Intentions of Students at a University in Hainan Province in China: Taking Social Support as a Moderator. *International Journal of Learning. Teaching and Educational Research., 18*(9), 183–200. doi:10.26803/ijlter.18.9.10

Zhao, H., Seibert, S. E., & Hills, G. E. (2005). The Mediating Role of Self-Efficacy in the Development of Entrepreneurial Intentions. *The Journal of Applied Psychology, 90*(6), 1265–1272. doi:10.1037/0021-9010.90.6.1265 PMID:16316279

Chapter 6
Study of Social Entrepreneurship Amongst Youth in Oman

Neelufer Kulkarni
Gulf College, Oman

Seema Varshney
Gulf College, Oman

Said Al Amri
Gulf College, Oman

ABSTRACT

Social entrepreneurship involves groundbreaking and pioneering methodologies to tackle concerns in the domains of education, environment, rational vocation, well-being, and health and human rights and is widely regarded as a building block of the sustainable development of a particular place. Social entrepreneurship is the aptitude an individual has which can transform several economic, environmental, social, and political issues at local and global levels. It is believed that acquaintance of youth to social entrepreneurial practice can impact this change. Social entrepreneurial orientation could be social vision, social attentiveness, innovativeness, and risk-taking. In this chapter, the authors have made an attempt to understand the youth's intention towards the social entrepreneurship. The data is collected from 123 students studying in different institutes and universities, as well as from the individual who are working or have their own startups. The study used partial least squares-based structural equation modelling.

DOI: 10.4018/978-1-6684-4666-9.ch006

1. INTRODUCTION

Social entrepreneurship is in the evolving stage as a field of investigation and it suggests a new level of innovation and novelty at the level of academic research, as it redefines and enhances the current economic theory (Swanson & Di Zhang, 2010, as cited in (lancu, Popescu, & Popescu, 2021).Social entrepreneurship can be understood as an entrepreneurial venture which aims to solve social and environmental problems. These enterprises concentrate on economic and social problems such as unemployment, access to education, environment preservation and drug abuse play a critical role in creation of social and economic value. According to the Sustainable Development Goals Report 2021 (https://unstats.un.org/sdgs/report/2021/) worldwide 14% of youth were neither engaged in education, training nor employment. In Oman, unemployment in the age group of eighteen to twenty-four years stood at 15.3% and 10.1% and 8.7% of job seekers possessed a higher diploma and bachelor's degree respectively (Statistical Year Book 2021). Entrepreneurship, especially Social Entrepreneurship, provides an excellent avenue for decent and productive employment. In light of this, the current study seeks to examine the factors which shape the attitudes and in turn the intention to start a social entrepreneurial venture in Oman.

Researchers have highlighted the importance of social entrepreneurship and have identified the role of personality traits (Luc, 2020), leadership traits (Cohen, Kaspi-Baruch, & Katz, 2019) and personal initiative (Nsereko, Balunywa, Munene, Orobia, & Muhammed, 2018) in influencing attitudes towards starting a social entrepreneurial venture. Studies such as Sahoo & Panda (2019), Herman (2019),Tu, Bhowmik, Hasan et al (2021) have identified the significant impact of entrepreneurial orientations on entrepreneurial intentions among students. Oman based studies focus on motivations entrepreneurial ecosystem (Issa Ala eddin & Thomas, 2018), entrepreneurial challenges (Matriano, 2019),advantages of encouraging start-ups (Magd & McCoy, 2014) and the impact of social media (Al Harrasi, Hakro, Srinivasan, Matriano, & AL Jabri, 2021). In the area of social entrepreneurship Varghese(2018) compared perceived challenges of social entrepreneurship and innovative entrepreneurship in Oman whereas Muthurman, Al Haziazi, & Al Hajri (2020) the importance of social entrepreneurship in Oman. To the best of the authors knowledge there is no empirical study modelling the impact of social entrepreneurial attitude on social entrepreneurial intentions. A plausible explanation can be that since social entrepreneurship is an emerging field in Oman it has not received much attention. The current study seeks to bridge the gap in existing literature by exploring the factor affecting social entrepreneurial attitude and its impact on entrepreneurial intention using Partial Least Square- Structural Equation Modeling. The remaining chapter is organized follows: Section 2 discusses the review of previous literature, Section

3 discusses the conceptual model and states the hypothesis which will be tested, section 4 discusses the research methodology adopted section 5 and 6 present the results and discuss the findings respectively, Section 7 And 8 present the directions for future research and conclusion.

2. LITERATURE REVIEW

VanSandt, Sud, & Marme (2009) regard social entrepreneurs as an important tool to alleivate the problems of capitalism. The study identified "effectual logic, enhanced legitimacy through appropriate reporting metrics, and information technology" as the three important catalysts which could predict social entrepreneurial intentions.

In research paper "Factors influencing social entrepreneurship intentions in Romania" Anica Lancu and Popescu & Posescu discusses fear of failure, not having stable income, lack of experience, lack of involvement in social projects are few of the barriers in social entrepreneurship. Lack of required funds is also mentioned as one of the major barrier in social entrepreneurship.

Mair & Noboa in their paper "Social Entrepreneurship: How Intentions to Create a Social Venture are Formed" merged traditional entrepreneurship theories with evidence to examine the factors which influence behavioral intentions. The study identified perceived social venture desirability and perceived social venture feasibility as the influential factors affecting intentions to start a social venture. The authors further state that social venture desirability is affected by attitudes such as empathy and moral judgment; and perceived social venture feasibility is facilitated by social support and self-efficacy beliefs

In their paper Boubker, Arroud, & Ouajdouni (2021) investigated whether entrepreneurship education had an impact on entrepreneurial intentions of Moroccan students. According to the proposed model, four variables "entrepreneurship education, attitude towards entrepreneurship, perceived social norms and perceived entrepreneurial capacity" were identified as having an effect on entrepreneurial intentions. The indicate PLS-SEM results indicate that "there is a statistically significant relationship between management student's entrepreneurship education, attitude towards entrepreneurship and entrepreneurial intention".

Herman (2019) examined the main determinants of entrepreneurial intentions in one hundred and thirty-eight engineering students in Romania. The study found entrepreneurship education, entrepreneurial family background and entrepreneurial personality traits had a direct effect on students' entrepreneurial intentions

Social innovation is not accepted in seclusion by single-handed entrepreneurs, rather it is an interactive process molded by the shared between number of Institutions and organizations that impact expansions in certain areas to meet a social need or to stimulate social development. Networking and interactions not only endorse the generation of new knowledge but also support social initiatives or social entrepreneurship attain and cultivate better competences. (Philips, Lee, Ghobadian, Regan, & James)

To encourage a socially conscious, sustainable economy where the matters of society are studied and observed, a study in Egypt shows only quality of education is not enough the purpose and process should also be taken care of. The students apart from learning about social entrepreneurship and entrepreneurs, should also be informed and taught about the skills, abilities and attempt should be made to develop a favourable attitude towards social enterprise (Kirby & Ibrahim).

In research paper "Intentions towards social entrepreneurship among university students in India" three important factors are as identified which restraints the intention of students towards initiating social entrepreneurship i.e., fear of risk, lack of financial and moral support and lack of knowledge about social entrepreneurship. Fear of risk was identified as the main cause restraining the youngsters to take up the idea of social entrepreneurship. (Chengalvala & Rentala, 2017)

Tu, Bhowmik, Hasan, Asheq, & Rahaman (2021) examined the dimensions of entrepreneurial orientations and their direct and indirect impact on social entrepreneurial orientation. Data was collected from a purposive sample of four hundred and sixty five graduate and post graduate students in Bangladesh using the online survey and PLS based SEM was used to assess the proposed model. The study findings releaved that social vision was a key determinantant of Social entrepreneurial attitude. The study suggests that educational institutions should incorporate social issues in their teaching pedagogy.

Tran & Korflesch (2016) proposed a conceptual model for social entrepreneurial intention based on social cognitive career theory. With the objective to identify social entrepreneurial intentions among graduate students in India, Tiwari, Bhatt, & Tikoria (2017) used a seventy item questionnaire to collect data from three hundred and ninety university students. Amongst Emotional Intelligence, creativity and social obligations, creativity showed the strongest positive effect on entrepreneurial orientation.In a futher study by the same author,cognitive styles and self-efficacy were used as antecedents to explain social entrepreneurial intention. The findings, based on a sample of five hundred and fifty students of premier higher educational institutions, reveal that self efficacy was an important determinant in shaping attitudes towards a social entrepreneurial venture.

3. CONCEPTUAL MODEL AND HYPOTHESIS DEVELOPMENT

The willingness and dedication to address a social problem is the stepping stone to create a social enterprise. Vision for a better society creates goals and shapes attitude towards social start up. The ability to offer new solutions is historically considered as an important factor in shaping entrepreneurial attitude. Similarly, Social Innovativeness or the ability to provide innovative solutions to a social problem can affect attitude towards social entrepreneurship. Risk and uncertainty are the twin problems which any business venture has overcome. The ability to foresee obstacles and devise plans for the same is a critical factor for success of a venture. The ability of handle risks and be prepared with action plan for obstacles or Risk-Taking motive can affect attitude towards social entrepreneurship. Potential entrepreneurs should have an optimistic picture of the future business conditions. Perception regarding availability of easy credit and financing options, favorable government policies and prestige associated with entrepreneurial activity act as a motivating factor to start a new venture. Universities offer entrepreneurship as a part of their curriculum. The effectiveness of entrepreneurial education and training can develop positive attitude and build confidence in starting an entrepreneurial venture. The current study seeks to identify the effect of social vision, social innovativeness, risk taking measure, entrepreneurial education and perception of business environment on social entrepreneurial attitude and the impact of social entrepreneurial attitude on social entrepreneurial intention.

Figure 1. Conceptual model

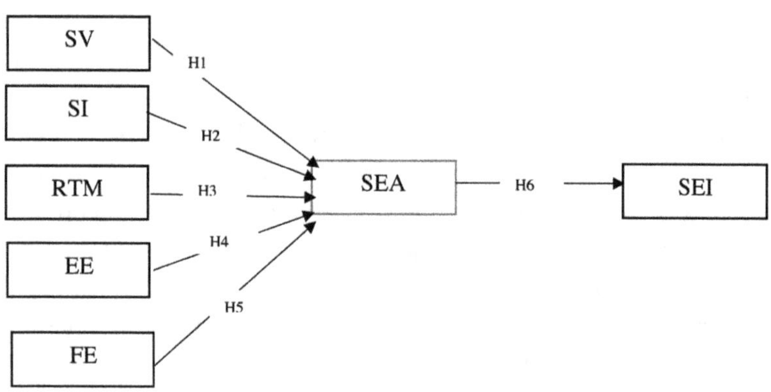

The study will test the following research hypothesis:

H_1: Social Vision has a statistically significant positive impact on social attitude
H_2: Innovativeness has a statistically significant positive impact on social attitude
H_3: Risk taking measure has a statistically significant positive impact on social attitude
H_4: Entrepreneurial Education has a statistically significant positive impact on social attitude
H_5: Financial Environment has a statistically significant positive impact on social attitude
H_6: Social Attitude has a statistically significant positive impact on social entrepreneurial intention

4. RESEARCH METHODOLOGY

The population for the study included youth residing in Muscat, Sultanate of Oman. The study used purposive sampling technique. The objective of this study is to examine the factors influencing social entrepreneurship attitude and the impact of social entrepreneurship attitude on Social entrepreneurial intention. Data was collected through an online survey which was emailed and shared on social media platforms. The questionnaire was divided into three sections. The first section included demographic and behavioral questions such as age, gender, educational qualification, employment status and involvement in social projects. Section two contained items on Social Vision, Innovativeness, Risk taking motive, financial environment, entrepreneurial education and Social Entrepreneurial Attitude. The constructs were defined as:

- **Social Vision**: Social Vision is the sturdy determination, willpower and resilience to solve social problems
- **Social Innovativeness:** It is being unique, innovative, creative and investigational in resolving issues and problems
- **Risk Taking Motive**: It is in the hope of greater achievements accepting the probability of loss and under uncertainty in decisions.
- **Social Entrepreneurial Attitudes**: Social Entrepreneurial Attitude is being affirmative, positive and optimistic towards social entrepreneurship.
- **Social Entrepreneurial Intention**: Social Entrepreneurial Intention is intention and determination towards creating a social entrepreneurial venture.
- **Entrepreneurial Education**: Formal or informal training related to entrepreneurship

- **Financial Environment:** It is ease and accessibility of financial resources to start the entrepreneurial start up

Social Vision, Innovativeness and Risk-Taking Motive scale was adopted from Sulphey & Salim (2021). These constructs were measured through three, five and four items respectively. Entrepreneurial Education and financial environment was measured through a three and five item scale adopted from Satar & Natasha (2019). Social entrepreneurial attitude consisted of items adopted from Miranda, Mera, & Rubio (2017). Section three consisted five items adpoted from Urban & Kujinga(2017) to measure social entrepreneurial intentions.All the items were measured on a 7-point Likert scale where 1= Strongly disagree and 7= Strongly Agree.

The study used partial least squares based structural equation modelling (PLS SEM) method for validating and testing the proposed model. The rationale for using for using PLS - SEM are: Firstly, the objective of the current study is to predict social entrepreneurial intention. Secondly, data is collected on a 7-point Likert scale and is most likely to violate the normality assumption. Lastly the proposed sample size of one hundred and twenty-three is greater than ten times the largest construct.

5. RESULTS

5.1. Demographic Profile

The study received one hundred and twenty-three responses. Data was checked for unengaged responses by calculating the standard deviation of scores of each respondent. All the respondents had attentively completed the survey. As for the demographic composition, sixty-one percent were females, thirty-nine percent had a bachelor's degree in business administration and seventy-three percent were nationals. After examining the respondent profile, the study assessed the measurement model.

5.2. Measurement Model Analysis

As the proposed model had eight reflective constructs, the study first examined the internal reliability. The indicator loadings were greater than the cut off value of 0.708, as recommended by Hair, Risher, Sarstedt, & Ringle (2019), implying that more than fifty percent of of the construct's variance was explained by the indicator's variance. Reliability and convergent validity was examined through cronbach's alpha,composite reliability and average variance extracted. As can be observed from table 2, the cronbach's alpha (α) and composite reliability (CR) lie between 0.7 and 0.93 demonstrating internal reliability of the constructs. The Average Vaariance extracted (AVE) is greater than the cut off value of 0.5 indicating the presence of convergent validity.

Table 1. Construct reliability and convergent validity

Construct	Items	Loadings	Cronbach's Alpha	CR	AVE
Social Vision	SV1	0.726			
	SV2	0.861	0.799	0.878	0.708
	SV3	0.925			
Social Innovativeness	SI1	0.890			
	SI2	0.905			
	SI3	0.812	0.823	0.842	0.764
	SI4	0.913			
	SI5	0.841			
Risk Taking Measure	RTM1	0.814			
	RTM2	0.800	0.868	0.908	0.711
	RTM3	0.852			
	RTM4	0.905			
Entrepreneurial Education	EE1	0.860			
	EE2	0.932	0.898	0.934	0.825
	EE3	0.931			
Financial Environment	FE1	0.884			
	FE2	0.917			
	FE3	0.847	0.915	0.934	0.742
	FE4	0.744			
	FE5	0.747			
Social Entrepreneurial Attitude	SEA1	0.775			
	SEA2	0.883			
	SEA3	0.895	0.887	0.916	0.685
	SEA4	0.763			
	SEA5	0.818			
Social Entrepreneurial Intention	SEI1	0.874			
	SEI2	0.904			
	SEI3	0.901	0.906	0.913	0.880
	SEI4	0.870			
	SEI5	0.838			

Source: Smart PLS Output

Discriminant validity was assessed through the Fornell-Larcker criterion and Heterotrait-Monotrait (HTMT) ratio. The HTMT ratio was lower than the cut off value of 0.85 and the sqaure root of AVE was greater than the paired co-relations between the constructs implying the constructs possessed discriminant validity.After ascertaining that the constructs were internal reliability, consistency and discriminant validity, the structural model was assessed.

Table 2. Discriminant validity

Fornell-Larcker Criterion							
	EE	**FE**	**RTM**	**SINV**	**SATT**	**SINV**	**SV**
EE	**0.909**						
FE	0.639	**0.861**					
RTM	0.356	-0.028	**0.843**				
SINV	0.317	-0.245	0.719	**0.828**			
SATT	0582	0.069	0.749	0.729	**0.938**		
SINV	0.246	0.067	0.629	0.595	0.437	**0.847**	
SV	0.351	-0.073	0.638	0.733	0.539	0.569	**0.842**
Heterotrait-Monotrait (HTMT) Ratio							
	EE	**FE**	**RTM**	**SINV**	**SATT**	**SINV**	**SV**
EE							
FE	0.702						
RTM	0.396	0.147					
SINV	0.348	0.268	0.765				
SATT	0.626	0.113	0.796	0.743			
SINV	0.275	0.171	0.731	0.685	0.451		
SV	0.392	0.200	0.691	0.820	0.521	0.672	

Source: Smart PLS Output

The assessment of the measurement model showed that the social entrepreneurial orientation, social entrepreneurial attitude and social entrepreneurial instentions scale had sound psychometric properties. The next step was to estimate the structural Model.

5.3. Structural Model Analysis

According to Hair, Risher, Sarstedt, & Ringle (2018) the structural model is assessed based on the coefficent of determination, cross validated redundancy measure Q^2

which is obtained through blindfolding and the statistical significance of the pathe coefficents.Each of these measures are discussed in the following paragraphs.

Before assessing the structural relationships the study ensured that collinearity among the constructs was absent. As the Variance Inflation Factor (VIF) was below 5 indicating low probability of collinearity among the constructs, the study examined the R^2. The R2 values can range between 0 and 1 and as a guideline and values above 0.75 can be considered as having substantial explanatory power (Hair, Risher, Sarstedt, & Ringle, 2018). From the R^2 , it can be implied that 75.2% of variation in Social Entrepreneurial Attitude can be explained by Social vision, Innovativeness, Risk taking measure, financial environment and economic environment. In turn Social entrepreneurial attitude can explain 53% of variation in the intention to start a social entrepreneurial venture. From the Q^2 values, moderate predictive consistency of the path model can be implied.

Table 3. Results of explanatory and predictive analysis

Construct	R^2	Q^2
Social Entrepreneurial Attitude	0.752	0.402
Social Entrepreneurial Intention	0.531	0.414

Source: Smart PLS Output

The following table presents the results of path analysis.The results show that Social Vision, Socicial Innovativeness and financial environment have statistically significant impact on social entrepreneurial attitude and social entrepreneurial attitude has a statistically significant impact on social entrepreneurial intention. The results also indicates that there is no statisticallly significant impact of Risk Taking measure on social entrepreneurial attitude.

Table 4. Hypothesis testing

Hypotheses			β	*t*-Statistic	p-Value	Inference
H_1:SV	→	SEA	0.27	3.82	0.00	Accepted
H_2:SI	→	SEA	0.19	2.27	0.03	Accepted
H_3:RTM	→	SEA	0.26	0.82	0.42	Rejected
H_4:EE	→	SEA	0.17	2.22	0.03	Accepted
H_5:FE	→	SEA	0.47	1.96	0.05	Accepted
H_6:SEA	→	SEI	0.75	8.930	0.00	Accepted

Source: Smart PLS Output

6. DISCUSSION OF THE FINDINGS

The objective of the study was to find the impact of social vision, social innovativeness, risk taking measure entrepreneurial education, financial environment on social entrepreneurial attitude. The study found that social vision has a statistically significant positive impact on social entrepreneurial attitude. Vision for a better society creates goals and shapes a positive attitude towards social start up. By creating an awareness of the problems facing the society and introducing social work as a part of the educational curriculum will help to create a vision better society. Students should be encouraged to take a social activity such as paper and plastic recycling awareness campaigns, tree plantations, blood donation drives to state a few so that a vision for better society is inculcated in them.

The study found a statically significant impact of social innovativeness on social entrepreneurial attitude. Youth can be encouraged to find innovative solutions for social problems. Competitions can be organized and the innovative solutions can be recognized and awarded. This will instill ability to provide innovative solutions to a social problem. Entrepreneurial education had a significant impact on attitude towards social entrepreneurship. Educational institutions can be effective in nurturing social entrepreneurship. They can include more hands-on training in starting a social venture. Perception regarding a favorable financial environment had a significant impact on attitude. Lastly Social entrepreneurial attitude had a significant impact on social entrepreneurial intention. This implies that due attention must be given to inculcate a positive attitude towards social entrepreneurship.

7. CONCLUSION

The present paper has identified the role of youth's social vision, innovativeness, social pro-activeness, entrepreneurial education, financial environment and risk-taking motive to craft encouraging social entrepreneurial attitudes and behavioral intention to adopt social entrepreneurship-based venture. This study intends to make a significant impact on the form of social entrepreneurship knowledge and insights regarding social entrepreneurial behavior. the study considers social entrepreneurial attitude and intention as consecutively dependent variables; however, other significant factors such as green or sustainable entrepreneurial behavior can be adopted as dependent variables in a single framework.

There exists a need to motivate and encourage those who have a yearning to start venture for a social cause. Universities and training institutes plays a important role in motivating and inspiring the youth to be social entrepreneurs and comprehend their goal. Social entrepreneurship has proven to be a promising and important global phenomenon that certainly deserves rigorous attention from academics, government and other training institutes.

To conclude, the findings, can be a basis of current knowledge, perceptions, and inferences for the researchers, entrepreneur, practitioners, managers, and policymakers of the social entities and social enterprises to metamorphose an individual's willingness and intention into action toward embracing career based on social entrepreneurship.

8. FUTURE RESEARCH DIRECTION

This paper examines social entrepreneurial attitude and intention as successively dependent variables. Future research topics can study other factors of substantial importance such as green or sustainable entrepreneurial behavior as dependent variables. In addition, cross nationality and cultural research as comparative study (developed versus developing country) can be taken up as future research attempt to inspect and validate effect generalization of the existing study. Finally, future research would be intended to investigate the mediating role of social entrepreneurial attitude, as well as the moderating role of nationality and cross culture on the current study's framework to understand whether youth's nationality or culture has any impact on the path relationship.

REFERENCES

Ajzen, I. (2011). The theory of planned behaviour: Reactions and reflections. *Psychology & Health*, 1113–1127.

Al Harrasi, N., Hakro, A. N., Srinivasan, V., Matriano, M. T., & Jabri, AL, M. (2021). Social Media Impact on Young Entrepreneurs in Oman. *Indian Journal of Economics and Business*, *20*(3), 1365–1392.

Boubker, O., Arroud, M., & Ouajdouni, A. (2021). Entrepreneurship education versus management students' entrepreneurial intentions. A PLS-SEM approach. *International Journal of Management Education*, *19*(1), 100450. doi:10.1016/j.ijme.2020.100450

Chengalvala, S., & Rentala, S. (2017). Intentions towards social entrepreneurship among university students in India. *International Journal of Research-Granthaalaya*, 406-413.

Cohen, H., Kaspi-Baruch, O., & Katz, H. (2019). The social entrepreneur puzzle: The background, personality and motivation of Israeli social entrepreneurs. *Journal of Social Entrepreneurship, 10*(2), 211–231. doi:10.1080/19420676.2018.1541010

Hair, J. F., Risher, J. J., Sarstedt, M., & Ringle, C. M. (2018). When to use and how to report the results of PLS-SEM. *European Business Review, 30*(1), 2–24. doi:10.1108/EBR-11-2018-0203

Hair, J. F., Risher, J. J., Sarstedt, M., & Ringle, C. M. (2019). When to use and how to report the results of PLS-SEM. *European Business Review, 31*(1), 2–24. doi:10.1108/EBR-11-2018-0203

Herman, E. (2019). Entrepreneurial Intention among Engineering Students and Its Main Determinants. *Procedia Manufacturing, 32*, 318–324. doi:10.1016/j.promfg.2019.02.220

Issa Ala eddin, M., & Thomas, B. J. (2018). A Review of the Entrepreneurship Ecosystem of Oman. *International Journal of Professional Management.*

Kirby, D. A., & Ibrahim, N. (n.d.). The case for (social) entrepreneurship education in Egyptian Universities. *Education + Training*, 403–415.

Lancu, A., Popescu, L., & Popescu, V. (2021). *Factors influencing social entrepreneurship intentions in Romania*. Economic Research-Ekonomska Istraživanja.

Luc, P. T. (2020). The influence of personality traits on social entrepreneurial intention among owners of civil society organisations in Vietnam. *International Journal of Entrepreneurship and Small Business, 40*(1), 291–308. doi:10.1504/IJESB.2020.107799

Magd, H. A., & McCoy, M. P. (2014). Entrepreneurship in Pman:Paving the Way for a Sustainable Future. *Emerging Market Queries in Finance and Business*, 1632-1640.

Mair, J., & Noboa, E. (n.d.). Social Entrepreneurship: How Intentions to Create a Social Venture are Formed. In *Social Entrepreneurship*. Palgrave Macmillan. doi:10.1057/9780230625655_8

Matriano, M. T. (2019). Oman Entrepreneurship Highlights: A Case Study of Nawa International. *Advances in Social Sciences Research, 6*(6), 1–12. doi:10.14738/assrj.66.6443

Miranda, F. J., Chamorro-Mera, A., & Rubio, S. (2017). Academic entrepreneurship in Spanish universities: An analysis of the determinants of entrepreneurial intention. *European Research on Management and Business Economics, 23*(2), 113–122. doi:10.1016/j.iedeen.2017.01.001

Miranda, F. J., Mera, C. A., & Rubio, S. (2017). Academic entrepreneurship in Spanish universities: An analysis of the determinants of entrepreneurial intention. *European Research on Management and Business Economics*, *23*(2), 113–122. doi:10.1016/j.iedeen.2017.01.001

Muthurman, S., Al Haziazi, M., & Al Hajri, A. (2020). Importance of Social Entrepreneurship in Oman towards the Sustainable Development. *Waffen-und Kostumkunde*, *11*(2), 138–150.

National Centre for Statistics and Information. (2021). *Statistical Year Book 2021*. National Centre for Statistics and Information.

Nsereko, I., Balunywa, W., Munene, J., Orobia, L., & Muhammed, N. (2018). Personal initiative: Its power in social entrepreneurial venture creation. *Cogent Business & Management*, *5*(1), 1443686. Advance online publication. doi:10.1080/23311975.2018.1443686

Philips, W., Lee, H., Ghobadian, A., Regan, N., & James, P. (n.d.). Social Innovation and Social Entrepreneurship: A Systematic Review. *Group & Organization Management*. doi:10.1177/1059601114560063

Sahoo, S., & Panda, R. K. (2019). Exploring entrepreneurial orientation and intentions among technical university students: Role of contextual antecedents. *Education + Training*, *61*(6), 719–736. doi:10.1108/ET-11-2018-0247

Satar, M. S., & Natasha, S. (2019). *Individual social entrepreneurship orientation: Towards development of a measurement scale. Asia Pacific Journal of Innovation and Entrepreneurship.*

Sulphey, M., & Salim, A. (2021). Development of a tool to measure social entrepreneurial orientation. *Journal of Entrepreneurship in Emerging Economies.*

Tiwari, P., Bhat, A. K., & Tikoria, J. (2017). Predictors of social entrepreneurial intention:an empirical study. *South Asian Journal of Business Studies*, *6*(1), 53–79. doi:10.1108/SAJBS-04-2016-0032

Tiwari, P., Bhatt, A. K., & Tikoria, J. (2017). An empirical analysis of the factors affecting social entrepreneurial intentions. *Journal of Global Entrepreneurship Research*, *7*(9), 1–25. doi:10.118640497-017-0067-1

Tran, A. P., & Korflesch, H. V. (2016). A conceptual model of social entrepreneurial intention based on the social cognitive career theory. *Asia Pacific Journal of Innovation and Entrepreneurship*, *10*(1), 17–38. doi:10.1108/APJIE-12-2016-007

Tu, B., Bhowmik, R., Hasan, M. K., Asheq, A. A., Rahaman, M. A., & Chen, X. (2021). Graduate Students' Behavioral Intention towards Social Entrepreneurship: Role of Social Vision, Innovativeness, Social Proactiveness, and Risk Taking. *Sustainability*, *13*(11), 13–36. doi:10.3390u13116386

Urban, B., & Kujinga, L. (2017). The institutional environment and social entrepreneurship intentions. *International Journal of Entrepreneurial Behaviour & Research*, *23*(4), 638–655. doi:10.1108/IJEBR-07-2016-0218

VanSandt, C. V., Sud, M., & Marme, C. (2009). Enabling the Original Intent: Catalysts for Social Entrepreneurship. *Journal of Business Ethics*, *90*(S3), 419–428. doi:10.100710551-010-0419-z

Varghese, T. (2018). Social Entrepreneurship Realities: Do a Country Need Social Entrepreneurs or Innovative Social Entrepreneurs? *International Review of Management and Business Research*, *7*(1), 186–190. doi:10.30543/7-1(2018)-17

Chapter 7
Green Entrepreneurship Paving a Way to Sustainable Development

Shweta Devendra Shirolkar
Dr. Vishwanath Karad MIT World Peace University, India

Madhuri Shete
Dr. Vishwanath Karad MIT World Peace University, India

Rajashri Kadam
Dr. Vishwanath Karad MIT World Peace University, India

Meenal Pendse
https://orcid.org/0000-0001-7225-311X
Dr. Vishwanath Karad MIT World Peace University, India

ABSTRACT

Entrepreneurship is defined as the process of starting or launching a new business with innovative products and services with an intention of not only generating profits but also value to different stakeholders along with its risk. Due to global concerns of climate change and sustainability, consumers have started consuming green products and showing their socially responsible behavior. There is a need to bring change in sustainable production and consumption. This problem can be solved at grass root level by new enterprises that are keen on solving these concerns. So, the transformation of green economy can be entrepreneur-driven by those who have innovative and sustainable ideas which are commercially viable. Hence, the objective of the chapter is to investigate the concept of green entrepreneurship, green innovations in business, and its significance. The chapter also explains the future perspectives and trends of green entrepreneurship paving a way to sustainable development.

DOI: 10.4018/978-1-6684-4666-9.ch007

INTRODUCTION

The Global environmental crisis is rising day by day and we as human beings are hard pressed to think on some innovative solutions for the issues. Unfortunately the crises which we are discussion the impact of the same is huge and massive. World of Business is the better place to start with and people should start thinking about unique solutions. Ideation and Unique solution to a given problem give rise to the complete domain of Entrepreneurship. Green Entrepreneurship is defined as "Businesses and start-up organizations coming up with innovative and unique solution for the environmental problems or concerned faced by all." The solutions are expected to have application at the global level and contribute towards environmental safety and pro- environmental behavior. The person who is behind setting up such ideas, such businesses which comprises all the products and services which has green design is termed as "A Green Entrepreneur."

Green innovations play very crucial role now a day as everyone is educated in terms of sustainable consumption and having concerns for the environment. The conception of green innovation is in the development of new and competitive products, services, processes, procedures and systems which are designed to use natural resources at a minimum level and to provide better quality of life to the society, Green innovation helps in developing competitive advantage and works more on environmental performance with the use of natural resources. The objectives of green innovations are decrease of pollution, energy productivity, decrease of waste, substitution of limited resources with sustainable resources and recycling (Kemp & Arundel, 1998). Green innovation helps in reducing environment effect of the company, solves the environmental problems of the company, and develops environment friendly process. It has been argued that green entrepreneurs, who aim to accomplish both business and environmental goals, have a transformative influence on their sectors and play a major role in sustainable development Green entrepreneurship and sustainable development are very closely linked. They think and all dimensions- economic, environmental and social needs balance for perfect functioning of sustainability (Johnson and Schaltegger, 2020).

Green entrepreneurship is relatively recent concept and started getting magnetism since 1990s. Green entrepreneurs are the economic actors who play central role in turning ideas in reality by transforming business designs or prototypes into commercial viable ventures. Green entrepreneurship, eco entrepreneurship and ecopreneurship are few of the names used interchangeably for same phenomenon. Green entrepreneurship is the process of defining and exploiting opportunities that are present in environmentally relevant market failures (Dean and McMullen, 2007) entrepreneurs using business tools to preserve open space, develop wildlife habitat, save endangered species and generally improve environmental quality. (Anderson and Leal, 1997) The earlier study has shown that a firm-level green entrepreneurship framework with three dimensions: green initiatives, government green support and green political influence factors directly enhance firm performance. (Mengli Zhao et. Al 2021)

Green entrepreneurship is getting more attention as it is considered as a way towards achieving sustainability. As an outcome of growing awareness of all these environmental changes, consumers are also changing their lifestyle and accepting eco-friendly products. This shift is leading towards the Green markets and entrepreneurs are entering in the Eco businesses. Recently Green entrepreneurs are considered as the catalyst in the economic development of the nation as they are the dynamic force in innovating and launching the new thoughts. Developed countries are focusing more on green whereas developing countries are focusing on entrepreneurship in developed countries and developing countries. The green entrepreneurs struggle to break through dominant trends, but regulative support at appropriate moments may help this transition by promoting a vision for collective action. Even though the environmental entrepreneurs facilitate processes of change through their actions, they are strongly influenced by broader business environment factors and their actions indicate role shifts between being proactive, influential actors and reactive, self-centered players. (Zahraie et al. 2016)

The concept is evolved around 1990 and highest contributions are from 2000. From a growth outlook of "Green entrepreneurship" is an increasingly apt phenomenon, which is still largely under-researched. Green entrepreneurship also plays a significant role in job creation. There are noticeable developments in environmental auditing as well as in technological research and implementation but still we can identify significant gap towards sustainability. So the understanding of pre-condition for the formation of "green innovation" is very critical along with its cause and barriers. Green entrepreneurship has become a vibrant field of research in the last few years Need to study what work has been done on the topic so far is the need recognized by the researchers. It seems important to do the bibliometric survey of the available literature in the field. The quantitative survey of available literature is done in this research which will be useful for other researchers and budding green entrepreneurs.

CONCEPTUAL OVERVIEW

The concept of green entrepreneurship is emerging as a hot cake and playing a vital role in terms of business development, which links sustainable development to entrepreneurship (Schaltegger & Wagner, 2008, Anil Kumar 2018). Green entrepreneurship has the potential to become the inspirational force behind the development of a new comprehensive sustainable system in all three aspects –

environment, economy, and society. In green entrepreneurship, more concern is given to ecological dimensions of sustainability which have the target to minimize the business impact on the natural environment (Gast et al., 2017). In traditional entrepreneurship, the main emphasis is on economic value creation and regional development, while in green entrepreneurship the economic aspect is considered as a means to achieve the social and environmental aspects. In addition to the economic perspectives, conventional entrepreneurs are more answerable to the sustainability requirements based on environmental legislation as well as consumer demands for green and sustainable products. However, the factors that make an entrepreneur green, in addition to the financial performance, are the environmental dimension in the core business strategy and that business opportunities are seized to eliminate the harm done to the natural environment (Cohen and Winn, 2007). In the 1990's Bennett (1991), Berle (1991), and Blue (1990) were the first to refer to the concepts of 'environmental entrepreneur', 'green entrepreneur', 'eco-entrepreneur', and 'ecopreneur'. Green Entrepreneurship is an activity that is consciously addressing environmental, and social problems and identifies the need to define its implementation. (Green Project, 2012). In enhancing sustainable environmental consciousness, it is necessary to discover the key issues, significance, and consequences of green washing and green entrepreneurship. Green entrepreneurship is a concept that needs to be practiced in every walk of business planning and execution of the course of the action plan.

REVIEW OF LITERATURE

A review of Literature was done on highly cited manuscripts published on Green Entrepreneurship. Out of the top highly cited 30 documents 6 manuscripts were the Review papers in which the academic literature on Green Entrepreneurship was synthesized to understand the current status of the academic literature on Green Entrepreneurship, and 10 manuscripts have followed the qualitative methodology to conduct in-depth interviews, phenomenological studies to explore the concept of Green Entrepreneurship and transition to Green Economy, 12 manuscripts followed the quantitative methodology to empirical conduct the studies on Green entrepreneurship, Eco- Entrepreneurship and only 2 conducted the mixed-method study deploying both qualitative and quantitative approach. This section consists of the details of all the manuscripts as per their methodology and respective findings associated with Green entrepreneurship.

REVIEW PAPERS

(Gast, Gundolf and Cesinger, 2017) conducted a review study on the concept of ecologically sustainable entrepreneurship. The analysis was conducted on 114 scientific articles to understand the drivers of ecological entrepreneurship for engagement and for conducting business. Challenges and enablers of ecological entrepreneurship and gave the future research agenda on the phenomenon while giving the integrative framework to conceptualize ecological entrepreneurship. (Demirel, Li, Rentocchini and Tamvada, 2017) conducted a study on existent literature to study the impact of factors like industry life cycle, knowledge spill-over, knowledge spillover, institution and external finance available, and how these factors are shaping the decision making of the green start-up which has steadily increased to address the issue of environmental concerns. (Alsaleh and Mahroum, 2014) conducted a review study on Green Policy instruments and Green Business Models. The article also aims to define the interplay between green policy instruments and green business models. (Antolin-Lopez, Martinez-del-Rio and Cespedes-Lorente, 2019) conducted a review study to have the conceptualization of environmental entrepreneurship. The need for the study was felt when it was found that the concept of environmental entrepreneurship is a very fragmented phenomenon that instills challenges in theoretical development, and empirical findings. The findings of the review suggested that environmental entrepreneurship is a multicomponent and dynamic construct that majorly has 3 interrelated components. The three components are the duality of goals, environmental agency, and environmental value creation. (De Bruin, 2016) in his study explains the transition toward the green economy and different factors impacting this transition. It presents the multi-level conceptual framework to advance the understanding of the transition to the green economy. (O'Neill and Gibbs, 2020) conducted a review study on the failure of a zero-carbon house in the United Kingdom. The authors integrated the literature on sustainability transition and policy dismantling and the role of government policies to bring in these changes. A different phase of the policy change was identified and reviewed to study the impact of these on the future of sustainability transition.

QUALITATIVE STUDIES

(Dixon and Clifford, 2007) conducted an exploratory study to understand how ecopreneurs can create an economically viable business while retaining the core social and environmental values. The study used the qualitative approach towards the research and found a strong link between entrepreneurialism and environmentalism. The study also posits that the entrepreneurial stint of the organization's head enables the achievement of economic, social, and environmental goals. (Allen and Malin, 2008) conducted a study to identify the patterns of social awareness of the green entrepreneurs and how that can be used in the management process of the natural resources. Case study analyses were conducted by the authors of small green entrepreneurs. In-depth, interviews were also conducted and several themes which emerged were low levels of interest in economic success; high degrees of awareness about the business's environmental impact; and high levels of concern for social justice. Additionally, some important constructs emerged as a finding of the study which are personal motivation, locality, mission, and forward-thinking orientation. (Gibbs and O'Neill, 2014) conducted 55 semi-structured interviews to study the development of green entrepreneurship and how it shapes the transition towards the green economy. The study assesses both the perspectives of entrepreneurial research and the socio-technical research specifically multi-level perspectives to better understand the role of green entrepreneurs to facilitate the transition towards a green economy. (O'Neill and Gibbs, 2016) conducted a follow-up study to rethink the role of green entrepreneurs to bring in the green economy transition. The study concluded that there is a need that policy developers should evaluate the complex nature of green entrepreneurship and its role in the transition. It should be seen as a collection of different actors involved not only the corporate reinventions. (Grinevich, Huber, Karataş-Özkan and Yavuz, 2017) conducted a study to understand the green potential of the sharing economy entrepreneurs. 30 semi-structured interviews were conducted to understand the green logic of sharing economy players. The results sharing economy players can grow with the green logic along with the social and economic goals in a flexible manner. (Mrkajic and Murtinu, 2016) conducted a study to understand the relationship between green entrepreneurship and venture capitalist funding. The research question which was taken to answer was is there any relation between and business being a green start-up and its capability to attract funding. The results of the study showed that there is no relationship between any business running on green technologies and any business positioning itself being a green business that has a higher capability to attract funding. (Hall, Matos and Bachor, 2017) studied the influential role of green entrepreneurs in shaping government policy documents to diffuse green technology. The study incorporates the technological, commercial, organizational, and societal framework of innovative uncertainties to identify hurdles opportunities, and challenges at a very young stage of technology development. (Staggenborg and Ogrodnik, 2015) studied the transition to environmentalism in Pittsburgh. Observation in-depth depth interviews were conducted to understand the openness toward the green movement. It was found that the orientation is positive towards the open space model but there is less efficacy to devise the strategies and grow the organization. (Kouri and Clarke, 2012) conducted a study on Green Jobs which are yet to be defined with clarity. The study utilizes discourse analysis and frame analysis to analyze the content on the aspect of Green Jobs. The results of the study identified 5 primary fames – environmental economy bridge, green entrepreneurship, nascent industry creation, internal industry transformation, and structural adjustments. (Haldar, 2019) conducted a study to highlight the ecological and social crises created by the profit-oriented industry and the need to have the intervention of the policymakers to incorporate the guidelines for sustainable innovations.

QUANTITATIVE STUDIES

(Ebrahimi and Mirbargkar, 2017) conducted an empirical investigation to study green innovations and SME development in market turbulence conditions. The author also studied the role of Green entrepreneurship to bring in SME development. 112 senior managers of SMEs were surveyed to take the data on green innovation, SME development, and views. The findings of the study revealed that there is a significant relationship between green innovation and SME development with the mediating effect of green entrepreneurship. (Nikolaou, Ierapetritis and Tsagarakis, 2011) conducted a research study to analyze strengths, weaknesses, opportunities, and threats to understand the public policy guidelines for local entrepreneurs for incorporating sustainable practices. The result of the study indicates that the institutional, structural, social, and economic factors play a crucial role in new business investing in activities associated with natural resource conservation. (Ge, Jiang, Gao and Tsai, 2016) determined a theoretical framework to conceptualize the relationship between green pro-activeness behavior, green performance, legitimacy, and transitional economies. Based on a survey conducted in China the result of the study posits green performance can be easily achieved if green start-ups have higher legitimacy. However, transitional economies can increase institutional uncertainty and hamper green performance by inculcating legitimacy issues. (Lotfi, Yousefi, and Jafari, 2018) studied the impact of the emerging market on green entrepreneurship and sustainable development. The authors try to develop a theoretical framework and also tested to study the relationship between the mentioned constructs. The findings of the study revealed that the emergence of the green market has a positive and significant impact on green entrepreneurship and sustainable development. Also, Green entrepreneurship has a positive significant impact on sustainable development. (Doukas, Tsiousi, Marinakis and Psarras, 2014) conducted a study for small and medium-sized enterprises. The research posits the need for State to support SMEs with appropriate policies for fostering green entrepreneurship. The study developed a model using a multi-criteria framework with linguistic variables to assess the corporate policies regarding green energy growth. (Zhao, Shang, and Song, 2020) studied China's urban ecological efficiency with the help of the panel data. The findings of the study propose that while promoting green entrepreneurship activity Chinese Government should give full play to industrial structure advancement to improve ecological efficiency. (Yi, 2020) conducted a research study on green entrepreneurship behavior of University students. The model was developed to understand the construct of green entrepreneurship behavior, university support, and external institutional support to foster green entrepreneurship among students. (Soomro, Ghumro and Shah, 2019) studied the inclination of the younger generation towards green entrepreneurship behavior.284 survey forms were collected from the respondents. The study's findings showed a significant relationship between sustainability education and sustainability orientation and inclination towards green entrepreneurship. There is an insignificant relationship between the self-efficacy of the respondent and the inclination toward green entrepreneurship. (Drăgoi et al., 2017) conducted an interesting study on agri- tourism. The focus of the study was to assess the constraints and factors impacting the growth of agri-tourism in rural communities of Romania. The factors like regional GDP and kilometers of National road support the Agritourism activity. (Papadopoulos, Karagouni, Trigkas, and Beltsiou, 2014) conducted a quantitative evaluation on the acceptance of green furniture in Greece and Cyprus which ultimately depends on several firms producing Greek and Cypriot furniture. Sectoral experts were also interviewed to give their opinions on the acceptability of the product. (Qazi et al., 2020) studied the role of personality traits, university green entrepreneurial support on the green entrepreneurial intention with the moderation role of environmental values. The findings of the study reveal that the personality traits are significantly associated with green entrepreneurial intention, but risk-averse students depict insignificant results towards green entrepreneurial intention. (Corradini, 2017) studies the location determinants of the green firms across the European region. The study intends to understand the distribution of new green technology-based firms are distributed and located across the European region.

MIXED-METHOD STUDIES

(Silajdžić, Kurtagić and Vučijak, 2015) conducted a study to answer some open questions knowledge on diffusing entrepreneurship activity, role, and mode of operations of public policies, externalities created for the society, and the connection between sustainability and entrepreneurship. The study aims to initiate the discussion on sustainable entrepreneurship in economies of transition. The authors conducted a review of literature, structured interviews, and case study analysis. The findings of the study reveal that entrepreneurs in the economies of transition are not ready to take the risk to invest in sustainable business. Also, Government and policymakers are not understanding their role to support sustainable business and its development. Forward-thinking orientation, personal motivation, locality, and mission are some of the constructs that can support the sustainability of green businesses.

(Braun, 2010) studied the women entrepreneurs to understand the gender attitudes and behavior towards green entrepreneurship. The study appointed exploratory method as well as quantitative data sets to analyze the attitude and behavior. The result of the study finds that women entrepreneurs are more inclined attitudinally toward green business concepts compared to their male counterparts. The generalizability of the study is required to be tested for the larger population. The implication of the study is on business innovation, a green marketplace, and a sustainable post-carbon future.

Various themes which emerged out of the review of literature done on Green Entrepreneurship are Review of Green Entrepreneurship as a concept, its drivers, actions, and challenges, green economy transition, SME development, Women entrepreneurship, Sustainable tourism, Governance, Policy issues, Support for Green business, Funding for Green business, Behavioral Studies.

As depicted in the Review of literature all kinds of methodologies have been deployed by the authors to work on the concept of Green Entrepreneurship. Several research studies are less using mixed methods compared to that qualitative and quantitative studies. This posits the method gap in the academic research published on Green Entrepreneurship. Also, the Review paper and research papers present the phenomenon of Green Entrepreneurship as contested and complex to understand when there are multiple criteria to understand the same. To clarify the academic fraternity on the bibliometric aspects of research done on Green entrepreneurship, this paper aims to analyze a few Scientometric indicators of the publications done on Green Entrepreneurship. Also, from the Review of Literature, it was observed that the Green Entrepreneurs face certain problems while practicing their businesses. The challenges and issues derived from the review are presented as follows-

CHALLENGES AND ISSUES RELATED TO GREEN ENTREPRENEURIAL

1. Green entrepreneurship is an under-researched phenomenon for sustainable development.
2. Consumers' dynamism in terms of changes and conscious consumption.
3. Green entrepreneurs need to adjust their strategies to save resources, and time to create better opportunities.
4. Green entrepreneurs can face the challenges of implementing the practices into their business on sustainable routes and communicating the same to society.

5. Green entrepreneurs should scan the abilities to overcome all the difficulties towards the society, as the decisions should not affect the environment.
6. Companies need to frame their plan given environmental strategies related to environmental and economic costs for the both company and the customers.
7. Companies can face challenges in developing green policies toward environmental concerns.

OBJECTIVES OF THE STUDY

The main objective of this study is to analyze the research publications on Green Entrepreneurship practices indexed in the Web of Science database and uncover trends or patterns in the realm of Green Entrepreneurship and sustainability knowledge progression and examine the structure of knowledge and derive knowledge synthesis that is presented in tabular and visual forms. Hence,

The objectives of the study are as follows

1. To find out the citations received for green entrepreneurship in the selected paper for the future scope of the study.
2. To know the author's publications in the areas of green entrepreneurship and sustainability development of the organizations.
3. To know the contribution of the prolific authors at the global level as well as at the country level.
4. To identify the keywords which are frequently used in scientific publications.
5. To identify the publication sources from 2007 to 2022.
6. To know the patterns of prolific authors and citations in their study field received by the authors.
7. To understand the issues and challenges faced by Green Entrepreneurs.

RESEARCH METHODOLOGY

The bibliometric methodology summarizes the research publications with the application of quantitative techniques. In this study, the bibliometric analysis will include citation analysis, network analysis, word cloud analysis, tree map, author's publication analysis in terms of keywords, source analysis from 2007 till 2022, and article citations at global as well as country-wise average citations. It is noteworthy that the emergence of scientific databases such as Scopus and Web of Science has made acquiring large volumes of bibliometric data. Data needed for this study was extracted from the WOS database after proper scrutiny. This was done by proper flow of the activities.

The following flow chart is used for further clarity about the documents for the bibliometric analysis-

Figure 1. Flow chart
Source – Authors

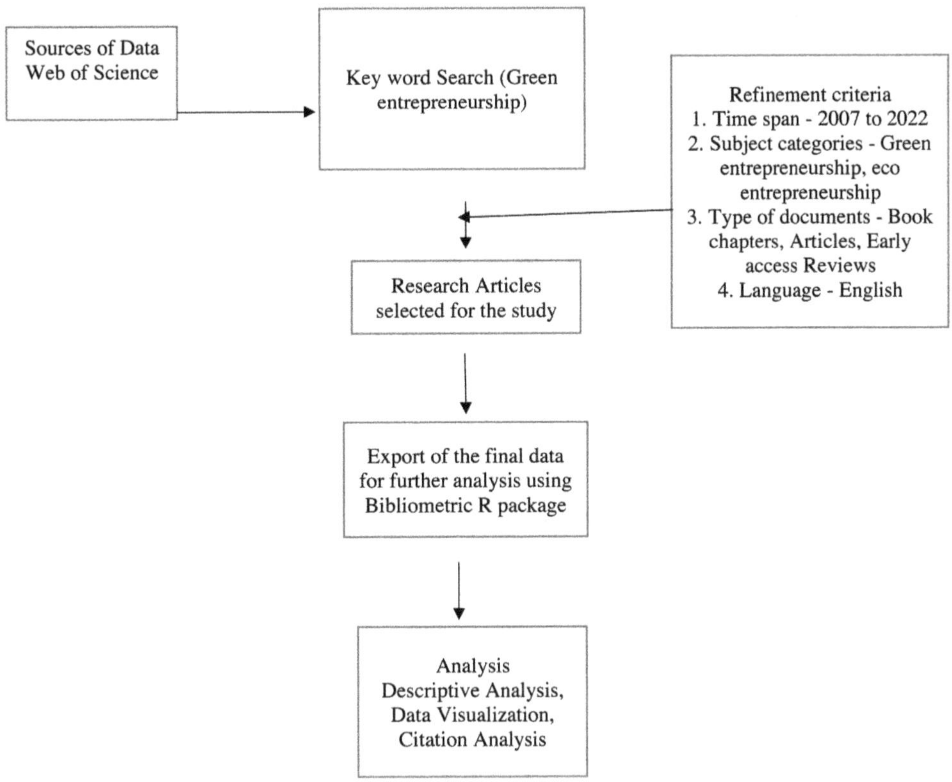

DATA ANALYSIS AND FINDINGS

Descriptive analysis and Network analysis are two types of data analysis used in this study.

Descriptive analysis entails looking at bibliometric data in terms of 1) Sources and 2) Authors. 3) Documents.

Network analysis focuses on extensive science mapping through visualization methods, namely, Co-occurrence network, Collaboration Network.

***A summary of Data Set*:** A quick synopsis (Refer. Table I: Dataset summary) shows a birds-eye perspective of the bibliometric data frame of 146 documents selected from the Web of Science database using a systematic search query. These documents were discovered in 93 sources, with an average year of publication of 3.67 years and a collaboration index of 2.83, indicating that significant research has been done in the past with active researcher participation.

***Average citations*:** The year 2007 showed (Refer to Figure 2) a surge in average citations per year to 9.5 followed by the year 2017 wherein the average citations per year were noted to be 6.4 indicating that a moderate number of studies were initiated on "Green entrepreneurship" during this period symbolizing a huge potential for the future studies.

Table 1. Dataset summary

Description	Results
MAIN INFORMATION ABOUT DATA	
Timespan	2007:2022
Sources (Journals, Books, etc)	93
Documents	146
Average years from publication	3.67
Average citations per document	0
Average citations per year per doc	0
References	1
DOCUMENT CONTENTS	
Keywords Plus (ID)	0
Author's Keywords (DE)	0
AUTHORS	
Authors	366
Author Appearances	404
Authors of single-authored documents	21
Authors of multi-authored documents	345
AUTHORS COLLABORATION	
Single-authored documents	24
Documents per Author	0.399
Authors per Document	2.51
Co-Authors per Documents	2.77
Collaboration Index	2.83

Source: Authors using Biblioshiny

Figure 2. Average citations per year
Source: Authors using Biblioshiny

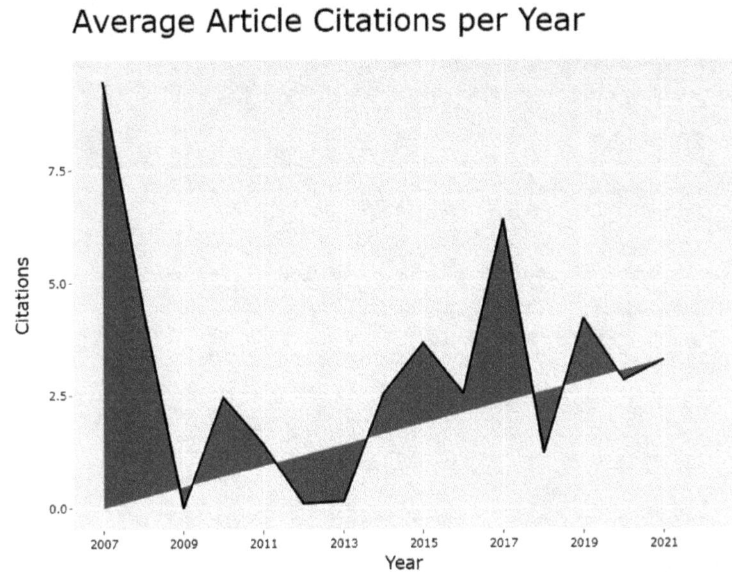

Figure 3. Most relevant sources
Source – Authors using Biblioshiny

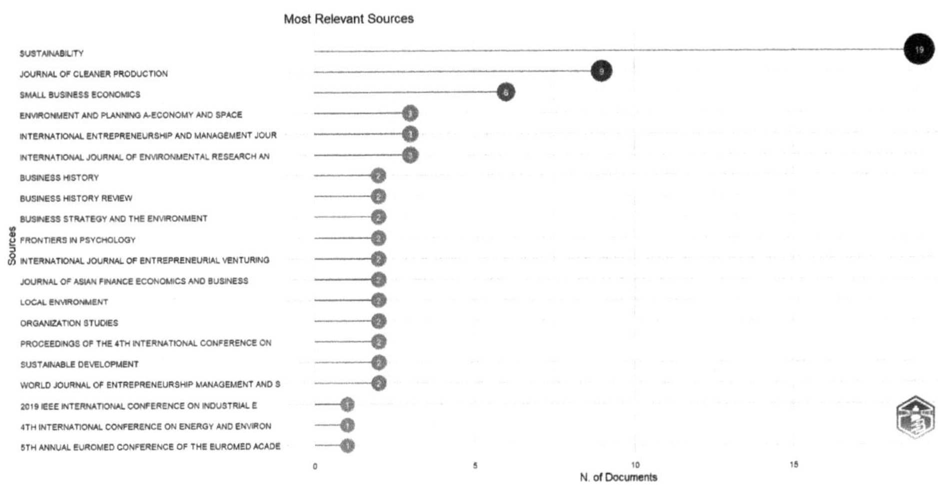

Most Relevant sources: The top 20 most relevant sources that are cited the most are shown in Figure 3. Sustainability is at the top of the list of the most influential journals followed by the Journal of Cleaner Production and Small Business Economies.

Figure 4. Source dynamics
Source – Authors using Biblioshiny

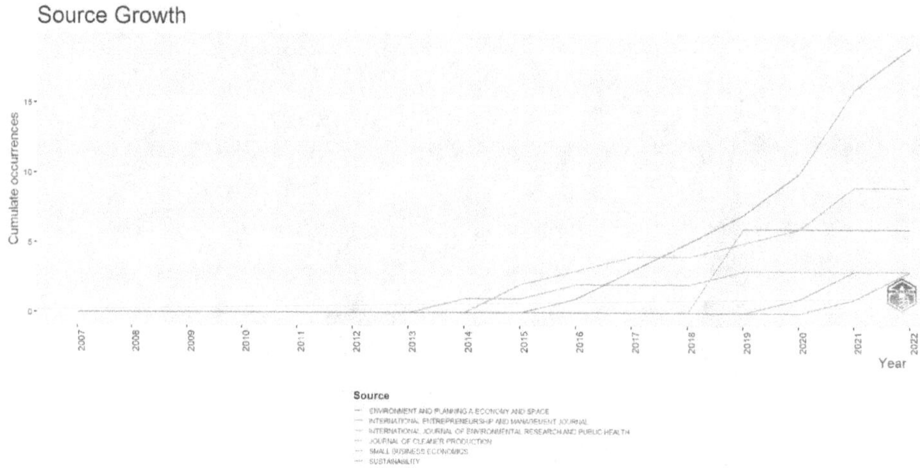

Source Dynamics: The above figure (Figure 4) shows the source dynamics of the top six journals using locally estimated scatter plot smoothing to specify the figure of publications related to the Green Entrepreneurship over the period. According to this figure, till 2013 there were no publications related to Green Entrepreneurship in any of the top six journals. The concept has evolved and came into the frame of research after 2013 and was a hot topic till 2020. *Sustainability* shows a very rapid boost in publications related to green entrepreneurship from 2015 onwards. It can be observed that before 2015 there was not even a single article related to green entrepreneurship, while several publications related to the same have been amplified very rapidly. *Environment and Planning, An Economy Space,* and *Journal of cleaner production* have shown consistent growth in their publications over some time. Whereas *Small Business Economies* has published the highest number of papers in one year and then its number remains same over next 3 years. *International Journal of Entrepreneurship and Management* is the one that has published articles related to Green entrepreneurship only after 2020. The above figure shows that the highest and rapidly increasing publications about the topic were in the year 2015 to 2020 and now the number of publications is comparatively consistent.

***Word Cloud*:** (Refer to Figure 5) Sustainable development, Corporate Social Responsibility, ecopreneurship, eco-innovation, and sustainability leading to innovative management come out as the most frequently used keywords in the literature related to green entrepreneurship. There is a phenomenal increase in the frequencies of these words in the literature since 2017. From the word cloud, one can interpret that the available literature has explored the various factors like firm performance, technology orientation, capability dynamics, climate change, field economy and eco-innovations are the determinants of green entrepreneurship. Also, self-efficacy, technology orientation, consumer behavior, and education are evolved as the factors playing a moderating role in changing the landscape of business towards green entrepreneurship.

Figure 5. Word cloud
Source –Authors using Biblioshiny

Social Network Analysis (SNA): SNA investigated Social Structure using networks and graph theory. Networked structures are described by nodes (such as authors, institutions, or publications sources), while ties or links that connect sets of nodes signify relevant relationships in the social network. Betweenness, a measure of centrality in Social Network Analysis (SNA), indicates the lead article network coverage with the influence of other articles (Ingale & Paluri, 2020);(Hu *et al.*, 2013). This could be observed from Figure 6 that there are connected relationships in the collaborative network with Authors Arabatiz. G, Chalikian.M, Galatsidas S, and Skordoulis M form the major connected relationships in the social network followed by Gao Y, Tsai SB, and Ges BS (Indicated by the orange cluster).

Co-occurrence Network: Based on betweenness and closeness the following keywords are represented as nodes and are linked through linkages forming a cluster (Refer to Figure 7). The keywords 'innovation, 'sustainable entrepreneurship', 'R&D', ' technology', 'dynamics', 'eco-innovations', ' business models, and 'finance represent the major cluster with significant closeness and betweenness. This indicates that significant studies have been done on these keywords.

Figure 6. Collaborative network- authors
Source –Authors using Biblioshiny

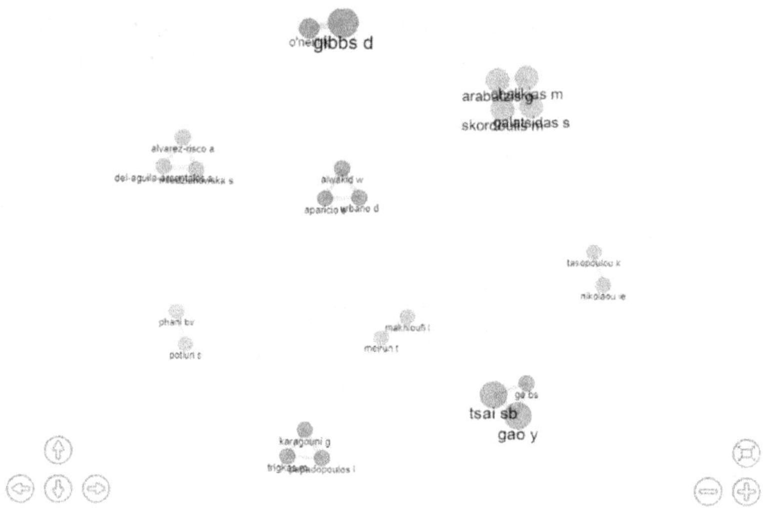

Figure 7. Co-occurrence network
Source –Authors using Biblioshiny

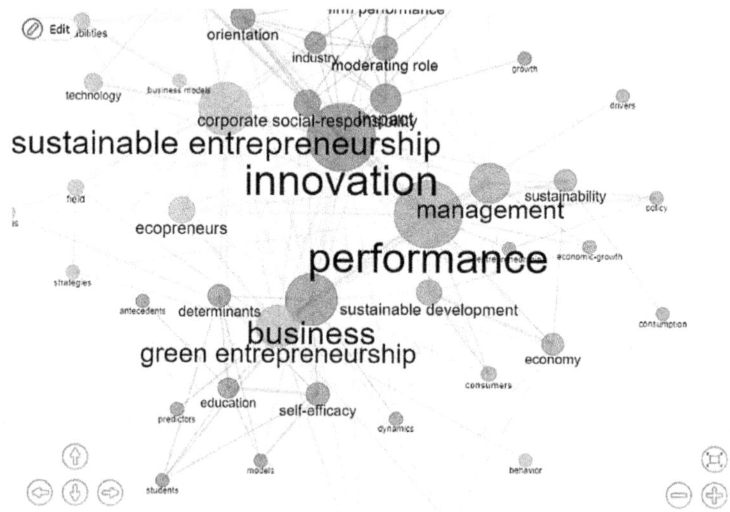

Countrywide contribution: The contribution of the various countries to the field is shown in Figure 8, indicating that developed countries have made the largest contribution to literature in the field. The majority (465) of the publication was contributed by the United Kingdom, while France (161), and China (124) were the second and third countries to get the work published in the area. The USA published 100 articles. Overall, it is indicated that, in terms of frequency and citations, France outperforms the rest of the globe with 80.5 average citations. According to citations, India is at the bottom of the leaderboard with a score of 39 in relevant production and last place in the top ten countries. This could represent underdeveloped countries' incremental progress toward high-quality research in this sector.

Figure 8. Most cited countries
Source –Authors using Biblioshiny

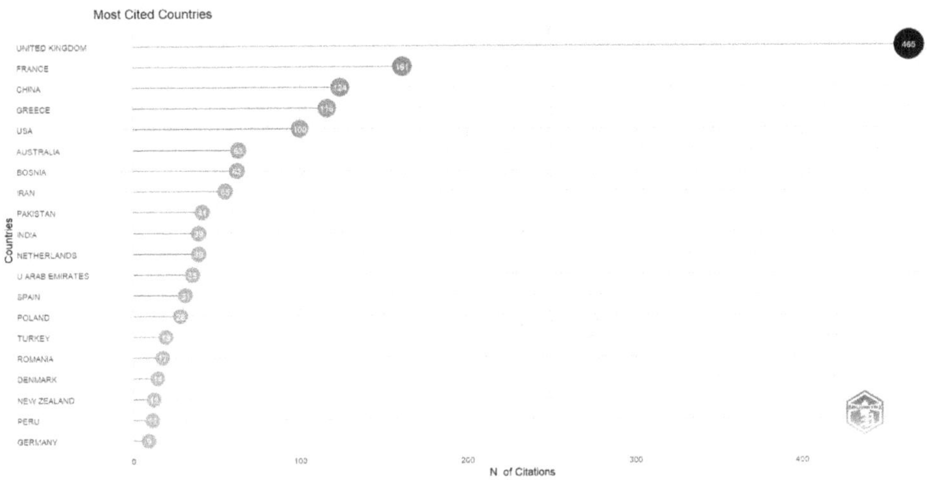

Treemap Analysis: Figure 9 depicts the tree map indicating the association of entrepreneurship with green entrepreneurship (26%), sustainable development, green economy, Eco entrepreneurship, environment, and green innovation. This kind of observation helps the authors to focus their studies on green entrepreneurship. The advent of green behavior is taking center stage in organizational practices, due to which there needs to be the adoption of green entrepreneurship amongst all the businesses to create future sustainable opportunities.

Most Relevant Authors: From figure 10, Haldar S, was the most productive author with maximum publication (5) in the field of green entrepreneurship, followed by Gibbs D (4) and Gao Y, Oneill K Tsai SB publishing three articles in the same filed. All the other authors have also taken an interest and doing research, as the subject is the hot cake from the business and sustainability perspective.

Figure 9. Treemap showing association of keyword
Source -Authors using Biblioshiny

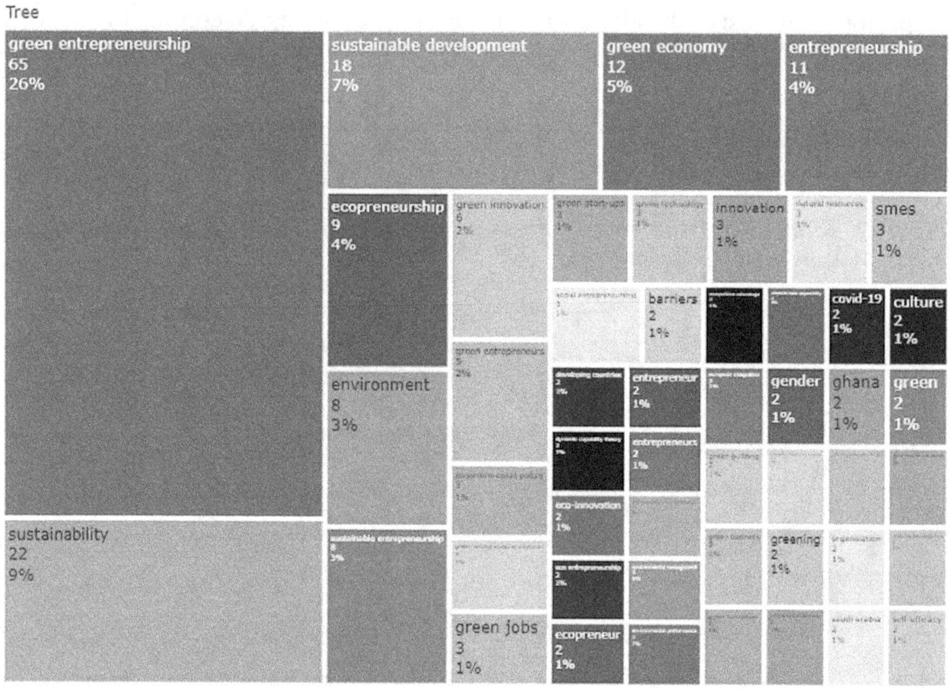

Figure 10. Most relevant article analysis
Source- Authors using Biblioshiny

CONCLUSION AND DISCUSSION

The present paper focuses on the evolution of Green entrepreneurship and sustainable innovative practices from 2007 to 2022. It also includes a thorough examination of the research topic's descriptive, conceptual, and social framework. The current study on Green entrepreneurship and sustainable development make a substantial contribution by consolidating fragmented material and highlighting essential papers, significant sources, and authors. Because of its ease, flexibility, and user-friendliness, Biblioshiny was employed under the Bibliometric R-Package, a tool used in Bibliometrics. The studies have been obtained from a Web of Science database that is structured and compatible with Bibliometric software, with high-quality research sources. The data set shows that research in this field began in 2007, that the results in the domain had seen near to zero studies before 2013 but after the year 2015 onwards the concept of green entrepreneurship gained momentum and a spurt was noticed during early 2020 in the publication in the said domain. This owes to the studies and research conducted on sustainability and studies on Millennium Development Goals implemented in 2000, and studies on Sustainable Development Goals implemented in 2015. The United Kingdom has made the most scholarly contributions and research work in this sector, followed by France and China, and its engagement with emerging economies is expanding. Social structure focuses upon collaboration networks based on authors. The conceptual structure revealed the co-occurrence network of keywords such as innovation, sustainable entrepreneurship, ecopreneurs, Green Entrepreneurship, business models, etc.

Most publications belonged to Sustainability, Journal of Cleaner Production, and Small Business Economies. This study aims to create a road map for academics and practitioners to comprehend what is already known. Researchers can then use bibliometric analyses to examine publication patterns with references to citations, authors, sources, nations, and a collaboration between authors, word cloud, and keyword analysis to explore research outlooks. The study's important insights into recent patterns will aid policymakers in developing policies concerning sustainable business practices, taking measures on encouraging Green entrepreneurship practices, and understanding in a better way the Sustainable Development Goals and challenges faced by practitioners.

REFERENCES

Allen, J., & Malin, S. (2008). Green Entrepreneurship: A Method for Managing Natural Resources? *Society &amp. Natural Resources*, *21*(9), 828–844. doi:10.1080/08941920701612917

Alsaleh, Y., & Mahroum, S. (2014). A Critical Review of the Interplay between Policy Instruments and Business Models: Greening the Built Environment a Case in Point. SSRN *Electronic Journal*. doi:10.2139/ssrn.2429275

Antolin-Lopez, R., Martinez-del-Rio, J., & Cespedes-Lorente, J. (2019). Environmental entrepreneurship as a multi-component and dynamic construct: Duality of goals, environmental agency, and environmental value creation. *Business Ethics (Oxford, England)*, *28*(4), 407–422. doi:10.1111/beer.12229

Aria, M. & Cuccurullo, C. (2017). Bibliometric: An R-tool for comprehensive science mapping Analysis. *Journal of Informatics*, *11*(4), 959–975. . doi:10.1016/j.joi.2017.08.007

Bennett, S. J. (1991). *Ecopreneuring: The Complete Guide to Small Business Opportunities from the Environmental Revolution*. John Wiley.

Berle, G. (1991). *The Green Entrepreneur: Business Opportunities that Can Save the Earth and Make You Money*. Liberty Hall Press.

Blue, J. (1990). *Ecopreneuring: Managing For Results*. Scott Foresman.

Braun, P. (2010). Going green: Women entrepreneurs and the environment. *International Journal of Gender and Entrepreneurship*, *2*(3), 245–259. doi:10.1108/17566261011079233

Cohen, B., & Winn, M. I. (2007). Market imperfections, opportunity, and sustainable entrepreneurship. *Journal of Business Venturing*, *22*(1), 29–49. doi:10.1016/j.jbusvent.2004.12.001

Corradini, C. (2017). Location determinants of green technological entry: Evidence from European regions. *Small Business Economics*, *52*(4), 845–858. doi:10.100711187-017-9938-7

De Bruin, A. (2016). Towards a framework for understanding transitional green entrepreneurship. *Small Enterprise Research*, *23*(1), 10–21. doi:10.1080/13215906.2016.1188715

Demirel, P., Li, Q., Rentocchini, F., & Tamvada, J. (2017). Born to be green: New insights into the economics and management of green entrepreneurship. *Small Business Economics*, *52*(4), 759–771. doi:10.100711187-017-9933-z

Dixon, S., & Clifford, A. (2007). Ecopreneurship – a new approach to managing the triple bottom line. *Journal of Organizational Change Management*, *20*(3), 326–345. doi:10.1108/09534810710740164

Doukas, H., Tsiousi, A., Marinakis, V., & Psarras, J. (2014). Linguistic multi-criteria decision-making for energy and environmental corporate policy. *Information Sciences*, *258*, 328–338. doi:10.1016/j.ins.2013.08.027

Drăgoi, M., Iamandi, I., Munteanu, S., & Ciobanu, R., Ţarţavulea (Dieaconescu), R., & Lădaru, R. (2017). Incentives for Developing Resilient Agritourism Entrepreneurship in Rural Communities in Romania in a European Context. *Sustainability*, *9*(12), 2205. doi:10.3390u9122205

Ebrahimi, P., & Mirbargkar, S. (2017). Green entrepreneurship and green innovation for SME development in market turbulence. *Eurasian Business Review*, *7*(2), 203–228. doi:10.100740821-017-0073-9

Gast, J., Gundolf, K., & Cesinger, B. (2017). Doing business in a green way: A systematic review of the ecological sustainability entrepreneurship literature and future research directions. *Journal of Cleaner Production*, *147*, 44–56. doi:10.1016/j.jclepro.2017.01.065

Ge, B., Jiang, D., Gao, Y., & Tsai, S. (2016). The Influence of Legitimacy on a Proactive Green Orientation and Green Performance: A Study Based on Transitional Economy Scenarios in China. *Sustainability*, *8*(12), 1344. doi:10.3390u8121344

Gibbs, D., & O'Neill, K. (2014). Rethinking Sociotechnical Transitions and Green Entrepreneurship: The Potential for Transformative Change in the Green Building Sector. *Environment and Planning A. Economy and Space*, *46*(5), 1088–1107. doi:10.1068/a46259

Grinevich, V., Huber, F., Karataş-Özkan, M., & Yavuz, Ç. (2017). Green entrepreneurship in the sharing economy: Utilizing a multiplicity of institutional logics. *Small Business Economics*, *52*(4), 859–876. doi:10.100711187-017-9935-x

Haldar, S. (2019). Towards a conceptual understanding of sustainability-driven entrepreneurship. *Corporate Social Responsibility and Environmental Management*.

Hall, J., Matos, S., & Bachor, V. (2017). From green technology development to green innovation: Inducing regulatory adoption of pathogen detection technology for sustainable forestry. *Small Business Economics*, *52*(4), 877–889. doi:10.100711187-017-9940-0

Ingale, K. K., & Paluri, R. A. (2020). Financial literacy and financial behavior: A bibliometric Analysis. *Review of Behavioral Finance*. doi:10.1108/RBF-06-2020-0141

Johnson, M. P., & Schaltegger, S. (2020). Entrepreneurship for sustainable development: A review and multilevel causal mechanism framework. *Entrepreneurship Theory and Practice*, *44*(6), 1141–1173. doi:10.1177/1042258719885368

Kouri, R., & Clarke, A. (2012). Framing 'Green Jobs' Discourse: Analysis of Popular Usage. *Sustainable Development*, *22*(4), 217–230. doi:10.1002d.1526

Kumar, A., & Kiran, P. (2018). Green Entrepreneurship: A Bibliometric Study. *Int. J. Appl. Bus. Econ. Res.*, *15*, 153–166.

Lotfi, M., Yousefi, A., & Jafari, S. (2018). The Effect of Emerging Green Market on Green Entrepreneurship and Sustainable Development in Knowledge-Based Companies. *Sustainability*, *10*(7), 2308. doi:10.3390u10072308

Mrkajic, B., & Murtinu, S. 2016. Is Green the New Gold? Venture Capital and Green Entrepreneurship. SSRN *Electronic Journal*. doi:10.2139/ssrn.2757653

Nikolaou, E., Ierapetritis, D., & Tsagarakis, K. (2011). An evaluation of the prospects of green entrepreneurship development using a SWOT analysis. *International Journal of Sustainable Development &amp. World Ecology*, *18*(1), 1–16.

O'Neill, K., & Gibbs, D. (2016). Rethinking green entrepreneurship – Fluid narratives of the green economy. *Environment and Planning A. Economy and Space*, *48*(9), 1727–1749.

O'Neill, K., & Gibbs, D. (2020). Sustainability transitions and policy dismantling: Zero carbon housing in the UK. *Geoforum*, *108*, 119–129. doi:10.1016/j.geoforum.2019.11.011

Papadopoulos, I., Karagouni, G., Trigkas, M., & Beltsiou, Z. (2014). Mainstreaming green product strategies. *EuroMed Journal of Business*, *9*(3), 293–317. doi:10.1108/EMJB-12-2013-0058

Qazi, W., Qureshi, J., Raza, S., Khan, K., & Qureshi, M. (2020). Impact of personality traits and university green entrepreneurial support on students' green entrepreneurial intentions: The moderating role of environmental values. *Journal of Applied Research in Higher Education*, *13*(4), 1154–1180. doi:10.1108/JARHE-05-2020-0130

Schaltegger, S., & Wagner, M. (2008). Managing the business case for sustainability. In *EMAN-EU 2008 Conference* (Vol. 7). Academic Press.

Silajdžić, I., Kurtagić, S., & Vučijak, B. (2015). Green entrepreneurship in transition economies: A case study of Bosnia and Herzegovina. *Journal of Cleaner Production*, *88*, 376–384. doi:10.1016/j.jclepro.2014.07.004

Soomro, B., Ghumro, I., & Shah, N. (2019). Green entrepreneurship inclination among the younger generation: An avenue towards a green economy. *Sustainable Development*, *28*(4), 585–594. doi:10.1002d.2010

Staggenborg, S., & Ogrodnik, C. (2015). New environmentalism and Transition Pittsburgh. *Environmental Politics*, *24*(5), 723–741. doi:10.1080/09644016.2015.1027059

Yi, G. (2020). From green entrepreneurial intentions to green entrepreneurial behavior: The role of university entrepreneurial support and external institutional support. *The International Entrepreneurship and Management Journal*, *17*(2), 963–979. doi:10.100711365-020-00649-y

Zahraie, B., Everett, A. M., Walton, S., & Kirkwood, J. (2016). Environmental entrepreneurs facilitating change toward sustainability: A case study of the wine industry in New Zealand. *Small Enterp. Dev.*, *23*(1), 39–57. doi:10.1080/13215906.2016.1188717

Zhao, M., Liu, J., & Chenglishu, D. (2021). Pursuing sustainable development through green entrepreneurship: An institutional perspective. *Business Strategy and the Environment*, *30*(8), 4281–4296. doi:10.1002/bse.2869

Zhao, X., Shang, Y., & Song, M. (2020). Industrial structure distortion and urban ecological efficiency from the perspective of green entrepreneurial ecosystems. *Socio-Economic Planning Sciences*, *72*, 100757. doi:10.1016/j.seps.2019.100757

Chapter 8
Does Green Entrepreneurship Have an Association With Sustainable Development and Its Components?
Evidence From a Country-Wise Panel Data Investigation

Ajay K. Singh
School of Liberal Arts and Management, DIT University, Dehradun, India

Sanjeev Kumar
School of Liberal Arts and Management, DIT University, Dehradun, India

Aditya Kumar Sharma
School of Liberal Arts and Management, DIT University, Dehradun, India

Shivani Sinha
Department of Economics, Banaras Hindu University, India

ABSTRACT

This study developed a global sustainable development index (GSDI), economic development index (EDI), social development index (SDI), environmental sustainability index (ESI), science and technological development index (STDI), entrepreneurship ecosystem index (EEI), and green entrepreneurship ecosystem index (GEI) for 34 countries during 2000–2019. Composite Z-score method was used to develop EDI, SDI, ESI, STDI, EEI, and GEI. It also observed the interaction among the estimated indexes using linear regression models.

DOI: 10.4018/978-1-6684-4666-9.ch008

1. INTRODUCTION

At present, the global economies are facing several challenges in maintaining environmental development due to high population growth, urbanisation, industrialisation, infrastructure development, modernisation of the agricultural sector, and anthropogenetic activities (Singh et al., 2019; Ivleva et al., 2019). Most economies focus on achieving high economic growth (Singh et al., 2020). In the era of globalisation, most countries use extensive natural resources and ecosystem services to maintain their production scale. The demand for goods and services has increased worldwide due to high population growth and change in consumption pattern of people. High population growth is caused to increase urbanisation, infrastructure development, and pressure on ecosystem services. Subsequently, population growth, urbanisation, and industrialisation have negative impact on environmental development (Singh et al., 2021). Agriculture is the sole sector to meet the food demand of the global population (Kumar et al., 2017; Singh & Issac, 2018; Singh & Kumar, 2022a). This sector's production activities require more ecosystem services to feed the present and growing population (Singh & Kumar, 2022a). High population growth is also caused to increase additional pressure on the government to create jobs for the growing population in all sectors. The agricultural sector provides seasonal jobs to unskilled workers, while, the service sector provides jobs to the skilled workforce. The industrial sector is highly likely to generate jobs for the skilled and unskilled workforce (Singh et al., 2019b).

Accordingly, most countries are executing their policies to increase high industrialisation while giving less attention to environmental development (Singh et al., 2019a). Industrialisation is highly supportive to increase economic development, social development and science & technological development (Singh & Singh, 2020). Science & technological development is also helpful in creating innovation, an entrepreneurship ecosystem, business opportunities, new goods and products, new markets and employment (Singh & Kumar, 2022b). The entrepreneurship ecosystem is also helpful for nurturing new business opportunities, innovation, ventures and start-ups, which are helpful to increase social-economic development (İyigün, 2015). Accordingly, it also positively impacts economic development and economic growth (Wennekers et al., 2010; Chen, 2014; Singh & Ashraf, 2020).

Furthermore, industrial development pays less attention to environmental development, which is considered a crucial component of sustainable development. Economic development, social development and science & technological development are also essential drivers of sustainable development (Singh & Kumar, 2022c). Hence, sustainable development has a multi-dimensional association with environmental economic, social and science & technological development (Drastichová, 2014; Armeanu et al., 2018; Omisore, 2018; Singh et al., 2021; Singh & Kumar, 2022b).

Sustainable development ensures sustainability in resources, leading sustainability in resources, leading to increase economic, social, environmental, science & technological development. Hence, sustainability is associated with the triple bottom line, which is essential to increasing sustainable development (İyigün, 2015; Roomi et al., 2020; Sridhara et al., 2022). Sustainable development *is the development that meets the needs of the present without compromising the ability of future generations to meet their needs* (U.N. Brundtland Report, 1987). It emphasises social justice, human development and social development. Later on, sustainable development is defined in the context of different sectors such as sustainable food security, sustainable entrepreneurship, sustainable agricultural development, environmental sustainability and sustainable livelihood security (İyigün, 2015; Singh et al., 2019a; Singh et al., 2020; Singh et al., 2021; Sridhara et al., 2022; Singh & Kumar, 2022a).

Economic, social, human, environmental, institutional, and technological development indicators are crucial determinants of sustainable development (Armeanu et al., 2018; Singh et al., 2019a; Jin et al., 2020; Roomi et al., 2020; Ullah et al., 2021; Singh & Kumar, 2022c). Economic development is useful to increase the flow of income by sustaining resource efficiency and productivity in the presence of scarce resources (Duran et al., 2015). It is a prime step in managing financial activities such as capital, stock, and tangible and intangible assets (İyigün, 2015). Social development is a situation in which all people have equal rights to use available resources to sustain their daily livelihood without any restriction. It provides social security for various stakeholders in a country (İyigün, 2015). Environmental development effectively maintains the quality and quantity of natural resources and ecological services (Ivleva et al., 2019; Singh & Kumar, 2022c). It also increases the attention of business communities and government to reduce the negative impact of production activities on ecosystem services and natural resources (İyigün, 2015). Science & technological development is helpful to increase a country's strength by using advanced technologies in production activities to increase productivity, efficiency and output (Singh et al., 2020; Singh & Kumar, 2022c).

Since the quality and quantity of ecosystem services are in a dangerous position due to high industrialisation, population growth and urbanisation. As a result, the scientific research communities have proposed that green and appropriate technology in producing goods and services would help to maintain environmental development and ecosystem services (Singh et al., 2022). Subsequently, it would reduce the negative impact of anthropogenetic activities on environmental factors and ecological services (Nuringsih et al., 2020). The practices of green entrepreneurship in the production sector are highly effective in increasing environmental sustainability and green growth (Ahmad et al., 2015; Demirel et al., 2017; Khan et al., 2020; Onsay, 2021; Tawiah et al., 2021). Therefore, green growth is an extensive application of green or environmental technology in production activities which help increase green GDP. Initiations of green entrepreneurship will bring several alternatives to increase environmental development and will abate the CO_2 and GHGs emissions from various activities (Ahmad et al., 2015). Green entrepreneurship or green growth ensures the protection of natural resources in sustainable ways (Tawiah et al., 2021). Cai et al. (2022) argued that green entrepreneurship has huge scope to resolve environmental and social issues. Hence, green entrepreneurship works as a crucial driver to increase sustainable development and its components (Alwakid et al., 2021). Existing studies have also used sustainable entrepreneurship, green growth and green economy to explain the concept of green entrepreneurship (Demirel et al., 2017; Moya-Clemente et al., 2020; Roomi et al., 2020; Tawiah et al., 2021). Sustainable and green entrepreneurship applies scientific processes, techniques, and methods that solve social, economic and environmental related issues in production activities in all sectors (İyigün, 2015).

An individual indicator may not be appropriate to defined green entrepreneurship ecosystem of a country. Therefore, previous studies could not provide uniform indicators of green entrepreneurship. However, indicators associated with green entrepreneurship ecosystem can be divided in two broad categories. First group of studies examine the sustainability of manufacturing firms as giving significant priority of environmental related indicators. For instance, Domańska et al. (2018) used green products manufacturing by SMEs to define green orientation of entrepreneurship in European unions. Ebrahimi and Mirbargkar (2017) used intention of SMEs to develop green products to assess the association between green innovation and SMEs development with respect to green entrepreneurship in Iran. Karimi and Chashmi (2019) considered environmental-social responsibilities and other characteristics to develop green entrepreneurship model in sustainable development in Iran. Demirel and Danisman (2019) considered replanning of water, renewable energy, replanning energy and minimizing waste and green loan to examine the influence of eco-innovation on growth SMEs in China. Alwakid et al. (2020) used ratio of SME that are environmentally friendly to total SMEs as proxy for green entrepreneurship to examine the relationship between cultural characteristics and green entrepreneurship in Saudi Arabia. Alwakid et al. (2021) examined the impact of green entrepreneurship practices on sustainable development in various firms. Yin et al. (2022) used total number of original green patents in last three years to capture the influence of green innovation on firm's performance in China. Skordoulis et al. (2022) used environmental issues and protection to explain association between green innovation and green entrepreneurship in firms in Greece.

Second group of studies assumes that any initiation which is conducive to increase green growth or green GDP can be useful to increase green entrepreneurship ecosystem. For example, application of green technology, environmental technology, carbon-free technology, and appropriate technology in production activities are better practices of green entrepreneurship (Söderholm, 2020). Galindo-Martín et al. (2020) used environmental performance index to examine relationship between green innovation and sustainable development in OECD countries. Onsay (2021) examine the association of green growth indicators with economic development in Southeast Asia. It used environmental resources productivity and environmental dimension of quality of life as proxy variables for green growth indicators in empirical investigation. Zeng and Ren (2022) explained that how environmental regulation stimulates green entrepreneurship in Chinses enterprises. This study used emissions of sulphur dioxide and nitrogen oxide as dependent variables which are the representative of green entrepreneurship. Cai et al. (2022) assessed the factors which promote the green entrepreneurial intension of students. Furthermore, environmental technologies and other activities (e.g., electricity, renewable sources of energy, renewable source of water, etc.) are essential to creating a green entrepreneurship ecosystem.

Prior studied claimed that green entrepreneurship significantly contributes to maintaining environmental sustainability and sustainable development (İyigün, 2015; Domańska et al. 2018; Nuringsih et al., 2020; Zhao et al., 2021; Tawiah et al., 2021; Alwakid et al., 2021; Gupta & Dharwal, 2022). Thus, creating a green entrepreneurship ecosystem and its applications has increased the attention of policymakers (Ahmad et al., 2015). As green entrepreneurship ecosystem may not be explained by an individual activity, thus, its measurement is debatable and controversial issues. Furthermore, existing studies could not provide scientific evidence on the association of green entrepreneurship and entrepreneurship ecosystem with sustainable development and its components in developing and developed countries. Therefore, this study addressed the answer to the following research questions:

- How can the scientific research community estimate the impact of green entrepreneurship ecosystem on sustainable development?
- What is the interconnection of sustainable development with green entrepreneurship ecosystem, entrepreneurship ecosystem, social development, economic development and science & technological development?
- What is the relative performance of selected countries in sustainable development and its components and green entrepreneurship ecosystem?
- What types of policy actions will be helpful to increase sustainable development, especially in developing countries?

With regards to the aforementioned research questions, this study achieved the following objectives:

- To develop the global sustainable development index (*GSDI*), economic development index (*EDI*), social development index (*SDI*), environmental sustainability index (*ESI*), science & technological development index (*STDI*), entrepreneurship ecosystem index (*EEI*) and green entrepreneurship Index (*GEI*) for selected 34 economies.
- To describe the comparative performance of selected countries based on estimated values of *GSDI, EDI, SDI, ESI, STDI, EEI* and *GEI*.
- To estimate the causal relationship of green entrepreneurship with sustainable development and its components.

2. CONCEPTUAL AND EMPIRICAL REVIEW

Evidence indicates that sustainable development may not be achieved without economic, social, environmental, scientific, & technological development. Sustainable development has a causal relationship with environmental sustainability in most economies (Singh et al., 2020; Singh et al., 2021; Singh & Kumar, 2022c). Furthermore, saving and investment, health expenditure, human development, poverty, population, pollution, market failures, and prevention and management of disasters are the crucial factors of sustainable development, economic prosperity, social equity and justice, and environmental sustainability is a crucial determinant of sustainable development (Singh et al., 2019; Khan & Khan, 2012; Ullah et al., 2021; Singh & Kumar, 2022c). It also covers a broad range of indicators about poverty eradication, quality of education, gender equality, and peace (Guijarro & Poyatos, 2018).

Existing studies observed the positive impact of the entrepreneurship ecosystem on economic development and growth (Wennekers et al., 2010; Farayibi, 2016; Bashir & Akhtar, 2016; Adusei, 2016; Omoruyi et al., 2017; Erken et al., 2018; Singh & Ashraf, 2020). The entrepreneurship ecosystem is also positively associated with social development (Dhahri & Omri, 2018). Bashir and Akhtar (2016) noticed the positive impact of entrepreneurship and innovation on economic growth. Also, the entrepreneurship ecosystem helps stimulate economic growth and increase the employment rate (Chen, 2014). Audretsch et al. (2015) reported a positive impact of entrepreneurship ecosystem on new firm start-ups' economic development in 127 European cities. Farayibi (2016) observed the positive impact of small-medium enterprises on economic growth in Nigeria. However, Zaki and Rashid (2016) found a negative association between entrepreneurship and economic growth in

Egypt, Hungry, India, Mexico, Indonesia, Turkey and Romania. Dvouletý (2017) observed that entrepreneurial activities help reduce the high unemployment rate in the Czech regions.

Prior studies have also assessed the influence of social-economic factors on entrepreneurship activities. Rusu and Roman (2017) observed the significant impact of the inflation rate, foreign direct investment, access to finance and tax rate on entrepreneurial activities. Tasnim and Afzal (2018) examined the impact of corruption levels on the entrepreneurship ecosystem in 50 countries. Dvouletý (2018) observed the association of foreign direct investment, net inflows (% of GDP), number of start-up procedures, unemployment rate, and economic freedom index with the entrepreneurship ecosystem in 11 European countries. Afzal et al. (2018) detected the determinants of entrepreneurial capability in selected economies. Erken et al. (2018) observed the impact of economic development, R&D capital, human capital and labour participation rate on the entrepreneurship ecosystem. Singh and Ashraf (2020) found a positive impact of social-economic development, science & technological development and IPRs related indicators on the entrepreneurship ecosystem.

Previous literature also explored that green entrepreneurship has a positive impact on sustainable development and its components (Tawiah et al., 2021; Cai et al., 2022). Ahmad et al. (2015) examined the influence of sustainable orientation, sustainable education and general self-efficacy on green entrepreneurship inclination among 100 business students. Nuringsih et al. (2020) explored the association of green entrepreneurship with sustainable development in Jakarta. Moya-Clemente et al. (2020) examined the influence of environmental and economic factors on sustainable entrepreneurship in 50 economies. For this investigation, it used factors associated with sustainable development goals performance for the measurement of sustainable entrepreneurship. It found that environmental and economic factors positively and significantly associated with sustainable entrepreneurship. Dhahri and Omri (2018) examined the influence of entrepreneurial activity on sustainable development, which was considered integration of economic growth, human development, and environmental quality in 20 developing countries.

Mahajan and Bandyopadhyay (2020) conclude that there is a requirement to find entrepreneurs from the gender perspective and discover how women entrepreneurs contribute to the economy, society, and the environment. Alwakid et al. (2021) observed the positive impact of green entrepreneurship on economic, social, and environmental components in Saudi Arabia. Exploring the impact of green entrepreneurship orientation on green innovation performance and environmental performance, Makhloufi et al. (2021) noted the significant impact of green absorptive capacity, environmental cooperation, and managerial environmental concerns on green entrepreneurship orientation. Further, green entrepreneurship orientation significantly impacts green innovation performance and environmental performance. Exploring the case of Southeast Asian Countries, Onsay (2021) concluded that green indicators are not playing a significant role in increasing GDP and GNP per capita.

Further, studying the case study of Gujarat, India, Haldar (2021) concluded that renewable energy entrepreneurs are motivated by economic, personal commitment, and environmental and social concerns. They have better opportunities for skill development programmes, subsidies, and entry-level barriers to shifting their conventional business to sustainable business. They face significant challenges, including access to finance, administrative hurdles, knowledge barriers, and limited technological upgrading. A recent study by Zhao et al. (2022) highlights how international venturing through 'green initiatives, green government support, and green political influence' promotes green entrepreneurship and helps firms achieve sustainable development goals.

Developing a conceptual model, Gupta and Dharwal (2022) conclude that green entrepreneurs, with the help of green production, green product, and a cyclic supply chain, can promote equitable economic growth, environmental conservation, and preservation, and help in the improvement of social and human life. Yin et al. (2022) showed the significant impact of utility-model innovation on SMEs' performance. However, overall firm performance is not growing with green invention innovation. Further, they have shown more impact of green invention innovation and green utility-model innovation on older firms as compared to younger firms. Zeng et al. (2022) found significant impact of green entrepreneurship on technological innovation and environmental regulation.

3. PROPOSED RESEARCH METHODOLOGY

3.1. Selection of Indicators and Countries

This study used economic development, social development, environmental sustainability, science & technological development, green entrepreneurship and entrepreneurship ecosystem associated indicators to develop *GSDI*, *EDI*, *SDI*, *STDI*, *EEI* and *GEI*. Thus, associated indicators were selected based on existing theoretical and empirical literature. Accordingly, 82 indicators seemed suitable to construct the aforementioned indexes. Thereupon, only 34 countries have been considered that have the data for identified indicators from 2000 to 2019. (Table: 1). Interpolation and extrapolation methods have been used to complete the time series for variables with the missing values (Singh et al., 2021; Singh & Kumar, 2022c).

3.2. Source of Data

This study is purely based on secondary data. Information on social-economic variables for selected economies has been collected from various sources such as World Development Indicators of the world Bank, Food and Agriculture Organization, United Nations Development Programme, World Trade Organization, Yale Center for Environmental Law and Policy, Center for International Earth Science Information Network, Colombia University. Intellectual property rights related data has been derived from World Intellectual Property Organization, Organization for Economic Co-Operation and Development, United Nations Development Programme, Department of Economic and Social Affairs of United Nations and others. Sustainable development goals (SDGs) related indicators have been sourced from the Department of Economic and Social Affairs, United Nations.

3.3. Hypothetical Framework on Index-Based Estimation

Previous studies have developed several indexes such as the sustainable livelihood security index (Singh & Issac, 2018), environmental sustainability index (Singh et al., 2019a; Singh & Kumar, 2022c), environmental performance index, food security index (Kumar et al., 2017), economic development index (Singh & Singh, 2020), social development index (Singh & Singh, 2020), agricultural sustainability index (Singh & Kumar, 2022a), global sustainable development index (Singh et al., 2020; Singh et al., 2021), entrepreneurship ecosystem development index (Singh & Ashraf, 2020), science & technological development index (Singh & Singh, 2020; Singh et al., 2020), human development index, water sustainability index, etc. to examine the relative performance of across entities or regions and countries. Prior studies have used principal component analysis and factors component analysis to develop various indexes (Tawiah et al., 2021; Sridhara et al., 2022). The composite Z-score method is useful to avoid aforesaid discrepancies in index estimation (Singh & Issac, 2018; Singh et al., 2020). In this technique, researchers assign weightage to each variable as per variation and eigen values in index-estimation. It also noticed that most studies had estimated the normalisation index or composite Z-score or standardisation index of undertaken variables in index-estimation (Singh & Issac, 2018; Singh et al., 2020; Singh & Kumar, 2022a). If a variable has a positive impact on expected output (as per the existing literature), then the composite score was estimated as (Singh et al., 2021; Sridhara et al., 2022):

$$CS_{ict} = \{[X_{ict} - Min(X_{ict})] / [Max(X_{ict}) - Min(X_{ict})]\} \quad (1)$$

Here, *CS* is the *composite-score* for a *i* variable, *c* is cross-sectional countries, and *t* is time. X_{ict} is the actual value; $Min(X_{ict})$ is minimum value; $Max(X_{ict})$ is the highest value for a specific variable across countries in a year. If a factor has a negative impact on expected output, then the *composite-score* was assessed as:

$$\text{Here, } CS_{ict} = \{[X_{ict} - Max(X_{ict})] / [Min(X_{ict}) - Max(X_{ict})]\} \quad (2)$$

The expression of variables is given in equation (1). The average linear sum of the composite score of all variables may be considered to develop an index (Singh et al., 2021). However, this study developed the final index as a linear sum of all composite scores multiplied by assigned weightage for corresponding variables. Weightage for each variable was assigned based on its proportion variation and eigenvalues among the set of selected variables. Therefore, the final index was estimated as:

$$(FI)_{ct} = w_1 {}^*(CS_1)_{ct} + w_2 {}^*(CS_2)_{ct} + ... + w_n {}^*(CS_n)_{ct} \quad (3)$$

Here, *FI* is a final index; *C.S.* is a composite index; $w_1, w_2, ..., w_n$ are the weightage for respective variables in equation (3). At the same time, the sum of all w_n was 1 (Singh et al., 2020). Previous studies emphasised variation and eigenvalues to estimate the weights for arbitrary variables in index estimation. As this study developed *GSDI, EDI, SDI, ESI, STDI, EEI* and *GEI* in a time series, thus, aforesaid process recursively applied for each year across countries.

3.4. Calculation of Weights for Variables

As this study develop *EDI, SDI, ESI, STDI, EEI* and *GEI* as an integration of 13, 11, 20, 10, 12 and 16 associated indicators, respectively. Undertaken variables do not have equal contribution in estimation of *EDI, SDI, ESI, STDI, EEI* and *GEI*. It is, therefore, appropriate to assign weights for individual indicator to increase the robustness of projected index (Kumar et al., 2017; Singh & Kumar, 2022c). Furthermore, it also increases the unanimity among the academicians and researchers on estimated index. It also shows the validity of created index. Since, composite score of corresponding variables were applied to estimate said indexes. Hence, weights for a particular variable were assigned as per its percentage variance among the set of undertaken variables. Accordingly, following formula was used for weights calculation of arbitrary variables:

$$wi = \frac{K}{\sqrt{Var\left(CS\right)}} \quad (4)$$

Here, w_i is weightage of ith variables; CS is the statistical variance of all composite score of all variables in a specific group; and sum of all w_i was 1 in equation (4). The value of K was assessed as:

Here,

$$K = \frac{1}{\left[\sum_{i=1}^{n}\left(\frac{1}{\sqrt{Var\left(CS\right)}}\right)\right]} \tag{5}$$

Previous studies such as Kumar et al. (2017), Singh and Issac (2018), Singh et al. (2019a), Singh and Ashraf (2020), Singh et al. (2021), and Singh and Kumar (2022a,c) pursued above-mentioned process to assign weights for specific variables in index estimation.

4. STATISTICAL AND EMPIRICAL ANALYSIS

4.1. Development of Economic Development Index (*EDI*)

Economic development includes several factors, such as employment, income stability and profitability (Moya-Clemente et al., 2020). Per capita income is an effective indicator to measure economic development, and it has a positive impact on sustainable development (Koirala & Pradhan, 2019; Jin et al., 2020; Baydoun and Aga, 2021; Singh and Kumar, 2022c). The real income of people decreases as inflation increases. Consequently, economic development is expected to be declined. Accordingly, it may negatively impact sustainable development (Koirala & Pradhan, 2019). Foreign direct investment net inflow also shows a positive influence on economic development. Hence, it appeared that a specific indicator might not capture economic development. Therefore, previous studies have developed *EDI* as an integration of the most relevant factors that positively impact economic development (Singh et al., 2019a; Singh et al., 2020; Singh et al., 2021; Singh & Kumar, 2022c). Therefore, in this study, *EDI* was developed to explain the relative performance of undertaken economies in economic development. The description of variables considered to develop *EDI* is given in Table: 2. In this study, *EDI* was assessed as:

$$(EDI)_{ct} = w_1 \times (CS\_EIPTE)_{ct} + w_2 \times (CS\_GDPPPE)_{ct} + w_3 \times (CS\_LFPRTPTP)_{ct} + w_4 \times (CS\_IGDPDAP)_{ct} + w_5 \times (CS\_ETPTE)_{ct} + w_6 \times (CS\_EGSPGDP)_{ct} + w_7 \times (CS\_FDINIPGDP)_{ct} + w_8 \times (CS\_FCEPGDP)_{ct} + w_9 \times (CS\_GDPPC)_{ct} +$$

$$w_{10} \times (CS\_GCFPGDP)_{ct} + w_{11} \times (CS\_SETPTE)_{ct} + w_{12} \times (CS\_VETPTE)_{ct} + w_{13} \times (CS\_WSWTPTE)_{ct} \quad (6)$$

Here, *EDI* is economic development index; *CS* is composite-score of corresponding variables; w_1, w_2, ..., w_{13} are the assigned weightage for associated variables in equation (6).

4.2. Development of Social Development Index (*SDI*)

Social development is defined as the allocation of resources (e.g., education, water, sanitation, heath, energy, jobs, etc.) which have an equal impact on social welfare, literacy rate, female employment, infant mortality rate, health facilities, female contribution in economic activities and age-dependency ratio to increase social welfare (Singh et al., 2019a; Jin et al., 2020; Singh & Singh, 2020; Singh & Singh, 2020; Singh et al., 2020; Singh et al., 2021; Sridhara et al., 2022; Singh & Kumar, 2022a; Singh & Kumar, 2022c). Health is a significant outcome and resource of sustainable development (Ullah et al., 2021). Social development also integrates factors associated with basic needs, women empowerment and child labour (Moya-Clemente et al., 2020). Hence, social development has a muti-interacting association with many activities. Therefore, Singh et al. (2020), Singh and Singh (2020), and Singh et al. (2021) have developed *SDI* to express the relative performance of selected economies in social development.

This study also develops *SDI* as a composite index of age-dependency ratio, education expenditure, fixed telephone subscriptions, the incidence of tuberculosis, mortality rate of infants, sex ratio at birth, unemployment youth and total unemployment, energy use, people using at least basic drinking water services and people using at least essential sanitation services to explore the cross-comparison of undertaken countries. Age-dependency ratio is a vital variable in increasing social development. The literacy rate measures overall social development (Singh & Kumar, 2022a). The fixed telephone is a better way to increase social communication among people. Social development is expected to be declined as the incidence of tuberculosis and infant mortality rate increase (Singh & Issac, 2018; Singh & Kumar, 2022a). Gender equality implies the overall women's empowerment and a better position of social development (Singh & Issac, 2018). Social development is negatively influenced due to an increase in youth unemployment and total unemployment. The availability of energy helps increase human health. Thus, energy use may be useful to increase social development. Furthermore, basic drinking water and sanitation services also significantly contribute towards social development. In this study, *SDI* is defined as a composite-index which explains the relative performance of undertaken countries in social development. While, it was evaluated as:

$$(SDI)_{ct} = w_1 \times (CS\_ADRPWAP)_{ct} + w_2 \times (CS\_EEPGNI)_{ct} + w_3 \times (CS\_FTSPHP)_{ct} + w_4 \times (CS\_ITPMP)_{ct} + w_5 \times (CS\_MRIPTLB)_{ct} + w_6 \times (CS\_SRB)_{ct} + w_7 \times (CS\_UYTPTLF)_{ct} + w_8 \times (CS\_UTPTLF)_{ct} + w_9 \times (CS\_EUKOEPC)_{ct} + w_{10} \times (CS\_PULBDWSPP)_{ct} + w_{11} \times (CS\_PULBSSPP)_{ct} \quad (7)$$

Here, *SDI* is the social development index; *CS* is the composite-score of corresponding variables; w_1, w_2, ..., w_{11} are the assigned weightage for associated variables in equation (7).

4.3. Development of Environmental Sustainability Index (*ESI*)

This study defines the environmental sustainability index (ESI) as a composite index of most related variables significantly impacting environmental development. Singh et al. (2019a), Jin et al. (2020), Singh et al. (2020), Singh et al. (2021), and Singh and Kumar (2022c) developed *ESI* to examine the position of environmental development across economies. CO_2 emissions from various sources are caused to increase environmental degradation (Akbostanci et al., 2009; Zhang & Lin, 2012; Baydoun & Aga, 2021).

The agricultural sector and fertiliser application are also caused to increase CO_2 emissions in the atmosphere. Demographical change, i.e., population growth, fertility rate, population density, and urbanisation, also negatively impacts environmental development (Zhang & Lin, 2012; Singh et al., 2019a; Singh et al., 2020; Singh & Singh, 2020; Singh et al., 2021; Singh & Kumar, 2022c). Therefore, variables associated with environmental development were considered to develop the *ESI* in the study (Table: 4). The *ESI* was estimated as:

$$(ESI)_{ct} = w_1 \times (CS\_PGAP)_{ct} + w_2 \times (CS\_ALPLA)_{ct} + w_3 \times (CS\_CDGEKPGDP)_{ct} + w_4 \times (CS\_CDGEMTPC)_{ct} + w_5 \times (CS\_CDGEGFC)_{ct} + w_6 \times (CS\_CDGEMIC)_{ct} + w_7 \times (CS\_CDGERBCPS)_{ct} + w_8 \times (CS\_CDGESFC)_{ct} + w_9 \times (CS\_CDGET)_{ct} + w_{10} \times (CS\_CDGEKPKOEU)_{ct} + w_{11} \times (CS\_CRWPTE)_{ct} + w_{12} \times (CS\_FRTBPW)_{ct} + w_{13} \times (CS\_PM2.5APMAE)_{ct} + w_{14} \times (CS\_FCPHAL)_{ct} + w_{15} \times (CS\_FAPLA)_{ct} + w_{16} \times (CS\_FFECPT)_{ct} + w_{17} \times (CS\_PM2.5APPELEWHO)_{ct} + w_{18} \times (CS\_PDPPSLA)_{ct} + w_{19} \times (CS\_UPPTP)_{ct} + w_{20} \times (CS\_CDGEPUMVA)_{ct} \quad (8)$$

Here, *ESI* is the environmental sustainability index; *CS* is the composite-score of corresponding variables; w_1, w_2, ..., and w_{20} are the assigned weightage for associated variables in equation (8).

4.4. Development of Science and Technological Development Index (*STDI*)

In this study, *STDI* is defined as a composite index of most related factors which are useful to increase a nation's technological advancement. It also measures the relative performance across economies in science & technological development (Singh & Kumar, 2022c). Science & technological development and intellectual property rights (IPRs) related factors can be considered to develop *STDI*. Scientific research articles and patent application files are the output of research & development (R&D) activity, depending on researchers and R&D expenditure. Also, patenting is an essential form of intellectual property rights (Dvouletý, 2018; Singh & Singh, 2020). ICT exports, merchandise trade, the share of manufacturing value-added in GDP, per capita manufacturing value-added, and share of medium and high-tech manufacturing value-added in total value-added are helpful to increase science & technological development. Therefore, factors associated with science & technological development and IPRs were considered to develop *STDI* in this study (Table: 5). The *STDI* was assessed as:

$$(STDI)_{ct} = w_1 \times (CS\_RRDPMP)_{ct} + w_2 \times (CS\_ICTGEPTGE)_{ct} + w_3 \times (CS\_MTPGDP)_{ct} + w_4 \times (CS\_RDEPGDP)_{ct} + w_5 \times (CS\_MVAPGDP)_{ct} + w_6 \times (CS\_MVAPC)_{ct} + w_7 \times (CS\_PMHTMVATVA)_{ct} + w_8 \times (CS\_STJAPPR)_{ct} + w_9 \times (CS\_PAFPTR)_{ct} + w_{10} \times (CS\_RDEPR)_{ct} \quad (9)$$

Here, *STDI* is the science & technological development index; *CS* is the composite-index; w_1, w_2, ..., and w_{10} are the assigned weightage for associated variables in equation (9).

4.5. Development of Global Sustainable Development Index (*GSDI*)

Sustainable development has a multi-dimensional association with a large number of factors which are positively associated with economic, social, human, science & technological, institutional and environmental development (Singh et al., 2020; Moya-Clemente et al., 2020; Misztal & Kowalska, 2020; Singh et al., 2021; Singh and Kumar, 2022c). The measurement of sustainable development depends upon selected indicators and methods (Miola & Schiltz, 2019). Evidence also reveals that the measurement of sustainable development is complex and controversial. However, Koirala and Pradhan (2019) have used the adjusted net saving to explain sustainable development performance in 12 Asian economies. Adjusted net saving comprises social, economic and environmental factors (Ullah et al., 2021).

Sustainable development integrates economic, social, environmental, and science & technological development (Guijarro & Poyatos, 2018; Singh et al., 2020; Singh et al., 2021; Singh & Kumar, 2022c). Dhahri and Omri (2018) integrated economic growth, human development, and environmental quality to recognise sustainable development performance. Accordingly, *GSDI* was considered a composite index of *EDI, SDI, ESI*, and *STD* in this study. Thus, *GSDI* was estimated as:

$$(GSDI)_{ct} = w_1 \times (CS\_EDI)_{ct} + w_2 \times (CS\_SDI)_{ct} + w_3 \times (CS\_ESI)_{ct} + w_4 \times (CS\_STDI)_{ct} \quad (10)$$

Here, *GSDI* is the global sustainable development index; *EDI* is the economic development index; *SDI* is the social development index; *STDI* is the science & technological development index; w_1, w_2, ..., w_4 are the assigned weightage for associated variables in equation (10). *GSDI* is defined as an integrated index of different indicators that best demonstrate sustainable development.

4.6. Development of Entrepreneurship Ecosystem Index (*EEI*)

Previous studies used different factors to define the entrepreneurship ecosystem. For instance, Wennekers et al. (2010) used self-employment or business ownership for the entrepreneurship ecosystem to assess its impact on economic development. Chen (2014) considered the employment rate and the number of company formations to explicate the role of the entrepreneurship ecosystem on economic growth in Taiwan. Audretsch et al. (2015) have used new business formation as a proxy indicator of the entrepreneurship ecosystem in 127 European cities. Adusei (2016) also used the number of new businesses registered to describe the entrepreneurship ecosystem in 12 African countries. Dvouletý (2017) also considered annual growth in registered business activities to examine the performance of the entrepreneurship ecosystem in the Czech regions. Credit to SMEs was also used as a proxy for the entrepreneurship ecosystem in Nigeria (Farayibi, 2016). Bashir and Akhtar (2016) used the global competitiveness index for the entrepreneurship ecosystem to examine its relationship with per capita GDP in G20 economies. Tasnim and Afzal (2018) considered the global entrepreneurship index to describe the entrepreneurship ecosystem in 50 cross-sectional economies. Zaki and Rashid (2016) used the number of new establishments to explain the entrepreneurship ecosystem. Rusu and Roman (2017) have applied total entrepreneurial activities to explain the position of the entrepreneurship ecosystem in 18 European countries. Dvouletý (2018) used self-employment activity to define entrepreneurship in 11 European economies. Erken et al. (2018) focused on business ownership rates to define the entrepreneurship ecosystem in 20 OECD economies. Roomi et al. (2020) measure the sustainable entrepreneurship and eco-innovation in business using indicators which proposed by UN. Singh and Ashraf (2020) also developed *EEI* using 12 indicators of the entrepreneurship ecosystem suggested by the Global Entrepreneurship Monitor survey. Therefore, this study also considered these indicators to create *EEI* (Table: 6). The *EEI* was estimated as:

$$(EEI)_{ct} = w_1 \times (CS\_BSEET)_{ct} + w_2 \times (CS\_CPI)_{ct} + w_3 \times (CS\_CSN)_{ct} + w_4 \times (CS\_FE)_{ct} + w_5 \times (CS\_GP)_{ct} + w_6 \times (CS\_GSP)_{ct} + w_7 \times (CS\_IMD)_{ct} + w_8 \times (CS\_IMO)_{ct} + w_9 \times (CS\_PSI)_{ct} + w_{10} \times (CS\_PSEET)_{ct} + w_{11} \times (CS\_RDE)_{ct} + w_{12} \times (CS\_TB)_{ct} \quad (11)$$

Here, *EEI* is the entrepreneurship ecosystem index; *CS* is the composite-index; w_1, w_2, ..., and w_{10} are the assigned weightage for related variables in equation (11).

4.7. Development of Green Entrepreneurship Index (*GEI*)

Green entrepreneurship emphasises increasing the use and practices of new technology or green technology to minimise the overwhelming use of natural resources. Accordingly, a green economy or green growth is a significant component of green entrepreneurship. A single variable cannot detect green entrepreneurship. Environmental technology, green technology and patented technology in the environmental field can be used as a proxy for green entrepreneurship to assess its impact on sustainable development (Ahmad et al., 2015; Nuringsih et al., 2020; Karimi & Chashmi, 2019; Alwakid et al., 2021). Moreover, factors such as sustainable growth and sustainable energy are also valuable for protect environmental development, which can be used to measure the performances of sustainable entrepreneurship or green entrepreneurship (Moya-Clemente et al., 2020; Roomi et al., 2020). Environmental technology helps to reduce GHGs emissions and increases the practice of green entrepreneurship (Demirel et al., 2017). The granted patents in environmental technology may be considered a proxy for environmental technologies (Singh et al., 2020). Adoption of renewable sources of energy through technological advancement may be conducive to reducing environmental degradation (Tawiah et al., 2021; Baydoun & Aga, 2021). Demirel and Danisman (2019) used replanning of water, renewable energy, replanning energy and minimizing waste to examine the impact of circular eco-innovations and external funding on the SMEs' growth. Skordoulis et al. (2022) used indicators linked with environmental issues, green product innovation and green process innovation to explain the relationship between green innovation and green entrepreneurship in firms in Greece. It found that previous literature focused on different indicators to defined green entrepreneurship ecosystem, sustainable entrepreneurship and eco-entrepreneurship. Thus, the green entrepreneurship index (*GEI*) was developed as an integration of factors which nurture the ecosystem of green entrepreneurship (Table: 7). *GEI* was estimated as:

$$(GEI)_{ct} = w_1 \times (CS\_ACFTC)_{ct} + w_2 \times (CS\_AEPP)_{ct} + w_3 \times (CS\_EPCPC)_{ct} + w_4 \times (CS\_EPFCSPT)_{ct} + w_5 \times (CS\_EPFHSPT)_{ct} + w_6 \times (CS\_EPFNGSPT)_{ct} + w_7 \times (CS\_EPFOSPT)_{ct} + w_8 \times (CS\_EPFOGCSPT)_{ct} + w_9 \times (CS\_EPFRSEHPT)_{ct} + w_{10} \times (CS\_REOPTEO)_{ct} + w_{11} \times (CS\_RECPTFEC)_{ct} + w_{12} \times (CS\_RIFWRPC)_{ct} + w_{13} \times (CS\_EILPE)_{ct} + w_{14} \times (CS\_PBCO2P)_{ct} + w_{15} \times (CS\_DERTPAT)_{ct} + w_{16} \times (CS\_SPGETTPGAT)_{ct} \quad (12)$$

Here, *GEI* is the environmental sustainability index; *CS* is the composite-score of corresponding variables; w_1, w_2, ..., and w_{16} are the assigned weightage for associated variables in equation (12).

4.8. Formulation of Empirical Models

Previous studies have applied estimated indexes as a dependent and independent variable to examine the causal relationship among them (Domańska et al., 2018; Singh et al., 2019a; Galindo-Martín et al., 2020; Moya-Clemente et al., 2020; Singh et al., 2021; Singh & Kumar, 2022a). For instance, Bashir and Akhtar (2016) examine the influence of the global competitiveness index on per capita GDP in G20 countries. Tasnim and Afzal (2018) examined the impact of the global entrepreneurship index on GDP in 50 cross-sectional economies. Dvouletý (2018) observed the influence of the economic freedom index on self-employment activity. Singh and Ashraf (2020) examined the causal relationship between the entrepreneurship ecosystem index and per capita GDP in 34 cross-sectional economies. Ullah et al. (2021) observed the impact of the governance index and e-government index on sustainable development. Therefore, several linear regression models were developed to examine the causal relationship among the estimated indexes in this study. The conceptual review claimed that green entrepreneurship and the entrepreneurship ecosystem have positive and significant impact on sustainable development. Therefore, the following linear regression model was used to examine the impact of *GEI* and *EEI* on *GSDI*:

$$(GSDI)_{ct} = \beta_0 + \beta_1 (EEI)_{ct} + \beta_2 (GEI)_{ct} + \mu_{ct} \quad (13)$$

Here, *GSDI* is the global sustainable development index; *EEI* is the entrepreneurship ecosystem index; *GEI* is the green entrepreneurship index; β_0 is the constant coefficient; β_1 and β_2 are the regression coefficients of associated variables; μ_{ct} is the error-term in equation (12). *GEI* was used as the dependent variable to assess its association with *GSDI*. The regression coefficient of *GEI* with *SDGI* and *EEI* was estimated as:

$$(GEI)_{ct} = \alpha_0 + \alpha_1 (GSDI)_{ct} + \alpha_2 (EEI)_{ct} + \chi_{ct} \tag{14}$$

Here, α_0 is constant-coefficient; α_1 and α_2 are the estimated regression coefficient of *GSDI* and *EEI*, respectively; χ_{ct} and is the error-term in equation (14). This study also examines the interconnection among the estimated indexes (i.e., *EDI*, *SDI*, *ESI*, *STDI*, *EEI*, and *GEI*). For the abovementioned investigations, the following regression models were used:

$$(SDI)_{ct} = \lambda_0 + \lambda_1 (GEI)_{ct} + \lambda_2 (EEI)_{ct} + \lambda_3 (EDI)_{ct} + \lambda_4 (ESI)_{ct} + \lambda_5 (STDI)_{ct} + \phi_{ct} \tag{15}$$

Here, λ_0 is the constant coefficient; λ_1, ..., λ_5 are the regression coefficients of associated variables; and is ϕ_{ct} error-term in equation (15).

$$(EDI)_{ct} = \theta_0 + \theta_1 (GEI)_{ct} + \theta_2 (EEI)_{ct} + \theta_3 (SDI)_{ct} + \theta_4 (ESI)_{ct} + \theta_5 (STDI)_{ct} + €_{ct} \tag{16}$$

Here, θ_0 is the constant coefficient; θ_1, ..., θ_5 are the regression coefficients of associated variables; and is $€_{ct}$ error-term in equation (16).

$$(STDI)_{ct} = \gamma_0 + \gamma_1 (GEI)_{ct} + \gamma_2 (EEI)_{ct} + \gamma_3 (SDI)_{ct} + \gamma_4 (ESI)_{ct} + \gamma_5 (EDI)_{ct} + \delta_{ct} \tag{17}$$

Here, γ_0 is constant-coefficient; γ_1, ..., γ_5 are the regression coefficients of associated variables; and is δ_{ct} error-term in equation (17).

$$(EEI)_{ct} = \xi_0 + \xi_1 (STDI)_{ct} + \xi_2 (GEI)_{ct} + \xi_3 (SDI)_{ct} + \xi_4 (ESI)_{ct} + \xi_5 (EDI)_{ct} + £_{ct} \tag{18}$$

Here, ξ_0 is the constant coefficient; ξ_1, ..., ξ_5 are the regression coefficients of associated variables; and is $£_{ct}$ error-term in equation (18).

$$(GEI)_{ct} = \eta_0 + \xi_1 (EEI)_{ct} + \eta_2 (STDI)_{ct} + \eta_3 (SDI)_{ct} + \eta_4 (ESI)_{ct} + \eta_5 (EDI)_{ct} + \varphi_{ct} \tag{19}$$

Here, η_0 is constant-coefficient; η_1, ..., η_5 are the regression coefficients of associated variables; and is φ_{ct} error-term in equation (19).

4.9. Selection of Appropriate Model

This study compiled social-economic development, science & technological development, intellectual property rights, environmental development, green entrepreneurship and entrepreneurship ecosystem associated variables in country-wise panel data from 2000 to 2019. These countries have high diversity in the aforementioned activities; therefore, it was expected that cross-sectional dependency, auto-correlation, and heteroskedasticity might be present in the country-wise panel data. Prior studies used a feasible generalised least squares estimation (*FGLSE*) model to reduce the cross-sectional dependency, auto-correlation and heteroskedasticity in the panel data (Kumar et al., 2017; Singh et al., 2021). Hence, regression coefficients of explanatory variables in the proposed regression equations were estimated through *FGLSE* model. SPSS and STATA statistical software were used to development of aforementioned indexes and run the proposed regression equations.

5. DISCUSSION ON DESCRIPTIVE RESULTS

Comparative performance of economies as per the estimated mean values of *EDI*, *SDI*, *ESI*, *STDI*, *GSDI*, *GEI* and *EEI* during 2000 – 2019 is given in Figure 1 and Figure 2. The values of *EDI* lie between 0.31 to 0.64 across countries. Thus, the estimates show a high diversity in economic development across countries. Switzerland has the highest value of *EDI*; thus, this country has the best performance in economic development. Luxembourg, Germany, Austria and Australia have 2nd, 3rd, 4th and 5th positions in economic development. Most high-income group economies, such as Estonia, Belgium, Netherland, Portugal, Hungary, Denmark, Finland, Canada, Sweden and, Spain, France, have the *EDI*'s values of more than 0.50. Therefore, these countries have relatively better performance in economic development. As India has the 34th position in economic development, thus, India's performance seems to be the poorest in economic development among the 34 countries. Argentina, Russia, Brazil, and Romania have 33rd, 32nd, 31st and 30th positions in economic development. It was also observed that mostly upper-middle-income countries have a poor position in economic development as per the values of *EDI*.

The *SDI*'s values lie between 0.242 to 0.791 across economies. There is high diversity in social development in these economies. The economies can be divided into four categories, i.e. (best, better, moderate and poor) as per the estimated values of SDI. Sweden, Denmark, Norway, Luxembourg, United States of America, Canada, Australia, Germany, Belgium, France, Switzerland, Japan, United Kingdom, Austria, and Finland have the best performance in social development. Estonia, Portugal, Hungry, Mexico, Greece, Spain, Croatia, Argentina, Poland and Latvia have a better position in social development. Russia, Lithuania, Romania, Brazil and China have moderate performance in social development. SDI's values were less than 0.50 for Tunisia, India and South Africa. Thus, this group of economies have a poor performance in social development. The estimates also infer that Sweden, Denmark, Norway, Luxembourg, and the United States of America have the 1st, 2nd, 3rd, 4th and 5th ranks in *SDI*. While, Tunisia, India and South Africa have 32nd 33rd and 34th ranks, respectively, in *SDI*. Tunisia, India and South Africa need to increase their position in social development.

The environmental performance of countries was measured through *ESI*. The *ESI*'s values lie between 0.413 to 0.756. Subsequently, the economies were segregated into four groups, i.e., the best environmentally sustainable group (Sweden, Finland, Estonia and Norway), the upper sustainable group (Lithuania, Portugal, Latvia, Canada, Austria, Spain, Switzerland, Croatia, Brazil, Japan, Romania, United States of America, France and Greece) middle environmentally sustainable group (Hungary, Russia, Germany, Denmark, Australia, Mexico, Poland, Argentina, United Kingdom, Belgium and Tunisia) and poorest sustainable group (Luxembourg, Netherlands, South Africa, China and India) as per the values of *ESI*. India's performance seemed relatively very poor in environmental sustainability as it has 34th rank in *ESI*. Also, China, South Africa and Netherland have 33rd, 32nd and 31st ranks, respectively, in *ESI*. Sweden, Finland and Estonia have the 1st, 2nd and 3rd positions in *ESI*.

The comparative status of selected countries in science & technological development was observed in *STDI*. The values of *STDI*'s lie between 0.138 to 0.619 across countries. The estimates reveal significant diversity in science & technological development in these economies. Accordingly, Switzerland has the highest value of *STDI*. Thus, the performance of this country was the best in science & technological development. Japan, Germany and Sweden have a relatively better performance in science & technological development. Finland, the United States of America, Netherlands, Denmark, Belgium, Austria, Hungary and China have a moderate position in science & technological development. Norway, Canada, the United Kingdom, France, Australia, Mexico and Estonia were relatively poor in science & technological development. Furthermore, Luxembourg, Spain, Romania, Poland, Lithuania, Croatia, Portugal, South Africa, Brazil, India, Greece, Latvia, Russia, Tunisia and Argentina have the lowest values of *STDI*. Accordingly, the performance of these economies appeared relatively poorest in science & technological development. Switzerland, Japan, and Germany have the 1st, 2nd and 3rd ranks in *STDI*. While Argentina, Tunisia and Russia have the 32nd, 33rd and 34th, ranks in *STDI*.

GSDI was the integrated index of *EDI*, *SDI*, *ESI* and *STDI*. Hence, it is noticeable that the performance and ranking of undertaken economies in sustainable development economies depend upon mentioned indexes. Subsequently, there was high diversity in sustainable development among the 34 countries. Switzerland has the highest value of *GSDI* as it has the 1st position in economic and social development and 11th position in environmental sustainability and science & technological development. After that, Sweden and Finland have 2nd and 3rd positions in sustainable development. Most high-income group economies (except Croatia, Greece and Poland) have a better position in sustainable development. All upper-middle-income group countries (South Africa) have a relatively moderate position in sustainable development. India, South Africa and Tunisia have the 34th, 33rd and 32nd ranks, respectively, in *GSDI*.

Undertaken economies have high diversity in the entrepreneurship ecosystem as per the *EEI*'s values. Estonia has the best performance in the entrepreneurship ecosystem. Switzerland, the Netherlands, the United States of America, Luxembourg and Tunisia have EEI values of more than 0.60. Therefore, there is a need to nurture a conducive ecosystem for entrepreneurship in these countries. Canada, Finland, Denmark, Belgium, China, Germany, Norway, Austria, Lithuania, the United Kingdom, India, and France have a better entrepreneurship ecosystem. Australia, Latvia, Mexico, Spain and Poland have a moderate position in the entrepreneurship ecosystem. The remaining economies need to increase their performance in the entrepreneurship ecosystem. Estonia, Switzerland, and the United States of America have the 1st, 2nd and 3rd ranks, respectively in the entrepreneurship ecosystem. Brazil, Croatia and Greece showed the poorest performance in the entrepreneurship ecosystem.

Furthermore, the estimates imply that Norway and Canada have the best position in green entrepreneurship. While most economies have the lowest values of *GEI*, less than 0.50, thus, these economies are required to think about applying more practices toward green entrepreneurship. France, Switzerland and India have the 34th, 33rd and 32nd ranks, respectively in *GEI*. Thus, these economies should give more priority to green entrepreneurship.

The estimates based on correlation coefficients among the estimated indexes indicate that *GSDI* was positively associated with *EDI*, *SDI*, *ESI*, *STDI*, *EEI* and *GEI* (Table: 9). Sustainable development cannot be achieved without implementing an integrated policy which should be conducive to increasing economic, social, environmental and science & technological development. *EDI* was also positively associated with *GSDI*, *SDI*, *ESI*, *STDI*, *EEI*, *GEI*. Furthermore, *SDI* has a positive association with *GSDI*, *EDI*, *ESI*, *STDI*, *EEI* and *GEI*. Environmental sustainability cannot be achieved through economic development, social development, science & technological development and practices of green entrepreneurship. Economic development, social development, and science & technological development also seemed optimistic about increasing the entrepreneurship ecosystem. In contrast, science & technological development and the entrepreneurship ecosystem negatively contribute to green entrepreneurship.

6. DISCUSSION ON EMPIRICAL RESULTS

The empirical results imply that the regression coefficient of *GSDI* with *EEI* and *GEI* appeared positive and significant (Table 9). The entrepreneurship ecosystem and green entrepreneurship have a positive impact on sustainable development. The estimate is consistent with previous studies such as İyigün (2015), Domańska et al. (2018), Nuringsih et al. (2020), Zhao et al. (2021), Tawiah et al. (2021), Alwakid et al. (2021), Gupta & Dharwal (2022) which also reported that sustainable development is positively associated with green entrepreneurship. Furthermore, the regression coefficients of *GEI* with *GSDI* seemed positive and statistically significant. Thus, sustainable development also showed a positive impact on green entrepreneurship. Accordingly, sustainable development has a causal relationship with green entrepreneurship.

The regression coefficients of *EEI* with *GSDI*, *SDI*, *EDI* and *STDI* were found positive. It emphasized that the entrepreneurship ecosystem plays a crucial role in increasing sustainable development, social development, economic development, and science & technological development. It also seems that the entrepreneurship ecosystem has a negative impact on green entrepreneurship. The aforesaid estimates are consistent with various existing studies such as Singh and Ashraf (2020) which noticed positive impact of entrepreneurship ecosystem on economic development. Cai et al. (2022) also argued that green entrepreneurship has positive contribution to increase social and environmental development. Singh and Singh (2020) also observed positive influence of science & technological development on growth of manufacturing sector.

The impact of green entrepreneurship on social development was found positive. Also, *EDI*, *ESI* and *STDI* have a positive impact on *SDI*. Singh et al. (2020), Singh et al. (2021), and Singh and Kumar (2022c) also reported positive influence of environmental sustainability development and science & technological development on social development. Further, the results infer that social development is expected to be improved as green entrepreneurship, economic development, science & technological development and environmental sustainability increase.

The regression coefficients of *EDI* with *EEI*, *ESI*, *STDI* and *SDI* were positive and statistically significant. Thus, economic development is expected to be increased as the entrepreneurship ecosystem, environmental sustainability, science & technological development and social development increase. The estimates are similar with previous studies like Singh et al. (2019a), Singh et al. (2020), Singh et al. (2021), and Singh and Kumar (2022c).

The regression coefficient of *STDI* with *EEI*, *EDI* and *SDI* were appeared positive and statistically significant. Thus, science & technological development is expected to be improved as the entrepreneurship ecosystem, economic development and social development increase. However, green entrepreneurship and environmental sustainability negatively influenced science & technological development.

EDI, *STDI* and *SDI* showed a positive impact on the entrepreneurship ecosystem. Thus, the estimates demonstrate that the entrepreneurship ecosystem is likely to improve as economic development, science & technological development and social development increase. The entrepreneurship ecosystem is negatively influenced due to an increase in green entrepreneurship and environmental sustainability. Environmental Sustainability and social development showed a positive impact on green entrepreneurship. Khan et al. (2020) also reported a positive association between green practices and environmental Sustainability in SAARC countries. While the entrepreneurship ecosystem, economic development, and science & technological development showed a negative impact on green entrepreneurship. The estimates can be acceptable in way that entrepreneurship ecosystem and science & technological development are essential to increase industrialization which may be caused to increase environmental degradation. Also, the process of economic development also needs more natural and ecosystem services to sustain the production scale (Singh et al., 2019a; Singh et al., 2020). Subsequently, natural and ecosystem services are projected to be declined as economic development increases. Therefore, it is understandable that initiations of green entrepreneurship ecosystem may be adversely affected due to increase in entrepreneurship ecosystem, economic development and science & technological development.

7. CONCLUDING REMARK, POLICY GUIDELINE AND FUTURE RESEARCH DIRECTION

The descriptive results showed high diversity in economic development across countries. Germany, Austria and Australia have 2nd, 3rd, 4th and 5th position, respectively in economic development. In economic development, Argentina, Russia, Brazil, and Romania have 33rd, 32nd, 31st and 30th positions, respectively. It was also witnessed that mostly upper-middle-income countries have a poor position in economic development. There was also appeared high diversity in social development among the 34 economies. In *SDI*, Sweden, Denmark, Norway, Luxembourg, and the United States of America have the 1st, 2nd, 3rd, 4th and 5th ranks, respectively. In *SDI*, Tunisia, India, and South Africa have 32nd, 33rd and 34th ranks, respectively. In *ESI*, China, South Africa and the Netherlands have 33rd, 32nd and 31st ranks, respectively. Sweden, Finland and Estonia have the 1st, 2nd and 3rd positions, respectively in *ESI*. Switzerland, Japan and Germany have the 1st, 2nd and 3rd ranks, respectively in *STDI*. While Argentina, Tunisia and Russia have the 32nd, 33rd and 34th, ranks in *STDI*. Subsequently, there was high diversity in sustainable development among 34 countries. Switzerland has the highest value of *GSDI*. In sustainable development, Sweden and Finland have 2nd and 3rd positions, respectively. India, South Africa and Tunisia have the 34th, 33rd and 32nd ranks, respectively in *GSDI*. Furthermore, Estonia, Switzerland and the United States of America have the 1st, 2nd and 3rd ranks, respectively in the entrepreneurship ecosystem. Brazil, Croatia and Greece showed the poorest performance in the entrepreneurship ecosystem. Norway and Canada have best position in green entrepreneurship. France, Switzerland and India have the 34th, 33rd and 32nd ranks, respectively. Hence, it was perceived a high diversity in sustainable development, economic development, social development, environmental sustainability, science & technological development, entrepreneurship ecosystem and green entrepreneurship in 34 countries. The aforementioned indexes are useful for policy makers to take effective and conducive policy action to maintain their position in sustainable development and its associated components, and entrepreneurship ecosystem and green entrepreneurship.

The correlation coefficients among the estimated indexes indicate that sustainable development was positively associated with economic, social, science & technological development; environmental sustainability; entrepreneurship ecosystem and green entrepreneurship. Economic and social development were positively associated with environmental sustainability, science & technological development, entrepreneurship ecosystem and green entrepreneurship. Furthermore, science & technological development also improved as social and economic development, and entrepreneurship ecosystem increase. However, the entrepreneurship ecosystem was negatively correlated with green entrepreneurship. Science & technological development and entrepreneurship ecosystem were also negatively correlated with green entrepreneurship.

The empirical results infer that green entrepreneurship and sustainable development have a positive and causal relationship. Social development and environmental sustainability would be improved as more green entrepreneurship practices increase. Social development, science & technological development and entrepreneurship ecosystem could be improved as economic development increases. Environmental sustainability is likely to be improved as social development, economic development, and green entrepreneurship increases. Economic development has a positive impact on social development and vice-versa. Moreover, economic development, social development, and entrepreneurship ecosystem seemed to increase as science & technological development increased. Hence, it was reported a complex association among the estimated indexes. Despite that, this study suggested that green entrepreneurship is highly effective in increasing sustainable development and its key components.

Following policy suggestions can be effective to increase green entrepreneurship and sustainable development: Economic development would improve as increase in employment in industrial sector and labour participation rate in economic activities. Furthermore, it would be helpful to increase consumption expenditure, and demand of goods and services in domestic and international market. Thus, it incentivizes to the manufacturing sector to increase production scale to meet the demand of goods and services. Accordingly, it would enhance the growth of industrial sector. Industrial sector should adopt green practices, environmental technology, appropriate technology and green technology to produce goods and service to increase the environmental development (Khan et al., 2020; Singh et al., 2022). Entrepreneurship ecosystem also would be effective to create business opportunities, new markets and new goods. The government should organize training programmes for new businessman to be green entrepreneurs. Education may be a most useful indicator to increase social development. For this, the government should increase extensive investment in education sector to increase social development. Also, initiations of better medical and health facilities for common people would reduce incidence of tuberculosis and infant mortality rate (Ivleva et al., 2019). Social development would also increase as providing the basic water drinking and sanitation facilities.

Abatement of CO_2 and GHGs emissions from various production activities would reduce the environmental degradation (Khan et al., 2020). Therefore, agricultural and industrial sectors should use green technology to increase environmental sustainability (Singh et al., 2022). Agricultural sector should avoid extensive application of fertilizer and pesticides in cultivation (Kumar et al., 2017; Singh et al., 2022). Largely populated country should adopt a conducive policy to control high population growth, urbanization and fossil fuel energy consumption to increase environmental sustainability. Science & technological development would improve as increase in number of researchers, R&D expenditure, scientific and technical research articles, transfer of technology from research organization to industrial field and implementation of strict IPRs regime (Singh & Kumar, 2022b). Subsequently, these variables would be helpful to create appropriate entrepreneurship ecosystem in global economies (Singh & Ashraf, 2020). Green practices can be discovered and used in several ways such as clean fuels technology, use of electricity in production activities, sources of renewable electricity and energy, renewable energy consumption, renewable internal freshwater resources, sustain energy intensity level, reduce waste material, development of environment-related technologies, green and environmental technology and forest cover to increase green entrepreneurship and sustainable development (Khan et al., 2020).

The empirical finding of this study provides complex association among the economic development, environmental sustainability, green entrepreneurship, entrepreneurship ecosystem, science & technological development, social development and sustainable development. In further study, existing researchers may use confirmatory factor analysis and principal component analysis to examine the performance of undertaken variables to increase green entrepreneurship ecosystem, and sustainable development and its components as including more countries. Aforementioned techniques would be helpful to identify the indicators which would be helpful to formulate an integrated policy to increase green entrepreneurship and sustainable development in global countries.

REFERENCES

Adusei, M. (2016). Does entrepreneurship promote economic growth in Africa? *African Development Review*, *28*(2), 201–214. doi:10.1111/1467-8268.12190

Afzal, M. N. I., Siddiqui, S., & Dutta, S. (2018). Determinants of entrepreneurial capability (EC) environment in ASEAN-05 economies-a log-linear stochastic frontier analysis. *Journal of Global Entrepreneurship Research*, *18*(1), 8–14. doi:10.118640497-018-0101-y

Ahmad, N. H., Halim, H. A., Ramayah, T., & Rahman, S. A. (2015). Green entrepreneurship inclination among generation Y: The road towards a green economy. *Problems and Perspectives in Management*, *13*(2), 211–218.

Akbostanci, E., Türüt-Asik, S., & Tunc, I. G. (2009). The relationship between income and environment in Turkey: Is there an environmental Kuznets curve? *Energy Policy*, *37*(2), 861–867. doi:10.1016/j.enpol.2008.09.088

Alwakid, W., Aparicio, S., & Urbano, D. (2020). Cultural antecedents of green entrepreneurship in Saudi Arabia: An institutional approach. *Sustainability*, *12*(9), 1–20. doi:10.3390u12093673

Alwakid, W., Aparicio, S., & Urbano, D. (2021). The influence of green entrepreneurship on sustainable development in Saudi Arabia: The role of formal institutions. *International Journal of Environmental Research and Public Health*, *18*(5433), 1–23. doi:10.3390/ijerph18105433 PMID:34069588

Armeanu, D. S., Vintila, G., & Gherghina, S. C. (2018). Empirical study towards the drivers of sustainable economic growth in EU-28 countries. *Sustainability*, *10*(4), 1-22.

Audretsch, D. B., Belitski, M., & Desai, S. (2015). Entrepreneurship and economic development in cities. *The Annals of Regional Science*, *55*(1), 3360. doi:10.100700168-015-0685-x

Bashir, H. A., & Akhtar, A. (2016). The role of innovative entrepreneurship in economic development: A study of G20 countries. *Management Studies and Economic System*, *2*(2), 91–100. doi:10.12816/0037559

Baydoun, H., & Aga, M. (2021). The effect of energy consumption and economic growth on environmental sustainability in the GCC countries: Does financial development matter? *Energies*, *14*(5897), 1–17. doi:10.3390/en14185897

Brundtland Report, U. N. (1987). *Our Common Future*. Oxford University Press.

Cai, X., Hussain, S., & Zhang, Y. (2022). Factors that can promote the green entrepreneurial intension of college students: A fuzzy set qualitative comparative analysis. *Frontiers in Psychology*, *12*(776886), 1–13.

Chen, C. C. (2014). Entrepreneurship, economic growth, and employment: A case study of Taiwan. *Hitotsubashi Journal of Economics*, *55*(1), 71–88.

Demirel, P., & Danisman, G. O. (2019). Eco-innovation and firm growth in the circular economy: Evidence from European small- and medium-sized enterprises. *Business Strategy and the Environment*, *28*(8), 1608–1618. doi:10.1002/bse.2336

Demirel, P., Li, Q. C., & Rentocchini, F. (2017). Born to be green: New insights into the economics and management of green entrepreneurship. *Small Business Economics*, *52*(1), 759–771.

Dhahri, S., & Omri, A. (2018). *Entrepreneurship contribution to the three pillars of sustainable development: What does the evidence really say?* MPRA Paper No. 84504. https://mpra.ub.uni-muenchen.de/84504/

Domańska, A., Żukowska, B., & Zajkowski, R. (2018). Green entrepreneurship as a connector among social, environmental and economic pillars of sustainable development. Why some countries are more agile? *Problemy Ekorozwoju*, *13*(2), 67–76.

Drastichová, M. (2014). Monitoring sustainable development and developing in EU. *Central European Review of Economic Issues*, *17*(1), 125–140. doi:10.7327/cerei.2014.09.03

Duran, D. C., Gogan, L. M., Artene, A., & Duran, V. (2015). The components of sustainable development – a possible approach. *Procedia Economics and Finance*, *26*(1), 806–811. doi:10.1016/S2212-5671(15)00849-7

Dvouletý, O. (2017). Relationship between unemployment and entrepreneurship dynamics in the Czech Regions: A panel var approach. *Acta Universitatis Agriculturae et Silviculturae Mendelianae Brunensis*, *65*(102), 987–995. doi:10.11118/actaun201765030987

Dvouletý, O. (2018). How to analyse determinants of entrepreneurship and self-employment at the country level? A methodological contribution. *Journal of Business Venturing Insights*, *9*(1), 92–99. doi:10.1016/j.jbvi.2018.03.002

Ebrahimi, P., & Mirbargkar, S. M. (2017). Green entrepreneurship and green innovation for SME development in market turbulence. *Eurasian Business Review*, *7*(2), 203–228. doi:10.100740821-017-0073-9

Erken, H., Donselaar, P., & Thurik, R. (2018). Total factor productivity and the role of entrepreneurship. *The Journal of Technology Transfer*, *43*(1), 1493–1521. doi:10.100710961-016-9504-5

Farayibi, A. (2016). *Entrepreneurship as a driver of economic growth: Evidence from enterprise development in Nigeria*. MPRA Paper No. 74591. https://mpra.ub.uni-muenchen.de/74591/

Galindo-Martín, M. A., Castaño-Martínez, M. S., & Méndez-Picazo, M. T. (2020). The Relationship between Green Innovation, Social Entrepreneurship, and Sustainable Development. *Sustainability*, *12*(11), 1–19. doi:10.3390u12114467

Guijarro, F., & Poyatos, J. A. (2018). Designing a sustainable development goal index through a Goal programming model: The case of EU-28 countries. *Sustainability*, *10*(3167), 1–17. doi:10.3390u10093167

Gupta, M., & Dharwal, M. (2022). Green entrepreneurship and sustainable development: A conceptual framework. *Materials Today: Proceedings*, *49*(1), 3603–3606. doi:10.1016/j.matpr.2021.08.148

Haldar, S. (2021). Sustainable entrepreneurship development in the renewable energy sector: Insights from Gujarat, India. *African Journal of Science, Technology, Innovation and Development*, *13*(7), 873–885. doi:10.1080/20421338.2020.1796004

Ivleva, M. L., Ivlev, V. Y., Inozemtsev, V., & Bagramiants, N. (2019). Environmental determinants of sustainable development. *Advances in Social Science, Education and Humanities Research*, *356*(1), 1082–1086.

İyigün, N. Ö. (2015). What could entrepreneurship do for sustainable development? A corporate social responsibility-based approach. *Procedia: Social and Behavioral Sciences*, *195*, 1226–1231. doi:10.1016/j.sbspro.2015.06.253

Jin, H., Qian, X., Chin, T., & Zhang, H. (2020). A global assessment of sustainable development based on modification of the human development index via the Entropy method. *Sustainability*, *12*(8), 1–20. doi:10.3390u12083251

Karimi, R. F., & Chashmi, S. A. N. (2019). Designing green entrepreneurship model in sustainable development consistent with the performance of Tehran industrial towns. *Journal of Business-To-Business Marketing*, *26*(1), 95–102. doi:10.1080/1051712X.2019.1565143

Khan, H., & Khan, U. (2012). From growth to sustainable development in developing countries: A conceptual framework. *Environment and Ecology*, *3*(1), 23–31.

Khan, S. A. R., Yu, Z., Sharif, A., & Golpîra, H. (2020). Determinants of economic growth and environmental Sustainability in South Asian for Regional Cooperation: Evidence from panel ARDL. *Environmental Science and Pollution Research International*, *27*(36), 1–13. doi:10.100711356-020-10410-1 PMID:32803598

Koirala, B. S., & Pradhan, G. (2019). Determinants of sustainable development: Evidence from 12 Asian countries. *Sustainable Development*, *28*(3), 1–7.

Kumar, A., Ahmad, M. M., & Sharma, P. (2017). Influence of climatic and non-climatic factors on sustainable food security in India: A statistical investigation. *International Journal of Sustainable Agricultural Management and Informatics*, *3*(1), 1–30. doi:10.1504/IJSAMI.2017.082917

Mahajan, R., & Bandyopadhyay, K. R. (2021). Women entrepreneurship and sustainable development: Select case studies from the sustainable energy sector. *Journal of Enterprising Communities: People and Places in the Global Economy*, *15*(1), 42–75. doi:10.1108/JEC-11-2020-0184

Makhloufi, L., Laghouag, A. A., Meirun, T., & Belaid, F. (2022). Impact of green entrepreneurship orientation on environmental performance: The natural resource-based view and environmental policy perspective. *Business Strategy and the Environment*, *31*(1), 425–444. doi:10.1002/bse.2902

Miola, A., & Schiltz, F. (2019). Measuring sustainable development goals performance: How to monitor policy action in the 2030 agenda implication? *Ecological Economics*, *164*(1), 1–10. doi:10.1016/j.ecolecon.2019.106373 PMID:31582878

Misztal, A., & Kowalska, M. (2020). Determinants of sustainable development of the industrial enterprises in Poland in the period from 2010 to 2019 – A statistical evaluation. *Prace Naukowe Uniwersytetu Ekonomicznego we Wrocławiu*, *64*(1), 160-173.

Moya-Clemente, I., Ribes-Giner, G., & Pantoja-Dıaz, O. (2020). Identifying environmental and economic development factors in sustainable entrepreneurship over time by partial least squares (PLS). *PLoS One*, *15*(9), 1–17. doi:10.1371/journal.pone.0238462 PMID:32886680

Nuringsih, K., & Nuryasman, M. N. (2020). Role of green entrepreneurship in raising the effect of green toward sustainable development. *International Journal of Economics, Business, and Entrepreneurship*, *3*(2), 29–46. doi:10.23960/ijebe.v3i2.69

Omisore, A. G. (2018). Attaining sustainable development goals in sub-Saharan Africa: The need to address environmental challenges. *Environmental Development*, *25*(1), 138–145. doi:10.1016/j.envdev.2017.09.002

Omoruyi, E. M. M., Olamide, K. S., Gomolemo, G., & Donath, O. A. (2017). Entrepreneurship and economic growth: Does entrepreneurship bolster economic expansion in Africa? *Journal of Socialomics*, *6*(4), 1–11.

Onsay, E. A. (2021). The analysis of green growth indicators in predicting the economic development of southeast Asian Countries. *Review of Socio-Economic Perspectives*, *6*(202190), 1–15.

Roomi, M. A., Saiz-Alvarez, J. M., & Coduras, A. (2020). Measuring sustainable entrepreneurship and eco-innovation: A methodological proposal for the global entrepreneurship monitor (GEM). *Sustainability*, *13*(4056), 1–15.

Rusu, V. D., & Roman, A. (2017). Entrepreneurial activity in the EU: An empirical evaluation of its determinants. *Sustainability*, *9*(1679), 1-16.

Singh, A. K., & Ashraf, S. N. (2020). Association of entrepreneurship ecosystem with economic growth in selected countries: An empirical exploration. *Journal of Entrepreneurship. Business Economics (Cleveland, Ohio)*, *8*(2), 36–92.

Singh, A. K., Ashraf, S. N., & Arya, A. (2019b). Estimating factors affecting technical efficiency in Indian manufacturing sector. *Eurasian Journal of Business and Economics*, *12*(24), 65–86. doi:10.17015/ejbe.2019.024.04

Singh, A. K., & Issac, J. (2018). Impact of climatic and non-climatic factors on sustainable livelihood security in Gujarat state of India: A statistical exploration. *Agriculture and Food Sciences Research*, *5*(1), 30–46. doi:10.20448/journal.512.2018.51.30.46

Singh, A. K., Issac, J., & Narayanan, K. G. S. (2019a). Measurement of environmental sustainability index and its association with socio-economic indicators in Asian economies: An empirical investigation. *International Journal of Environment and Sustainable Development*, *18*(1), 57–100. doi:10.1504/IJESD.2019.098641

Singh, A. K., & Kumar, S. (2022a). Influence of climate change on agricultural Sustainability in India: A state-wise panel data analysis. *Asian Journal of Agriculture*, *6*(1), 15–27.

Singh, A. K., & Kumar, S. (2022b). Expert's perception on technology transfer and commercialisation, and intellectual property rights in India: Evidence from selected research organisations. *Journal of Management, Economics, and Industrial Organization*, *6*(1), 1–33. doi:10.31039/jomeino.2022.6.1.1

Singh, A. K., & Kumar, S. (2022c). Exploring the impact of sustainable and environmental sustainability development on social-economic, science and technological development in selected countries: A country-wise panel data analysis. *Society & Sustainability*, *4*(1), 55–83. doi:10.38157s.v4i1.405

Singh, A. K., Kumar, S., Ashraf, S. N., & Jyoti, B. (2022). Implications of farmer's adaptation strategies to climate change in agricultural sector of Gujarat: Evidence from farm level data. *Research on World Agricultural Economy*, *3*(1), 42–57. doi:10.36956/rwae.v3i1.498

Singh, A. K., & Singh, B. J. (2020). Implications of intellectual property protection, and science and technological development in the manufacturing sector in selected economies. *Journal of Advocacy. Research in Education*, *7*(1), 16–35.

Singh, A. K., Singh, B. J., Kumar, S., & Lenka, S. K. (2021). Assessment of global sustainable development, environmental Sustainability, economic development and social development index in selected economies. *International Journal of Sustainable Development and Planning*, *16*(1), 123–138. doi:10.18280/ijsdp.160113

Singh, A. K., Singh, B. J., & Negi, V. (2020). Does sustainable development have a causal relationship with environmental development? Evidence from a country-wise panel data analysis. *International Journal of Technology Management & Sustainable Development*, *19*(2), 147–171. doi:10.1386/tmsd_00020_1

Skordoulis, M., Kyriakopoulos, G., Ntanos, S., Galatsidas, S., Arabatzis, G., Chalikias, M., & Kalantonis, P. (2022). The mediating role of firm strategy in the relationship between green entrepreneurship, green innovation, and competitive advantage: The case of medium and large-sized firms in Greece. *Sustainability*, *14*(6), 1–18. doi:10.3390u14063286

Söderholm, P. (2020). The green economy transition: The challenges of technology change for sustainability. *Sustainable Earth*, *3*(6), 1–11. doi:10.118642055-020-00029-y

Sridhara, S., Gopakkali, P., Manoj, K. N., Patil, K. K. R., Paramesh, V., Jha, P. K., & Prasad, P. V. V. (2022). Identification of sustainable development priorities for agricultural through sustainable livelihood security indicators for Karnataka, India. *Sustainability*, *14*(1831), 1-23.

Tasnim, N., & Afzal, M. N. I. (2018). An empirical investigation of country level efficiency and national systems of entrepreneurship using data envelopment analysis (DEA) and the tobit model. *Journal of Global Entrepreneurship Research*, *8*(37), 1–17. doi:10.118640497-018-0138-y

Tawiah, V., Zakari, A., & Adedoyin, F. F. (2021). Determinants of green growth in developed and developing countries. *Environmental Science and Pollution Research International*, *28*(1), 39227–39242. doi:10.100711356-021-13429-0 PMID:33751350

Ullah, A., Pinglu, C., Ullah, S., & Hashmi, S. H. (2021). Nexus of regional integration, socioeconomic determinants and sustainable development in belt and road initiative countries. *PLoS One*, *16*(7), 1–29. doi:10.1371/journal.pone.0254298 PMID:34242342

Wennekers, S., van Stel, A., Carree, M., & Thurik, R. (2010). The relationship between entrepreneurship and economic development: Is it u-shaped? *Foundations and Trends in Entrepreneurship*, *6*(3), 167–237. doi:10.1561/0300000023

Yin, C., Salmador, M. P., Li, D., & Lloria, M. B. (2022). Green entrepreneurship and SME performance: The moderating effect of firm age. *The International Entrepreneurship and Management Journal*, *18*(1), 255–275. doi:10.100711365-021-00757-3

Zaki, I. M., & Rashid, N. H. (2016). Entrepreneurship impact on economic growth in emerging countries. *The Business and Management Review*, *7*(2), 31–39.

Zeng, J., & Ren, J. (2022). How does green entrepreneurship affect environmental improvement? Empirical findings from 293 enterprises. *The International Entrepreneurship and Management Journal*, *18*(1), 409–434. doi:10.100711365-021-00780-4

Zhang, C., & Lin, Y. (2012). Panel estimation for urbanisation, energy consumption and CO2 emissions: A regional analysis in China. *Energy Policy*, *49*(1), 488–498. doi:10.1016/j.enpol.2012.06.048

Zhao, M., Liu, J., & Shu, C. (2021). Pursuing sustainable development through green entrepreneurship: An institutional perspective. *Business Strategy and the Environment*, *30*(8), 4281–4295. doi:10.1002/bse.2869

APPENDIX

Table 1. Description of selected countries

List of Countries	Income Group of the Country
Croatia	High income: non-OECD
Australia	High income: OECD
Austria	
Belgium	
Canada	
Denmark	
Estonia	
Finland	
France	
Germany	
Greece	
Hungary	
Japan	
Luxembourg	
Netherlands	
Norway	
Poland	
Portugal	
Spain	
Sweden	
Switzerland	
United Kingdom	
United States of America	
India	Lower middle income
Argentina	Upper middle income
Brazil	
China	
Latvia	
Lithuania	
Mexico	
Romania	
Russian Federation	
South Africa	
Tunisia	

Table 2. Economic development associated factors

Indicator Name	Units	Symbol	Expected Impact
Employment in industry (% of total employment)	%	*EIPTE*	Positive
GDP per person employed (constant 2017 PPP $)	US $	*GDPPPE*	Positive
Labour force participation rate (% of total population ages 15-64)	%	*LFPRTPTP*	Positive
Inflation GDP deflator (annual %)	%	*IGDPDAP*	Negative
Employers (% of total employment)	%	*ETPTE*	Positive
Exports of goods and services (% of GDP)	%	*EGSPGDP*	Positive
Foreign direct investment net inflows (% of GDP)	%	*FDINIPGDP*	Positive
Final consumption expenditure (% of GDP)	%	*FCEPGDP*	Positive
GDP per capita (constant 2015 US$)	US $	*GDPPC*	Positive
Gross capital formation (% of GDP)	%	*GCFPGDP*	Positive
Self-employed (% of total employment)	%	*SETPTE*	Positive
Vulnerable employment (% of total employment)	%	*VETPTE*	Negative
Wage and salaried workers (% of total employment)	%	*WSWTPTE*	Positive

Source: Singh et al. (2019a); Koirala and Pradhan (2019); Singh et al. (2020); Moya-Clemente et al. (2020); Singh and Singh (2020); Baydoun and Aga (2021); Tawiah et al. (2021); Singh et al. (2021).

Table 3. Social development associated factors

Indicator Name	Units	Symbol	Expected Impact
Age dependency ratio (% of working-age population)	%	*ADRPWAP*	Positive
Education expenditure (% of GNI)	%	*EEPGNI*	Positive
Fixed telephone subscriptions (per 100 people)	%	*FTSPHP*	Positive
Incidence of tuberculosis (per 100,000 people)	%	*ITPMP*	Negative
Mortality rate infant (per 1,000 live births)	%	*MRIPTLB*	Negative
Sex ratio at birth (male births per female births)	%	*SRB*	Positive
Unemployment youth (% of total labor force ages 15-24)	%	*UYTPTLF*	Negative
Unemployment total (% of total labor force)	%	*UTPTLF*	Negative
Energy use (kg of oil equivalent per capita)	%	*EUKOEPC*	Positive
People using at least basic drinking water services (% of population)	%	*PULBDWSPP*	Positive
People using at least basic sanitation services (% of population)	%	*PULBSSPP*	Positive

Source: Singh and Issac (2018); Singh et al. (2019a); Singh et al. (2020); Moya-Clemente et al. (2020); Singh and Singh (2020); Baydoun and Aga (2021); Singh et al. (2021).

Table 4. Environmental sustainability associated factors

Indicator Name	Units	Symbol	Expected Impact
Population growth (annual %)	%	*PGAP*	Negative
Agricultural land (% of land area)	%	*ALPLA*	Negative
CO_2 emissions (kg per 2015 US$ of GDP)	Kg.	*CDGEKPGDP*	Negative
CO_2 emissions (metric tons per capita)	Metric tons	*CDGEMTPC*	Negative
CO_2 emissions from gaseous fuel consumption (% of total)	%	*CDGEGFC*	Negative
CO_2 emissions from manufacturing industries and construction (% of total fuel combustion)	%	*CDGEMIC*	Negative
CO_2 emissions from residential buildings and commercial and public services (% of total fuel combustion)	%	*CDGERBCPS*	Negative
CO_2 emissions from solid fuel consumption (% of total)	%	*CDGESFC*	Negative
CO_2 emissions from transport (% of total fuel combustion)	%	*CDGET*	Negative
CO_2 intensity (kg per kg of oil equivalent energy use)	Kg.	*CDGEKPKOEU*	Negative
Combustible renewables and waste (% of total energy)	%	*CRWPTE*	Negative
Fertility rate total (births per woman)	Number	*FRTBPW*	Negative
sFertiliser consumption (kilograms per hectare of arable land)	Kg./Ha.	*FCPHAL*	Negative
Forest area (% of land area)	%	*FAPLA*	Positive
Fossil fuel energy consumption (% of total)	%	*FFECPT*	Negative
PM2.5 air pollution, mean annual exposure (micrograms per cubic meter)		*PM2.5APMAE*	Negative
PM2.5 air pollution, population exposed to levels exceeding WHO guideline value (% of total)	Micrograms per cubic meter	*PM2.5APPELEWHO*	Negative
Population density (people per sq. km of land area)	Number	*PDPPSLA*	Negative
Urban population (% of total population)	%	*UPPTP*	Negative
CO_2 emissions per unit of manufacturing value added (kilogrammes of CO_2 per constant 2015 United States dollars)	Kg.	*CDGEPUMVA*	Negative

Source: Akbostanci et al. (2009); Singh and Issac (2018); Singh et al. (2019a); Singh et al. (2020); Khan et al. (2020); Singh and Singh (2020); Moya-Clemente et al. (2020); Singh et al. (2021); Tawiah et al. (2021); Sridhara et al. (2022).

Table 5. Science & technological development associated factors

Indicator Name	Units	Symbol	Expected Impact
Researchers in R&D (per million people)	Number	*RRDPMP*	Positive
ICT goods exports (% of total goods exports)	%	*ICTGEPTGE*	Positive
Merchandise trade (% of GDP)	%	*MTPGDP*	Positive
Research and development expenditure (% of GDP)	%	*RDEPGDP*	Positive
Manufacturing value added as a proportion of GDP (%)	%	*MVAPGDP*	Positive
Manufacturing value added per capita	US $	*MVAPC*	Positive
Proportion of medium and high-tech manufacturing value added in total value added (%)	%	*PMHTMVATVA*	Positive
Scientific and technical journal articles published by per researcher	Number	*STJAPPR*	Positive
Patent applications files (non-residents + residents)/1000 Researchers	Number	*PAFPTR*	Positive
Research and development expenditure per researcher (current US$)	US $	*RDEPR*	Positive

Source: Singh et al. (2020); Misztal and Kowalska (2020); Singh and Singh, 2020; Singh et al. (2021).

Table 6. Entrepreneurship ecosystem associated factors

Indicator Name	Units	Symbol	Expected Impact
Basic school entrepreneurial education and training	Number	*BSEET*	Positive
Commercial and professional infrastructure	Number	*CPI*	Positive
Cultural and social norms	Number	*CSN*	Positive
Financing for entrepreneurs	Number	*FE*	Positive
Governmental programs	Number	*GP*	Positive
Governmental support and policies	Number	*GSP*	Positive
Internal market dynamics	Number	*IMD*	Positive
Internal market openness	Number	*IMO*	Positive
Physical and services infrastructure	Number	*PSI*	Positive
Post school entrepreneurial education and training	Number	*PSEET*	Positive
R&D transfer	Number	*RDE*	Positive
Taxes and bureaucracy	Number	*TB*	Positive

Source: Singh and Ashraf (2020).

Table 7. Green entrepreneurship associated factors

Indicator Name	Units	Symbol	Expected Impact
Access to clean fuels and technologies for cooking (% of population)	%	*ACFTC*	Positive
Access to electricity (% of population)	%	*AEPP*	Positive
Electric power consumption (kWh per capita)	kWh	*EPCPC*	Positive
Electricity production from coal sources (% of total)	%	*EPFCSPT*	Positive
Electricity production from hydroelectric sources (% of total)	%	*EPFHSPT*	Positive
Electricity production from natural gas sources (% of total)	%	*EPFNGSPT*	Positive
Electricity production from oil sources (% of total)	%	*EPFOSPT*	Positive
Electricity production from oil, gas and coal sources (% of total)	%	*EPFOGCSPT*	Positive
Electricity production from renewable sources, excluding hydroelectric (% of total)	%	*EPFRSEHPT*	Positive
Renewable electricity output (% of total electricity output)	%	*REOPTEO*	Positive
Renewable energy consumption (% of total final energy consumption)	%	*RECPTFEC*	Positive
Renewable internal freshwater resources per capita	Cubic meters	*RIFWRPC*	Positive
Energy intensity level of primary energy (megajoules per constant 2017 purchasing power parity GDP)	Megajoules	*EILPE*	Positive
Production-based CO2 productivity, GDP per unit of energy-related CO2 emissions (US dollars/Kg. 2015)	US$/Kg	*PBCO2P*	Negative
Development of environment-related technologies, % all technologies (%)	%	*DERTPAT*	Positive
Share of patent grants in environmental technology with total patent grants in all sector (%)	%	*SPGETTPGAT*	Positive

Source: Ahmad et al. (2015); Singh et al. (2019a); Ivleva et al. (2019) Nuringsih et al. (2020); Singh et al. (2020); Alwakid et al. (2021); Singh et al. (2021); Baydoun and Aga (2021).

Table 8. Pearson correlation coefficients among the indexes

Indicators	GSDI	EDI	SDI	ESI	STDI	EEI	GEI
GSDI	1	0.780**	0.896**	0.586**	0.806**	0.329**	0.130**
EDI	0.780**	1	0.661**	0.363**	0.525**	0.309**	0.028
SDI	0.896**	0.661**	1	0.453**	0.599**	0.337**	0.194**
ESI	0.586**	0.363**	0.453**	1	0.179**	-0.026	0.276**
STDI	0.806**	0.525**	0.599**	0.179**	1	0.335**	-0.054
EEI	0.329**	0.309**	0.337**	-0.026	0.335**	1	-0.092**
GEI	0.130**	0.028	0.194**	0.276**	-0.054	-0.092**	1

Source: Estimated by authors. **Note:** ** indicates that the correlation coefficient is statistically significant at the 1%.

Table 9a. Causal relationship among the indicators

Dependent Variables	GSDI		GEI		SDI		EDI	
No. of obs.	680		680		680		680	
Wald Chi²	105.60*		26.53*		1079.53*		641.59*	
Log likelihood	803.7325		941.619		771.5458		1104.738	
Dependent Variables	*Reg. Coef.*	*Std. Err.*	*Reg. Coef.*	*Std. Err.*	*Reg. Coef.*	*Std. Err.*	*Reg. Coef.*	*Std. Err.*
GSDI	-	-	0.1397*	0.031	-	-	-	-
EEI	0.1896*	0.020	-0.0647*	0.017	0.1158*	0.022	0.0383*	0.014
GEI	0.2096*	0.046	-	-	0.3076*	0.051	-0.0917*	0.032
EDI	-	-	-	-	0.6762*	0.057	-	-
ESI	-	-	-	-	0.3417*	0.041	0.1129*	0.026
STDI	-	-	-	-	0.3148*	0.027	0.0908*	0.018
SDI	-	-	-	-	-	-	0.2538*	0.021
Con. Coef.	0.3456*	0.021	0.3403*	0.016	-0.1506*	0.031	0.2358*	0.017

Source: Estimated by authors. **Note:** * and *** indicate that the regression coefficients are statistically significant at the 1% and 5% level respectively.

Table 9b. Causal relationship among the indicators

Dependent Variables	STDI		EEI		GEI	
No. obs.	680		680		680	
Wald Chi²	504.12*		161.26*		107.90*	
Log likelihood	597.758		421.7042		978.6815	
Dependent Variables	*Reg. Coef.*	*Std. Err.*	*Reg. Coef.*	*Std. Err.*	*Reg. Coef.*	*Std. Err.*
GSDI	-	-	-	-	-	-
EEI	0.0843*	0.029	-	-	-0.0402*	0.017
GEI	-0.2675*	0.066	-0.2068**	0.087	-	-
EDI	0.4032*	0.079	0.2856*	0.104	-0.1329*	0.046
ESI	-0.1319*	0.055	-0.3510*	0.071	0.1540*	0.031
STDI	-	-	0.1415*	0.049	-0.0873*	0.022
SDI	0.5248*	0.045	0.3240*	0.063	0.1673*	0.028
Con. Coef.	-0.0659748**	0.041	0.3713929*	0.051	0.2929*	0.020

Source: Estimated by authors. **Note:** * and *** indicate that the regression coefficients are statistically significant at the 1% and 5% level respectively.

Figure 1. Comparation of economies in term of GSDI, EDI, SDI, ESI and STDI
Source: Estimated by authors.

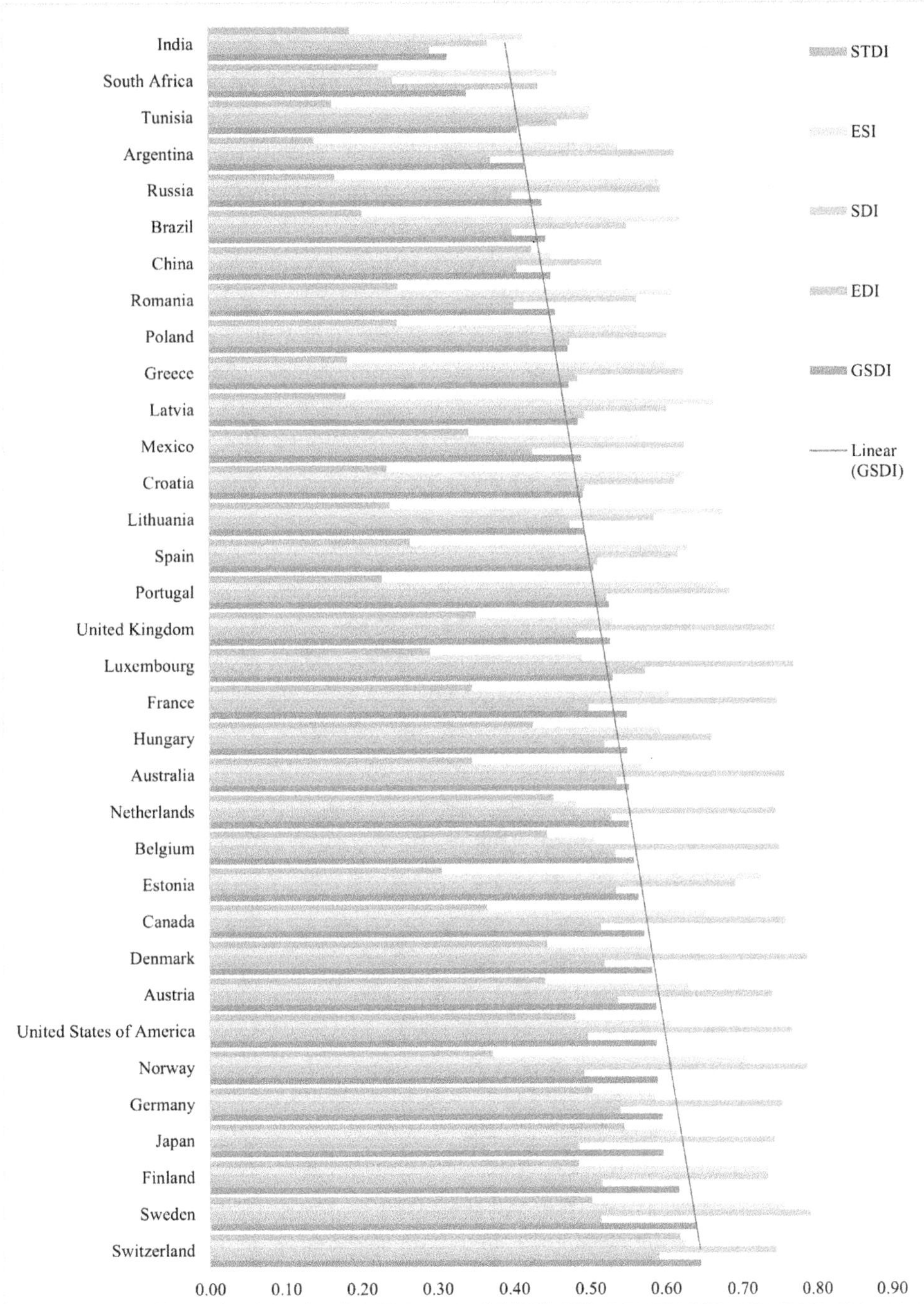

Figure 2. Comparation of economies in term of GSDI, EDI, SDI, ESI and STDI
Source: Estimated by authors.

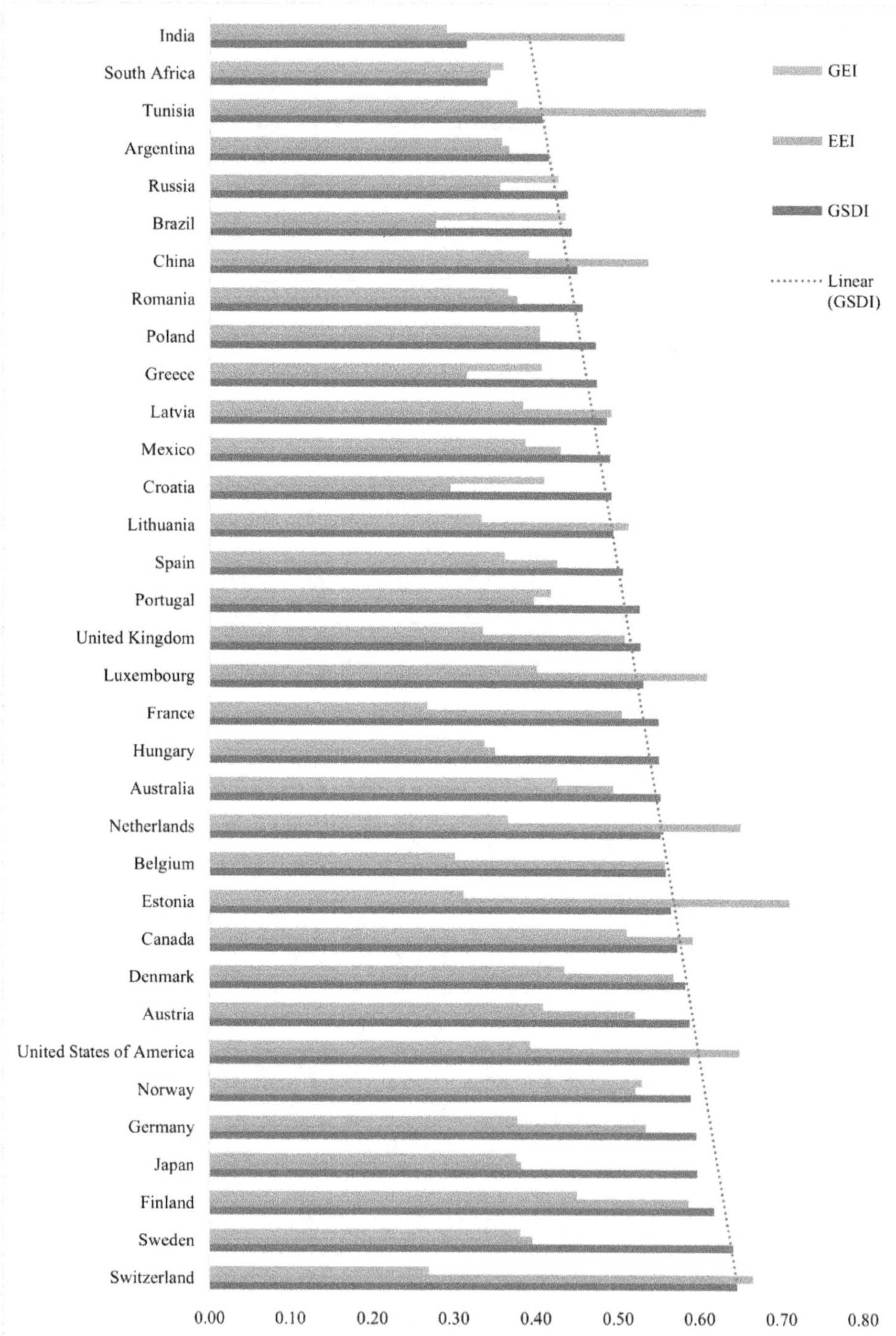

Chapter 9
Green Entrepreneurship and Sustainable Development

Tarana Afrin Chandel
https://orcid.org/0000-0002-8605-6018
Integral University, India

ABSTRACT

The environmental problems and employment crises throughout the world have been growing. Economic growth is one of the key parameters for economic policies expected for beneficial effects having good impact on the employment and economic well-being. Changes are required and need to find solutions for the problem instead of creating. These changes affect the environment while facilitating industries/ business. To overcome the environmental hazard, green entrepreneurship came to light. The concept of green entrepreneurship came into existence from environmental hazards such as pollution, global warning, depletion of ozone layer, and climatic changes occurring due to disturbance within the ecosystem. This study also aims to analyze the relationship between entrepreneurship, transformation, and green development along with the relation between social, traditional entrepreneurship, and in-between institutions and industries.

1. INTRODUCTION

Sustainable development is a development which fulfils the requirement of the current generation without harming the further generations. Sustainable development (SD) motivates everyone to preserve, safeguard and boost the resources. Each and every human being should have the basic needs i.e. employment, food, water, sanitation and energy. Plenty of definitions of SD exist. Trzyna, in 1995 defined SD as Caring for

DOI: 10.4018/978-1-6684-4666-9.ch009

the Earth (A. Jibril, 2011; Trzyna, T. C., 1995) aimed towards changing the quality of human life (A. Jibril, 2011). The spine of the sustainable development is social, economic and environment developments. The author Tarana A Chandel, defines sustainable development as 3P i.e. People, Profit and Planet. People, Profit and Planet relates to Social, Economic and Environment respectively. The first meeting regarding SD was held in 1987 and the report was published as "Our Common Future" from the World Commission on Environment and Development by Brundtland Commission (Rachel Emaet al, 2015; Keith Burgess, 2017). Green entrepreneurship is the action taken towards social and environment problems, upcoming with new technical ideas to implement and solve the related problems. These technical ideas are cost effective, support environment issues and at the same time balance economic sustainability at social level. Weather scientists made responsible to human being for climate change. The economic development is related with RE energy demand. Reduction in carbon emission itself is a challenging movement for businessman, private and government companies and also international organization globally. This challenge, impact and bearing capacity cannot be allocated evenly among different societies, countries and also generations. These challenges interconnected the duties and facilities given to human for survival and environment resources. In the last few decades, we see improvements in financial growth taking out 400 millions of people from poverty zone (Jennifer A. Elliott, 2013). Countries having financial growth are Russia, Brazil, India, China and the Global South (Jennifer A. Elliott, 2013). Now the scenario has changed. Low income countries especially Africa are successful in economic developments in trade and foreign investments. Difference in economic success between different countries is easily visible due to sustainable developments. Poverty has diverse paradigm beyond wealth; moral concern, human rights, peace and security. Work for poor for their better life should be global responsibility for the sustainable developments in future. Sustainability development is not only for poor people but for the global community with respect to environment hazard regarding climatic change (J. Mensah, 2019). The idea of green entrepreneurship came into existence from the ecosystem hazards or we can say disturbance in the environment regarding global warming, pollution in air, ozone layer and carbon dioxide emission all around due to fossil fuel. These hazards had brain washed the consumers toward ecosystem, making them more perceptive toward green and eco-friendly devices. This was the existence of emerging green market. This emerging market changed the human behaviour such as increased income of household women, values and also uplift in lifestyle. It showed improvements in business (private and government), designing new green products or re-designing the old products. This green market transformed into green supply chain management system (GSCMS), waste management system (WMS), changing the market policies. The motive of this chapter is to highlight progress on eco-system lifestyle of human globally, advancement in emerging technology, economic developments, sustainable developments goals, policies and green entrepreneurship.

1.1 CONCEPT OF SUSTAINABILITY DEVELOPMENT

Sustainable improvement is considered a principal and vital mission for worldwide organisations together with the United Nations and other governments globally. The conceptualization of sustainable development does not have any absolute limit but limits toward innovative technology, social development, environment and the ability of eco-system to accept the after effect activities of human (Johannesburg, 2002; A. Leiserowitz, 2005). A study report by the board of Sustainable Development of U.S. National Academy of Science reviewed "Our Common Journey: A Transition toward Sustainability'. The report focussed on what at present is? And what has to be done in future? (A. Leiserowitz, 2005), the duration of this present and future is depicted is 25 years (A. Leiserowitz, 2005). Our Common Journey: A Transition toward Sustainability' is shown in figure 1.Sustainable Development is categorized by social, economic and environment sustainability as shown in figure 2. Sustainability development can also be defined as an intersection of social, economic and environment developments as shown in figure 3. Social sustainability includes food, education, employment, human lifestyle, consumable product services, eco-friendly nature for survival and equality among human in society. Economic sustainability includes employment, financial uplift, business enhancement (private and government) and finally economic growth of individual human as well as country. Environment sustainability includes green and clean atmosphere, pollutant free air, waste management system and consumable recycle system. However approach toward sustainability development may vary. The UK government describes sustainability development based on five factors. These involve (i) Living within limits of ecosystem (ii) Guaranty of well-built healthy and fair-minded society (iii) Achieving a green finance, (iv) Upgrading good governance (v) Using flawless science liability.These principal incorporates excellent governance (A framework involving rules, procedures, regulations which are executed by the government) and an innovative science and technology.

Figure 1. A transition toward sustainability
(U.S NRC, 1999)

What is to be sustained	**Duration** for present and future 25 Years	What is to be developed
NATURE Ecosystem Biodiversity Earth		**PEOPLE** Children survival Food Education Employment Equality
LIVELYHOOD SUPPORT Resources Environment Eco-friendly services	Linked with all human	**ECONOMY** Manufacturing- sectors Employment Finance

Source: U.S. National Research Council, Policy Division, Board on Sustainable Development, Our Common Journey: A Transition Towards Sustainability (Washington, DC: National Academy Press, 1999)

Figure 2. Concept of sustainable development
(Rachel Emaet, January 2015)

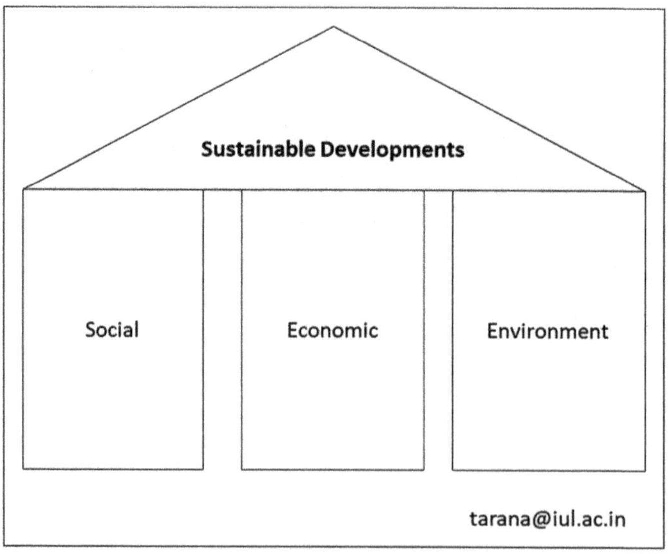

Figure 3. Sustainability development with its components
(Trzyna, T. C., 1995)

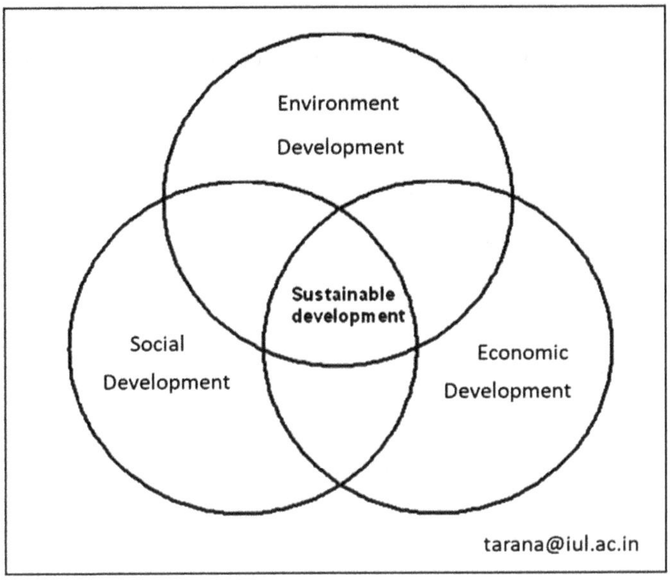

1.2 EVOLUTION OF SUSTAINABLE DEVELOPMENT (SD)

The evolution of the SD in China was the concept of "Heaven and Earth in one" (L Shi, 2019; Wu, J, 2014). The emperor Western Zhou Dynasty (BC1100-771) noticed that the nature gifts of god i.e. mountain, river and forest and claimed to use following the laws of environment rather than exploiting them (L Shi, 2019;). Since then initiative has been taken to protect the natural resources and the sustainability management system started imposing policies, collecting taxes to maintain mountain, forest and gardens (L Shi, 2019; Niu, W, 2015). As environmental degradation continued due to different causes, measures were taken towards forest sustainability. In 1713 the word sustainability was firstly utilized by Carlowitz monograph as Afforestation and Economy and addressing the issues of forest sustainability (Von Carlowitz, 2014). In 1980 the phrase sustainable development became distinct when the World Conservation Strategy (WCS) was presented by an International Union of the Conservation of Nature and Natural Resources focussing to achieve SD by protecting the living resource (Von Carlowitz, 2014). Critics confessed associating SD as the basic goal of society (Von Carlowitz, 2014) and the World Conservation Strategy wholeheartedly contributed its interest in development of the community. Report paid emphasis on the condition of the population, spices, energy, industry and human habitation at global level (Von Carlowitz, 2014; WCED, 1987) A part of this, the report also debated on major issues of social, economic and environment that humans are facing. These are three major debate points; i. the calamity of energy, environment and developments cannot be segregated ii energy and other resources are not sufficient for human survival and development iii. Present development policies should be modified for the sake of present and future human (WCED, 1987).

1.3 SUSTAINABLE DEVELOPMENTS IN A GLOBALIZING WORLD

In 1992, United Nation organised a conference in Rio de Janeiro, Brazil. In this conference, they talked about environment and development and began the journey towards Sustainable Development globally (J.Mensah, 2019; Sun, X, 2012). The agreement was passed and signed as 'Rio Declaration on Environment and Development' and 'Agenda 21 known as the Johannesburg Plan' (J.Mensah, 2019). Agenda 21 had an agreement of recognizing the common with different responsibilities for both developing and developed countries towards environmental issues as well as financial support and technology transfer to the developing countries by the developed countries. This conferencing had goals and plans to execute sustainable development, making partnership globally to find solutions of global environment problems (10, Sun, X, 2012). This became a global history for implementing action to sustainable development strategy (Sun, X, 2012; Hu D. 2004). United Nation Millenium Summit was held in the year September 2000 at U.N. Headquarter, New York. In this summit, 189 countries participated, accepting Millennium Development goals (MDGs), focussing to get rid of poverty (Li. C., 2005). These goals were recognised as an international framework providing guidelines for national development and cooperation for coming 15 years in favour of human development in the beginning of the century (Li, C., 2005). After 1992, a dispute of interest arose gradually in action among social, economy and environment developments. The World Summit on Sustainable Development was organized in Johannesburg, South Africa, from 26 August to 4 September 2002 (Johannesburg, 2002). This summit agenda was "From our origins to the future". The general assembly had a commitment for human equality, caring global society and awareness of human self-esteem to all (Johannesburg, 2002). Acknowledging that humanity is at a crossway, the general assembly fully committed to achieving a goal to develop a practical and visible plan in eliminating poverty and social development. Eliminating poverty has become the biggest challenge globally and necessary for sustainable development especially for developing countries. The requirement to add the policies of cooperative governance of stakeholders globally became critical (U N, 2012). On behalf of these disputes, United Nation again organised a summit known as Rio Summit 2012 (J. Mensah,

2019; Sun, X, 2012, 22). This summit laid emphasis on green economy as the basic parameters for the solution of dispute among environment and development (Barbier E.B, 2012). At the end of the summit one more component was added in SD i.e. governance. Now SD was social, economic, environment and governance (Zhu. D, 2016). A meeting was again held at the UN headquarter in New York as United Nation Sustainable Development Summit in September 2015, above 150 leaders of the nation joined the summit (U N, 2015). This summit evaluated the execution Millennium Development goals and fostering Transforming our World' - 2030 Agenda for sustainable development (U N, 2015). Transforming our world set the sustainable development goals changing the traditional concept of development. New concept of growth, sustainable development came into existence with three component as social, economic and environment development (U N, 2015)

1.4 SUSTAINABLE DEVELOPMENT GOALS

The establishment of SD in 2015, in New York as United Nation Sustainable Development Summit, the 2030 Agenda is for the prosperity in the sustainable world. The people in the world are having peaceful, protective and spirited lives on the earth. Table 1 shows the sustainable development goals (U N, 2019; M. Prabhakar, 2018; Tomislav Klarin, 2018).

1.5 ENERGY TRANSFORATION AND LOW-CARBON DEVELOPMENT

Technologies have the ability to supply green, low-carbon, resilient electricity structures, transport and buildings. Improvements in value and overall performance are surpassing expectancies in areas which include solar harnessing electrical power, wind farms and electrical battery storage. Energy transformation leads toward low carbon emission and environmental injustice. Energy transformation is a fundamental system involving technologies, policies and infrastructure supporting sustainable development (F.W. Geels, 2004; A. Smith, 2007; A. Smith 2005). These systems vary from place to place, culture, economic structure, and stakeholders. The effects of policy transformation at state or national level are less noticed. At the same time different policies and political issues may have clear results in low carbon transition and outcome (Jehling, 2019). Energy transformation to a clean and green energy system utilizing renewable energy (Sovacool, 2009; Painul, 2001) resources such as solar and wind energy, electric vehicle (Sovacool, 2016) require innovative technology but in political ordinance tariff and pricing are major issues.

Table 1. Sustainable development goals

S. No.	Goals	Description
1.	No Poverty	End poverty in all its forms everywhere
2.	Zero Hunger	End hunger, achieve food security and improved nutrition and promote sustainable agriculture
3.	Good Health and Well Being	Ensure healthy lives and promote well-being for all at all ages
4.	Quality Education	Ensure inclusive and equitable quality education and promote lifelong learning opportunities for all
5.	Gender Equality	Achieve gender equality and empower all women and girls
6.	Clean Water and Sanitation	Ensure availability and sustainable management of water and sanitation for all
7.	Affordable and Clean Energy	Ensure access to affordable, reliable, sustainable and modern energy for all
8.	Decent Work & Economic Growth	Promote sustained, inclusive and sustainable economic growth, full and productive employment and decent work for all
9.	Industry, Innovation and Infrastructure	Build resilient infrastructure, promote inclusive and sustainable industrialization and foster innovation
10.	Reduce Inequalities	Reduce inequality within and among countries
11.	Sustainable Cities and Communities	Make cities and human settlements inclusive, safe, resilient and sustainable
12.	Responsible Consumption and Production	Ensure sustainable consumption and production patterns
13.	Climate Action	Take urgent action to combat climate change and its impacts
14.	Life Below Water	Conserve and sustainably use the oceans, sea and marine resources for sustainable development
15.	Life On Land	Protect, restore and promote sustainable use of terrestrial ecosystems, sustainably manage forests, combat desertification, and halt and reverse land degradation and halt biodiversity loss
16.	Peace, Justice and Strong Institutions	Promote peaceful and inclusive societies for sustainable development, provide access to justice for all and build effective, accountable and inclusive institutions at all levels
17.	Partnerships for the goal	Strengthen the means of implementation and revitalize the Global Partnership for Sustainable Development

(M. Prabhakar, 2018; U N, 2019, Tomislav Klarin, 2018)

1.5.1 Importance of the Renewable Energy in the Sustainable Development

The role of electricity and thermal energy generated by solar energy systems even at higher cost is of incomparable importance in rural and remote areas where electricity is not available. Children are able to educate themself in the brightness of solar lantern, community halls are illuminated by solar PV's electricity, water is heated by solar water heating systems and lives saving drugs in hospitals are kept in refrigerators. Solar energy systems designed and developed for these applications even at higher cost are helping in raising the standards of living in villages. Lots of job opportunities are generated based on solar energy technologies. It helps in alleviating poverty of rural masses. Similarly, it has been found that the renewable energy systems may contribute to green tourism development of hilly areas, historical place of remote areas, zoological and botanical parks, tourist places on islands and near sea and rivers, etc. Consequently, a community economic development is feasible. Solar energy can meet the significant amount of energy need of tourism infrastructure, such as warm water and space for warming themself in winter and central air conditioning during summer. Solar energy systems and devices can also be used for water displacement pumps, water sterilization, and providing distilled water which is very important since water shortage is one of the major issues of tourist places. These are the novel areas for entrepreneurs to invest money.

1.5.2 Growth of Solar Energy Worldwide

From 1992 till 2018, solar energy had an exponential growth worldwide (Brent Wanne, 2019) as shown in figure 4. This duration was famous as solar era evolving small scale industry and merged into large scale industry with larger market value in generation of electric power. . The solar PV system was potentially recognized by the subsidy programs regarding tariffs. This was implemented by many governments to provide economic incentives for investments. The growth of renewable electricity is enhancing faster with time than ever worldwide, hold the new global energy economy (IEA, 2021). The worldwide capacity to produce electricity from solar panels, wind turbines and other renewable technologies is growing with time and will be on verge in the coming years. IEA 2021 predicts the renewable energy technologies in the field electricity, transport and heat till 2026 and challenges for industries in identifying the hurdles for fast growth in energy sector. Renewable energy plays a vital role in elimination greenhouse gas emission and ensuring a smooth pathway to net zero as the world is stepping back from utilizing fossil fuel energy. Apart of providing market analysis and forecasts, Renewables 2021 also explores emerging trends towards storage, producing hydrogen from renewable electricity, stimulus packages, aviation biofuels and residential heating. Along with it, renewable power generating capacity is on way to set further another annual record in 2021, driven by solar PV.

Almost 290 Gigawatt (GW) of new renewable power will be produced this year, 3% more than 2020's. Solar PV alone reports more than half of all renewable power expansion in 2021 globally, followed by wind and hydropower. The start-up initiative of the Jawaharlal Nehru National Solar Mission (JNNSM) taken by the Government of India and state government has been an important event for the renewable energy sector, promoting solar energy in Indian. The objective of this mission is to develop

India in the market of solar energy and becoming a one of the global leader, by making the policies and spreading across the country. The mission was designed in three phase; one was from 2012-2013, next phase was from 2013 to 2017 third and the last phase was from 2017 till 2022. Inaugurated in January 2010, the JNNSM has been revised twice and now boasts a target of 100 GW of solar PV by 2022 (IRENA, 2021). A target of 20000 GW on grid solar plant was achieved. Government of India, State Government and various agencies are making efforts to aware consumers as well as investors about the benefits of using renewable energy resources including solar energy in the light of increasing pollution, effects of global warming due to over exploitation of fossil fuels for economic development. The motive of JNNSM is to make India a world leader in solar energy market by making the policies for its distribution across the country (IRENA, 2021). Capacity of renewable energy from 2014 to 2026 (IEA, 2021) is shown in figure 5.

Figure 4. Growth in solar photovoltaic energy exponentially
(Brent Wanne, 2019)

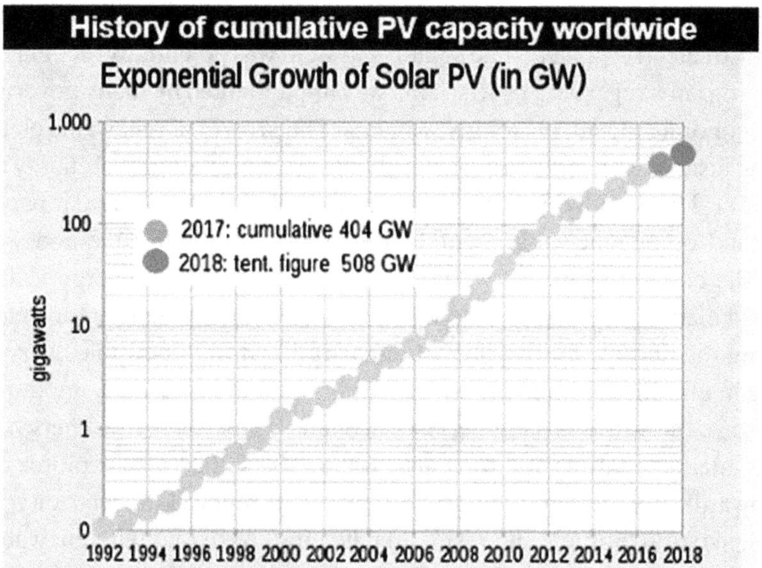

Figure 5. Capacity of renewable energy from 2014 to 2026
(IEA, 2021)

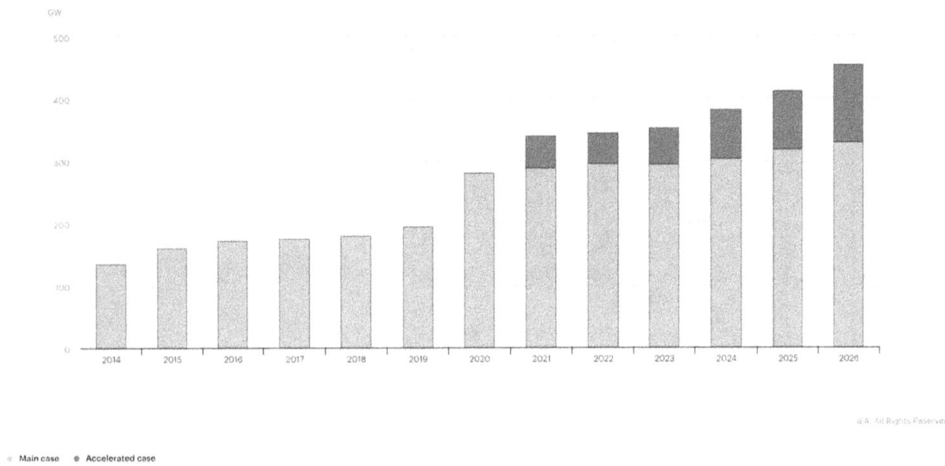

1.6. INVESTMENT IN RENEWABLE ENERGY SECTOR

The transition of energy globally requires accelerating to great extent to fulfil the objectives of the Paris Agreement to restrict the increasing average global temperatures below 2°C, and ideally to 1.5 °C, by the end of the century, in contrast to pre-industrial proportion (IRENA, 2020). Renewable energy supply, enhanced electricity services, and renewable energy efficiency can bring more than 90% of global greenhouse carbon emission reductions needed in the energy sector. To proceed the energy transformation globally, investment in RE is required to escalade significantly and essentially. In the present analysis of "A Roadmap to 2050: Energy Transformation globally", IERNA aligned the world to follow the objectives of the Paris Agreement with collective investment of USD 27 trillion in the period of 2016 to 2050 on renewable energy necessities. The investment in fossil fuel, electrification and infrastructure, renewables and energy efficiency are 20, 26, 27 and 37 Trillion USD respectively (IRENA, 2020) as shown in figure 6.

The energy transformation globally in the power sector require approximately USD 22.5 trillion for new capacity installation by the end of 2050. Annual investments for 2050 installation capacity doubles compared to the present investment i.e. from USD 310 billion to USD 660 billion.

Figure 6. Investment in RE: A roadmap 2016-2050 (USD Trillion)
(IRENA, 2020)

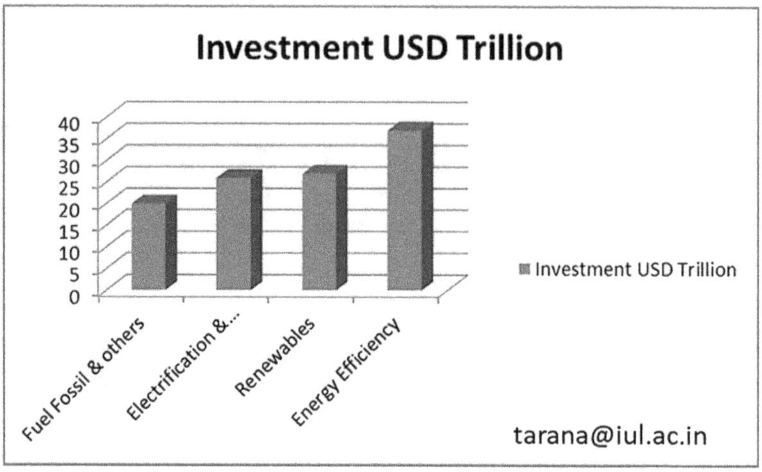

1.6.1. Investment to Implement Renewable Energy Targets in NDCs

Nationally Determined Contributions (NDCs) is accountable for the foundation of the Paris Agreement on climate change. Most certifier to the Paris climate deal have involved renewable energy in their NDCs, admitting that growing energy transition will be essential for acquiring the climate goals. Efforts for climatic action: RE in NDC, approximately USD 1.7 trillion is required for implementing RE target in between 2015 and 2030, an average of USD 110 billion/year. USD 1.2 trillion (approx. 70% of total investment) is circulated to fulfil the target. Furthermore USD 500 billion is needed for developing countries as international finance to support the restricted targets. Figure 7 shows the investment for implementing conditional and unconditional targets (IRENA, 2021). A worldwide plan, to invest USD 95 trillion worth on RE till the mid-century but these plans and related investments are not always funded for climate proof systems (IRENA, 2019). This survey has two pathways. First is the current plan (plans and policies set presently) and second is the clean and green energy transformation (IRENA, 2019). IRENA also planned to redirect the fossil fuel investment towards RE investment but double for the future decades. An overall energy transition can develop superior energy system assuring global temperature not more than ideal temperature of 1.5 degree Centigrate beyond industrial limits. To achieve this global temperature investment in RE should be done without any delay.

Figure 7. Investment for implementing conditional and unconditional targets (IRENA, 2021)

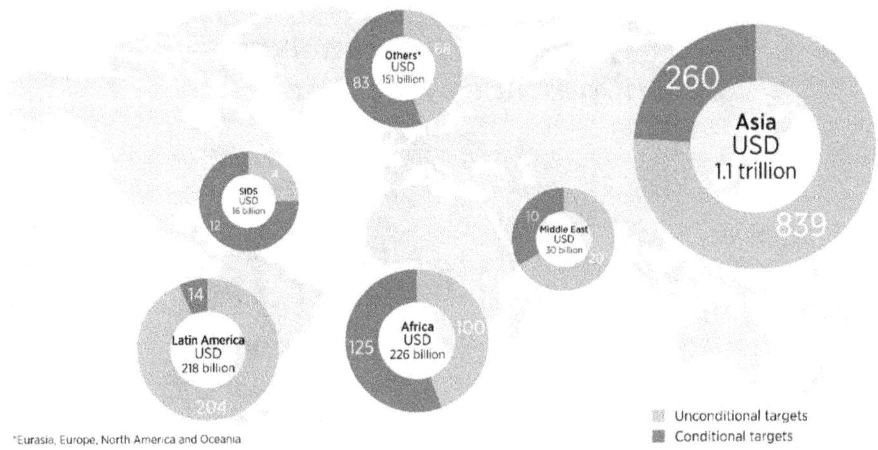

1.6.2 Investors Impact on Energy Transformation

Business man (big or small), companies (private or government) and investors are investing more money on RE sector rather than any other sector and observed 70% everlasting promising investment. At present energy sector is on boom and this is a perfect and secured time for the stake holder to shift and hold energy sector. On 11 May 2021, IEA announces discarding of all fossil fuel projects (IRENA, 2019; ET, 2021) as the world wishes net-zero CO_2 emission and limiting the global temperature up to 1.5°C. Following the above statement, IEA forecasted decline in fossil fuel, whereas 2040 is the dead line for the RE sector globally in reaching zero carbon emission. Impact investors are investing their capital in enhancing new technologies. It is called a fast and huge elevation of RE investment and capacity bringing happiness in wealth, health and development. Bridgespan jointly worked with many impact investors for last several years and scrutinized 70 effective investments in energy sector (Sam Whittemore, 2021). These investors spread globally and fund companies at different levels. Analysis of Bridgespan regarding impact investors investing their capital in different category of energy sector is shown in figure 8 (Sam Whittemore, 2021). Large numbers of investor have motive to mobilize large capital so that they can decrease carbon emission and avoid worst effect of climate change. They spotlight in three main directions; first is energy generation such as solar energy, wind energy, waste energy and power utilities, second is transportation such as electric vehicle and third is energy efficiency technology (Sam Whittemore, 2021). Electric vehicles decline fossil fuel carbon emission.

Figure 8. Energy investment category
(Moose, 2021)

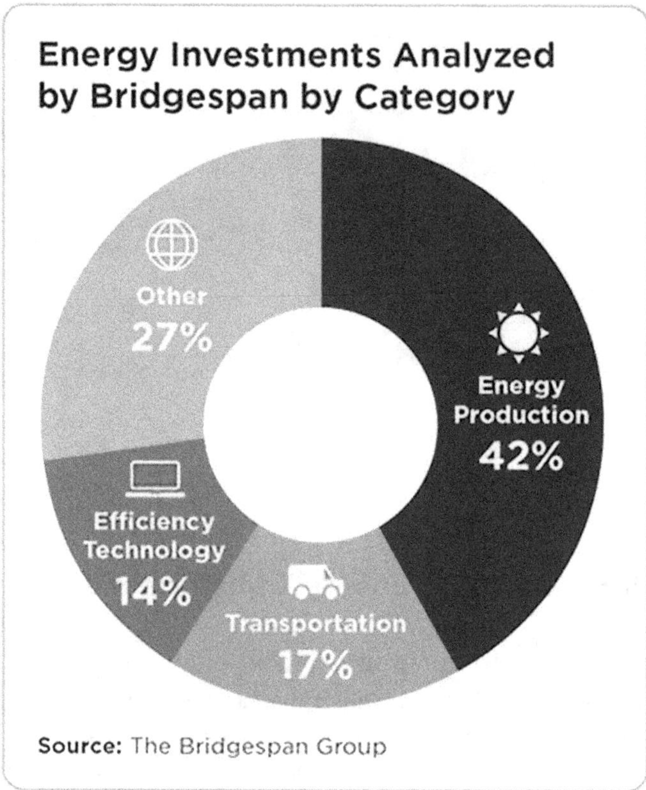

1.7 GREEN ENTREPRENEURSHIP

Green entrepreneurship is the trading firm of actively conveying environmental hazards or requires economic sustainable marketing strategy having positive effect on the environment, community, and financial system. Green entrepreneur is a person who establishes and executes the business drafted to bear the environmental hazards or need its device and tactics from the beginning of the marketing strategy. We can also say that green entrepreneur is a person who finds solution to the problems of people and environment and fully implement it by green products. Five categories of green entrepreneurial business are solar energy and other renewable energy, organics, recycling and reusing, "clean" products and green knowledge (Moose, 2021).

1.7.1 Solar Energy and Other Renewable Energy

United State management has made plan of making energy self-dependent. President Obama in 2009 said excess dependency on traditional energy is unsustainable (Neville, 2021). Thus, he committed to move toward renewable energy. With the change in technology, businessman and investors having strong interest in green energy technology, made solar energy their priority area; designed, manufactured green product and launched in the market. The process of entrepreneur in RE and sustainability is the desire to start a new project with full passion or transform the present product of the company. Entrepreneurs and entrepreneurial managers change the future of their business with strong vision, designing and implementing new innovative products or model with full enthusiasm and passion. The gross outcome of the company is the company's development, growth and regeneration that are hold up by using new competitive merits leading to new constructive possibilities. The research and the entrepreneurial process in renewable energy has achieved the top most success on the sunrise of the new millennium, stretching it perimeter from a borderline of sub-field of control research into one of the most applicable spheres of strategic advertising, commercial enterprise and management

1.7.2 Organics

Green entrepreneurship in green organic products is on the rising horizon. With education and training given, consciousness of the blessings of consuming organically grown ingredients increases, cost-effectiveness in producing them to satisfy that demand. There are presently many approaches to get into the organic agriculture enterprise. There are organic grocery wholesales, dairy farms, cattle farms, fish farms, markets, and stores. The most common is a natural produce farm. Organic food is produced by farmers who use renewable resources and the conservation of soil and water to enhance environmental quality for future generations.

Owning your personal sustainable organic farm is a feasible and favourite commercial enterprise alternative while locals purchase part of the organic produce (Neville, 2021). This is as same as farming without fertilizers and chemical pesticides. Frey Family farm in Ashford, Washington are the present examples of organic farming (Moose, 2021). Products of Frey Family farm are certified organic products as they utilize only organic seed, principal and practices (Moose, 2021). Their motive is to produce healthy food for their family and community with the concern for the land which they steward. Frey family share their certified organic products in the community under Community Supported Agriculture Program (CSAP) and CSA program continues for 20 weeks (Moose, 2021). Other green enterprise are accessible in organic product organisation such as beauty product, garden treatments and also and textiles. Organic meat, poultry, eggs, and dairy products come from animals that are free from antibiotics or hormones for growth. Green products are label 'Organic' only after a government approved certifier inspector inspect farming land and ensures the products are grown following the rules satisfying USDA organic standards (Melissa C S, 2022). Restaurant and market providing organic products must be certified too. Other industries where organic products are manufactured are textile industry, cosmetic industry, agriculture.

Figure 9. Use of plastic in various sector
(Arokiaraj David, 2019)

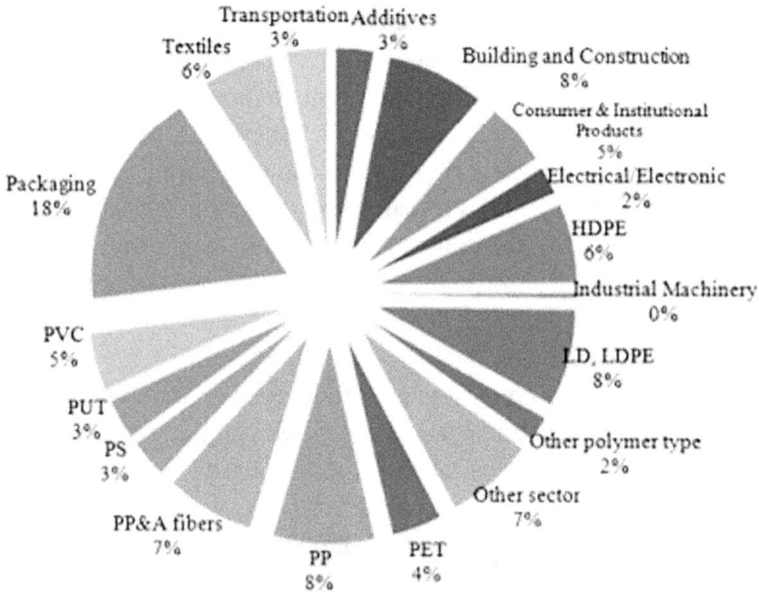

1.7.3. Recycling and Reusing

Waste materials are the biggest problem of present and future world. The transition towards industrialization has great impact on environment creating global warming, carbon emission, polluted air for breathing, water, land and noise pollution. Green entrepreneur reuse this waste product. The waste products are paper, plastic, batteries, used electronics products, woods, construction materials, food products, textile and many more. Some of them are not biodegrading materials. On the other side, biodegrading waste materials are food, natural plants and materials, and feces.

Figure 10. Global plastic production till 2020
(Ian Tiseo, 2021)

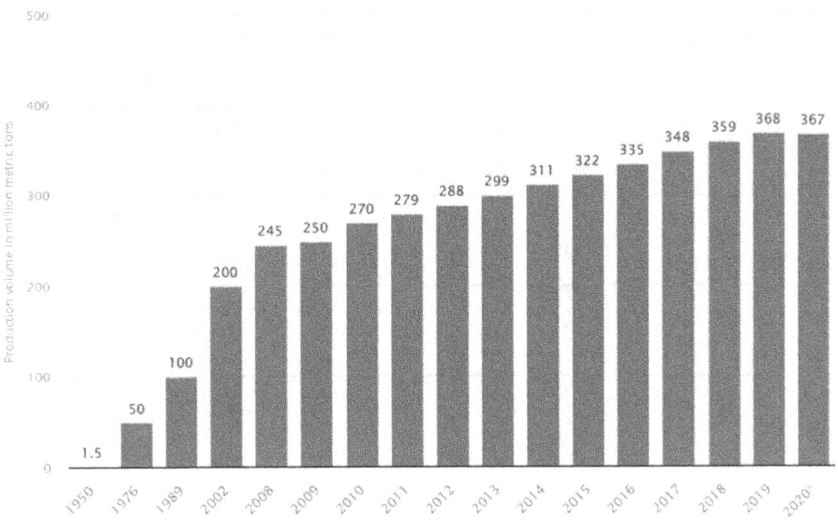

Plastic and rubber waste: Plastic is one of the non-biodegradable material. The production of plastic globally in 1950s was 1.5 million metrics, 336 million metrics in 2016 (D. Arokiaraj, 2019) and reaching 367 million metrics ton in 2020 (D. Arokiaraj, 2019). 9% was recycled, 12% was destroyed by burning and the remainder are still dumped on lands. The production has declined 3% only in 2020 due to COVID-19. The utilization of plastic in various sectors is shown in figure 9 (D. Arokiaraj, 2019). The global plastic production in 2010 was 270 million metric tons which has increases up to 370 million metric tons in 2020 (Ian Tiseo, 2022; Ian Tiseo, 2021). As per statistical data source statista 2022, global forecasting of plastic production in 2025 is 445.25 million tons and 590 million metric ton by 2050 (Ian Tiseo, 2021) is shown in figure 10. The forecasting of plastic production globally from 2025 to 2050 (Ian Tiseo, 2022) is shown in figure 11.

Food Loss and waste: In current scenario, issues on food loss and waste are focused as a main feature of the challenges and in capabilities which identifies the global food system and also its impact on social, economic and environment. Food waste is a measure of food loss and waste (FLW) (Per Pinstrup, 2014) or we can say edible part of the food is in short or wasted. Food loss is declination of quantity and quality of raw food products that is not directly consumed by human where as food waste refers to the amount of food consumed by human is discarded. This declination may be due to insects, birds, mold, and inadequate climate condition. Food losses may occur from production to storage, processing and during transport (Emilie Wieben, 2017), shown in figure 12.

Figure 11. Forecasting of plastic production globally
(Ian Tiseo, 2022)

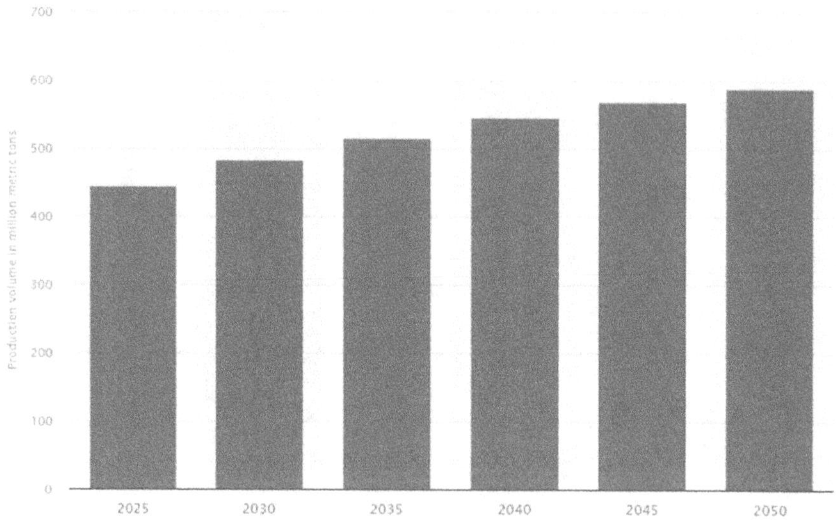

Figure 12. Food waste during processing
(Emilie Wieben, 2017)

Food that are produced but somehow not consumed shows a powerful contributor towards greenhouse gas (GHG) emissions globally shown in figure 13 and reduces the productive outcome of food pile, which undoubtedly will effect each human life and eco-friendly capabilities to cope with climatic change. Removing large amount of food that are ruined and wasted is on top priorities for improving sustainability within the food organization, fulfilling the growing request for food and riding the climatic movement ahead. This is focused inside the 2030 Agenda for sustainability development (SD), setting the mark in reduction of food wastage and loss globally (Emilie Wieben, 2017). The Paris Agreement also accept the value of food production and security system regarding climatic change, while many other countries have finally registered food value chain intercession in their proposed Nationally Determined Contributions (INDCs) (Emilie Wieben, 2017). This confirms the growing global acknowledgement towards the action inside the food production and security system fulfilling the objectives for SD and environment stabilization. Tackling the issues of food waste and loss globally requires some calls and meeting for joint action towards the integrated food technology covering all risk, demand, business and opportunities toward SD. This is relevant towards worldwide climatic change, reaction towards food waste and loss and scaling up weather technologies and weather-smart practices within the food organization. Finance chain infrastructure, regulation and capacity restriction are major sources of food waste and loss in the developing countries. Focussing smart solution for weather across food organization may strongly support to enhance economic flow required for the implementation. However, this will reinforced regulatory framework in addition to policy coherence to support the incentive required for financial investments from private organization. In this aspect, support will be crucial to ensure policy framework and financial incentives are in line with the dreams for food waste and loss reduction and climate action.

***Contributions to climate change*:** Good food production is based on natural resources along with best environmental condition. Water, sunlight, power energy and other inputs are essential to sustain the process and other activities within the food organization. Withdrawal from natural resource endowments will lead towards greenhouse gas (GHG) emissions contributing to climate change.

When computing the aggregate carbon emission contributing the environmental change all through life cycle, unconsumed food is predicted to be 3.6 Gt of CO_2 eq per year in addition to 0.8 Gt of CO_2 eq per year from the associated land use and forestry (Emilie Wieben, 2017). Food waste and loss has major contribution towards carbon emission, whereas country wise China is on top and India rank third position in the world where carbon emission is maximum from food waste and loss as shown in figure 13. Food waste decomposing in the landfills also produces greenhouse gas as methane. Larger the food waste greater is the greenhouse gas emission. A different source of carbon emission is shown in figure 14 (Emilie Wieben, 2017).

Figure 13. Carbon emission globally from food waste
(Emilie Wieben, 2017)

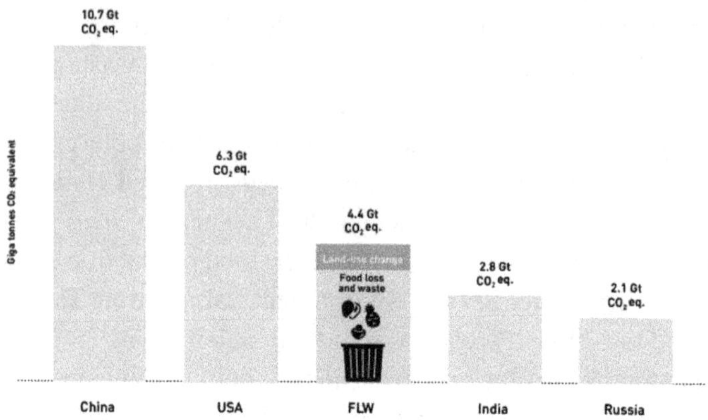

Source: FAO, 2015a and CAIT Climate Data Explorer (2017).

Figure 14. Sources of carbon emission
(Emilie Wieben, 2017)

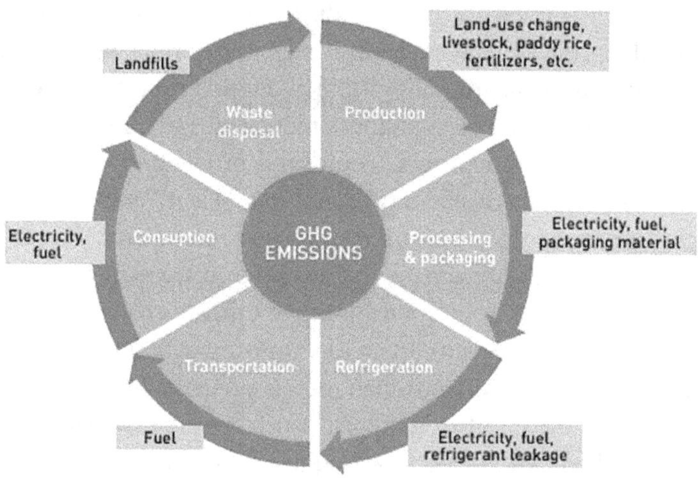

***Solutions to Food Waste*:** Minimizing food waste is lead to sustainable food future. On 4th June 2013, Department of Agriculture and Environment Protection Agency in US organised the U.S Food Waste Challenge, calling on individuals involved in food chain including farmer, agriculture processors, food manufactures, grocery stores, restaurants, universities, school and local government (Chan, 2022). The goals (Chan, 2022) are as follows

1. Minimize food waste by correcting product development, storage, shopping, marketing, labelling and cooking process
2. Connect strong food donors to hunger relief camps/organisation / food banks / pantries
3. Recycle food waste by feeding animal or generate clean and green energy, natural fertilizers.

Department of Agriculture and Environment Protection Agency announced the goal set on 16 September 2015 for 50% reduction and improvement in food security and protect natural resources (Chan, 2022). The guidelines for reducing food waste throughout the process of food production chain was issued by the National Resources Defence Council are given below (Chan, 2022)

1. **State and local governments** can include education expedition and prevention of food waste and implement municipal mulch program. Farmers who donate surplus amount of product to the food bank can be benefitted through the government by tax credit
2. **Businesses** such as restaurants, grocery stores, and institutional food services can figure out the amount of their food waste and implement best practices
3. **Farmers** can figure out food loss while processing, distribution, storage and can implement best practices
4. **Consumers** should know how to cook food and store it properly, develop awareness when the food is not in the state of edible and to generate organic fertilizer.

1.7.4. Green Architecture

Green architecture or green building deals with the study of design and construction with an eco-friendly environment leading to sustainability development. Green architecture utilized the construction material that does not harm the environment and human health, providing full ventilation for sun to penetrate and exhaust greenhouse gas. Green architect pay emphasis on filter water, clean and green air, green roof and integrating eco-friendly system into the building while constructing it. The approach behind this to maintain temperature in summers and winters, indoor and outdoor climate, eliminate GHS (Md R. Ghaffar, 2017; Amany Ragheb, 2016) leading towards sustainability development. The word green roof indicate that the roof of the building is constructed utilizing green technology such as solar photovoltaic panel (Mohammad Reza Ghaffar, 2017)and solar water heater for providing green energy and hot water. Some of the real time green building globally is mentioned below

Pixel Building (Melbourne, Australia): this is first building in Australia made carbon-neutral office building producing water and energy on its site. This building is aesthetically good having multiple features in the building (G. Green, 2020). This building have proper shading and allowing daylight in the building as required, support the collected rain water on roof and helps the proper process of water waste and wind turbine to provide green energy to the building. This building is shown in figure 15 (G. Green, 2020)

Central Park (Sydney, Australia): this is a residential building, designed by Ateliers Jean Nouvel with PTW Architects and is in use since 2014.This residential building is known as Central Park as it is having 250 species of plants and flower making it attractive look as shown in figure 16 (G. Green, 2020)

Figure 15. Pixel Building (Melbourne, Australia)
(G. Green, 2020)

Suzlon One Earth (Pune, India): this building is constructed in India in 2009, designed by Christopher Benninger (G. Green, 2020) shown in figure 17. This building has a top-tier green headquarters. it is having platinum LEED certification and utilizes 80% of power energy generated through wing and 20% power energy generated through solar.

Bosco Verticale (Milan, Italy): This building is a duplex residential apartment, designed by Stefano Boeri and is under use since 2014 shown in figure 18. This is the tallest residential building with lot of space to accommodate, plenty of herbs and shrubs, full grown trees.

Figure 16. Central Park (Sydney, Australia)
(G. Green, 2020)

Figure 17. Suzlon One Earth (Pune, India)
(Going Green, 2020)

Figure 18. Bosco Verticale (Milan, Italy)
(Going Green, 2020)

1.8 GREEN MARKET

In view of current economy and environmental sustainability demand in the recent year, national and global effort are made to upgrade green development as a new source of growth. The transition of green economy has become a policy debate in present scenario. It is a path way towards sustainability development, declination in poverty and new economic growth through it. Looking towards international economy crisis, the UN general assembly and many other UN agencies had 2nd Preparatory Committee Meeting UN Conference on Sustainable Development on 7 March 2011 - 8 March 2011, NEW YORK, USA, (UNEP, 2022) which was based on the conclusion of the Intergovernmental Preparatory Meeting held on 28 February-4 March 2011. This meeting was the combine effort. In 2008-09, green market was promoted on the basis of short term growth. This was done to enhance the potential of employment and income of human through investment in green innovative technology while other proceeded toward green growth with environment point of view maintaining sustainability development. Investment in green innovative technology (e.g. green energy, climatic change, green architecture, green food) undoubtedly will increase long term financial performance leading towards enhanced worldwide economy, according to the macroeconomic model reported in Green Economy Report documents (UNEP, 2011) (UNEP, 2022). The world Trade Organization (WTO) is on fast track in achieving UN's Agenda 2030 for SD with combine effort of UN's Department of Economic and Social Affair in monitoring and achieving SD Goals (SDGs) (UNEP, 2022, S. U-tantada, 2019) such as poverty declination, green health, elevating education and climatic change. These goals place great emphasis on green trade economy globally to fulfil the 2030 Agenda. The use of green market economy can be expressed with the references of the United Nations-Department of Economic and Social Affairs (UN-DESA, 2015) (UNEP, 2022) having 17 goals. These 17 goals create awareness about worldwide financial, social and environment conditions and how it can be improved globally with conjugate work on three different factors.

- Improving social and economic condition i.e. decline in poverty and removing hunger under the goal (no.: 1, 2 and 8)
- Human welfare including green energy, green consumable products, clean healthy environment, gender equality, employment, green health under the goal (no.: 3, 4, 5, 7, 9, 10, 11, 16 and 17)
- Green environment include sanitation, filtered water, pollution free air to breath, life's in water, on land under goal (no.: 6, 12, 13, 14 and 17)

Top politicians and business leaders globally can collaboratively frame policies and implementing it and transit towards green trade and green economy.

1.9 IMPACT OF COVID-19 ON ENTREPRENEURSHIP

COVID-19 pandemic had a great impact on global economy. It has pulled the worldwide economy years back. As per International Labour Organization (ILO), 5 million to 25 million jobs were lost, dropping down the labour income from $860 billion to $3.4 trillion (UNGA, 2020). More than 70 million people were drop back into poverty. Medium and small scale industry was the root and pillars of the worldwide economy with 66% employment for developing countries with low income (UNGA, 2020). Side by side, the fully enthusiasm entrepreneur of small and medium scale industry can be capitalized (on) to handle the global problems and implement on the goals of SD for social and environment recovery. This small and medium scale industry was the base of the employment and living. Entrepreneur was growing with time. In 2018-19, within 15% of the youth population took initiative toward entrepreneurial activity. Alas, this entrepreneurial activity growth was 40% further fallen down in some countries (UNGA, 2020; Donna Kelley, 2019) in 2019 due to COVID-19 pandemic.

Figure 19. Annual change in economic growth globally
(Mukhisa Kituy, 2020)

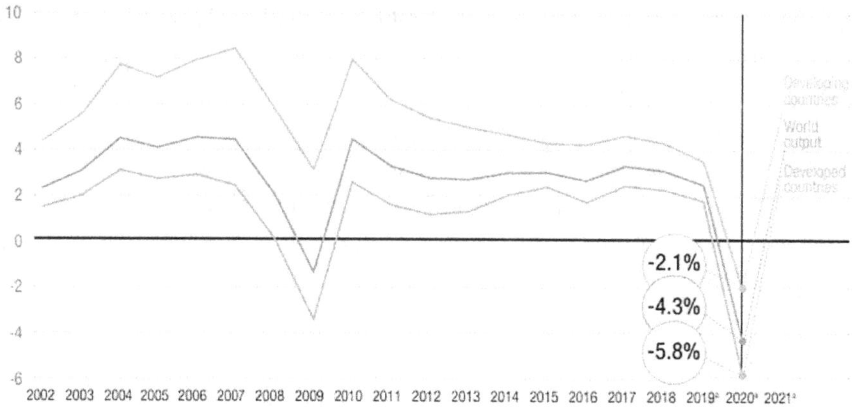

Source: UNCTAD (2020).
Note: Calculations for country aggregates are based on GDP at constant 2015 dollars
ª Forecasts.

Gender biasing was also one of the major issues in many countries. After surveying 62 countries, the rate of entrepreneurship for women equivalent to men was only in 6 countries (Donna Kelley, 2019). Entrepreneur within age of 25-34 were on top in 36/50 countries which declined gradually due to COVID-19 pandemic (UNCTAD, 2020). COVID-19 pandemic has negative impact on the newly upcoming entrepreneurs whether men or women due to lockdown and financial crises. Approximately 27% of women entrepreneurs were financially thrashed and bankruptcy. 4.3% of global economy has shattered down in 2020 with only 4.1% recovery in 2021 (Mukhisa Kituy, 2020) as shown in figure 19. Developed countries were more affected competitively to developing countries in 2020. Economic downfall in developed countries was 5.8% whereas developing countries had 2.1%. Similarly the recovery rate in developed countries was +3.1% compared with +5.7% in developing countries. Unlike the global financial crisis of 2008/09, developing countries are expected to experience negative growth in 2020, and developed economies are expected to experience a much deeper fall in output, at -3.4 per cent in 2009 compared with -5.8 per cent in 2020. Positive growth in economy of China and republic of Korea by +1.3% and +0.1% respectively in 2020 whereas Argentina, Brazil, Mexico, France, Germany, Italy, suffered from negative economy by -10.4%, -5.7%, -10%, -8.1, -4.9, -8.6 respectively. United Kingdom of Great Britain and Northern Ireland had -9.9% economy downfalls. Lives in all corners of spheres have been affected, resulting impact on social and economic condition by COVID-19 pandemic. The corona virus disease originated in China (Asia) and spread out in Europe and America, this was the bingeing of economy fall down. Gradually it spread as fire leading to recession. The World Health Organization, on 23 September confirmed 31 million people infected with corona virus disease and 963,000 deaths globally (Mukhisa Kituy, 2020) the same day whose data can be reflected in figure 20. America was on top among infected people in the nation and accounted 53% of world's confirmrd infected cases and 53% death also whereas Europe was the 2nd largest and accounted 20% of the world infected cases and 24% of death (Mukhisa Kituy, 2020).

Figure 20. Number of reported cases of COVID-19 by WHO
(Mukhisa Kituy, 2020)

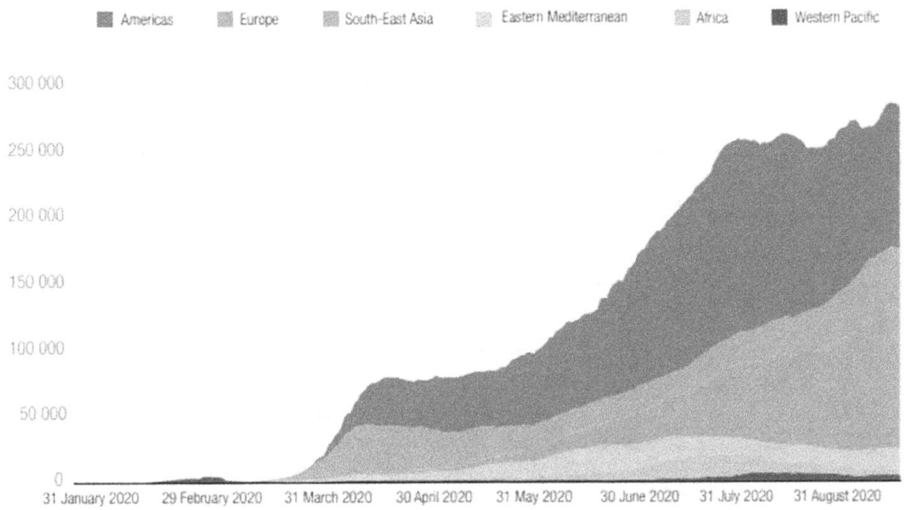

Source: World Health Organization, COVID-19 Dashboard (as at 23 September 2020).
Note: Regions according to World Health Organization designations.

The COVID-19 pandemic has had an immediate and negative impact on foreign direct investment (FDI) in 2020. Due to pandemic the on-going investment projects were delayed and the new projects were on racked on shelves. As the result, forecasting of FDI flow has decrease 40% in 2020 since 2019 as the closed value was $1.6 trillion (Mukhisa Kituy, 2020) as shown in figure 21.

The above graph shows that FDI has fallen down below $1 trillion in 2020 since 2005 and is further expected to fall in 2021. From the beginning of the year 2022, FDI is expected to be recovered at the earliest. The lockdown during COVID-19 had blocked the investment flow; thereby downfall in economy globally.

Figure 21. Foreign direct investment globally
(Mukhisa Kituy, 2020)

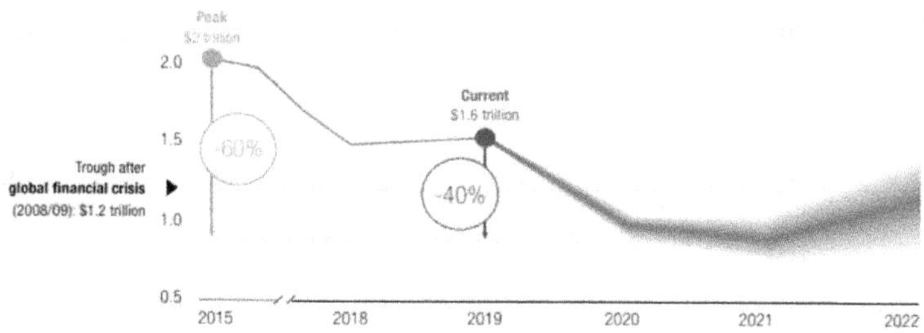

Source: UNCTAD (2020a).

Figure 22. Foreign direct investment flow
(Mukhisa Kituy, 2020)

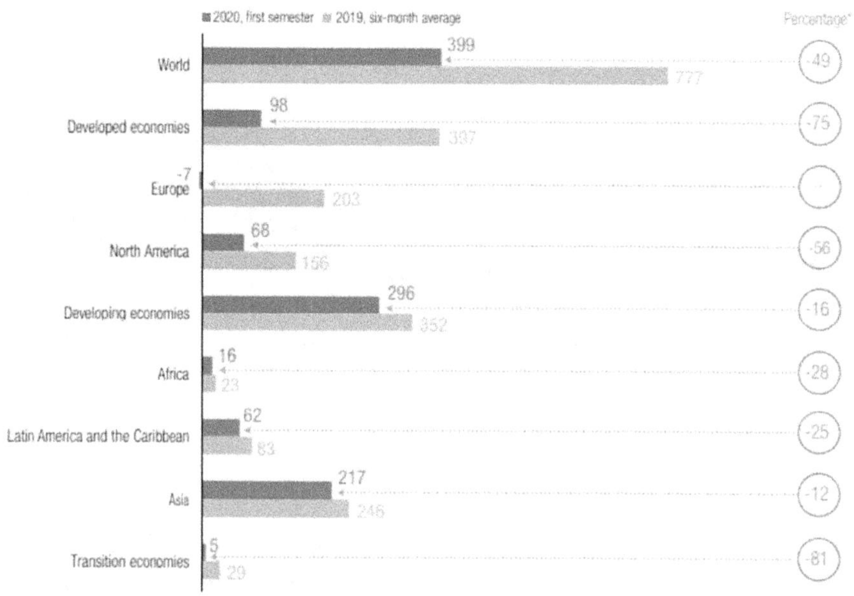

Source: UNCTAD Global Investment Trends Monitor, No. 36, October 2020.
* Data not available.

Data from UNCTAD 2020 certify the immediate impact of COVID-19, reflecting on FDI with 49% downfall as compared to 2019 as shown in figure 22. Decline in FDI flow in developed as well as developing countries was 75% and 16% respectively whereas 28% reduction in FDI Africa, 25% in Latin America and Caribbean and only 12% in Asia. The less declination in FDI flow Asia was due to strong investment China. The overall study show greater impact of COVID-19 pandemic in developed countries rather than developing countries in 2019-2021.

Due to COVID-19 many people lost their job and became handicap. Government of India introduced Atmanirbhar Bharat Abhiyaan or Self-reliant India. The Hon'ble Prime Minister Shri Narendra Modi introduced Atmanirbhar Bharat Abhiyaan or Self-reliant India campaign for A Vision of New India. On 12 May 2020, Prime Minister contributed 2.5 Million USD economic package under the 'Atmanirbhar Bharat Abhiyaan', to support the citizen of our country during the Coronavirus crisis (by making self-reliant) and to resist with COVID-19 pandemic in India. The motive behind this is to make the country and its citizens self-supporting and self-sustaining in all aspects. The backbone of this Aatma Nirbhar Bharat is Economy, Infrastructure, System, Vibrant Demography and Demand. Finance Minister further announces Government Reforms and Enablers across Seven Sectors under Atmanirbhar Bharat Abhiyaan.

1.10 GREEN PRODUCTION AND EMPLOYMENT

More the 200 million students are enrolled in higher education and expected to twice by 2030. Higher educational institute should study and have research in collaboration with the business, government bodies, NGOs with the vision to implement policies, regulations and framework for green economy. These job require technical training for technician through technical educational institute and business managers, economists, engineers and marketers are trained during education from universities. Approximately 71 million youth are having completed their education and are unemployed, struggling for suitable job (Mari Nishimura, 2021). As per International Labour Organization (ILO), transition towards green economy will generate 60 million of job by 2030 (Mari Nishimura, 2021). Green job has become one of the subjects of economic research during last one and a half decades. Economist Mathew Forstater proposed a green public carrier employment application which was reflected in the notable report of peer reviewed journal since 2004 (Michael Forstater, 2004). Political Economy research Institute made a proposal of two years recovery program worth $100 billion generating 2 million green jobs in power sector in 2008 (Robert Pollin, 2008). Before, the Bureau of Labour Statistics (BLS) presented the study on green job, there was no global and consolidated way to follow green job in the economy sector. Since then the term green jobs are often used in green economy reports (ILO, 2010). Policies to boost renewable energy production were included while implementing 2009 American Recovery and Reinvestment Act (ARRA) under the advisory-ship of Van Jones. The initiative of green job by BLS (ILO, 2009) was to create awareness towards

1. Transition toward jobs in renewable energy with time

2. Industrialization, employment and geological distribution of jobs
3. Earning of the labours in these job

BLS had two approaches to measure green jobs (ILO, 2009). These two approaches are mentioned below

1. Output approach: recognizes the foundation of produced green products, services and associated jobs
2. Process approach: recognizes the foundation of eco-friendly production process, following the procedure and associated jobs.

Green employment are divided in three categories

1. Renewable energy generation
2. Energy efficiency
3. Environment management

Renewable energy generation employment involves all jobs in solar, wind, water, tides, geothermal, biomass and nuclear energy. Generation of renewable energy requires surveying and mapping, technical consulting, geological services, lawyers, accountants and financial services, electrical, mechanical, and project engineers, construction, marketing, sales, transportation, permitting, installation, quality assurance, and maintenance.

Energy efficiency employment involves the job of heating and air conditioning mechanics and installers, plumbers and pipefitters, roofers, and manufacturers of energy efficient products, including household Energy Star appliances, manufacturers that use recycled products as inputs, public transportation workers, workers making and selling electric and hybrid cars or car parts, and workers building and maintaining a more resilient energy grid.

Environment management employment involves jobs in environment and health sectors. These include waste material collectors, sweeper, pipes and waste water cleaner, scientist, engineer, educators, regulators and legislator

Green employment upgrade energy, raw materials efficiency, environment providing pollution free air to breath and live, reduce GHG emission, waste and pollution, supporting ecosystem for climatic change and making eco-friendly and healthy environment. RE sectors have 11.5 million jobs in 2019 and it will enhance and reach up to 42 million jobs by 2050, 21.3 million employments in power efficiency sectors and 14.5 millions in power grids and variable/ flexible renewable energy. Organic agriculture, sustainable agriculture and green food production are based on labour incentive. For installation we require infrastructure thereby generating employment in construction, transport and sanitation. Sustainable development management provide 362 to 630 million jobs by 2050.

1.11 CONCLUSION AND FUTURE SCOPE

This study has illuminated a positive, regionally heterogeneous relationship between green and non-green entrepreneurship and sustainable development. In particular, green entrepreneurship had a stronger influence than non-green entrepreneurship on all the domain of sustainable development. Our results are consistent with previous studies that have shown tight links and interrelations between green entrepreneurship and sustainable development. The findings also correspond with more recent work that has recognised the bidirectional nature of green entrepreneurship and sustainable development in urban contexts. Policies makers from government and private agencies should think and consider what activities should be taken into consideration as green. People working in RE power sectors can help the society in making economically and environmentally sustainable. Young leader are increasingly occupy high position in International Politics, Education, Economics, Government & Corporate field. This change is influencing the scenario completely that will change the current work values and ethics. The top leader, politician and businessman of the nation can make prosperous future with green economy. On the other side when consumers are aware of importance of green products, they will give the priorities to the Eco-Friendly product and will help to develop the stable sustainable environment and social value. Green-Thinker Entrepreneurs will increase in number. Eco-Business will grow strongly. Combining the policies, social, government and private enterprises, one can reach to stable global green economy growth rate. Green business will enhance green entrepreneur, will come forward with the justice and responsibility towards the future generation and society. Once the green business capture the market, green economy growth enhances. People are having lead projects with bottom-top approach rise for green innovative technology, enhancing the value prosperous green business future. "A JUST TRANSITION CREATES DECENT WORK OPPORTUNITIES FOR ALL AND ENSURES THAT SOCIAL PROTECTION EXISTS WHERE NEEDED. IT ALSO INCLUDES MECHANISMS FOR SOCIAL DIALOGUE FROM THE PRIVATE SECTORS AND WORKER'S UNION THROUGHOUT POLICYMAKING PROCESS AT ALL LEVELS' (Mari Nishimura, 2021).

ACKNOWLEDGMENT

I would like to thank the editors for their cooperation

REFERENCES

Barbier, E. B. (2012). The green economy post Rio+20. *Science, 2012*(338), 887–888. doi:10.1126cience.1227360 PMID:23161980

Burgess, K. (2017). *Foundation for Democracy and Sustainable Development.* https://www.fdsd.org/the-challenge/what-is-sustainable-development/

Carlowitz, V. (2014). Encyclopedia of Public Health. Springer.

Chan, H. (2022). *The Nutrition Source> Sustainability > Food Waste.* https://www.hsph.harvard.edu/nutritionsource/sustainability/food-waste/

David, A. (2019). Recover, Recycle and Reuse: An Efficient Way to Reduce the Waste. *International Journal of Mechanical and Production Engineering Research and Development, 9*(3), 31-42. http://www.tjprc.org/publishpapers/2-67-1554700771-4IJMPERDJUN20194.pdf

Elliott, J. A. (2013). *An Introduction to Sustainable Development* (4th ed.). Routledge, Taylor and Francis.

Emaet. (2015). *The Concept of Sustainable Development: Definition and Defining Principles.* United Nations' 2015 Global Sustainable Development Report. doi:10.13140/RG.2.2.34980.22404

Geels, F. W. (2004, September). From sectoral systems of innovation to socio-technical systems: Insights about dynamics and change from sociology and institutional theory. *Research Policy, 33*(6–7), 897–920. doi:10.1016/j.respol.2004.01.015

Ghaffar. (2017). Studying green architecture factors in order to achieving sustainable. *International Journal of Scientific & Engineering Research, 8*(6).

Going Green 9. (2020). *Green buildings: examples of sustainable architecture around the world.* https://edition.cnn.com/style/article/green-buildings-world-sustainable-design/index.html

Hu, D., & Deng, M. (2004). A review of sustainable development theory and sustainable development of hospitals. *Chin. Hosp. Manag., 2004*(24), 42–45.

Investment needs for the global energy transformation. (2020). *International Renewable Energy Agency.* https://www.irena.org/financeinvestment/Investment-Needs

IRENA. (2019). *Transforming the energy system.* https://www.irena.org/publications/2019/Sep/Transforming-the-energy-system

Jawaharlal Nehru National Solar Mission. (2021). https://www.iea.org/policies/4916-jawaharlal-nehru-national-solar-mission-phase-i-ii-and-iii

Jehling, M., Hitzeroth, M., & Brueckner, M. (2019). Applying institutional theory to the analysis of energy transitions: From local agency to multi-scale configurations in Australia and Germany. *Energy Research & Social Science*, *53*(July), 110–120. doi:10.1016/j.erss.2019.01.018

Jibril, A. (2011). *The Concept And Principles Of Sustainable Development.* Conference: 52nd Annual Conference Organised by the Association of Nigerian Geographers (ANG) on "Climate Change and Sustainable Development, Sokoto, Nigeri.a

Johannesburg. (2002). *Report of the World Summit on Sustainable Development.* United Nations.

Kater, S., Kelly, E., & Whittemore, S. (2021). *Impact Investors and the Coming Energy Sector Transformation*. https://www.bridgespan.org/insights/library/impact-investing/impact-investors-and-the-energy-sector

Kaur. (2013). Current role of entrepreneurship in global greenmarket. *International Journal ofManagement, 4*(5), 1-5. https://www.academia.edu/4752352/CURRENT_ROLE_OF_ENTREPRENEURSHIP_IN_GLOBAL_GREEN_MARKET?email_work_card=thumbnail

Klarin, T. (2018). The Concept of Sustainable Development:From its Beginning to the Contemporary Issues. *Zagreb International Review of Economics & Business*, *21*(1), 67–94. doi:10.2478/zireb-2018-0005

Leiserowitz, A. (2005, April). What is Sustainable Development? Goals, Indicators, Values, and Practice. *Environment*, *47*(3), 8–21. doi:10.1080/00139157.2005.10524444

Lele, S. M. (1991, June). Sustainable development: A critical review. *World Development*, *19*(6), 607–621. doi:10.1016/0305-750X(91)90197-P

Li, C. (2005). United Nations summit seeks global development. *Contemp. World*, *2005*, 4–6.

Mensah. (2019). Sustainable development: Meaning, history, principles, pillars, and implications for human action: Literature review. *Cogent Social Sciences, 5*(1). https://www.tandfonline.com/doi/full/10.1080/23311886.2019.1653531

Moose. (2021). *Clean Air Lawn Care*. https://cleanairlawncare.com/what-is-green-entrepreneurship

Neville. (2021). *Introduction to Renewable Energy entrepreneurship*. https://www.savannahstate.edu/academic-affairs/documents/ENGT2803-IntroductiontoRenewableEnergyEntrepreneurshipSyllabus.pdf

Niu, W., Ma, N., & Yijun, L. (2015). Sustainable development from action to science—Sustainability science and the annual report for world sustainable development 2015. *Bull. Chin. Acad. Sci.*, *2015*(30), 573–585.

Painul, J. P. (2001, September). Barriers to renewable energy penetration; a framework for analysis. *Renewable Energy*, *24*(1), 73–89. doi:10.1016/S0960-1481(00)00186-5

Pinstrup-Andersen. (2014). F*ood losses and waste and sustainable food systems*. HLPE Reports. https://www.fao.org/3/i3901e/i3901e.pdf

Press release IEA. (2021). https://www.iea.org/news/renewable-electricity-growth

Ragheb, A., El-Shimy, H., & Ragheb, G. (2016). Green architecture: A concept of sustainability. *Procedia: Social and Behavioral Sciences*, *216*, 778–787. doi:10.1016/j.sbspro.2015.12.075

Renewable. (2021). *IEA, Annual renewable electricity capacity additions, main and accelerated cases, 2014-2026*. https://www.iea.org/data-and-statistics/charts/annual-renewable-electricity-capacity-additions-main-and-accelerated-cases-2014-2026

Sanyal, A. (2021). *Green Entrepreneurship: A Path towards Sustainable Development*. https://www.globsyn.edu.in/blog/green-entrepreneurship-a-path-towards-sustainable-development

Shi, L., Han, L., Yang, F., & Gao, L. (2019). The Evolution of Sustainable Development Theory: Types, Goals, and Research Prospect. *Sustainability*, *2019*(11), 7158. doi:10.3390u11247158

Smith, A. (2007). Translating sustainabilities between green niches and socio-technical regimes. *Technology Analysis and Strategic Management*, *19*(4), 427–450. doi:10.1080/09537320701403334

Smith, A., Stirling, A., & Berkhout, F. (2005, December). A. Stirling, F. Berkhout (2005)The governance of sustainable socio-technical transitions. *Research Policy*, *34*(10), 1491–1510. doi:10.1016/j.respol.2005.07.005

Sovacool, B. K. (2009). Rejecting renewables: The socio-technical impediments to renewable electricity in the United States. *Energy Policy*, *37*(11), 4500–4513. doi:10.1016/j.enpol.2009.05.073

Sovacool, B. K. (2016). How long will it take? Conceptualizing the temporal dynamics of energy transitions. *Energy Research & Social Science*, *13*(March), 202–215. doi:10.1016/j.erss.2015.12.020

Stöppler. (2022). *What Is the Definition of Organic Food?* MedicineNet. https://www.medicinenet.com/what_is_the_definition_of_organic_food/views.htm

Sun, X. (2012). Review and prospect on the UN's efforts for sustainable development. *China Popul. Environ.*, *22*, 1–6.

The Economic Time News. (2021). *No new fossil fuel projects for net-zero 2050 goal: IEA*. https://economictimes.indiatimes.com/news/international/business/no-new-fossil-fuel-projects-for-net-zero-2050-goal-iea/articleshow/82730817.cms

The Sustainable Development Goals Report. (2019). *United Nations*. https://unstats.un.org/sdgs/report/2019/The-Sustainable-Development-Goals-Report-2019.pdf

Tiseo, I. (2021). *Global plastic production 1950-2020*. https://www.statista.com/statistics/282732/global-production-of-plastics-since-1950/

Tiseo, I. (2022). *Plastic production forecast worldwide 2025-2050*. https://www.statista.com/statistics/664906/plastics-production-volume-forecast-worldwide/

Trzyna, T. C. (1995). *A Sustainable World: Defining and Measuring Sustainable Development*. Earthscan Publication, Ltd.

U-tantada. (2019). Green Market Economy and Emerging Market Environment: Sustainable Adaptive Complex Systems. *International Review of Research in Emerging Markets and the Global Economy*, *5*(1). https://www.researchgate.net/publication/333561173_Green_Market_Economy_and_Emerging_Market_Environment_Sustainable_Adaptive_Complex_Systems

UNEP. (2022). *The Transition to a Green Economy: Benefits, Challenges and Risks from a Sustainable Development Perspective*. https://www.unep.org/resources/report/transition-green-economy-benefits-challenges-and-risks-sustainable-development, https://wedocs.unep.org/bitstream/handle/20.500.11822/9310/-Transition%20to%20a%20green%20economy:%20benefits,%20challenges%20and%20risks%20from%20a%20sustainable%20development%20perspective-2012UN-DESA,%20UNCTAD%20Transition%20GE.pdf?sequence=3&amp%3BisAllowed=

UNGA. (2020). *Entrepreneurship for sustainable development Report of the Secretary-General, United Nations General Assembly A/75/257, 27 July 2020, Seventy-fifth session*. UNGA.

United Nations. (2012). *The Future we Want*. United Nations.

United Nations. (2015). *Transforming Our World: The 2030 Agenda for Sustainable Development*. United Nations.

Wanne, B. (2019). *Is exponential growth of solar PV the obvious conclusion?* https://www.iea.org/commentaries/is-exponential-growth-of-solar-pv-the-obvious-conclusion

Wieben, E. (2017). *Save Food For A Better Climate, Converting the food loss and waste challenge into climate action*. Food and Agriculture Organization of the United Nations. https://www.fao.org/3/i8000e/i8000e.pdf

World Commission on Environment and Development. (2018). Our Common Future. Oxford University Press.

Wu, J. (2014). What is sustainability science? *Ying Yong Sheng Tai Xue Bao*, *2014*(25), 1–11. PMID:24765835

Zhu, D. (2016). Sustainability science: An object-process-subject analytical framework. *China Popul. Environ.*, *2016*(26), 1–9.

Chapter 10
Social Entrepreneurship Through Innovations in Agriculture

Shad Ahmad Khan
https://orcid.org/0000-0001-7593-3487
University of Buraimi, Oman

Hesham Magd
Modern College of Business and Science, Oman

Ibrahim Rashid Al Shamsi
University of Buraimi, Oman

Kaneez Masoom
Babu Banarasi Das University, India

ABSTRACT

The social entrepreneurs consider solving the social problem first rather than minting profits. As the world today is suffering from the problem of rising population, the food demands are destined to rise in the times to come. The shrinking arable land, less availability of fresh water, concentration of population in towns and cities, etc. are becoming a threat to the agriculture sector. Thus, the agriculture sector requires innovative practices that at times comes with cost. Entrepreneurship with an objective of minting profit might escalate the price of the agricultural produce, and being a primary sector, it might further lead to inflation in other sectors as well. To these issues, social entrepreneurship appears to be a potential solution that has been discussed considering literature and reports in this chapter.

DOI: 10.4018/978-1-6684-4666-9.ch010

INTRODUCTION

Social Entrepreneurship is a branch of entrepreneurship that appears to be the need for the hour, as its motive is more noble than conventional entrepreneurship. The social entrepreneurs, consider solving the social problem first, rather than minting profits in a less span of time (Barberá-Tomás et al. 2019). As the world today is suffering from the problem of rising population, the food demands are destined to rise in the times to come. The shrinking arable land, less availability of fresh water, concentration of population in towns and cities etc is becoming a threat to the agriculture sector (Khan et al., 2020). The new techniques like aeroponics, aquaponics, and vertical farming are emerging as a potential solution to the emerging problem of food availability in times to come. The recent trends have compelled the researchers to observe that the new forms of agriculture techniques are overtaken by the large business houses, who mainly are involved in this process to exploit the existing demand of food and extract high levels of profit margin.

Food availability needs to be considered as a right for individual under "Right to live", as guaranteed by the constitution of various countries across the globe. It is believed that the modern techniques in agriculture can maximise the yield to 36 times from the same piece of land and can use as little as 5% of the total water requirements to support irrigation (Stories, 2016). With the support of the government and Non-profit organisations, the establishment cost can be subsidised. This study considers the involvement of social entrepreneurs in the innovative agricultural practices would ensure that the purpose of innovative agricultural practices is not defeated. This study will have an implication on all the nations across the globe, especially the lower income nations, where the basic facilities is not available to the general masses.

The present study considers the needs, challenges, and innovative agricultural practices by focusing on aeroponic vertical farming, and checks the relationship between social entrepreneurs, and agriculture, and social entrepreneurs, agriculture and innovations through bibliometric analysis of Scopus database. The main idea of this paper is to explore the key words in the arena of social entrepreneurs and agriculture, and find the studies conducted considering vertical farming as an element of study.

BACKGROUND OF THE STUDY

Entrepreneurship and Social Entrepreneurship

Entrepreneurship has always been in the centre of discussion and a major area of attention for the government across the world. In the recent years, the entrepreneurship development has caught up attention in the countries that otherwise had other priorities. The entrepreneurship education is one such areas where a lot of development and emphasis have been given (Khan et al., 2019). However, the entrepreneurship business and start-ups suffer obstacles that often lead to discouragement amongst the potential entrepreneurs (Singh et al., 2020). With the concerns over planetary sustainability, inclusive growth, and other socio-economic factors, the policy makers are now giving increased importance to entrepreneurship and a lot of measures are taken across the globe to harness the potential solutions that entrepreneurship offers.

In the words of Galindo and Méndez-Picazo (2013) stated that "Entrepreneurship acts as a mechanism for socio-economic development, reduction in poverty, and employment generation". Entrepreneurship in the developing countries is instrumental in realising economic growth, employment creation and poverty reduction (Omoruyi et al., 2017). As the globally many social and ecological problems are emerging the social entrepreneurship has emerged as an important subset of the entrepreneurship. Social Entrepreneurship is found to be focusing on the social problems that is hampering the economies around the world, such as hunger, poverty, housing problems, racial and ethnical discrimination, deprivation of education and so on (Hamirul 2020). The social entrepreneurship hits the very social problem that has emerged. The social problem is the significant gap between the ideals of the society and the actual achievements or status. An attempt to lower down such gaps is a social cause. Social entrepreneurs work towards reducing such gap through positive social orientation (Kerbo, and Coleman, 2006).

In the words of Schumpeter (1936), "Creation of new business is an important driver of economies". shows that entrepreneurship positively explains the variations in the growth and further it is reasonable to contend that entrepreneurship in developing economies is instrumental to unlocking economic growth, create employment and reduce poverty. To understand social entrepreneurship, it is important to understand the way social entrepreneurship is difference from conventional entrepreneurship or commercial entrepreneurship. Although both types of entrepreneurships undergo the process of identifying, analysing, and exploiting of the opportunities, but the conventional entrepreneurship is more oriented towards generation of profit, whereas social entrepreneurship is oriented towards solving the social issue or gaining social values. The intention of the entrepreneurs i.e., creation of personal wealth or deliver social welfare marks the difference between the two (Austin, et al., 2006). Social entrepreneurs establish creative solutions to benefit the individuals as well the society, along with benefiting the social businesses through social value creation as the main objective (Dobele, L., 2016). The similar trend has been observed through the concept of Self-Help Groups (SHGs) and micro enterprises that aims to overcome the societal problems (Gangwar & Khan, 2022).

NEED FOR INNOVATION IN AGRICULTURE

Increasing Food Demand: It is estimated that by the year 2050, close to 80% of the world's population will live in urban areas and the total population of the world will increase 9.8 billion people (United Nations). The world population as of November 2017 is 7.6 billion (Worldometers, 2017). According to Wikipedia world population (2017), the population of the world will be 11.2 billion by 2100. To put it in perspective, the demand for food will rise by 30% by 2050 and almost 50% by 2100. This has a direct and positive correlation with agriculture i.e., more population more agriculture.

Water Shortage: According to World Wildlife (2017), although 70% of planet earth is covered with water but only 3% of the world water is fresh water (the water we drink, we bathe in, use in agriculture etc), two-thirds of that are tucked away in the frozen glaciers, in other words unavailable for our use (WWF, 2017). The results are 1.1 billion people worldwide lack access to clean water and a total of 2.7 billion people find water scarce for at least one month of the year. In addition to this 2.4 billion people face the problem of Inadequate sanitation, they are exposed to diseases, such as cholera, typhoid fever, and other water-borne illnesses. Two million people, mostly children, die each year from diarrheal diseases alone (WWF, 2017).

The WWF report further adds that many of the water system that keeps ecosystem thriving and feed a growing human population have become stressed. Rivers, lakes, and aquifers are either drying up or are becoming polluted, further, more than half the world's wetlands have disappeared. Agriculture consumes more water than any other source and is responsible for withdrawal of 70% global water (The water Project, 2017). The inefficiencies in agriculture have led to more waste of water. Climate change is altering patterns of weather and water around the world, causing shortages and droughts in some areas and floods in others (WWF, 2017).

Shrinking Arable Land: For the purpose agriculture arable land is required. By definition, arable land is referred as land capable of being ploughed and used to grow crops. The world has lost a third of its arable land due to erosion or pollution in the past 40 years, with potentially disastrous consequences as global demand for food soars, scientists have warned (The Guardian, 2015). Increasing population and growing food demands have led to increase in requirement of arable land. It is important for any country to convert its non-arable land into arable land to meet with the growing demand.

Innovation in Agriculture: Vertical Farming

Vertical farming is a practice of growing food in vertically stacked layers as well as vertically inclined surfaces, theoretically supporting farming of every kind of crops, vegetables, herbs, and fruits. In the modern arena, vertical farming harness the technologies like artificial control of light, environmental control (temperature, gases, humidity, etc.) and fertigation. This technology is referred as CEA (controlled-environment agriculture) technology in indoor farming techniques (Khan et.al, 2020). Vertical farming is possible in any kind of closed structures like buildings, skyscrapers, warehouse, or any structures. Organizations like Aerofarm claim that in their vertical farming the crops need 95% less water and no soil (The Guardian, 2016), Aero farm can achieve this through root misting system, instead of soil the crops are grown on a reusable recycled plastic cloth (Khan et.al, 2020). For photosynthesis, in place of sun there are rows of LED lightening, this along with Climate control system reduces the growing process turned almost to half (Stories, 2016). The system makes the growing to harvest to happen at any time during the year, as the dependency on the weather conditions is almost zero (Khan et.al, 2020).

CHALLENGES FOR INNOVATIVE AGRICULTURAL PRACTICES

Economics: One of the important concerns is potential profitability of vertical farming. There are different figures leading to different estimates for establishment of vertical farming farm. According to Hughes (1998) the initial building costs will be easily over $100 million, for a 60-hectare vertical farm, this may vary depending upon the type of city. The cost for cities such as Tokyo, Moscow, Mumbai, Dubai, Milan, Zurich, and Sao Paulo ranging from $1850 to $880 per square meter, respectively. According to Aero Farm (2016), it will cost $25 million for a 70-100 sq. ft. this covers the cost land acquisition, site preparation, construction, capital equipment, working capital, soft costs, tenant improvement including HVAC. The cost of establishment may vary depending on the country and location where the vertical farming setup is to be established, but one thing to agree on is that the initial establishment expenses are huge as compared to any typical agricultural setup. The era where the concepts like Break Even Point (BEP) or Return on Investment (ROI) exists, it won't be wrong to raise question on the economic feasibility of the vertical farming.

Energy use: Another challenge is the use of energy to power the supplemental lights to obtain viable yield. Bruce Bugbee, a crop physiologist at Utah State University, believes that the power demands of vertical farming will be too expensive and uncompetitive with traditional farms using only free natural light. The environmental writer George Monbiot calculated that the cost of providing enough supplementary light to grow the grain for a single loaf would be about $15. An article in the Economist argued that "even though crops growing in a glass skyscraper will get some natural sunlight during the day, it won't be enough" and "the cost of powering artificial lights will make indoor farming prohibitively expensive". The controlled environment system i.e., HVAC will be as costly as any other tower at the same time expensive plumbing and elevator systems to distribute food and water throughout will be also expensive. Some others have an opinion that to fulfill the energy requirement the farms will have to resort to fossil fuel-based generators to keep the farm supplied with uninterrupted electricity.

Pollution: There are mainly two factors influencing the pollution through vertical farming; 1) the greenhouse gases because of electricity of generation; and 2) CO_2 Supplemented by growers to 3-4 times the rate normally found in the atmosphere to increase photosynthesis and subsequently increasing the yield. Even if the farms are powered by green energy, it is expected that the source of required CO_2 will be from combustion. There are high chances that through necessary ventilation much CO_2 will be leaked into the atmosphere adding to city's pollution. Another type of pollution that is added by vertical farm growers is light pollution. Greenhouse growers commonly exploit photoperiodism in plants to control whether the plants are in a vegetative or reproductive stage. As part of this control, growers will have the lights on past sunset and before sunrise or periodically throughout the night. Single story greenhouses are already a nuisance to neighbors because of light pollution, a 30-story vertical farm in a densely populated area will surely face problems because of its light pollution. Hydroponics greenhouses regularly change the water, meaning there is a large quantity of water containing fertilizers and pesticides that must be disposed of. While solutions are currently being worked on, the most common method of simply spreading the mixture over a sufficient area of neighboring farmland or wetlands would be more difficult for an urban vertical farm.

METHODOLOGY FOR BIBLIOMETRIC ANALYSIS

A bibliometric assessment includes applying real procedures to conclude emotional and quantitative changes in each intelligent investigation subject, spread out the profile of appropriations on the point, and distinguish tendencies inside a discipline. This review uses the Scopus database collection across all disciplines. For this purpose, the csv files were generated through the Scopus database using two sets of key words i.e., "Agriculture" AND "Social entrepreneurship", and "Agriculture" AND "Social entrepreneurship" AND "innovation". The generated files were uploaded into Vos viewer to check the Co-Occurrence of all key words to extract the most popular words in the domain, country analysis has been done to check the national background of the authors, and citations analysis has been conducted to check the strength of the document as per the standard recommendations of Donthu et al., (2021) and Khan et al., (2021). The main objective of the study is to identify the gaps in literature through checking the number of documents in the arena of agriculture and social entrepreneurship. Also, an attempt has been made to identify the number of countries where such studies are being carried on.

BIBLIOMETRIC ANALYSIS:

Agriculture and Social Entrepreneurship

As a starting point of this study the Scopus database (Donthu et al., 2021; Khan et al., 2021) was explored using the key word as "Agriculture" AND "Social entrepreneurship", only 49 documents were found related to these two fields suggesting the limited work done in this area. To achieve majority of the words the occurrence was set at 3 and above, that was able to give us 16 words as presented in the table 1. As visible from table 1, after social entrepreneurship and agriculture the most repeated words were: rural areas; rural development; entrepreneur; social farming; regional planning; economic and social effects; alternative agriculture; sustainability; economics and education. The bibliometric graph as presented in Figure 1, explained the relationship between these keywords, and a healthy interconnection of words was identified.

Agriculture, Social Entrepreneurship, and Innovation

As a second part of this study the Scopus database was explored using the key word as "Agriculture" AND "Social entrepreneurship" AND "innovation", only 19 documents were found related to these three fields suggesting research scope in this area. In order to achieve majority of the words the occurrence was set at 2 and above, that was able to give us 7 words as presented in the table 2

Table 1. Co-Occurrence analysis of agriculture and social entrepreneurship

S. No.	Items	Occurrences	Total Link Strength
1.	social entrepreneurship	26	47
2.	Agriculture	15	34
3.	Rural areas	6	27
4.	Rural development	4	22
5.	Entrepreneur	5	19
6.	Social farming	4	19
7.	Regional planning	4	18
8.	Economic and social effects	3	14
9.	Alternative agriculture	3	13
10.	Rural area	3	13
11.	Sustainability	4	11
12.	Agricultural worker	3	10
13.	Social enterprise	4	9
14.	Economics	3	8
15.	Education	3	7
16.	Entrepreneurship	3	7

Source: Extracted from scopus.com via Vos Viewer (authors calculation)

Figure 1. Bibliometric graph- Agriculture and Social Entrepreneurship (showing the links and network of the studies)
Source: *Extracted from scopus.com via Vos Viewer (authors calculation)*

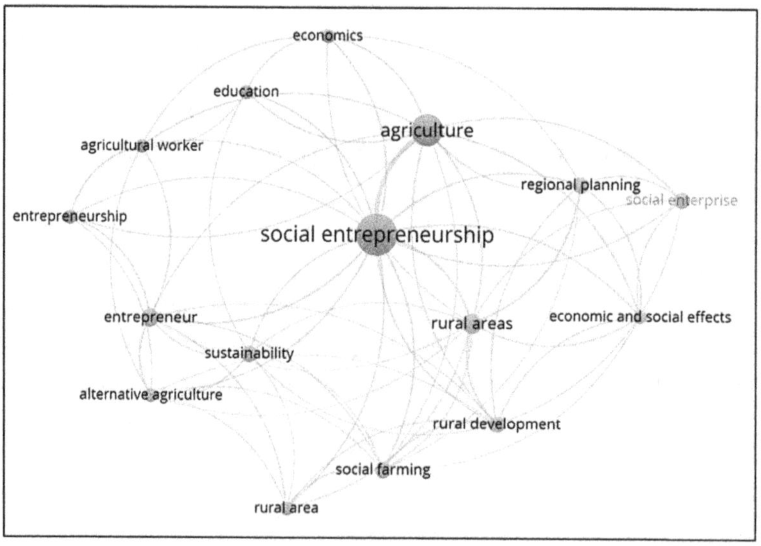

Table 2. Co-occurrence analysis of agriculture, social entrepreneurship and innovation

S. No.	Items	Occurrences	Total Link Strength
1.	Social entrepreneurship	9	7
2.	Agriculture	3	4
3.	Engineering education	2	4
4.	Innovation	2	3
5.	Entrepreneurship	2	2
6.	Social innovation	2	2
7.	Sustainability	2	0

Source: Extracted from scopus.com via Vos Viewer (authors calculation)

As visible from table 2, after social entrepreneurship and agriculture the most repeated words were: engineering education; innovation; entrepreneurship; social innovation; sustainability. The bilbliometric graph as presented in Figure 2, explained the relationship between these keywords, and a healthy interconnection of words was identified, however, in as represented in the graph and the table the sustainability could find any substantial link strength.

Figure 2. Bibliometric graph- agriculture, social entrepreneurship and innovation (showing the links and network of the studies)
Source: *Extracted from scopus.com via Vos Viewer (authors calculation)*

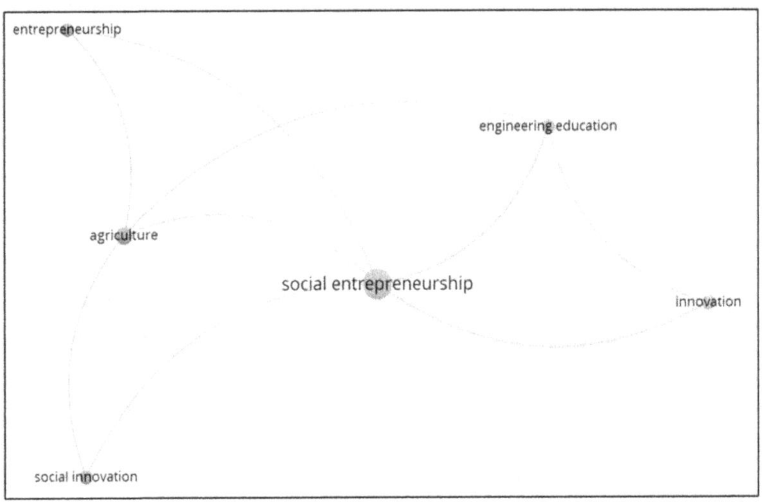

Countries Involved in Conducting Research on Agriculture and Social Entrepreneurship

Out of 200+ recognized countries in the world, only thirteen countries were found working on the field of Agriculture, Social Entrepreneurship, and Innovation, this has been achieved on a very liberal side, where even one contribution of the country has been recognised. In terms of producing the work, Indonesia tops the list, however, Portugal is ranked 1, based on the highest citations as compared to other nations.

Table 3. Countries involved in studies on agriculture, social entrepreneurship and innovation

S. No	Country	Documents	Citations	Total Link Strength
1.	Portugal	1	57	0
2.	Spain	1	24	0
3.	Canada	2	10	0
4.	India	1	7	0
5.	Puerto Rico	1	6	0
6.	China	1	5	1
7.	United States	3	5	1
8.	Senegal	1	1	0
9.	Bulgaria	1	0	0
10.	Finland	1	0	0
11.	Indonesia	4	0	1
12.	Japan	1	0	1
13.	Lithuania	1	0	0

Source: Extracted from scopus.com via Vos Viewer (authors calculation)

DISCUSSION

It is now a fact that the food demand will continue to grow globally with the increase in the population, to cater it the corresponding pressure on the agriculture will also go up. This would require agriculture sector to adopt latest technology and innovative techniques. At the same time, it also cannot be ignored that the technology will come with a cost, majorly cost related to finances and ecology. The users need to identify whether the proposed cost will be able to combat the existing and expected issues with minimum damage to the ecology. Another aspect is that the agriculture and related challenges are more social in nature than scientific, as the social beings will be the most affected if the agricultural policy and plans are not made in time. As the innovative agricultural practices will also incur heavy expenditure in terms of resources, the conventional entrepreneurship (profit oriented) will further add on the cost that will be transferred as a burden to the buyers. As a solution to this social entrepreneurship appears a more viable approach to tackle this issue, as the principle of social entrepreneurship is social value creation. Further, the SHGs and micro enterprises based on social entrepreneurship could be also a solution to this issue. When checked into the body of knowledge i.e., the existing literature, social entrepreneurship and agriculture as combination have been less studied. Perhaps, the researchers didn't consider agricultural issues as a social problem. This was further justified with the involvement of the countries and the number of documents contributed. This field emerged to be a very less researched area leaving a lot of scope and opportunity for the future researchers.

IMPLICATIONS

The managerial implication of this study is mainly on the government, funding agencies and other allied agencies working in the arena of agriculture and entrepreneurship. Further, this study has a serious implication on the existing social entrepreneurs who might be interested in trying their feat in the field of innovative agricultural practices and can take the advantage of the already established social value. This study can also influence the conventional agripreneurs who might come up with measures to reduce the burden of cost from their buyers through achieving efficiency and effectiveness.

CONCLUSION

The world is undergoing a period of crisis, and if no constructive steps are taken the situation will become worse. The human population is growing, and the resources to support agriculture i.e., water bodies, fertile soil, and arable land is shrinking. To this issue, vertical farming through the modern techniques appears to be a feasible solution. The problem is the cost involved in such process as deputing technology in any form of process requires financial cost. Although there are other challenges as well, but the cost recovery from the buyers makes the challenge bigger. To these issues the social entrepreneurship appears to be a feasible solution. This area however has attracted very less attention of the researchers across the globe with very limited quality studies and low country representation. The need for the hour would be to promote studies in the arena of social entrepreneurship and agriculture. Also, the government and private players need to join hands in supporting these initiatives.

LIMITATION FOR FUTURE RESEARCH

Conducting a study based on secondary data for a field which is less researched and studied was a major limitation for this study. Further, the idea of social entrepreneurs in the field of innovative agriculture appeared to be novel, as no living examples could be identified for the purpose of case study. The social entrepreneurs already involved in agriculture are mainly into the conventional form of agriculture and usually don't prefer the innovative techniques for variety of ecological reasons.

DIRECTIONS FOR FUTURE RESEARCH

The proposed area i.e., agriculture and social entrepreneurship is very less studied area as per the bibliometric analysis. This speaks loud about the scope and opportunity lies in this area. The contextual studies, case studies, and general studies, all can be focused. Also, very limited empirical findings have been discovered, that could be another direction for the future research.

REFERENCES

AeroFarms. (2016). *Farms That Rise to the Challenge*. https://www.aerofarms.com/2016/05/17/vertical-farming-challenge/

Austin, J., Stevenson, H., & Wei–Skillern, J. (2006). Social and Commercial Entrepreneurship: Same, Different, or Both? *Entrepreneurship Theory and Practice*, *30*(1), 1–22. doi:10.1111/j.1540-6520.2006.00107.x

Barberá-Tomás, D., Castelló, I., de Bakker, F. G., & Zietsma, C. (2019). Energizing through visuals: How social entrepreneurs use emotion-symbolic work for social change. *Academy of Management Journal*, *62*(6), 1789–1817. doi:10.5465/amj.2017.1488

Dobele, L. (2016). A New Approach in Higher Education: Social Entrepreneurship Education. In *Proceedings- 11th International Conference on Mangement, Enterprise and Benchmarking (MEB 2016)*. Óbuda University, Keleti Faculty of Business and Management.

Donthu, N., Kumar, S., Mukherjee, D., Pandey, N., & Lim, W. M. (2021). How to conduct a bibliometric analysis: An overview and guidelines. *Journal of Business Research*, *133*, 285–296. doi:10.1016/j.jbusres.2021.04.070

Galindo, M. Á., & Méndez-Picazo, M. T. (2013). Innovation, entrepreneurship and economic growth. *Management Decision, 51*(3), 501–514. doi:10.1108/00251741311309625

Gangwar, V. P., & Khan, S. A. (2022). Analyzing the Role of Micro-Entrepreneurship and Self-Help Groups (SHGs) in Women Empowerment and Development. In M. Arafat (Ed.), Driving Factors for Venture Creation and Success in Agricultural Entrepreneurship (pp. 213–226). IGI Global. doi:10.4018/978-1-6684-2349-3.ch011

Graham, L. (2017). *UN raises world population forecast to 9.8 billion people by 2050 due to rapid growth in Africa*. Retrieved from https://www.cnbc.com/2017/06/22/un-raises-world-population-forecast-to-9-point-8-billion-people-by-2050.html

Hamirul, M., Roslan, H., Hamid, S., Ijab, M. T., Yusop, F. D., & Norman, A. A. (2020). Social entrepreneurship in higher education: Challenges and opportunities. *Asia Pacific Journal of Education*, 1–16.

Kerbo, H. R., & Coleman, J. W. (2006). *Social Problems: A brief introduction* (2nd ed.). Pearson.

Khan, M. A., Patnaik, D., Ashraf, R., Ali, I., Kumar, S., & Donthu, N. (2021). Value of special issues in the Journal of Business Research: A bibliometric analysis. *Journal of Business Research, 125*, 295–313. doi:10.1016/j.jbusres.2020.12.015

Khan, S. A., Devi, T. P., & Sharma, P. P. (2020). Vertical farming: Why it matters for Bhutan. *Studies in Indian Place Names, 40*(1), 1323-1329.

Khan, S. A., Sharma, P. P., & Thoudam, P. (2019). Role of Attitude and Entrepreneurship Education towards Entrepreneurial Orientation among Business Students of Bhutan. *International Journal of Recent Technology and Engineering, 8*(3S), 335–345. doi:10.35940/ijrte.C1072.1083S19

Omoruyi, E. M. M., Olamide, K. S., Gomolemo, G., & Donath, O. A. (2017). Entrepreneurship and Economic Growth: Does Entrepreneurship Bolster Economic Expansion in Africa? *J Socialomics, 6*(04), 219. doi:10.4172/2167-0358.1000219

Patil, V. (2015). *Which Is The Only Carbon-Negative Country?* Retrieved from https://www.scienceabc.com/social-science/carbon-negative-country.html

Pem, S. (2017). *Bhutan's 71 percent forest cover confirmed*. Retrieved from http://www.bbs.bt/news/?p=67069

Schumpeter, J. A. (1936). *The Theory of Economic Development*. Harvard University Press.

Singh, E. H., Wangda, S., Khan, S., & Khan, S. A. (2020). Exploring the obstacles for start-ups in Bhutan: From a prevented entrepreneurs perspective. *International Journal of Innovation, Creativity and Change, 4.*

Stories. (2016). *This Farm of the Future Uses No Soil and 95% Less Water.* Retrieved from https://www.youtube.com/watch?v=-_tvJtUHnmU

The Guardian. (2014). *World largest vertical farm New Ark green revolution.* Retrieved from https://www.theguardian.com/environment/2016/aug/14/world-largest-vertical-farm-newark-green-revolution

The Guardian. (2015). *Arable land soil food security shortage.* Retrieved from https://www.theguardian.com/environment/2015/dec/02/arable-land-soil-food-securityshortage

The Water Project. (2017). https://thewaterproject.org/water-scarcity/water-scarcity-andagriculture

Times of Oman. (2019). Retrieved from https://timesofoman.com/article/1900951/Business/Food-consumption-in-Oman-to-grow-46-annually-until-2023

UNDESA. (2016). *World Population Prospects: The 2016 Revision – Key Findings and Advance Tables.* United Nations Department of Economic and Social Affairs, Population Division.

Urban Land Institute. (2016). *The Changing World with David Rosenberg of AeroFarms.* Retrieved from https://www.youtube.com/watch?v=HLL3CEhlNz0

Wikipedia. (2017). Retrieved from https://en.wikipedia.org/wiki/World_population

World Bank. (2014). *Arable land (% of land area).* Retrieved from https://data.worldbank.org/indicator/AG.LND.ARBL.ZS

World bank. (2019). *Oman Food Products Imports by country in US$ Thousand 2018.* Retrieved from https://wits.worldbank.org/CountryProfile/en/Country/OMN/Year/LTST/TradeFlow/Import/Partner/by-country/Product/16-24_FoodProd

Worldometers. (2017). Retrieved from https://www.worldometers.info/world-population/

WWF. (2017). Retrieved from https://www.worldwildlife.org/threats/water-scarcity

Youn. (2017). *Visit the World's Only Carbon-Negative Country.* Retrieved from https://www.nationalgeographic.com/travel/destinations/asia/bhutan/carbon-negative-country-sustainability/

Chapter 11
Waste to Wealth Enterprises:
A Study on Solid Waste Management Initiatives

Ritesh Dwivedi
https://orcid.org/0000-0003-3921-5458
Amity University, Noida, India

Balvinder Shukla
Amity University, Noida, India

Garima Malik
Amity University, Noida, India

ABSTRACT

The government of India (GoI) launched Swachh Bharat Mission on October 2014 to improve the prevailing sanitation, hygiene, and waste management state in the country. There has been an increased thrust of the authorities in the field of waste collection and management. The main objective of writing this study is to analyze initiatives in India of municipalities or areas with less than 3 Lakhs populations where exemplary solid waste management practices have been deployed through existing government machinery. The study tries to look into the role played by both government and community and smaller municipal corporations which have set an example and benchmarks for larger urban conglomerates to adopt their intervention model/strategy. Also, the chapter tries to bring out the attribute of a decentralized approach in all the cases which has been the basic reason of success in all the projects. Additionally, this study is an attempt to identify and study the best practices across the country to boost the chances of their replication wherever possible.

DOI: 10.4018/978-1-6684-4666-9.ch011

A. INTRODUCTION

The Prime Minister of India, in his highly spirited approach, brought up the issue of sanitation and hygiene in the country from the red fort podium on the 68th Independence Day of India. The responsibility towards waste management including its collection and disposal lies with lowest tier of Government in the country. The municipal corporations and Zilla Parishads have their revenue generation models but despite that almost all these bodies in the country have always been with inadequate funds which brings out the fact that sustainability is the most challenging factor in Waste collection and management initiatives.

From a conventional point of view, waste is defined as items without any value, but when waste is handled meaningfully and scientifically from the origination point, segregation and disposal a lot of value can be derived from the same.

India has grown larger gradually and it has more than 1.27 billion populations at present approximately. After 1991 when India opened up its economy to foreign investments the population in Urban Conglomerates has risen exponentially. Large number of people have already or are continually migrating to city area for better opportunities. Moreover, with increase in colleges and other bodies of higher education has resulted in more migration toward cities. Due to an uncontrolled Urbanisation, lack of proper infrastructure, improvement in living standards the waste generated by cities has increased manifold (Agarwal et al, 2015).

Right now only some part of solid waste generated is disposed through proper treatment. Waste segregation is biggest issue that must be taken up on urgent basis as it is the major challenge towards successful implementation of solid waste management initiatives. Improper disposal of waste not only causes pollution, it affects ground water, and causes diseases and has huge environmental and economic cost (NIUA, 2020).

Urban India contributes nearly 80- 85% of India's tax revenue. On the other hand, poor sanitation and waste management cost India 5.2% of its GDP. In fact, due to sanitation and hygiene issues India's GDP lost US $106.7 billion in 2015. As per a World Bank Report (2006) (the cost escalated to current prices), the per capita per annum burden of poor sanitation is estimated to be Rs. 8,700/.

In India, In India, an estimated 62 million tonnes/year of Municipal Solid Waste is currently generated in urban areas which is set to spiral to thrice the amount, that is, 165 million tonnes by 2030 and 436 million tonnes by 2050, leading to amplified public health and environment challenges. India is losing 1,250 hectares of precious land every year to landfill the processed/un- processed municipal solid wastes. In fact, the National Green Tribunal (NGT) has estimated that more than 10,000 hectares of valuable urban land is locked up as current dumpsites in India (Pamnani & Mika, 2014).

The country is finding it difficult to cope with large volumes of waste generated by the increasing urban population, which does not only pose a threat to public health at larger level and the environment conservation but is also a significant opportunity for economic gains (Tripathy, 2018). India generates 60 million tons of trash every year; the landfills are overflowing with no territorial space for addition land. Delhi produces 9,000 metric tons of municipal solid waste, which is going to major landfill sites. Three out of the four sites were needed to be been stopped by 2005 to 2009. Mumbai generates 6,500 metric tons of garbage daily out of which 4,500 metric tons is dumped at Deonar dumping ground, scheduled to expire at the end of 2016. The landfills have turned into mountains of trash which is increasing in height day by day (Kumar et al, 2009).

The solid waste generated in an Urban Setting are categorised into following types: -

1. Municipal Solid Waste: - Waste coming out of private homes, commercial establishments and institutions, as well as industrial facilities.
2. Hazardous Wastes like Medical Waste, Corrosive Wastes like chemicals and acids or toxic wastes like pesticides etc.
3. Agricultural Waste
4. Industrial Waste

After large scale funding and focus from the Government with Swachh Bharat Mission and the implementation of CSR policy by Ministry of Corporate affairs in 2014 the involvement of Corporate Sector in the domain has also increased.

B. SUCCESSFUL INITIATIVES FROM THE GRASSROOTS

Case – 1: Swachh Ambikapur Model - From Trash to Cash

Ambikapur is situated in Sarguja District in Chhatisgarh state. As per the 2011 census, Ambikapur is having population of 264,575. As a remarkable feat, city has achieved 100% segregation of waste at the start point itself (households) and that is why municipality has no landfills. After these attempts Ambikapur has been declared as a zero waste city since 2016. Ambikapur handles 45 metric ton Solid waste every day but remarkably 90% of waste gets segregated at households. 447 SHG women of 48 wards were involved into a registered Society called **Swachh Ambikapur Mission Sahakari Samiti Maryadit.** Ambikapur Municipal Corporation has signed an agreement with the mentioned samiti. This drive is actively monitored and guided by the Collector of Ambikapur District, and supported by Chhattisgarh State Urban Development Agency; and the Government of Chhattisgarh (Purohit, 2018).

The strength of the project lies in its simplicity. After the launch of Swachh Bharat Mission in 2015 the model practised widely for improving the Urban Infrastructure and Waste Management was Public Private Partnership (PPP). Although PPP model seems logical as it brings in the Private Sector's expertise and finances and helps bringing in new innovative technologies and approaches to the domain but a review of similar models in other Municipal Corporations demonstrated the profit orientation largely of the PPP mode rather than expected Service orientation and moreover it would not enable larger public participation. Taking cognisance of this authorities in government adopted a Public driven model in place of typical Government driven system. Solid waste management practices at Municipal level was divided into two parts: -

1. Door to Door Collection from households and other establishments in the city.
2. City Sanitation which comprised of cleaning of roads and other public places.

During 2015, door to door waste collection by SHGs was launched in 17 wards out of 48 in Ambikapur and for the rest a private contractor was deployed for collecting waste from common containers placed in the city. In 2016 Door to Door collection was extended to all the 48 wards. City Sanitation was kept entirely under the purview of the Municipal Corporation.

The main components of the Project are: -

1. Formation of Women Self Help Group SHGs – 623 women formed the SHG. Out of this number 123 Women were designates as Supervisors. All members were given exhaustive training for 15 days.
2. The city was divided into 17 zones each comprising of around 600 households and few commercial establishments. Further 17 Solid and Liquid Resource Management Centres (SLRMs) were constructed. The SLRM Center is the hub of the entire project. It is an industrial work shed built on an open land, fenced on all sides, with a broad gate on the front side. The area of the land required for each varied from 3,000 - 5,000 square feet. Designating areas for SLRMs within the city was a major challenge, hence all the unauthorised occupation over Government land in the city was mapped and the encroachments were either removed or rehabilitated to a different area (Purohit, 2018).
3. Each centre operates through two vehicles, first one is a manual pedal-tricycle and second is a battery-operated rickshaw. Two containers: one for inorganic and another for organic refuse are installed on the rickshaw. All homes and institutions have been asked to use two bin system; red bin and green bin for

inorganic and organic refuse, respectively. Three women accompany each rickshaw.

4. The SLRM works in the form of segregation centre where recyclable Organic and non – recyclable items are segregated. A Tertiary segregation centre has also been started where the recyclable waste further classified into 156 categories.
5. Organic waste is fed to cattle and poultry. The remaining waste is either fed to the bio-gas plant or is used for composting.
6. The resources recovered at the SLRMs are later sold and each worker receives their share of the revenue as per their contribution to the resource sold.

Key Achievements of the Project:

1. Through the initiative the city has become free of open dumping yards and landfills. The 15 acres of landfill site which was used earlier has been re-developed as a park.
2. Ambikapur Municipal Corporation has reclaimed a lot of valuable land by removal of land encroachment.
3. As it is decentralised model the cost of transportation of waste for Municipal Corporation has gone down drastically.
4. Jobs for 623 women who are paid Rs.5000 per month and also earn through the sale of items which are recycled.

Case – 2: Petlad Municipality

Petlad is a Municipality city in district of Anand, Gujarat. The Petlad city is divided into 12 wards constituted regularly every fifth year through elections. The Petlad Municipality has population of 55,330 of which 28,763 are males while 26,567 are females as per Census India 2011 data.

Literacy rate of Petlad city is 88.92% higher than state average of 78.03%.

Petlad Municipality handles facilities for over 11,100 houses and take decisions related to road construction within Municipality limits (CEPT University, 2011).

Petlad municipality has implemented lot many initiatives and innovations. The municipality has its own Pyrolysis plant Organic waste / food waste is converted into manure and plastic is used to generate energy from waste. i.e. bio fuel is made which is further used as fuel. The waste plastic decomposes at high temperature in Pyrolysis plant and produces a sort of bio – diesel. The Municipality has achieved 100% waste collection. The waste is segregated at the source and the plastic is being treated through the Pyrolysis plant which heats the waste at a high temperature The exhausts generated in this process is condensed and transformed into oil. The fuel generated has the same calorific value as normal diesel and is used in low powered diesel engines like Water Pumps and Generators.

There are two notable initiatives taken at Petland which have won various accolades and have been widely appreciated. These are: -

1. **'Waste to Best':** - It is an innovative programme wherein the scrap collected from households is used in waste collection is the city. The plastic including rubber waste is also recycled turning waste into wealth. Generally, government grants are used for waste management works, but Petlad Nagarpalika thought of not utilizing the grants / funds for the waste management in budget and using waste scrap as a resource instead. Petlad became the only municipality in Gujarat who was using scrap for making equipment out of waste material.

In their previous model like in Ambikapur (Case – I) the scrap metal would be sold off to easily available scrap dealers at a very low cost. The municipality came up with an innovative idea to convert these into useful items like dustbins, drain grills, gates etc. Self Help groups were identified and after their consent they were also involved. For this purpose, they hired a fabricator for welding and a painter on daily and a workshop for the initiative was developed. Items like Wall-mounted small dustbins were made which were further installed at 50 locations. These bins were installed at various places and Government employees, students from schools and members of the community were involved in to paint them.

The program has led to cost savings also when it was analysed with previous such expenditure. The results were achieved at only 10% of cost of new infrastructure and also helped in community awareness and involvement.

1. **Door to Door Collection Bio – Waste:** - Petlad Municipality has also undertaken a very innovative initiative to collect bio-hazardous waste, segregate at source and dispose scientifically through incinerator. Petlad municipality is the first in Gujarat to start a home-to-home service for collecting used sanitary pads and diapers and disposing it off scientifically. These items take a very long for bio – degradation and are serious concern for surface pollution and also poses a serious health risk. The problem is further increased as these items are generally disposed of with the common household waste which make the segregation difficult (CEPT University, 2011).

For the collection of this waste the Municipality decided to deploy e-rickshaws which were painted yellow in colour. These yellow coloured rickshaws are exclusively designated for collection of diapers and sanitary napkins only. Self Help Groups (SHGs) were again considered and involved in the process and small incinerators have been installed at bus depots, railway stations, schools and colleges. A wide awareness campaign was initiated wherein social media and various other means were used for promotion and a helpline number was designated wherein citizen can call for the collection of these items.

Due to the sensitive nature of the subject, participation from women was limited but gradually the initiative picked up as the awareness campaigns started by the municipal corporation gathered more traction and the community at large understood the message behind the initiative.

Petlad Municipal Corporation has exemplified the importance of the effectiveness of simple methods when implemented with the correct approach can make a big difference. Petlad has achieved 100% door to door collection. The model is simple, replicable and cost effective.

Case – 3: Alappuzha – Nirmala Bhavanam Nirmala Nagaram

Alappuzha with a population of 1.74 Lakhs has 52 wards of which 23 fall in the city limits produces around 58 tonnes per day of Solid wasted and has implemented the programme 'Nirmala Bhavanam Nirmala Nagaram' to implement the sanitation drive across the city.

The Municipal Corporation had been using a 6 Hectare landfill site in Sargodayapuram Village for dumping the waste, collected from the City. Due to years of continuous dumping had caused serious environmental concerns, contamination of water resources and stench in the surrounding areas. There were large scale protests at the site for more than 100 days by the villagers in 2012 and it was decided by the Gram Panchayat that waste up-to 5 Tons only will be dumped at the site, which was stopped by the Gram Panchayat completely by the year 2014. As the city ran out of public places to use for dumping of waste a strategic change in approach was required. SHGs started a survey initiate to study the waste disposal practises of households and the nature of waste that was being generated. After a thorough deliberation, a decentralised approach towards waste management was felt necessary and adopted for future programs.

The 'Nirmala Bhavanam Nirmala Nagaram' programme was launched in in 12 specifically selected wards which are mostly urbanised) as a pilot project. The maximum number of households who own lands were asked to set up biogas plants. Agency for Non-Conventional Energy and Rural Technology (ANERT) has developed innovative biogas plants at cost of Rs. 17,500 and these plants can treat 8-10 kg waste matter. Supply of gas from the plant continues for two-three hours daily. Another type of portable biogas plants was developed by Integrated Rural Technology centre (IRTC) the capacity of this plant is about 1,000 litres and costs Rs.13,500. The state gives 75% subsidy on the biogas plants (Ganesan, 2017).

For smaller households the 'Pipe Composting' method was adopted. The system has two PVC pipes of 1.25 m length and eight inches' diameter with two caps. The pipes are fixed in a vertical position on the ground with some part remaining under the ground. Considering a family size of four, the waste generated can be filled in one of the pipe for 30-35 days till it is full. Once it is full, the first pipe is closed and then for the next 30 days' waste is filled into the other pipe. By the time the second pipe is full, waste in the first one would be converted into compost. The people who cannot afford the plants due to space or financial constraints were asked to group together and install one plant in the neighbourhood and use it.

Kerala Veterinary and Animal Science University developed one more model which consists of a tank made of bricks. Under this model, air enters into the tank by specifically created gaps on the sides. It treats about two tons of waste and process it into compost in 90 days. Bottom of the tank is filled with a layer of fresh cow dung to generate microbes for composting

12 waste collection centres with 165 of these bins at public places are established on suitable locations. Those workers who used to transport the waste earlier to Sarvodayapuram landfill site were used to maintain these bins. About 10,000 households not having any alternate waste treatment facilities were associated with collection centres where waste is treated through aerobic bins. Generated compost is distributed to farmers free of cost thereby reducing the dependency on chemical fertilisers and will in turn lead to an increase in their household income.

It was observed that plastic was 5% out of the total generated waste in the city. The Municipal Corporation conducts a Plastic collection drive once every two months and the plastic waste collected is sent to a recycling facility in Erode, Tamil Nadu. Clubs have been formed in Schools and Colleges and students are often roped in for the collection drives for plastic wastes.

There are two key aspects in this model, first, small and cost effective innovations were done by the involved agencies like ANERT, IRTC and Kerala Veterinary and Animal Science University which made waste management possible at the origination level and second, the efforts of the Municipal Corporation to increase participation of the citizens. WATSAN (Water and Sanitation) clubs were introduced in the schools to create awareness. Student cadets were formed to prevent public from throwing waste as well as Self Help Groups were also involved to provide technical support and required services at the household level. They took over the responsibility of identifying beneficiaries, installing the technology and providing support services after installation to households. CCTVs were installed at public spaces and squads were formed to monitor and penalise those who do not dispose waste at the designated spots.

The 12 wards where this programme was implemented have been declared as Total Sanitation Wards. More than 80% of the households in these wards now have either the pipe composting or the biogas plant.

Case - 4: Multi -Pronged Sanitation and Hygiene Initiatives by Rec Limited (Rec Limited: Formerly Known as Rural Electrification Corporation)

REC remains as one of the very old and committed stakeholder in Government India's drive under the massively ambitious programmes SBMG (Swachh Bharat Mission-Gramin). Through it's CSR initiatives this remains as one of the critical component. While the Gramin mission entered to the phase 2 with focus on ODF-Plus (Open-defecation free), the main focus holds on promoting the right behaviour among masses and development of safe management practices of solid and liquid waste in rural areas. REC limited has been very consistent and working sincerely towards the phase 2 mandate of ODF-Plus through various innovative initiatives (recindia.nic.in).

- Behaviour change communication: For enhancing the dissemination and adoption of key message around safe sanitation practices, REC got involved in development of 26 episodes of 20 minutes each in season 3 of a unique programme, "*Main Kuch Bhi Kar Sakti Hoon*" (mkbksh.org).
- It also has adopted an entire slum under Swachha Action Plan (SAP) for cleanliness of toilets through use of diverse IEC materials. Sanitation, hygiene and drinking water facility were also the key areas of intervention under the plan and improvements targeted.
- It has constructed about 12,500 girls' and boys' toilets in Government Schools under Swachh Vidyalaya Abhiyaan in six states namely, Bihar, Telangana, Rajasthan, Madhya Pradesh, Punjab, Uttar Pradesh (recindia.nic.in).
- It has worked on provisioning of running water arrangement facility in toilets constructed in schools
- Provisioning support to Mechanized Sweeping, collection and transportation of Municipal Solid Waste
- Provisioning assistance for procurement of e-rickshaws for garbage pick-up in Delhi
- Setting-up of an electric crematorium in Ghaziabad

Impact of these multi-pronged initiatives of REC in and around the intervened rural communities are as below:

- Significant Reduction in open defecation in intervened areas
- Improvement in overall hygienic practices
- Increase in school enrolment and attendance
- Reduction in drop outs, especially amongst girls
- Water and sanitation facility's access increased considerably
- Reduction in poor sanitation related diseases like diarrhoea, soil transmitted helminths, trachoma and scabies
- Better understanding in the households pertaining to sanitation and hygiene

Table 1.

S	Segregate waste
P	Practise composting
A	Awareness generation
R	Reduce, reuse & recycle
S	Safe sanitation
H	Hygiene for all

Case – 5: Sparsh by Apollo Tyre Foundation

SPARSH is the initiative under the CSR wing (Apollo Tyre Foundation) of Apollo Tyres which aims at providing the associated stakeholders and community services around waste management and better hygiene. This initiative was launched in year 2013 and have reached out to a diverse and large community in past many years. The outreach under initiatives spans across multiple states in India wherever the private entity has the key communities associated with (apollotyres.com).

The key objectives of SPARSH has been

- To create awareness on solid waste management
- To improve the overall quality of life of people
- To promote cleanliness and green cover
- To develop hygiene practices
- To introduce scientific waste disposal methods
- To eradicate open defecation

SPARSH has 4 major programmes under its umbrella which are Clean My Village Project (CMV), Clean My Transport Nagar Project (CMTN), sanitation management and End-of-Life Tyre (ELT) playground. CMTN and CMV focuses on waste management and proper cleanliness in identified villages and areas of the company which represent its trans-shipment areas and also community in surrounding areas of manufacturing zone. Under these initiatives, the implementers carry out the collection of door-to-door waste, road sanitisation and cleaning, information and awareness drive, segregation of waste and composting.

Further, under its total sanitation programme, the Company focuses on building toilets and bathing areas for under privileged community to eradicate defecation and promote overall hygiene, induce better quality of life.

The 4th project under SPARSH is making of End-of-Life Tyre (ELT) spaces where recycling of waste to be taken up and further linked to several income generation opportunities for community.

During 2019-20, initiative has reached out to 13,378 people while adopting door-to-door method for waste collection activity and awareness promotion has resulted in covering 13,310 people. Some very specific products like Paper Mache products and plastic derived tiles have been made using collected waste and processing them. Compost material and incense sticks are being prepared under the project from floral waste.

Under SPARSH construction of 122 toilets has been completed in last year only for vulnerable class of the society in the Chennai industrial area. Approximately 488 beneficiaries have been directly benefited with these toilets having extra bathing space. Additionally, two operation playgrounds (made of ELT) have been constructed at different locations during last years to promote recycling.

C. DURING AND POST PANDEMIC (COVID 19) WASTE MANAGEMENT TRENDS AND FUTURE STRATEGY

During the pandemic waste management has become more challenging as the plastic usage has gone drastically up during the pandemic and the trend is continuing till today. This is because of packaging requirements, medical gears waste and demand of single-use items and medicinal waste etc. Lot of waste has been generated during diagnosis and treatment at different healthcare facilities, hospitals, testing centres, laboratories etc. Covid-19 virus has added lot many challenges in handling the medical waste and lot many countries have started following the WHO guidelines for waste management in infected areas specifically. In this direction, use of landfills has gone up considerably and it was found most safe for the contagious waste coming out of healthcare institutions (WHO, 2020).

International Practices

At the international level also, lot many countries have adopted numerous new practices to contain this type of waste. Waste generated out of medical facilities must be strictly kept is specific bags or collection units and sealed properly before any movement. Use of high temperature burners has also been a good way to handle the critical waste. Apart from landfills cement kilns and factory based furnaces have been found good alternative for disposal of this waste.

Centres for Disease control and Prevention, USA has issued guidelines to treat the all medical waste with same protocol with strict safety measures (Commendatore, 2020). Jordon has followed rigorous ways to handle the solid waste by segregating the different type of waste, using all kind of safety gears, disinfectant sprays for facilities, staff and separate transport facilities on daily basis (ISWA Jordon, 2020). Philippines has established separate waste transport unit for handling medical waste during the pandemic with separately registered vehicles, trained staff and dedicatedly disposing at distant remote islands (EMB, 2020).

Future Strategy to Improve Further

All across the world, civic authorities have faced lot many challenges as they were in an unprecedented situation during the pandemic. Going with the best available resources, authorities requisitioned separate gears (like PPE kits, gloves, face-shields etc.), transport vehicles and dedicated trained staff in large numbers to manage the solid waste of this nature. Indeed, waste management infrastructure like latest gears, machines, transport vehicles, waste disposal applications have to be added in adequate numbers so that positives of this development can be felt for many decades.

New measures like use of colour specific plastic bags or container (mostly used red or yellow packs for infectious waste) for waste segregation, time bound waste disposal (most likely daily), proper training of staff, strict and efficient waste disposal protocols and development of technology based immediate waste disposal methods and exploring innovative recycling techniques have been touched upon and further work on it will be hallmark of the waste management strategies during and post pandemic scenario.

D. DISCUSSION AND SUGGESTIONS

It is evident that the first requirement of any project in Solid Waste management is the will of the existing government machinery, the concerned civic bodies. If the Municipalities or concerned civic bodies in rural or semi-urban areas take lead, the community participation is bound to come. SWM Rules 2016 mandate waste segregation at the household level in three specific categories such as biodegradable, non-biodegradable and hazardous waste. Further, segregated waste must reach to the relevant stakeholders such as vendors / workers authorised to collect the locality level waste. If the waste generators i.e. households are sensitised about this and a clear system is established the waste management becomes easier and more effective. The lack of awareness in public regarding the process of segregation needs to be addressed to make any project successful. Also improvement in segregation also improves the value and quality of material that can be recycled which further improves the sustainability of the project. Hence awareness campaigns need to be regular to emphasise the need of segregation at the source.

Moreover, waste pickers, who are key workers in the entire programme, must be aligned with Deendayal Antyodaya Yojana-National Urban Livelihoods Mission to improve their livelihoods and lifestyle as well as their skills and capabilities.

A number of technologies are available today for scientific waste collection and management but a suitable and balanced approach as per the local conditions and the type of the waste generated must be adopted. Although the cases taken up for consideration belong to areas with smaller populations but the same can be extrapolated for bigger cities as well. A cluster based approach can be devised for bigger cities. Innovations adopted in discussed interventions are very effective and can be replicated very easily.

As the sustainability of the discussed interventions are dependent on the revenue obtained from salvaged recyclable items sale to the suitable customers, as a support measure, creation of an online portal for the sale of items to a wider public will help in getting higher revenues. Also SHGs can be encouraged and trained to create units which can add further value to the products and market linkages can be provided to facilitate the sale of end products. Improving the involvement of local community by providing more jobs can be counted as the key outcome at the end.

E. CONCLUSION

Proper management of waste is very important for a sustainable development, to prevent growing public health hazards and ecological imbalance. Operating of waste management services requires innovative technologies to provide efficient integrated systems & sustainable model, and needs to be socially accepted also. Government of India and some of the key stake holders including CSR entities (Csrbox, 2021) have been working relentlessly to optimize the resource utilization for a better waste management under Swachh Bharat Abhiyan. Civic bodies have also started competing with each other better for Swachh Survey Ranking as fund disbursement has been linked with the performance of the civic body towards waste management and sanitation initiates. Absence of bigger players in waste management sector has facilitated lot many small enterprises to prove their metal (Swach Survekshan, 2020).

Different countries also adopting environment friendly innovative measures towards medical and other solid waste management. Lot of experience sharing and dialogues have produced robust waste management and disposal protocols which have used extensively across the world during and post pandemic days. Lot of resources have been invested in waste management to safeguard citizens during the pandemic and currently further value addition is still a possibility.

Green funds availability in this sector opens up a great opportunity for socially sensitive entrepreneurs and enterprises having passion and expertise in this sector. Lot many enterprises have already accepted the challenges prevailing and planned or started working on their own or in collaboration with civic bodies. Media has also played a great role in spreading the positive environment and reporting about good initiatives on the theme. These developments are presenting the silver lining of this journey from waste to wealth which is getting stronger day by day.

REFERENCES

Arti, P., & Meka, S. (2014). *Municipal Solid Waste Management In India: A Review And Some New Results.* Retrieved from https://www.researchgate.net/publication/260230170_MUNICIPAL_SOLID_WASTE_MANAGEMENT_IN_INDIA_A_REVIEW_AND_SOME_NEW_RESULTS

CEPT University. (2011). *What works.* Leading Practices Catalogue from Municipalities and Municipal Corporations of Gujarat For Performance Assessment System Project. Retrieved from https://pas.org.in/Portal/document/ResourcesFiles/GoodPracticeDocs/pdfs/Leading%20Practices_What%20Works.pdf

Commendatore, C. (2020). *Coronavirus Impacts Hit Solid Waste Managers, Generators.* https://www.waste360.com/medical-waste/coronavirus-impacts-hit-solid-waste-managers-generators

Csrbox. (2021). *Top 10 Waste Management Projects Though CSR in India.* Retrieved from https://csrbox.org/India_CSR_news_Top-10-Waste-Management-Projects-Though-CSR-in-India_1020

EMB. (2020). *Management of Infectious Healthcare Waste During Covid-19 Pandemic*. https://emb.gov.ph/management-of-infectious-healthcare-waste-during-covid-19-pandemic/

Ganesan, P. (2017). *Implementation of Decentralized Waste Management in Kerala: A Comparative Analysis of Alappuzha and Thiruvananthapuram*. Academic Press.

ISWA-Jordan. (2020). *Country Specific Waste Management Responses, COVID-19 Response International knowledge sharing on Waste Management*. https://www.iswa.org/fileadmin/galleries/0001_COVID/Jordan_Solid_Waste_Handling_Manual_Coronavirus_crisisENG.pdf

Kumar, S., Bhattachryya, J. K., Vaidya, A.N., Chakrabarti, T., Devotta, S., & Akolkar, A.B. (2009). *Assessment of the status of municipal solid waste management in metro cities, state capitals, class I cities, and class II towns in India: An insight Waste Management*. Retrieved from https://www.sciencedirect.com/science/article/abs/pii/S0956053X08001529

MKBKSH Website. (n.d.). *The Journey So Far*. Retrieved from https://mkbksh.org/about-main-kuch-bhi-kar-sakti-hoon/#season-1-and-2

NIUA. (2020). *Swachh Bharat Mission – Urban - "Guidance on Efficient Collection And Transportation Of Municipal Solid Waste" – July 2020*. Retrieved from https://www.niua.org/csc/assets/pdf/key-documents/phase-2/Waste/SBM-Guidance-on-Efficient-Collection-and-Transportation-of-MSW.pdf

Purohit, M. (2018). *Lessons in waste management from a small town in Chhattisgarh*. Retrieved from https://yourstory.com/2018/03/ambikapurwaste-management/amp

Raveesh, Mona, & Jayveer. (2015). *Waste Management Initiatives in India for Human Well Being*. Retrieved from https://smartnet.niua.org/content/a94538d0-540c-408d-9534-5be38586d8e4

REC Website. (n.d.). *Sanitation & Hygiene*. Retrieved from https://www.recindia.nic.in/sanitation-and-hygiene

Survekshan, S. (2020). Innovation and Best Practices. Report by Ministry of Housing and Urban Affairs, Government of India.

Tripathy, U. (2018). *A 21st Century Vision on Waste to Energy in India: A Win- Win Strategy for Energy Security and Swachh Bharat Mission (Clean India Mission).* Background paper for Eighth Regional 3R Forum in Asia and the Pacific. United Nations Centre For Regional Development. Retrieved from https://www.uncrd.or.jp/content/documents/6717FINAL-Background%20paper_Tripathy.pdf

Tyres, A. (2013). *Environment.* Retrieved from https://corporate.apollotyres.com/responsibility/environment/

WHO. (2020). *Water, sanitation, hygiene, and waste management for the COVID-19 virus: Interim guidance.* World Health Organization. https://www.who.int/publications-detail/water-sanitation-hygiene-and-waste-management-for-covid-19

Conclusion

SUMMARY AND FUTURE RESEARCH DIRECTIONS

Social entrepreneurship is construed as an innovative activity aimed at addressing or mitigating social issues and offers the potential to shift civil society through innovative social ventures that pursue profit and purpose (Alberti and Varon Garrido, 2017). Social entrepreneurs drive social innovation and transformation in various fields, including education, tourism, health, the environment, and enterprise development (Bansal, Garg, and Sharma, 2019). The United Nations General Assembly adopted the 2030 Agenda for Sustainable Development and 17 Sustainable Development Goals (SDGs) as a universal and transformative development strategy (Fischer *et al.*, 2021). The 2030 Agenda commits the global community to "achieving sustainable development in its three dimensions—economic, social and environmental—in a balanced and integrated manner" (Tate and Bals, 2018). Research on social entrepreneurship vastly agrees on entrepreneurs with a social agenda to solve a public goods problem caused by a combination of market and government failure (Santos, 2012).

There is a strong connection between government agenda, corporate responsibility, social entrepreneurship, value creation, and sustainable development (Baima *et al.*, 2020). All enterprises should have an agenda for fulfilling their social responsibility and satisfying the triple bottom line requirements (TBL) defined by Elkington's 1997 framework: economic, environmental, and social sustainability (Tate and Bals, 2018). In social enterprises, social value initiatives are rooted at the time of enterprise creation, while in commercial enterprises, it comes later as an operational strategy (Alberti and Varon Garrido, 2017). The conventional form of corporate social responsibility seems less relevant in the changed scenario, with increased awareness and expectation of people from the government and institutions (Legrand, Sloan, and Chen, 2018). The actions and social responsibility of corporates and universities should be centered on social innovations, sustainable social change, and social inclusiveness (Calic and Mosakowski, 2016).

Educational institutes and universities play a vital role in developing students' ethical behavior, which is crucial for a person to think and work for a social cause (Aubry *et al.*, 2021). Social entrepreneurship courses have a growing presence in developed countries like USA and UK (Forliano, De Bernardi and Yahiaoui, 2021). The convergence of values, skills, and knowledge delivered in these programs is highly significant to students who endeavor to be social entrepreneurs (Bansal, Garg and Sharma, 2019). There are many instances where academic entrepreneurs have undertaken commercial activities and have contributed to social innovation (Skute, 2019). The role of entrepreneurial universities as incubators is crucial in the process of social innovation and in the development of social entrepreneurship mindset (Jabeen, Faisal and Katsioloudes, 2017). Thus, it is imperative to recognize the strong relationship between entrepreneurial universities' activities and economic growth driven by social innovation (Witkamp *et al.*, 2017). This would pave the way for universities to contribute toward the fulfillment of SDGs.

CHAPTER SUMMARIES

The first chapter provides a comprehensive overview of Social Entrepreneurship, Sustainability, and Value Creation using a systematic review and thematic mapping of the literature. The chapter contributes to the field primarily in two ways. First, the publication patterns spread across the last 20 years were examined by categorizing and analyzing the literature according to the author, journal, institution, and country. Second, the most influential authors and works were identified by carrying out citation analysis. The findings and analysis suggest that authors from across the world have contributed to this field; however, their relational ties are not heterogeneous and significant impact is confined to a few authors. The most influential works were also identified, which were pivotal in developing this research field and had a global impact. The keyword and co-occurrence analyses illustrate that the focus of critical researchers has been on social enterprise and sustainable development.

The book's second chapter addresses the social entrepreneurs' use of private wealth. The chapter has addressed the research gap of how the private wealth of an individual might affect the probability of becoming a social entrepreneur. The two-research hypothesis have been tested; First, to test the link between an individual's private wealth and the probability of becoming a social entrepreneur, and second is about, whether the probability of becoming a social entrepreneur is embedded in their core beliefs and, therefore not linked to their personal level of wealth. The study affirms that a particular group of individuals to become entrepreneurs don't care about amassing financial resources before becoming self-employed. They rather become entrepreneurs and start a social venture solely based on their altruistic and compassionate motives. On the other hand, the second group starts a social venture only if they have reached a certain amount of private wealth and then starts to engage in more social endeavors, as they consider this a personal fulfillment activity and less critical than a basic need.

The book's third chapter has helped showcase the research development in the field of social entrepreneurship in the last five years (2017-2021). The data was extracted from the Scopus database using the search string; "Social entrepreneurship" OR "Social entrepreneur" OR "Social entrepreneurial". The chapter has contributed to displaying the current trends in social entrepreneurship, influential authors and articles, and conceptual and social structures of social entrepreneurship. The findings suggest that research on social entrepreneurship has been extensively carried out in developed countries like the United States, the United Kingdom, and Spain. The publication trends on social entrepreneurship have been upward sloping in the last five years. This reflects an overall increased interest in this research domain. Findings also reflect that the active work on social entrepreneurship has also picked up in developing countries like India.

The fourth chapter in this book has provided an overview of the effect of Covid-19 on HEIs & Entrepreneurship education in the GCC countries. This paper is based on the literature published in the arena of entrepreneurship education in the context of covid-19 lacks empirical evidence from the GCC countries. The article has evaluated the aspects of online and offline teaching and has tried to contextualize the same with the GCC scenario. The study recommends that the aspirations from entrepreneurship education can be fulfilled only with proper coordination of different stakeholders, the strategic intervention of the policymakers, and the involvement of higher education institutions in an aligned manner.

The fifth chapter in this book is a primary data-based study measuring the impact of social entrepreneurial education on the entrepreneurial intention with a mediating role of entrepreneurial self-efficacy. The database has been drawn from the University of Buraimi and Modern College of Business and Science, Oman. One of the recommendations from the analysis is that social entrepreneurship education is inefficient in stimulating the social entrepreneurship intentions among students in Oman. Unless those students have social entrepreneurship self-efficacy, they will not take social entrepreneurship as a career option. Individuals' confidence in their ability to deal with or manage entrepreneurial activities, known as entrepreneurial self-efficacy, has been found to mediate between education and entrepreneurial intention. Therefore, the authors believe that extra efforts are required to build students' confidence, and civic responsibility needs to be developed among the youngsters. In addition, an increased interface with government programs, access to CSR funds, and corporate governance are also required.

The sixth chapter in the book is based on quantifying the effect of social vision, social innovativeness, risk-taking, entrepreneurial education, and perception of business environment on social entrepreneurial attitude and further the impact of social entrepreneurial attitude on social entrepreneurial intention. The study has used the most advanced techniques for the data analysis; structural equation modeling (PLS-SEM) and purposive sampling techniques have been used for the data collection. The study has given promising results; the positive and significant impact of social vision, social innovativeness, and entrepreneurial education on attitude towards social entrepreneurship. Findings have recognized the role of universities in encouraging students and building their attitude towards social entrepreneurship.

The seventh chapter in the book is a qualitative paper based on 114 articles (2007-2022) drawn from the literature. The chapter helps to unearth the field of green entrepreneurship in terms of its principal authors, publications, prominent journals, and the essential keywords forming the conceptual structure of the research domain. Green entrepreneurship has the potential to become the inspirational force behind the development of a new comprehensive sustainable system in all three aspects –environment, economy, and society. The concept of green entrepreneurship has gained momentum, and a spike in publications was noticed in early 2020. The United Kingdom has made the most scholarly contributions, research work in this sector, followed by France and China, and its engagement with emerging economies is now expanding.

The eighth chapter in the book provides evidence from a country-wise panel data investigation' is an attempt to establish the relationship between sustainable development and green entrepreneurship, entrepreneurship ecosystem, social development, and economic development. The empirical results infer that green entrepreneurship and sustainable development have a positive and causal relationship. Social development and environmental sustainability would be improved as more green entrepreneurship practices increase. Social development, science & technological development, and entrepreneurship ecosystem could be improved as economic development increases. Environmental sustainability is likely to be improved as social development, economic development, and green entrepreneurship increase. Therefore, agricultural and industrial sectors should use green technology to increase environmental sustainability (Singh et al., 2022). The agricultural sector should avoid extensively applying fertilizer and pesticides in cultivation (Kumar et al., 2017; Singh et al., 2022).

The ninth chapter in the book has illuminated a positive relationship between green entrepreneurship and sustainable development. In particular, green entrepreneurship had a more decisive influence than non-green entrepreneurship in all the domains of sustainable development. The findings also confirm the bidirectional nature of the relationship between green entrepreneurship and sustainable development in urban contexts. Policymakers from government and private agencies should think and consider what activities should be taken into consideration as green. Green entrepreneurs will increase in number, and eco-friendly businesses will grow strongly. One can achieve stable global green economic growth by combining the policies, social, government, and private enterprises. On the other side, when consumers are aware of the importance of green products, they will prioritize the Eco-Friendly product and help develop a stable, sustainable environment and social value.

The tenth chapter in the book adds value to the discussion on social entrepreneurship; this chapter focuses on the need for innovations in the agricultural sector and suggests vertical farming as one of the solutions for increasing productivity. The human population is growing, and the resources to support agriculture, i.e., water bodies, fertile soil, and arable land, are shrinking. To this issue, vertical farming through modern techniques appears to be a feasible solution. However, this area has attracted very little attention from researchers across the globe, with minimal quality studies and low country representation. The need for the hour would be to promote studies in social entrepreneurship and agriculture.

The eleventh chapter of the book emphasizes that waste segregation is one of the most significant issues that poses a major challenge to successfully implementing solid waste management initiatives. The chapter demonstrates ways to tackle the issues in a solid waste management system with the help of two live cases from different parts of the states in India. Proper waste management is crucial for sustainable development, preventing growing public health hazards and ecological imbalance. The government of India and some critical stakeholders, including CSR entities (Csrbox, 2021), have been working relentlessly to optimize resource utilization for better waste management under Swachh Bharat Abhiyan. Civic bodies have also started competing proactively for higher Swachh Survey Ranking as fund disbursement has been linked with the performance of the civic body towards waste management and sanitation initiatives.

FUTURE RESEARCH DIRECTIONS

The contributed chapters have addressed the various dimensions and issues in the field of social entrepreneurship. Based on the chapter's findings and available literature, various gaps have been identified in the literature and framed as future research directions. First and foremost, since the research field is still growing, there is a lot of scope to incorporate variables like demographic, personality, income sources, and behavioral factors that have not been studied so far. Secondly, the literature lacks cross-country and cross-cultural studies in this domain. There is much scope for comparative studies between countries, like developing and developed and low-income and high-income countries.

Contextual factors highly influence social entrepreneurial activities; therefore, under-explored countries and sectors require quick attention in the future. Most of the research in social entrepreneurship has been from developed countries and selected sectors like micro-finance, education, tourism, and the health industry. Most studies on social entrepreneurship have focused on health, poverty, and education problems; other problems like gender discrimination, women empowerment, and child abuse also require immediate attention by future researchers. Moreover, researchers may use different analysis techniques on a more extensive sample set, which will provide confirmation and robustness to the existing findings, thereby helping in decision-making by the policymakers.

The Editors

REFERENCES

Alberti, F. G., & Varon Garrido, M. A. (2017). Can profit and sustainability goals co-exist? New business models for hybrid firms. *The Journal of Business Strategy*, *38*(1), 3–13. doi:10.1108/JBS-12-2015-0124

Aubry, M. (2021). Higher Education For Sustainability: A Global Perspective. *Journal of Cleaner Production. Elsevier Ltd*, *2*(3), 41–51. doi:10.1002/pmj

Baima, G., Forliano, C., Santoro, G., & Vrontis, D. (2020). Intellectual capital and business model: A systematic literature review to explore their linkages. *Journal of Intellectual Capital*, *22*(3), 653–679. doi:10.1108/JIC-02-2020-0055

Bansal, S., Garg, I., & Sharma, G. D. (2019). Social entrepreneurship as a path for social change and driver of sustainable development: A systematic review and research agenda. *Sustainability (Switzerland)*, *11*(4), 1091. Advance online publication. doi:10.3390u11041091

Calic, G., & Mosakowski, E. (2016). Kicking Off Social Entrepreneurship: How A Sustainability Orientation Influences Crowdfunding Success. *Journal of Management Studies*, *53*(5), 738–767. doi:10.1111/joms.12201

Fischer, B., Guerrero, M., Guimón, J., & Schaeffer, P. R. (2021). Knowledge transfer for frugal innovation: Where do entrepreneurial universities stand? *Journal of Knowledge Management*, *25*(2), 360–379. doi:10.1108/JKM-01-2020-0040

Forliano, C., De Bernardi, P., & Yahiaoui, D. (2021). Entrepreneurial universities: A bibliometric analysis within the business and management domains. *Technological Forecasting and Social Change. Elsevier Inc., 165*, 120522. doi:10.1016/j.techfore.2020.120522

Jabeen, F., Faisal, M. N., & Katsioloudes, M. I. (2017). Entrepreneurial mindset and the role of universities as strategic drivers of entrepreneurship: Evidence from the United Arab Emirates. *Journal of Small Business and Enterprise Development, 24*(1), 136–157. doi:10.1108/JSBED-07-2016-0117

Legrand, W., Sloan, P., & Chen, J. S. (2018). Corporate social responsibility and social entrepreneurship. *Sustainability in the Hospitality Industry, 16*(3), 297–334. doi:10.9774/gleaf.9781315690261_13

Santos, F. M. (2012). A Positive Theory of Social Entrepreneurship. *Journal of Business Ethics, 111*(3), 335–351. doi:10.100710551-012-1413-4

Skute, I. (2019). 'Opening the black box of academic entrepreneurship: A bibliometric analysis', *Scientometrics. Springer International Publishing, 120*(1), 237–265. doi:10.100711192-019-03116-w

Tate, W. L., & Bals, L. (2018). Achieving Shared Triple Bottom Line (TBL) Value Creation: Toward a Social Resource-Based View (SRBV) of the Firm. *Journal of Business Ethics. Springer Netherlands, 152*(3), 803–826. doi:10.100710551-016-3344-y

Witkamp, M. J. (2017). Strategic niche management of social innovations : the case of social entrepreneurship Strategic niche management of social innovations : the case of social entrepreneurship. *Technology Analysis and Strategic Management, 7325*(August), 37–41.

Compilation of References

A., L., & D., D. (2012). *Social Entrepreneurship. In Entrepreneurship - Gender, Geographies and Social Context*. InTech. doi:10.5772/36056

Abuzayed, B., & Al-Fayomi, N. (2021). Risk spill over from crude oil prices to GCC stock market returns: New evidence during the COVID-19 outbreak. *The North American Journal of Economics and Finance*, *58*, 101476. doi:10.1016/j.najef.2021.101476

Acs, Z. J., Boardman, M. C., & McNeely, C. L. (2013). The social value of productive entrepreneurship. *Small Business Economics*, *40*(3), 785–796. doi:10.100711187-011-9396-6

Adusei, M. (2016). Does entrepreneurship promote economic growth in Africa? *African Development Review*, *28*(2), 201–214. doi:10.1111/1467-8268.12190

AeroFarms. (2016). *Farms That Rise to the Challenge*. https://www.aerofarms.com/2016/05/17/vertical-farming-challenge/

Afzal, M. N. I., Siddiqui, S., & Dutta, S. (2018). Determinants of entrepreneurial capability (EC) environment in ASEAN-05 economies-a log-linear stochastic frontier analysis. *Journal of Global Entrepreneurship Research*, *18*(1), 8–14. doi:10.118640497-018-0101-y

Ahmad Khan, S., & Magd, H. (2021). Empirical examination of MS Teams in conducting webinar: Evidence from international online program conducted in Oman. *Journal of Content Community and Communication*, *14*(8), 159–175. doi:10.31620/JCCC.12.21/13

Ahmad, N. H., Halim, H. A., Ramayah, T., & Rahman, S. A. (2015). Green entrepreneurship inclination among generation Y: The road towards a green economy. *Problems and Perspectives in Management*, *13*(2), 211–218.

Ajzen, I. (2011). The theory of planned behaviour: Reactions and reflections. *Psychology & Health*, 1113–1127.

Akbostanci, E., Türüt-Asik, S., & Tunc, I. G. (2009). The relationship between income and environment in Turkey: Is there an environmental Kuznets curve? *Energy Policy*, *37*(2), 861–867. doi:10.1016/j.enpol.2008.09.088

Al Harrasi, N., Hakro, A. N., Srinivasan, V., Matriano, M. T., & Jabri, AL, M. (2021). Social Media Impact on Young Entrepreneurs in Oman. *Indian Journal of Economics and Business, 20*(3), 1365–1392.

Alberti, F. G., & Varon Garrido, M. A. (2017). Can profit and sustainability goals co-exist? New business models for hybrid firms. *The Journal of Business Strategy, 38*(1), 3–13. doi:10.1108/JBS-12-2015-0124

Albort-Morant, G., & Ribeiro-Soriano, D. (2016). A bibliometric analysis of international impact of business incubators. *Journal of Business Research. Elsevier Inc., 69*(5), 1775–1779. doi:10.1016/j.jbusres.2015.10.054

Al-Kharusi, S., & Murthy, S. R. (2020, December). Financial Stability of GCC Banks in the COVID-19 Crisis: A Simulation Approach. *The Journal of Asian Finance, Economics and Business, 7*(12), 337–344. doi:10.13106/jafeb.2020.vol7.no12.337

Allen, J., & Malin, S. (2008). Green Entrepreneurship: A Method for Managing Natural Resources? *Society &amp. Natural Resources, 21*(9), 828–844. doi:10.1080/08941920701612917

Alon, I., Farrell, M., & Li, S. (2020). *Regime type and COVID-19 response*. FIIB Business Review. doi:10.1177/2319714520928884

Alsaleh, Y., & Mahroum, S. (2014). A Critical Review of the Interplay between Policy Instruments and Business Models: Greening the Built Environment a Case in Point. SSRN *Electronic Journal*. doi:10.2139/ssrn.2429275

Alwakid, W., Aparicio, S., & Urbano, D. (2020). Cultural antecedents of green entrepreneurship in Saudi Arabia: An institutional approach. *Sustainability, 12*(9), 1–20. doi:10.3390u12093673

Alwakid, W., Aparicio, S., & Urbano, D. (2021). The influence of green entrepreneurship on sustainable development in Saudi Arabia: The role of formal institutions. *International Journal of Environmental Research and Public Health, 18*(5433), 1–23. doi:10.3390/ijerph18105433 PMID:34069588

Anand, A., Argade, P., Barkemeyer, R., & Salignac, F. (2021). Trends and patterns in sustainable entrepreneurship research: A bibliometric review and research agenda. *Journal of Business Venturing, 36*(3), 106092. Advance online publication. doi:10.1016/j.jbusvent.2021.106092

Angelidou, M., & Psaltoglou, A. (2017). An empirical investigation of social innovation initiatives for sustainable urban development. Sustainable Cities and Society, 33(December), 113–125. doi:10.1016/j.scs.2017.05.016

Anggadwita, G., Luturlean, B., Ramadani, V., & Ratten, V. (2017a). Socio-cultural environments and emerging economy entrepreneurship: Women entrepreneurs in Indonesia. *Journal of Entrepreneurship in Emerging Economies, 9*(1), 85–96. doi:10.1108/JEEE-03-2016-0011

Anggadwita, G., Ramadani, V., Alamanda, D. T., Ratten, V., & Hashani, M. (2017b). Entrepreneurial intentions from an Islamic perspective: A study of Muslim entrepreneurs in Indonesia. *International Journal of Entrepreneurship and Small Business, 31*(2), 165–179. doi:10.1504/IJESB.2017.10004845

Antolin-Lopez, R., Martinez-del-Rio, J., & Cespedes-Lorente, J. (2019). Environmental entrepreneurship as a multi-component and dynamic construct: Duality of goals, environmental agency, and environmental value creation. *Business Ethics (Oxford, England), 28*(4), 407–422. doi:10.1111/beer.12229

Archambault, & Campbell, Y. G., & V. L. (2013). Full-Text Citation Analysis : A New Method to Enhance. *Journal of the American Society for Information Science and Technology, 64*(July), 1852–1863. doi:10.1002/asi

Aria, M., & Cuccurullo, C. (2017). bibliometrix: An R-tool for comprehensive science mapping analysis. *Journal of Informetrics. Elsevier Ltd, 11*(4), 959–975. doi:10.1016/j.joi.2017.08.007

Armeanu, D. S., Vintila, G., & Gherghina, S. C. (2018). Empirical study towards the drivers of sustainable economic growth in EU-28 countries. *Sustainability, 10*(4), 1-22.

Arti, P., & Meka, S. (2014). *Municipal Solid Waste Management In India: A Review And Some New Results.* Retrieved from https://www.researchgate.net/publication/260230170_MUNICIPAL_SOLID_WASTE_MANAGEMENT_IN_INDIA_A_REVIEW_AND_SOME_NEW_RESULTS

Aubry, M. (2021). Higher Education For Sustainability: A Global Perspective. *Journal of Cleaner Production. Elsevier Ltd, 2*(3), 41–51. doi:10.1002/pmj

Audretsch, D. B., Belitski, M., & Desai, S. (2015). Entrepreneurship and economic development in cities. *The Annals of Regional Science, 55*(1), 3360. doi:10.100700168-015-0685-x

Austin, J., Stevenson, H., & Wei–Skillern, J. (2006). Social and Commercial Entrepreneurship: Same, Different, or Both? *Entrepreneurship Theory and Practice, 30*(1), 1–22. doi:10.1111/j.1540-6520.2006.00107.x

Austin, J., Stevenson, H., & Wei-Skillern, J. (2012). Social and commercial entrepreneurship: Same, different, or both? *Revista ADM, 47*(3), 370–384.

Bacq, S., & Alt, E. (2018). Feeling capable and valued: A prosocial perspective on the link between empathy and social entrepreneurial intentions. *Journal of Business Venturing, 33*(3), 333–350. doi:10.1016/j.jbusvent.2018.01.004

Bacq, S., Geoghegan, W., Josefy, M., Stevenson, R., & Williams, T. (2020). The COVID-19 virtual idea blitz: Marshalling social entrepreneurship to rapidly respond to urgent grand challenges. *Business Horizons, 63*(6), 705–723. doi:10.1016/j.bushor.2020.05.002 PMID:32398883

Bacq, S., & Janssen, F. (2011). The multiple faces of social entrepreneurship: A review of definitional issues based on geographical and thematic criteria. *Entrepreneurship and Regional Development, 23*(5-6), 373–403. doi:10.1080/08985626.2011.577242

Bacq, S., & Lumpkin, G. T. (2020). Social entrepreneurship and COVID-19. *Journal of Management Studies*. Advance online publication. doi:10.1111/joms.12641 PMID:32398883

Badr, N., El-Gharbawy, A., Wahba, M., & Bary, A. A. (2018). The impact of entrepreneurship education on planned behavior. *The Business and Management Review*, *9*(4), 213–222.

Bahrini, R., & Filfilan, A. (2020). Impact of the novel coronavirus on stock market returns: Evidence from GCC countries. *Quantitative Finance and Economics.*, *4*(4), 640–652. doi:10.3934/QFE.2020029

Baima, G., Forliano, C., Santoro, G., & Vrontis, D. (2020). Intellectual capital and business model: A systematic literature review to explore their linkages. *Journal of Intellectual Capital*, *22*(3), 653–679. doi:10.1108/JIC-02-2020-0055

Bansal, S., Garg, I., & Sharma, G. D. (2019). Social entrepreneurship as a path for social change and driver of sustainable development: A systematic review and research agenda. *Sustainability (Switzerland)*, *11*(4), 1091. Advance online publication. doi:10.3390u11041091

Baptista, R., Karaöz, M., & Mendonça, J. (2014). The impact of human capital on the early success of necessity versus opportunity-based entrepreneurs. *Small Business Economics*, *42*(4), 831–847. doi:10.100711187-013-9502-z

Barberá-Tomás, D., Castelló, I., de Bakker, F. G., & Zietsma, C. (2019). Energizing through visuals: How social entrepreneurs use emotion-symbolic work for social change. *Academy of Management Journal*, *62*(6), 1789–1817. doi:10.5465/amj.2017.1488

Barbier, E. B. (2012). The green economy post Rio+20. *Science*, *2012*(338), 887–888. doi:10.1126cience.1227360 PMID:23161980

Bashir, H. A., & Akhtar, A. (2016). The role of innovative entrepreneurship in economic development: A study of G20 countries. *Management Studies and Economic System*, *2*(2), 91–100. doi:10.12816/0037559

Bates, T. (1990). Entrepreneur human capital inputs and small business longevity. *The Review of Economics and Statistics*, *72*(4), 551–559. doi:10.2307/2109594

Baydoun, H., & Aga, M. (2021). The effect of energy consumption and economic growth on environmental sustainability in the GCC countries: Does financial development matter? *Energies*, *14*(5897), 1–17. doi:10.3390/en14185897

Belz, F. M., & Binder, J. K. (2017). Sustainable Entrepreneurship: A Convergent Process Model. *Business Strategy and the Environment*, *26*(1), 1–17. doi:10.1002/bse.1887

Bennett, S. J. (1991). *Ecopreneuring: The Complete Guide to Small Business Opportunities from the Environmental Revolution*. John Wiley.

Berle, G. (1991). *The Green Entrepreneur: Business Opportunities that Can Save the Earth and Make You Money*. Liberty Hall Press.

Blue, J. (1990). *Ecopreneuring: Managing For Results*. Scott Foresman.

Bocar, A. C., Khan, S. A., & Epoc, F. (2022). (in press). COVID-19 Work from Home Stressors and the Degree of its Impact: Employers and Employees Actions. *International Journal of Technology Transfer and Commercialisation. Inderscience.*

Bosma, N., Van Praag, M., Thurik, R., & De Wit, G. (2004). The value of human and social capital investments for the business performance of startups. *Small Business Economics, 23*(3), 227–236. doi:10.1023/B:SBEJ.0000032032.21192.72

Boubker, O., Arroud, M., & Ouajdouni, A. (2021). Entrepreneurship education versus management students' entrepreneurial intentions. A PLS-SEM approach. *International Journal of Management Education, 19*(1), 100450. doi:10.1016/j.ijme.2020.100450

Braun, P. (2010). Going green: Women entrepreneurs and the environment. *International Journal of Gender and Entrepreneurship*, *2*(3), 245–259. doi:10.1108/17566261011079233

Brundtland Report, U. N. (1987). *Our Common Future*. Oxford University Press.

Brush, C. G., Manolova, T. S., & Edelman, L. F. (2008). Properties of emerging organizations: An empirical test. *Journal of Business Venturing*, *23*(5), 547–566. doi:10.1016/j.jbusvent.2007.09.002

Burgess, K. (2017). *Foundation for Democracy and Sustainable Development*. https://www.fdsd.org/the-challenge/what-is-sustainable-development/

Cai, X., Hussain, S., & Zhang, Y. (2022). Factors that can promote the green entrepreneurial intension of college students: A fuzzy set qualitative comparative analysis. *Frontiers in Psychology*, *12*(776886), 1–13.

Campbell, L., Gulas, C. S., & Gruca, T. S. (1999). Corporate giving behavior and decision-maker social consciousness. *Journal of Business Ethics*, *19*(4), 375–383. doi:10.1023/A:1006080417909

Canela, M. Á., Alegre, I., & Ibarra, A. (2019). Dummy variables. In *Quantitative methods for management* (pp. 57–63). Springer. doi:10.1007/978-3-030-17554-2_6

Canestrino, R., Ćwiklicki, M., Magliocca, P., & Pawełek, B. (2020). Understanding social entrepreneurship: A cultural perspective in business research. *Journal of Business Research*, *110*, 132–143. doi:10.1016/j.jbusres.2020.01.006

Cardon, M. S., Glauser, M., & Murnieks, C. Y. (2017). Passion for what? Expanding the domains of entrepreneurial passion. *Journal of Business Venturing Insights*, *8*, 24–32. doi:10.1016/j.jbvi.2017.05.004

Carlowitz, V. (2014). Encyclopedia of Public Health. Springer.

Cascavilla, I., Hahn, D., & Minola, T. (2022). How You Teach Matters! An Exploratory Study on the Relationship between Teaching Models and Learning Outcomes in Entrepreneurship Education. *Administrative Sciences*, *12*(1), 12. doi:10.3390/admsci12010012

Cassar, G. (2007). Money, money, money? A longitudinal investigation of entrepreneur career reasons, growth preferences and achieved growth. *Entrepreneurship and Regional Development, 19*(1), 89–107. doi:10.1080/08985620601002246

Castriotta, M. (2019). *What's in a name? Exploring the conceptual structure of emerging organizations, Scientometrics*. Springer International Publishing. doi:10.100711192-018-2977-2

CEPT University. (2011). *What works.* Leading Practices Catalogue from Municipalities and Municipal Corporations of Gujarat For Performance Assessment System Project. Retrieved from https://pas.org.in/Portal/document/ResourcesFiles/GoodPracticeDocs/pdfs/Leading%20 Practices_What%20Works.pdf

Cerqueti, R., Lucarelli, C., Marinelli, N., & Micozzi, A. (2020). Teams in new ventures: Gender, human capital and motivation. *International Journal of Gender and Entrepreneurship, 12*(2), 145–171. doi:10.1108/IJGE-07-2019-0115

Certo, T., & Miller, T. (2008). Social Entrepreneurship: Key Issues and Concepts. *Business Horizons, 51*(4), 267–271. doi:10.1016/j.bushor.2008.02.009

Chan, H. (2022). *The Nutrition Source> Sustainability > Food Waste*. https://www.hsph.harvard.edu/nutritionsource/sustainability/food-waste/

Chao, C. C., Patricia, G. G., & Ann, C. (1998). Does entrepreneurial self-efficacy distinguish entrepreneurs from managers? *Journal of Business Venturing, 13*(4), 295–316. doi:10.1016/S0883-9026(97)00029-3

Chen, C. C. (2014). Entrepreneurship, economic growth, and employment: A case study of Taiwan. *Hitotsubashi Journal of Economics, 55*(1), 71–88.

Chengalvala, S., & Rentala, S. (2017). Intentions towards social entrepreneurship among university students in India. *International Journal of Research-Granthaalaya*, 406-413.

Choi, N., & Majumdar, S. (2014). Social entrepreneurship as an essentially contested concept: Opening a new avenue for systematic future research. *Journal of Business Venturing. Elsevier Inc., 29*(3), 363–376. doi:10.1016/j.jbusvent.2013.05.001

Cisneros, L., & … . (2018). *Bibliometric study of family business succession between 1939 and 2017: mapping and analyzing authors' networks, Scientometrics*. Springer International Publishing. doi:10.100711192-018-2889-1

Cohen, B., & Winn, M. I. (2007). Market imperfections, opportunity, and sustainable entrepreneurship. *Journal of Business Venturing, 22*(1), 29–49. doi:10.1016/j.jbusvent.2004.12.001

Cohen, H., Kaspi-Baruch, O., & Katz, H. (2019). The social entrepreneur puzzle: The background, personality and motivation of Israeli social entrepreneurs. *Journal of Social Entrepreneurship, 10*(2), 211–231. doi:10.1080/19420676.2018.1541010

Comerio, N., & Strozzi, F. (2019). Tourism and its economic impact: A literature review using bibliometric tools. *Tourism Economics, 25*(1), 109–131. doi:10.1177/1354816618793762

Commendatore, C. (2020). *Coronavirus Impacts Hit Solid Waste Managers, Generators*. https://www.waste360.com/medical-waste/coronavirus-impacts-hit-solid-waste-managers-generators

Corradini, C. (2017). Location determinants of green technological entry: Evidence from European regions. *Small Business Economics*, *52*(4), 845–858. doi:10.100711187-017-9938-7

Cortez, R., & Johnston, W. (2020). The coronavirus crisis in B2B settings: Crisis uniqueness and managerial implications based on social exchange theory. *Industrial Marketing Management*, *88*, 125–135. doi:10.1016/j.indmarman.2020.05.004

Csrbox. (2021). *Top 10 Waste Management Projects Though CSR in India*. Retrieved from https://csrbox.org/India_CSR_news_Top-10-Waste-Management-Projects-Though-CSR-in-India_1020

Cumming, D., Meoli, M., & Vismara, S. (2021). Does equity crowdfunding democratize entrepreneurial finance? *Small Business Economics*, *56*(2), 533–552. doi:10.100711187-019-00188-z

Dacin, M. T., Dacin, P. A., & Tracey, P. (2011). Social entrepreneurship: A critique and future directions. *Organization Science*, *22*(5), 1203–1213. doi:10.1287/orsc.1100.0620

Dacin, P. A., Dacin, M. T., & Matear, M. (2010). Social entrepreneurship: Why we don't need a new theory and how we move forward from here. *The Academy of Management Perspectives*, *24*(3), 37–57.

Dana, L. P. (1992). Entrepreneurial education in Europe. *Journal of Education for Business*, *68*(2), 74–78. doi:10.1080/08832323.1992.10117590

David, A. (2019). Recover, Recycle and Reuse: An Efficient Way to Reduce the Waste. *International Journal of Mechanical and Production Engineering Research and Development, 9*(3), 31-42. http://www.tjprc.org/publishpapers/2-67-1554700771-4IJMPERDJUN20194.pdf

Davis, A. E., & Shaver, K. G. (2012). Understanding gendered variations in business growth intentions across the life course. *Entrepreneurship Theory and Practice*, *36*(3), 495–512. doi:10.1111/j.1540-6520.2012.00508.x

De Bruin, A. (2016). Towards a framework for understanding transitional green entrepreneurship. *Small Enterprise Research*, *23*(1), 10–21. doi:10.1080/13215906.2016.1188715

Dees, J. G. (1998). Enterprising Nonprofits. *Harvard Business Review*, (January-February), 55–67. PMID:10176919

Dees, J. G. (1998). *The Meaning of "Social Entrepreneurship"*. The Kauffman Center for Entrepreneurial Leadership.

Demirel, P., & Danisman, G. O. (2019). Eco-innovation and firm growth in the circular economy: Evidence from European small- and medium-sized enterprises. *Business Strategy and the Environment*, *28*(8), 1608–1618. doi:10.1002/bse.2336

Demirel, P., Li, Q., Rentocchini, F., & Tamvada, J. (2017). Born to be green: New insights into the economics and management of green entrepreneurship. *Small Business Economics, 52*(4), 759–771. doi:10.100711187-017-9933-z

Dhahri, S., & Omri, A. (2018). *Entrepreneurship contribution to the three pillars of sustainable development: What does the evidence really say?* MPRA Paper No. 84504. https://mpra.ub.uni-muenchen.de/84504/

Diamantopoulos, A. (2008). Formative indicators: Introduction to the special issue. *Journal of Business Research, 61*(12), 1201–1202. doi:10.1016/j.jbusres.2008.01.008

Dickel, P., Sienknecht, M., & Hörisch, J. (2021). The early bird catches the worm: An empirical analysis of imprinting in social entrepreneurship. *Journal of Business Economics, 91*(2), 127–150. doi:10.100711573-020-00969-z

Dimov, D. (2010). Nascent entrepreneurs and venture emergence: Opportunity confidence, human capital, and early planning. *Journal of Management Studies, 47*(6), 1123–1153. doi:10.1111/j.1467-6486.2009.00874.x

Dixon, S., & Clifford, A. (2007). Ecopreneurship – a new approach to managing the triple bottom line. *Journal of Organizational Change Management, 20*(3), 326–345. doi:10.1108/09534810710740164

do Paço, A., Ferreira, J. M., Raposo, M., Rodrigues, R. G., & Dinis, A. (2015). Entrepreneurial intentions: Is education enough? *The International Entrepreneurship and Management Journal, 11*(1), 57–75. doi:10.100711365-013-0280-5

Dobele, L. (2016). A New Approach in Higher Education: Social Entrepreneurship Education. In *Proceedings- 11th International Conference on Management, Enterprise and Benchmarking (MEB 2016)*. Óbuda University, Keleti Faculty of Business and Management.

Dobele, L. (2016). A New Approach in Higher Education: Social Entrepreneurship Education. In *Proceedings- 11th International Conference on Mangement, Enterprise and Benchmarking (MEB 2016)*. Óbuda University, Keleti Faculty of Business and Management.

Domańska, A., Żukowska, B., & Zajkowski, R. (2018). Green entrepreneurship as a connector among social, environmental and economic pillars of sustainable development. Why some countries are more agile? *Problemy Ekorozwoju, 13*(2), 67–76.

Donthu, N., Kumar, S., Mukherjee, D., Pandey, N., & Lim, W. M. (2021). How to conduct a bibliometric analysis: An overview and guidelines. *Journal of Business Research, 133*, 285–296. doi:10.1016/j.jbusres.2021.04.070

Douglas, E., & Prentice, C. (2019). Innovation and profit motivations for social entrepreneurship: A fuzzy-set analysis. *Journal of Business Research, 99*, 69–79. doi:10.1016/j.jbusres.2019.02.031

Doukas, H., Tsiousi, A., Marinakis, V., & Psarras, J. (2014). Linguistic multi-criteria decision-making for energy and environmental corporate policy. *Information Sciences, 258*, 328–338. doi:10.1016/j.ins.2013.08.027

Doyle, K. O. (1999). *The Social Meanings of Money and Property in Search of a Talisman*. Sage. doi:10.4135/9781483328324

Drăgoi, M., Iamandi, I., Munteanu, S., & Ciobanu, R., Țarțavulea (Dieaconescu), R., & Lădaru, R. (2017). Incentives for Developing Resilient Agritourism Entrepreneurship in Rural Communities in Romania in a European Context. *Sustainability*, *9*(12), 2205. doi:10.3390u9122205

Drastichová, M. (2014). Monitoring sustainable development and developing in EU. *Central European Review of Economic Issues*, *17*(1), 125–140. doi:10.7327/cerei.2014.09.03

Duran, D. C., Gogan, L. M., Artene, A., & Duran, V. (2015). The components of sustainable development – a possible approach. *Procedia Economics and Finance*, *26*(1), 806–811. doi:10.1016/S2212-5671(15)00849-7

Durán-Sánchez, A., Del Río-Rama, M. C., Álvarez-García, J., & García-Vélez, D. F. (2019). Mapping of scientific coverage on education for Entrepreneurship in Higher Education. *Journal of Enterprising Communities*, *13*(1–2), 84–104. doi:10.1108/JEC-10-2018-0072

Dvouletý, O. (2017). Relationship between unemployment and entrepreneurship dynamics in the Czech Regions: A panel var approach. *Acta Universitatis Agriculturae et Silviculturae Mendelianae Brunensis*, *65*(102), 987–995. doi:10.11118/actaun201765030987

Dvouletý, O. (2018). How to analyse determinants of entrepreneurship and self-employment at the country level? A methodological contribution. *Journal of Business Venturing Insights*, *9*(1), 92–99. doi:10.1016/j.jbvi.2018.03.002

Ebrahimi, P., & Mirbargkar, S. (2017). Green entrepreneurship and green innovation for SME development in market turbulence. *Eurasian Business Review*, *7*(2), 203–228. doi:10.100740821-017-0073-9

Elert, N., Andersson, F. W., & Wennberg, K. (2015). The impact of entrepreneurship education in high school on long-term entrepreneurial performance. *Journal of Economic Behavior & Organization*, *111*, 209–223. doi:10.1016/j.jebo.2014.12.020

Elliott, J. A. (2013). *An Introduction to Sustainable Development* (4th ed.). Routledge, Taylor and Francis.

Elliott, J. W. (1980). Wealth and wealth proxies in a permanent income model. *The Quarterly Journal of Economics*, *95*(3), 509–535. doi:10.2307/1885091

Emaet. (2015). *The Concept of Sustainable Development: Definition and Defining Principles*. United Nations' 2015 Global Sustainable Development Report. doi:10.13140/RG.2.2.34980.22404

EMB. (2020). *Management of Infectious Healthcare Waste During Covid-19 Pandemic*. https://emb.gov.ph/management-of-infectious-healthcare-waste-during-covid-19-pandemic/

Erken, H., Donselaar, P., & Thurik, R. (2018). Total factor productivity and the role of entrepreneurship. *The Journal of Technology Transfer*, *43*(1), 1493–1521. doi:10.100710961-016-9504-5

Eroglu, O., & Piçak, M. (2011). Entrepreneurship, national culture and Turkey. *International Journal of Business and Social Science, 2*(16).

Erpf, P., Butkevičienė, E., & Pučėtaitė, R. (2022). Between *de Jure* and *de Facto* : Embedding Western Concepts of Social Entrepreneurship in Post-Socialist Reality. *Journal of Social Entrepreneurship, 13*(1), 1–28. doi:10.1080/19420676.2020.1751245

Etzkowitz, H. (2003). Innovation in innovation: The Triple Helix of university-industry-government relations. *Social Sciences Information. Information Sur les Sciences Sociales, 42*(3), 293–337. doi:10.1177/05390184030423002

Eyal, O. (2008). When parents choose to start up a school: A social-capital perspective on educational entrepreneurship. *Journal of Educational Administration, 46*(1), 99–118. doi:10.1108/09578230810849835

Faisal, M.N., Jabeen, F., & Katsioloudes, M. (2017). Strategic interventions to improve women entrepreneurship in GCC countries: A relationship modeling approach. *Journal of Entrepreneurship in Emerging Economies, 9*(2), 161–180. doi:10.1108/JEEE-07-2016-0026

Farayibi, A. (2016). *Entrepreneurship as a driver of economic growth: Evidence from enterprise development in Nigeria.* MPRA Paper No. 74591. https://mpra.ub.uni-muenchen.de/74591/

Faul, F., Erdfelder, E., Buchner, A., & Lang, A.-G. (2009). Statistical power analyses using G*Power 3.1: Tests for correlation and regression analyses. *Behavior Research Methods, 41*(4), 1149–1160. doi:10.3758/BRM.41.4.1149 PMID:19897823

Faul, F., Erdfelder, E., Lang, A.-G., & Buchner, A. (2007). G*Power 3: A flexible statistical power analysis program for the social, behavioral, and biomedical sciences. *Behavior Research Methods, 39*(2), 175–191. doi:10.3758/BF03193146 PMID:17695343

Fayolle, A., & Gailly, B. (2008). From craft to science: Teaching models and learning processes in entrepreneurship education. *Journal of European Industrial Training, 32*(7), 569–593. doi:10.1108/03090590810899838

Ferreira, J. J. M., Fernandes, C. I., & Kraus, S. (2019). Entrepreneurship research: Mapping intellectual structures and research trends. *Review of Managerial Science, 13*(1), 181–205. doi:10.100711846-017-0242-3

Ferreira, J. J., Fayolle, A., Ratten, V., & Raposo, M. (Eds.). (2018). *Entrepreneurial Universities.* Edward Elgar Publishing. doi:10.4337/9781786432469

Fessler, P., & Schürz, M. (2018). Private wealth across European countries: The role of income, inheritance and the welfare state. *Journal of Human Development and Capabilities, 19*(4), 521–549. doi:10.1080/19452829.2018.1507422

Forliano, C., De Bernardi, P., & Yahiaoui, D. (2021). Entrepreneurial universities: A bibliometric analysis within the business and management domains. *Technological Forecasting and Social Change. Elsevier Inc., 165*, 120522. doi:10.1016/j.techfore.2020.120522

Fornell, C. G., & Larcker, D. F. (1981). Evaluating Structural Equation Models with Unobservable Variables and Measurement Error. *JMR, Journal of Marketing Research, 18*(1), 39–50. doi:10.1177/002224378101800104

Frączkiewicz-Wronka, A., & Wronka-Pośpiech, M. (2014). The use of ICT for achieving the objectives of the business model: Social enterprise perspective. *Polish Journal of Management Studies, 10.*

Fried, V. H., & Hisrich, R. D. (1994). Toward a model of venture capital investment decision making. *Financial Management, 23*(3), 28–37. doi:10.2307/3665619

Galindo, M. Á., & Méndez-Picazo, M. T. (2013). Innovation, entrepreneurship and economic growth. *Management Decision, 51*(3), 501–514. doi:10.1108/00251741311309625

Galindo-Martín, M. A., Castaño-Martínez, M. S., & Méndez-Picazo, M. T. (2020). The Relationship between Green Innovation, Social Entrepreneurship, and Sustainable Development. *Sustainability, 12*(11), 1–19. doi:10.3390u12114467

Ganesan, P. (2017). *Implementation of Decentralized Waste Management in Kerala: A Comparative Analysis of Alappuzha and Thiruvananthapuram.* Academic Press.

Gangi, Y. A. (2017). The role of entrepreneurship education and training on creation of the knowledge economy: Qatar leap to the future. *World Journal of Entrepreneurship, Management and Sustainable Development, 13*(4), 375–388. doi:10.1108/WJEMSD-06-2017-0032

Gangwar, V. P., & Khan, S. A. (2022). Analyzing the Role of Micro-Entrepreneurship and Self-Help Groups (SHGs) in Women Empowerment and Development. In M. Arafat (Ed.), Driving Factors for Venture Creation and Success in Agricultural Entrepreneurship (pp. 213–226). IGI Global. doi:10.4018/978-1-6684-2349-3.ch011

García-González, A., & Ramírez-Montoya, M. S. (2021). Social entrepreneurship education: Changemaker training at the university. *Higher Education, Skills and Work-based Learning, 11*(5), 1236–1251. doi:10.1108/HESWBL-01-2021-0009

Gartner, W. B., Frid, C. J., & Alexander, J. C. (2012). Financing the emerging firm. *Small Business Economics, 39*(3), 745–761. doi:10.100711187-011-9359-y

Gartner, W. B., Gartner, W. C., Shaver, K. G., Carter, N. M., & Reynolds, P. D. (Eds.). (2004). *Handbook of entrepreneurial dynamics: The process of business creation.* Sage. doi:10.4135/9781452204543

Gast, J., Gundolf, K., & Cesinger, B. (2017). Doing business in a green way: A systematic review of the ecological sustainability entrepreneurship literature and future research directions. *Journal of Cleaner Production, 147*, 44–56. doi:10.1016/j.jclepro.2017.01.065

Ge, B., Jiang, D., Gao, Y., & Tsai, S. (2016). The Influence of Legitimacy on a Proactive Green Orientation and Green Performance: A Study Based on Transitional Economy Scenarios in China. *Sustainability, 8*(12), 1344. doi:10.3390u8121344

Geels, F. W. (2004, September). From sectoral systems of innovation to socio-technical systems: Insights about dynamics and change from sociology and institutional theory. *Research Policy*, *33*(6–7), 897–920. doi:10.1016/j.respol.2004.01.015

Germak, A. J., & Robinson, J. A. (2014). Exploring the motivation of nascent social entrepreneurs. *Journal of Social Entrepreneurship*, *5*(1), 5–21. doi:10.1080/19420676.2013.820781

Ghaffar. (2017). Studying green architecture factors in order to achieving sustainable. *International Journal of Scientific & Engineering Research, 8*(6).

Ghauri, P. N., Tasavori, M., & Zaefarian, R. (2014). Internationalisation of service firms through corporate social entrepreneurship and networking. *International Marketing Review*, *31*(6), 576–600. doi:10.1108/IMR-09-2013-0196

Gibbs, D., & O'Neill, K. (2014). Rethinking Sociotechnical Transitions and Green Entrepreneurship: The Potential for Transformative Change in the Green Building Sector. *Environment and Planning A. Economy and Space*, *46*(5), 1088–1107. doi:10.1068/a46259

Glavas, A., & Mish, J. (2015). Resources and Capabilities of Triple Bottom Line Firms: Going Over Old or Breaking New Ground? *Journal of Business Ethics*, *127*(3), 623–642. doi:10.100710551-014-2067-1

Going Green 9. (2020). *Green buildings: examples of sustainable architecture around the world.* https://edition.cnn.com/style/article/green-buildings-world-sustainable-design/index.html

Gold, A. H., Malhotra, A., & Segars, A. H. (2001). Knowledge management: An organizational capabilities perspective. *Journal of Management Information Systems*, *18*(1), 185–214. doi:10.1080/07421222.2001.11045669

Graham, L. (2017). *UN raises world population forecast to 9.8 billion people by 2050 due to rapid growth in Africa*. Retrieved from https://www.cnbc.com/2017/06/22/un-raises-world-population-forecast-to-9-point-8-billion-people-by-2050.html

Gras, D., & Lumpkin, G. T. (2012). Strategic foci in social and commercial entrepreneurship: A comparative analysis. *Journal of Social Entrepreneurship*, *3*(1), 6–23. doi:10.1080/19420676.2012.660888

Grilli, L., Mrkajic, B., & Giraudo, E. (2022). Industrial policy, innovative entrepreneurship, and the human capital of founders. *Small Business Economics*, 1–22. doi:10.100711187-022-00611-y

Grimes, M. G., McMullen, J. S., Vogus, T. J., & Miller, T. L. (2013). Studying the origins of social entrepreneurship: Compassion and the role of embedded agency. *Academy of Management Review*, *38*(3), 460–463. doi:10.5465/amr.2012.0429

Grinevich, V., Huber, F., Karataş-Özkan, M., & Yavuz, Ç. (2017). Green entrepreneurship in the sharing economy: Utilizing a multiplicity of institutional logics. *Small Business Economics*, *52*(4), 859–876. doi:10.100711187-017-9935-x

Guijarro, F., & Poyatos, J. A. (2018). Designing a sustainable development goal index through a Goal programming model: The case of EU-28 countries. *Sustainability, 10*(3167), 1–17. doi:10.3390u10093167

Gupta, M., & Dharwal, M. (2022). Green entrepreneurship and sustainable development: A conceptual framework. *Materials Today: Proceedings, 49*(1), 3603–3606. doi:10.1016/j.matpr.2021.08.148

Gupta, P., Chauhan, S., Paul, J., & Jaiswal, M. P. (2020). Social entrepreneurship research: A review and future research agenda. *Journal of Business Research, 113*, 209–229. doi:10.1016/j.jbusres.2020.03.032

Guzman, A., & Trujillo, M. (2008). Social Entrepreneurship – Literature Review. *Estudios Gerenciales, 24.*

Hair, J. F., Hult, G. T. M., Ringle, C. M., & Sarstedt, M. (2022 in press). *A Primer on Partial Least Squares Structural Equation Modeling (PLS-SEM)* (3rd ed.). Sage.

Hair, J. F., Hult, G. T. M., Ringle, C., & Sarstedt, M. (2017). *A primer on partial least squares structural equation modeling (PLS-SEM)* (2nd ed.). SAGE Publications.

Hair, J. F. Jr, Howard, M., & Nitzl, C. (2020). Assessing measurement model quality in PLS-SEM using confirmatory composite analysis. *Journal of Business Research, 109*, 101–110. doi:10.1016/j.jbusres.2019.11.069

Hair, J. F., Risher, J. J., Sarstedt, M., & Ringle, C. M. (2018). When to use and how to report the results of PLS-SEM. *European Business Review, 30*(1), 2–24. doi:10.1108/EBR-11-2018-0203

Hair, J. F., Sarstedt, M., & Ringle, C. M. (2019). Rethinking some of the rethinking of partial least squares. *European Journal of Marketing, 53*(4), 566–584. doi:10.1108/EJM-10-2018-0665

Haldar, S. (2019). Towards a conceptual understanding of sustainability-driven entrepreneurship. *Corporate Social Responsibility and Environmental Management.*

Haldar, S. (2021). Sustainable entrepreneurship development in the renewable energy sector: Insights from Gujarat, India. *African Journal of Science, Technology, Innovation and Development, 13*(7), 873–885. doi:10.1080/20421338.2020.1796004

Hall, J., Matos, S., & Bachor, V. (2017). From green technology development to green innovation: Inducing regulatory adoption of pathogen detection technology for sustainable forestry. *Small Business Economics, 52*(4), 877–889. doi:10.100711187-017-9940-0

Hall, J., Matos, S., Sheehan, L., & Silvestre, B. (2012). Entrepreneurship and innovation at the base of the Pyramid: A recipe for inclusive growth or social exclusion? *Journal of Management Studies, 49*(4), 785–812. doi:10.1111/j.1467-6486.2012.01044.x

Hardy, M., & Reynolds, J. (2004). Incorporating categorical information into regression models: The utility of dummy variables. Handbook of Data Analysis, 229-55.

Hasnan, B. (2020). Spillover effect of COVID19 on the Global Economy. *Transnational Marketing Journal.*, *8*(2), 177–196. doi:10.33182/tmj.v8i2.1067

Hassan, H. M. K. (2020). Intention towards social entrepreneurship of university students in an emerging economy: The influence of entrepreneurial self-efficacy and entrepreneurship education. *On the Horizon*, *28*(3), 133–151. doi:10.1108/OTH-04-2020-0012

Haugh, H. (2005). A research agenda for social entrepreneurship. *Social Enterprise Journal*, *1*(1), 1–12. doi:10.1108/17508610580000703

He, H., & Harris, L. (2020). The impact of covid-19 pandemic on corporate social responsibility and marketing philosophy. *Journal of Business Research*, *116*, 176–182. doi:10.1016/j.jbusres.2020.05.030 PMID:32457556

Herman, E. (2019). Entrepreneurial Intention among Engineering Students and Its Main Determinants. *Procedia Manufacturing*, *32*, 318–324. doi:10.1016/j.promfg.2019.02.220

Hermann, R. R., & Bossle, M. B. (2020). Bringing an entrepreneurial focus to sustainability education: A teaching framework based on content analysis. *Journal of Cleaner Production*, *246*. . doi:10.1016/j.jclepro.2019.119038

Heuer, A., & Kolvereid, L. (2014). Education in entrepreneurship and the Theory of Planned Behaviour. *European Journal of Training and Development*, *38*(6), 506–523. doi:10.1108/EJTD-02-2013-0019

Hockerts, K. (2018). The Effect of Experiential Social Entrepreneurship Education on Intention Formation in Students. *Journal of Social Entrepreneurship*, *9*(3), 234–256. doi:10.1080/19420676.2018.1498377

Hofstede, G., Noorderhaven, N. G., Roy, A., Thurik, L. M. U., & Alexander, R. M. (2004). 8. Culture's role in entrepreneurship: self-employment out of. *Innovation, entrepreneurship and culture: The interaction between technology, progress and economic growth*, 162.

Hofstede, G. (1980). *Culture's consequences: International differences in work-related values*. Sage.

Hofstede, G. (1983). National cultures revisited. *Behavior Science Research*, *18*(4), 285–305. doi:10.1177/106939718301800403

Holgersson, H. E. T., Nordström, L., & Öner, Ö. (2014). Dummy variables vs. category-wise models. *Journal of Applied Statistics*, *41*(2), 233–241. doi:10.1080/02664763.2013.838665

Hossain, M. U., Arefin, M. S., & Yukongdi, V. (2021). Personality Traits, Social Self-Efficacy, Social Support, and Social Entrepreneurial Intention: The Moderating Role of Gender. *Journal of Social Entrepreneurship*, 1–21. doi:10.1080/19420676.2021.1936614

Hsieh, C. W., Yang, K., & Fu, K. J. (2012). Motivational bases and emotional labor: Assessing the impact of public service motivation. *Public Administration Review*, *72*(2), 241–251. doi:10.1111/j.1540-6210.2011.02499.x

Hu, D., & Deng, M. (2004). A review of sustainable development theory and sustainable development of hospitals. *Chin. Hosp. Manag., 2004*(24), 42–45.

Huitt, W. (2007). Maslow's hierarchy of needs. *Educational Psychology Interactive, 23.*

Ingale, K. K., & Paluri, R. A. (2020). Financial literacy and financial behavior: A bibliometric Analysis. *Review of Behavioral Finance*. doi:10.1108/RBF-06-2020-0141

Investment needs for the global energy transformation. (2020). *International Renewable Energy Agency*. https://www.irena.org/financeinvestment/Investment-Needs

IRENA. (2019). *Transforming the energy system*. https://www.irena.org/publications/2019/Sep/Transforming-the-energy-system

İrengün, O., & Arıkboğa, Ş. (2015). The effect of personality traits on social entrepreneurship intentions: A field research. *Procedia: Social and Behavioral Sciences, 195*, 1186–1195. doi:10.1016/j.sbspro.2015.06.172

Issa Ala eddin, M., & Thomas, B. J. (2018). A Review of the Entrepreneurship Ecosystem of Oman. *International Journal of Professional Management.*

ISWA-Jordan. (2020). *Country Specific Waste Management Responses, COVID-19 Response International knowledge sharing on Waste Management*. https://www.iswa.org/fileadmin/galleries/0001_COVID/Jordan_Solid_Waste_Handling_Manual_Coronavirus_crisisENG.pdf

Ivleva, M. L., Ivlev, V. Y., Inozemtsev, V., & Bagramiants, N. (2019). Environmental determinants of sustainable development. *Advances in Social Science, Education and Humanities Research, 356*(1), 1082–1086.

İyigün, N. Ö. (2015). What could entrepreneurship do for sustainable development? A corporate social responsibility-based approach. *Procedia: Social and Behavioral Sciences, 195*, 1226–1231. doi:10.1016/j.sbspro.2015.06.253

Jair Duque Oliva, E., Cervera Taulet, A., Rodríguez Romero, C., Mba Dea, M., & de la, Profesor. (n.d.). *Estudio bibliométrico de los modelos de medición del concepto de calidad percibida del servicio en Internet.*

Janssen, F., Fayolle, A., & Wuilaume, A. (2018). Researching bricolage in social entrepreneurship. *Entrepreneurship and Regional Development, 30*(3-4), 450–470. doi:10.1080/08985626.2017.1413769

Jawaharlal Nehru National Solar Mission. (2021). https://www.iea.org/policies/4916-jawaharlal-nehru-national-solar-mission-phase-i-ii-and-iii

Jehling, M., Hitzeroth, M., & Brueckner, M. (2019). Applying institutional theory to the analysis of energy transitions: From local agency to multi-scale configurations in Australia and Germany. *Energy Research & Social Science, 53*(July), 110–120. doi:10.1016/j.erss.2019.01.018

Jibril, A. (2011). *The Concept And Principles Of Sustainable Development.* Conference: 52nd Annual Conference Organised by the Association of Nigerian Geographers (ANG) on "Climate Change and Sustainable Development, Sokoto, Nigeri.a

Jindal, S. K. (1990). Money usage: A psychological analysis. *Indian Journal of Applied Psychology.*

Jin, H., Qian, X., Chin, T., & Zhang, H. (2020). A global assessment of sustainable development based on modification of the human development index via the Entropy method. *Sustainability, 12*(8), 1–20. doi:10.3390u12083251

Johannesburg. (2002). *Report of the World Summit on Sustainable Development.* United Nations.

Johnson, B. R. (1990). Toward a multidimensional model of entrepreneurship: The case of achievement motivation and the entrepreneur. *Entrepreneurship Theory and Practice, 14*(3), 39–54. doi:10.1177/104225879001400306

Johnson, M. P., & Schaltegger, S. (2020). Entrepreneurship for sustainable development: A review and multilevel causal mechanism framework. *Entrepreneurship Theory and Practice, 44*(6), 1141–1173. doi:10.1177/1042258719885368

Karabulut, A. T. (2016). Personality Traits on Entrepreneurial Intention. *Procedia: Social and Behavioral Sciences, 229*, 12–21. doi:10.1016/j.sbspro.2016.07.109

Karimi, R. F., & Chashmi, S. A. N. (2019). Designing green entrepreneurship model in sustainable development consistent with the performance of Tehran industrial towns. *Journal of Business-To-Business Marketing, 26*(1), 95–102. doi:10.1080/1051712X.2019.1565143

Kassean, H., Vanevenhoven, J., Liguori, E., & Winkel, D. E. (2015). Entrepreneurship education: A need for reflection, real-world experience and action. *International Journal of Entrepreneurial Behaviour & Research, 21*(5), 690–708. doi:10.1108/IJEBR-07-2014-0123

Kater, S., Kelly, E., & Whittemore, S. (2021). *Impact Investors and the Coming Energy Sector Transformation.* https://www.bridgespan.org/insights/library/impact-investing/impact-investors-and-the-energy-sector

Kaur. (2013). Current role of entrepreneurship in global greenmarket. *International Journal of Management, 4*(5), 1-5. https://www.academia.edu/4752352/CURRENT_ROLE_OF_ENTREPRENEURSHIP_IN_GLOBAL_GREEN_MARKET?email_work_card=thumbnail

Kedmenec, I., & Strašek, S. (2017). Are some cultures more favourable for social entrepreneurship than others? *Economic research-. Ekonomska Istrazivanja, 30*(1), 1461–1476. doi:10.1080/1331677X.2017.1355251

Kent Baker, H. (2020). A bibliometric analysis of board diversity: Current status, development, and future research directions. *Journal of Business Research, 108*(August), 232–246. . doi:10.1016/j.jbusres.2019.11.025

Kerbo, H. R., & Coleman, J. W. (2006). *Social Problems: A brief introduction* (2nd ed.). Pearson.

Khan, M. A. I., Azharuddin, S., Khan, S. S., & Ali, M. M. (2021). Influence of Entrepreneur Traits on SME's Financial Performance: Case Study of GCC Entrepreneurs Who Survived during COVID-19. *International Journal of Advance Research and Innovative Ideas in Education, 7*(1).

Khan, S. A., Devi, T. P., & Sharma, P. P. (2020). Vertical farming: Why it matters for Bhutan. *Studies in Indian Place Names, 40*(1), 1323-1329.

Khan, H., & Khan, U. (2012). From growth to sustainable development in developing countries: A conceptual framework. *Environment and Ecology, 3*(1), 23–31.

Khan, M. A., Patnaik, D., Ashraf, R., Ali, I., Kumar, S., & Donthu, N. (2021). Value of special issues in the Journal of Business Research: A bibliometric analysis. *Journal of Business Research, 125*, 295–313. doi:10.1016/j.jbusres.2020.12.015

Khan, S. A. R., Yu, Z., Sharif, A., & Golpîra, H. (2020). Determinants of economic growth and environmental Sustainability in South Asian for Regional Cooperation: Evidence from panel ARDL. *Environmental Science and Pollution Research International, 27*(36), 1–13. doi:10.100711356-020-10410-1 PMID:32803598

Khan, S. A., Epoc, F., Gangwar, V. P., Ligori, T. A. A., & Ansari, Z. A. (2021). Will Online Banking Sustain in Bhutan Post Covid-19? A Quantitative Analysis of The Customer E-Satisfaction and E-Loyalty in The Kingdom of Bhutan. *Transnational Marketing Journal, 9*(3). Advance online publication. doi:10.33182/tmj.v9i3.1288

Khan, S. A., Sharma, P. P., & Thoudam, P. (2019). Role of Attitude and Entrepreneurship Education towards Entrepreneurial Orientation among Business Students of Bhutan. *International Journal of Recent Technology and Engineering, 8*(3S), 335–345. doi:10.35940/ijrte.C1072.1083S19

Kilenthong, P., Hills, G., & Monllor, J. (2008). Impact Of Entrepreneurship Education on Entrepreneurial Self-Efficacy and Intention (Summary). *Frontiers of Entrepreneurship Research., 28*(4), 11.

Kirby, D. A., & Ibrahim, N. (2011). The case for (social) entrepreneurship education in Egyptian universities. *Education + Training, 53*(5), 403–415. doi:10.1108/00400911111147712

Kirby, D. A., & Ibrahim, N. (n.d.). The case for (social) entrepreneurship education in Egyptian Universities. *Education + Training*, 403–415.

Kirk, C. P., & Rifkin, L. S. (2020). I'll trade you diamonds for toilet paper: Consumer reacting, coping and adapting behaviors in the COVID-19 pandemic. *Journal of Business Research, 117*, 124–131. doi:10.1016/j.jbusres.2020.05.028 PMID:32834208

Klarin, T. (2018). The Concept of Sustainable Development:From its Beginning to the Contemporary Issues. *Zagreb International Review of Economics & Business, 21*(1), 67–94. doi:10.2478/zireb-2018-0005

Koirala, B. S., & Pradhan, G. (2019). Determinants of sustainable development: Evidence from 12 Asian countries. *Sustainable Development, 28*(3), 1–7.

Konakli, T. (2015). Effects of Self-Efficacy on Social Entrepreneurship in Education: A Correlational Research. *Research in Education, 94*(1), 30–43. doi:10.7227/RIE.0019

Kouri, R., & Clarke, A. (2012). Framing 'Green Jobs' Discourse: Analysis of Popular Usage. *Sustainable Development, 22*(4), 217–230. doi:10.1002d.1526

Kraus, S., Filser, M., O'Dwyer, M., & Shaw, E. (2014). Social Entrepreneurship: An exploratory citation analysis. *Review of Managerial Science, 8*(2), 275–292. doi:10.100711846-013-0104-6

Kumar, S., Bhattachryya, J. K., Vaidya, A.N., Chakrabarti, T., Devotta, S., & Akolkar, A.B. (2009). *Assessment of the status of municipal solid waste management in metro cities, state capitals, class I cities, and class II towns in India: An insight Waste Management*. Retrieved from https://www.sciencedirect.com/science/article/abs/pii/S0956053X08001529

Kumar, A., Ahmad, M. M., & Sharma, P. (2017). Influence of climatic and non-climatic factors on sustainable food security in India: A statistical investigation. *International Journal of Sustainable Agricultural Management and Informatics, 3*(1), 1–30. doi:10.1504/IJSAMI.2017.082917

Kumar, A., & Kiran, P. (2018). Green Entrepreneurship: A Bibliometric Study. *Int. J. Appl. Bus. Econ. Res., 15*, 153–166.

Lancu, A., Popescu, L., & Popescu, V. (2021). *Factors influencing social entrepreneurship intentions in Romania*. Economic Research-Ekonomska Istraživanja.

Legrand, W., Sloan, P., & Chen, J. S. (2018). Corporate social responsibility and social entrepreneurship. *Sustainability in the Hospitality Industry, 16*(3), 297–334. doi:10.9774/gleaf.9781315690261_13

Leiserowitz, A. (2005, April). What is Sustainable Development? Goals, Indicators, Values, and Practice. *Environment, 47*(3), 8–21. doi:10.1080/00139157.2005.10524444

Leiva, J. C., & Mora-Esquivel, R. (2022). The entrepreneurial activity of university students in Costa Rica: The role of the university ecosystem. *International Journal of Intellectual Property Management, 12*(1), 109–128. doi:10.1504/IJIPM.2022.120986

Lele, S. M. (1991, June). Sustainable development: A critical review. *World Development, 19*(6), 607–621. doi:10.1016/0305-750X(91)90197-P

Letts, C. W., Ryan, W., & Grossman, A. (1997). Virtuous capital: What foundations can learn from venture capitalists. *Harvard Business Review, 75*, 36–50. PMID:10165448

Lewis, J. A., Packard, T. R., & Lewis, M. D. (2011). *Management of Human Service Programs*. Cengage Learning.

Li, C. (2005). United Nations summit seeks global development. *Contemp. World, 2005*, 4–6.

Ligouri, E., & Winkler, C. (2020). From Offline to Online: Challenges and Opportunities for Entrepreneurship Education Following the COVID-19 Pandemic. *Entrepreneurship Education and Pedagogy, 3*(4), 1–6. doi:10.1177/2515127420916738

Li, L., & Yuan, F. (2019). Integrating Social Entrepreneurship into Higher Education in the New Era. *Proceedings of the 2019 3rd International Conference on Education, Economics and Management Research*. 10.2991/assehr.k.191221.039

Lim, Y. (2022). Relational composition and member turnover of entrepreneurial founder teams at the nascent stage: A typology and empirical evidence. *Journal of Small Business and Entrepreneurship*, 1–24. doi:10.1080/08276331.2022.2045543

Lins, E., & Lutz, E. (2016). Bridging the gender funding gap: Do female entrepreneurs have equal access to venture capital? *International Journal of Entrepreneurship and Small Business*, *27*(2-3), 347–365. doi:10.1504/IJESB.2016.073993

Littlewood, D., & Holt, D. (2018). Social Entrepreneurship in South Africa: Exploring the Influence of Environment. *Business & Society*, *57*(3), 525–561. doi:10.1177/0007650315613293

Lotfi, M., Yousefi, A., & Jafari, S. (2018). The Effect of Emerging Green Market on Green Entrepreneurship and Sustainable Development in Knowledge-Based Companies. *Sustainability*, *10*(7), 2308. doi:10.3390u10072308

Lozano, R., Lozano, F. J., Mulder, K., Huisingh, D., & Waas, T. (2013). Advancing Higher Education for Sustainable Development: International insights and critical reflections. *Journal of Cleaner Production*, *48*, 3–9. doi:10.1016/j.jclepro.2013.03.034

Luc, P. T. (2020). The influence of personality traits on social entrepreneurial intention among owners of civil society organisations in Vietnam. *International Journal of Entrepreneurship and Small Business*, *40*(1), 291–308. doi:10.1504/IJESB.2020.107799

Lynn & Howard. (2004). *Is the social entrepreneur a new type of leader?* Academic Press.

Magd, H. A., & McCoy, M. P. (2014). Entrepreneurship in Pman:Paving the Way for a Sustainable Future. *Emerging Market Queries in Finance and Business*, 1632-1640.

Mahajan, R., & Bandyopadhyay, K. R. (2021). Women entrepreneurship and sustainable development: Select case studies from the sustainable energy sector. *Journal of Enterprising Communities: People and Places in the Global Economy*, *15*(1), 42–75. doi:10.1108/JEC-11-2020-0184

Mahmood, N., Elahi, R. M., Mukhtar, B., Khan, M. M., Javaid, O., & Hyder, I. (2020). Bottom-up framework for experiential & project-based 4-year BS entrepreneurship program: An intrapreneurial conceptualization at institute of business management (IOBM). *Journal of Entrepreneurship Education*, *23*(5).

Mair, J., & Marti, I. (2006). Social entrepreneurship research: A source of explanation, prediction, and delight. *Journal of World Business*, *41*(1), 36–44. doi:10.1016/j.jwb.2005.09.002

Mair, J., & Noboa, E. (n.d.). Social Entrepreneurship: How Intentions to Create a Social Venture are Formed. In *Social Entrepreneurship*. Palgrave Macmillan. doi:10.1057/9780230625655_8

Makhloufi, L., Laghouag, A. A., Meirun, T., & Belaid, F. (2022). Impact of green entrepreneurship orientation on environmental performance: The natural resource-based view and environmental policy perspective. *Business Strategy and the Environment*, *31*(1), 425–444. doi:10.1002/bse.2902

Maresch, D. (2016). The impact of entrepreneurship education on the entrepreneurial intention of students in science and engineering versus business studies university programs. Technological Forecasting and Social Change, 104, 172–179. doi:10.1016/j.techfore.2015.11.006

Maritz, A., Perenyi, A., Waal, G., & Buck, C. (2020). Entrepreneurship as the Unsung Hero during the Current COVID-19 Economic Crisis: Australian Perspectives. *Sustainability*, *12*(11), 4612. doi:10.3390u12114612

Maslow, A. H. (1943). A theory of human motivation. *Psychological Review*, *50*(4), 370–396. doi:10.1037/h0054346

Matriano, M. T. (2019). Oman Entrepreneurship Highlights: A Case Study of Nawa International. *Advances in Social Sciences Research*, *6*(6), 1–12. doi:10.14738/assrj.66.6443

McFadyen, M. A., & Cannella, A. A. Jr. (2004). Social capital and knowledge creation: Diminishing returns of the number and strength of exchange relationships. *Academy of Management Journal*, *47*(5), 735–746.

McMullen, J. S., & Bergman, B. J. Jr. (2017). Social entrepreneurship and the development paradox of prosocial motivation: A cautionary tale. *Strategic Entrepreneurship Journal*, *11*(3), 243–270. doi:10.1002ej.1263

Mensah. (2019). Sustainable development: Meaning, history, principles, pillars, and implications for human action: Literature review. *Cogent Social Sciences*, *5*(1). https://www.tandfonline.com/doi/full/10.1080/23311886.2019.1653531

Miao, C., Qian, S., & Ma, D. (2017). The relationship between entrepreneurial self-efficacy and firm performance: A meta-analysis of main and moderator effects. *Journal of Small Business Management*, *55*(1), 87–107. doi:10.1111/jsbm.12240

Miller, T. L., Grimes, M. G., McMullen, J. S., & Vogus, T. J. (2012). Venturing for others with heart and head: How compassion encourages social entrepreneurship. *Academy of Management Review*, *37*(4), 616–640. doi:10.5465/amr.2010.0456

Miola, A., & Schiltz, F. (2019). Measuring sustainable development goals performance: How to monitor policy action in the 2030 agenda implication? *Ecological Economics*, *164*(1), 1–10. doi:10.1016/j.ecolecon.2019.106373 PMID:31582878

Miranda, F. J., Chamorro-Mera, A., & Rubio, S. (2017). Academic entrepreneurship in Spanish universities: An analysis of the determinants of entrepreneurial intention. *European Research on Management and Business Economics*, *23*(2), 113–122. doi:10.1016/j.iedeen.2017.01.001

Misztal, A., & Kowalska, M. (2020). Determinants of sustainable development of the industrial enterprises in Poland in the period from 2010 to 2019 – A statistical evaluation. *Prace Naukowe Uniwersytetu Ekonomicznego we Wrocławiu*, *64*(1), 160-173.

MKBKSH Website. (n.d.). *The Journey So Far*. Retrieved from https://mkbksh.org/about-main-kuch-bhi-kar-sakti-hoon/#season-1-and-2

Molecke, G., & Pinkse, J. (2017). Accountability for social impact: A bricolage perspective on impact measurement in social enterprises. *Journal of Business Venturing*, *32*(5), 550–568. doi:10.1016/j.jbusvent.2017.05.003

Monroe-White, T., & Zook, S. (2018). Social Enterprise Innovation: A Quantitative Analysis of Global Patterns. *Voluntas. Springer US*, *29*(3), 496–510. doi:10.100711266-018-9987-9

Moose. (2021). *Clean Air Lawn Care*. https://cleanairlawncare.com/what-is-green-entrepreneurship

Mosey, S., & Wright, M. (2007). From Human Capital to Social Capital : A. *Entrepreneurship Theory and Practice*, *31*(6), 909–935. doi:10.1111/j.1540-6520.2007.00203.x

Moss, T. W., Short, J. C., Payne, G. T., & Lumpkin, G. T. (2011). Dual identities in social ventures: An exploratory study. *Entrepreneurship Theory and Practice*, *35*(4), 805–830. doi:10.1111/j.1540-6520.2010.00372.x

Moya-Clemente, I., Ribes-Giner, G., & Pantoja-Dıaz, O. (2020). Identifying environmental and economic development factors in sustainable entrepreneurship over time by partial least squares (PLS). *PLoS One*, *15*(9), 1–17. doi:10.1371/journal.pone.0238462 PMID:32886680

Mrkajic, B., & Murtinu, S. 2016. Is Green the New Gold? Venture Capital and Green Entrepreneurship. SSRN *Electronic Journal*. doi:10.2139/ssrn.2757653

Muthurman, S., Al Haziazi, M., & Al Hajri, A. (2020). Importance of Social Entrepreneurship in Oman towards the Sustainable Development. *Waffen-und Kostumkunde*, *11*(2), 138–150.

Nasra, R., & Dacin, M. T. (2010). Institutional arrangements and international entrepreneurship: The state as institutional entrepreneur. *Entrepreneurship Theory and Practice*, *34*(3), 583–609. doi:10.1111/j.1540-6520.2009.00354.x

National Centre for Statistics and Information. (2021). *Statistical Year Book 2021*. National Centre for Statistics and Information.

Naveed, M., Zia, M. Q., Younis, S., & Shah, Z. A. (2021). Relationship of individual social entrepreneurial orientations and intentions: Role of social entrepreneurship education. *Asia Pacific Journal of Innovation and Entrepreneurship*, *15*(1), 39–50. doi:10.1108/APJIE-07-2020-0118

Ndofirepi, T. M. (2020). Relationship between entrepreneurship education and entrepreneurial goal intentions: Psychological traits as mediators. *Journal of Innovation and Entrepreneurship*, *9*(2), 1–20. doi:10.118613731-020-0115-x

Neck, H. M., Greene, P. G., & Brush, C. G. (Eds.). (2014). *Teaching entrepreneurship: A practice-based approach*. Edward Elgar Publishing.

Neville. (2021). *Introduction to Renewable Energy entrepreneurship*. https://www.savannahstate.edu/academic-affairs/documents/ENGT2803-IntroductiontoRenewableEnergyEntrepreneurship Syllabus.pdf

Nicholls, A. (2010). The legitimacy of social entrepreneurship: Reflexive isomorphism in a pre–paradigmatic field. *Entrepreneurship Theory and Practice*, *34*(4), 611–633. doi:10.1111/j.1540-6520.2010.00397.x

Nikolaou, E., Ierapetritis, D., & Tsagarakis, K. (2011). An evaluation of the prospects of green entrepreneurship development using a SWOT analysis. *International Journal of Sustainable Development &amp. World Ecology*, *18*(1), 1–16.

Nitzl, C., Roldan, J. L., & Cepeda, G. (2016). Mediation analysis in partial least squares path modeling: Helping researchers discuss more sophisticated models. *Industrial Management & Data Systems*, *116*(9), 1849–1864. doi:10.1108/IMDS-07-2015-0302

NIUA. (2020). *Swachh Bharat Mission – Urban - "Guidance on Efficient Collection And Transportation Of Municipal Solid Waste" – July 2020*. Retrieved from https://www.niua.org/csc/assets/pdf/key-documents/phase-2/Waste/SBM-Guidance-on-Efficient-Collection-and-Transportation-of-MSW.pdf

Niu, W., Ma, N., & Yijun, L. (2015). Sustainable development from action to science—Sustainability science and the annual report for world sustainable development 2015. *Bull. Chin. Acad. Sci.*, *2015*(30), 573–585.

Nowiński, W., Haddoud, M., Lančarič, D., Egerová, D., & Czeglédi, C. (2017). The impact of entrepreneurship education, entrepreneurial self-efficacy and gender on entrepreneurial intentions of university students in the Visegrad countries. *Studies in Higher Education*, *44*, 1–19.

Nsereko, I., Balunywa, W., Munene, J., Orobia, L., & Muhammed, N. (2018). Personal initiative: Its power in social entrepreneurial venture creation. *Cogent Business & Management*, *5*(1), 1443686. Advance online publication. doi:10.1080/23311975.2018.1443686

Nuringsih, K., & Nuryasman, M. N. (2020). Role of green entrepreneurship in raising the effect of green toward sustainable development. *International Journal of Economics, Business, and Entrepreneurship*, *3*(2), 29–46. doi:10.23960/ijebe.v3i2.69

Nuringsih, K., Nuryasman, M. N., & Amelinda, R. (2020). The propensity for social entrepreneurship during the coronavirus outbreak. *J. Manaj*, *24*(2), 174–193.

O'Neill, K., & Gibbs, D. (2016). Rethinking green entrepreneurship – Fluid narratives of the green economy. *Environment and Planning A. Economy and Space*, *48*(9), 1727–1749.

O'Neill, K., & Gibbs, D. (2020). Sustainability transitions and policy dismantling: Zero carbon housing in the UK. *Geoforum*, *108*, 119–129. doi:10.1016/j.geoforum.2019.11.011

Oleson, M. (2004). Exploring the relationship between money attitudes and Maslow's hierarchy of needs. *International Journal of Consumer Studies*, *28*(1), 83–92. doi:10.1111/j.1470-6431.2004.00338.x

Omisore, A. G. (2018). Attaining sustainable development goals in sub-Saharan Africa: The need to address environmental challenges. *Environmental Development*, *25*(1), 138–145. doi:10.1016/j.envdev.2017.09.002

Omoruyi, E. M. M., Olamide, K. S., Gomolemo, G., & Donath, O. A. (2017). Entrepreneurship and Economic Growth: Does Entrepreneurship Bolster Economic Expansion in Africa? *J Socialomics*, *6*(04), 219. doi:10.4172/2167-0358.1000219

Omoruyi, E. M. M., Olamide, K. S., Gomolemo, G., & Donath, O. A. (2017). Entrepreneurship and economic growth: Does entrepreneurship bolster economic expansion in Africa? *Journal of Socialomics*, *6*(4), 1–11.

Onsay, E. A. (2021). The analysis of green growth indicators in predicting the economic development of southeast Asian Countries. *Review of Socio-Economic Perspectives*, *6*(202190), 1–15.

Oyedotun, T. D. (2020). Sudden change of pedagogy in education driven by COVID-19: Perspectives and evaluation from a developing country. *Research in Globalization*, *2*, 1–5. doi:10.1016/j.resglo.2020.100029

Painul, J. P. (2001, September). Barriers to renewable energy penetration; a framework for analysis. *Renewable Energy*, *24*(1), 73–89. doi:10.1016/S0960-1481(00)00186-5

Palacios-Callender, M., & Roberts, S. A. (2018). Scientific collaboration of Cuban researchers working in Europe: Understanding relations between origin and destination countries. *Scientometrics*, *117*(2), 745–769. doi:10.100711192-018-2888-2 PMID:30595611

Palali´c, R., Ramadani, V., Đilovi´c, A., Dizdarevi´c, A., & Ratten, V. (2017). Entrepreneurial intentions of university students: A case-based study. *Journal of Enterprising Communities: People and Places in the Global Economy*, *11*(3), 393–413. doi:10.1108/JEC-12-2016-0046

Papadopoulos, I., Karagouni, G., Trigkas, M., & Beltsiou, Z. (2014). Mainstreaming green product strategies. *EuroMed Journal of Business*, *9*(3), 293–317. doi:10.1108/EMJB-12-2013-0058

Parhankangas, A., & Renko, M. (2017). Linguistic style and crowdfunding success among social and commercial entrepreneurs. *Journal of Business Venturing*, *32*(2), 215–236. doi:10.1016/j.jbusvent.2016.11.001

Patil, V. (2015). *Which Is The Only Carbon-Negative Country?* Retrieved from https://www.scienceabc.com/social-science/carbon-negative-country.html

Pem, S. (2017). *Bhutan's 71 percent forest cover confirmed*. Retrieved from http://www.bbs.bt/news/?p=67069

Phillips, W., Lee, H., Ghobadian, A., O'Regan, N., & James, P. (2015). Social Innovation and Social Entrepreneurship: A Systematic Review. *Group & Organization Management*, *40*(3), 428–461. doi:10.1177/1059601114560063

Pinstrup-Andersen. (2014). *Food losses and waste and sustainable food systems*. HLPE Reports. https://www.fao.org/3/i3901e/i3901e.pdf

Pittaway, L., & Cope, J. (2007). Simulating entrepreneurial learning: Integrating experiential and collaborative approaches to learning. *Management Learning, 38*(2), 211–233. doi:10.1177/1350507607075776

Press release IEA. (2021). https://www.iea.org/news/renewable-electricity-growth

Pret, T., & Carter, S. (2017). The importance of "fitting in": Collaboration and social value creation in response to community norms and expectations. *Entrepreneurship and Regional Development. Routledge, 29*(7–8), 639–667. doi:10.1080/08985626.2017.1328903

Purohit, M. (2018). *Lessons in waste management from a small town in Chhattisgarh.* Retrieved from https://yourstory.com/2018/03/ambikapurwaste-management/amp

Puumalainen, K., Sjögrén, H., Syrjä, P., & Barraket, J. (2015). Comparing social entrepreneurship across nations: An exploratory study of institutional effects. *Canadian Journal of Administrative Sciences/Revue Canadienne des Sciences de l'Administration, 32*(4), 276-287.

Qazi, W., Qureshi, J., Raza, S., Khan, K., & Qureshi, M. (2020). Impact of personality traits and university green entrepreneurial support on students' green entrepreneurial intentions: The moderating role of environmental values. *Journal of Applied Research in Higher Education, 13*(4), 1154–1180. doi:10.1108/JARHE-05-2020-0130

Rae, D., Gee, S., & Moon, R. (2009). Creating an enterprise culture in a university: The role of an entrepreneurial learning team. *Industry and Higher Education, 23*(3), 183–197. doi:10.5367/000000009788640279

Ragheb, A., El-Shimy, H., & Ragheb, G. (2016). Green architecture: A concept of sustainability. *Procedia: Social and Behavioral Sciences, 216*, 778–787. doi:10.1016/j.sbspro.2015.12.075

Rasoolimanesh, S. M., Jaafar, M., Kock, N., & Ahmad, A. G. (2017). The effects of community factors on residents' perceptions toward World Heritage site inscription and sustainable tourism development. *Journal of Sustainable Tourism, 25*(2), 198–216. . 1195836 doi:10.1080/09669582.2016

Ratten, V. (2017). Entrepreneurial universities: The role of communities, people and places. *Journal of Enterprising Communities: People and Places in the Global Economy, 11*(3), 310–315. doi:10.1108/JEC-03-2017-0021

Ratten, V. (2020). Coronavirus (Covid-19) and the entrepreneurship education community. *Journal of Enterprising Communities: People and Places in the Global Economy, 14*(5), 753–764. doi:10.1108/JEC-06-2020-0121

Raveesh, Mona, & Jayveer. (2015). *Waste Management Initiatives in India for Human Well Being.* Retrieved from https://smartnet.niua.org/content/a94538d0-540c-408d-9534-5be38586d8e4

REC Website. (n.d.). *Sanitation & Hygiene.* Retrieved from https://www.recindia.nic.in/sanitation-and-hygiene

Renewable. (2021). *IEA, Annual renewable electricity capacity additions, main and accelerated cases, 2014-2026.* https://www.iea.org/data-and-statistics/charts/annual-renewable-electricity-capacity-additions-main-and-accelerated-cases-2014-2026

Renko, M. (2013). Early challenges of nascent social entrepreneurs. *Entrepreneurship Theory and Practice, 37*(5), 1045–1069. doi:10.1111/j.1540-6520.2012.00522.x

Rey-Martí, A., Ribeiro-Soriano, D., & Palacios-Marqués, D. (2016). A bibliometric analysis of social entrepreneurship. *Journal of Business Research, 69*(5), 1651–1655. doi:10.1016/j.jbusres.2015.10.033

Reynolds, P. D. (2011). Informal and early formal financial support in the business creation process: Exploration with PSED II data set. *Journal of Small Business Management, 49*(1), 27–54. doi:10.1111/j.1540-627X.2010.00313.x

Ribeiro, A. T. V. B., Uechi, J. N., & Plonski, G. A. (2018). Building builders: Entrepreneurship education from an ecosystem perspective at MIT. *Triple Helix (Heidelberg), 5*(1), 1–20. doi:10.118640604-018-0051-y

Richter, N. F., Cepeda, G., Roldán, J. L., & Ringle, C. M. (2016). European Management Research Using Partial Least Squares Structural Equation Modeling (PLSSEM). *European Management Journal, 34*(6), 589–597. doi:10.1016/j.emj.2016.08.001

Rigdon, E. E. (2016). Choosing PLS Path Modeling as Analytical Method in European Management Research: A Realist Perspective. *European Management Journal, 34*(6), 598–605. doi:10.1016/j.emj.2016.05.006

Ringle, C. M., Wende, S., & Becker, J.-M. (2015). *SmartPLS 3.* Bönningstedt: SmartPLS. Retrieved from http://www.smartpls.com

Robinson, P. B., & Sexton, E. A. (1994). The effect of education and experience on self-employment success. *Journal of Business Venturing, 9*(2), 141–156. doi:10.1016/0883-9026(94)90006-X

Roomi, M. A., Saiz-Alvarez, J. M., & Coduras, A. (2020). Measuring sustainable entrepreneurship and eco-innovation: A methodological proposal for the global entrepreneurship monitor (GEM). *Sustainability, 13*(4056), 1–15.

Roslan, M. H. H., Hamid, S., Ijab, M. T., Yusop, F. D., & Norman, A. A. (2020). Social entrepreneurship in higher education: Challenges and opportunities. *Asia Pacific Journal of Education*, 1–16. doi:10.1080/02188791.2020.1859354

Ruskovaara, E., & Pihkala, T. (2013). Teachers implementing entrepreneurship education: Classroom practices. *Education + Training, 55*(2), 204–216. doi:10.1108/00400911311304832

Rusu, V. D., & Roman, A. (2017). Entrepreneurial activity in the EU: An empirical evaluation of its determinants. *Sustainability, 9*(1679), 1-16.

Saebi, T., Foss, N. J., & Linder, S. (2019). Social Entrepreneurship Research: Past Achievements and Future Promises. *Journal of Management, 45*(1), 70–95. doi:10.1177/0149206318793196

Sahoo, S., & Panda, R. K. (2019). Exploring entrepreneurial orientation and intentions among technical university students: Role of contextual antecedents. *Education + Training*, *61*(6), 719–736. doi:10.1108/ET-11-2018-0247

Salamzadeh, A., Salamzadeh, Y., & Nejati, M. (2011). *Social entrepreneurship: Analyzing literature and proposing a comprehensive model*. Academic Press.

Santos, F. M. (2012). A Positive Theory of Social Entrepreneurship. *Journal of Business Ethics*, *111*(3), 335–351. doi:10.100710551-012-1413-4

Sanyal, A. (2021). *Green Entrepreneurship: A Path towards Sustainable Development*. https://www.globsyn.edu.in/blog/green-entrepreneurship-a-path-towards-sustainable-development

Sassmannshausen, S. P., & Volkmann, C. (2018). The scientometrics of social entrepreneurship and its establishment as an academic field. *Journal of Small Business Management*, *56*(2), 251–273. doi:10.1111/jsbm.12254

Satar, M. S., & Natasha, S. (2019). *Individual social entrepreneurship orientation: Towards development of a measurement scale. Asia Pacific Journal of Innovation and Entrepreneurship.*

Schaltegger, S., & Wagner, M. (2008). Managing the business case for sustainability. In *EMAN-EU 2008 Conference* (Vol. 7). Academic Press.

Schumpeter, J. A. (1936). *The Theory of Economic Development*. Harvard University Press.

Scott, E. (2020). *How to Handle the Stress of Working from Home*. Available from: https://www.verywellmind.com/the-stress-of-working-from-home-4141174

Scott, S., Hughes, M., & Kraus, S. (2019). Developing relationships in innovation clusters. *Entrepreneurship and Regional Development*, *31*(1/2), 22–45. doi:10.1080/08985626.2018.1537145

Seghers, A., Manigart, S., & Vanacker, T. (2012). The impact of human and social capital on entrepreneurs' knowledge of finance alternatives. *Journal of Small Business Management*, *50*(1), 63–86. doi:10.1111/j.1540-627X.2011.00344.x

Sen, S., & Cowley, J. (2013). The Relevance of Stakeholder Theory and Social Capital Theory in the Context of CSR in SMEs: An Australian Perspective. *Journal of Business Ethics*, *118*(2), 413–427. doi:10.100710551-012-1598-6

Setiawan, G., & Lestari, E. (2021). The Effect of Entrepreneurship Education to Student's Entrepreneurial Intention With Self-Efficacy As Mediating Variable. *DeReMa (Development Research of Management) Jurnal Manajemen*, *16*, 158–178.

Shahverdi, M., Ismail, K., & Qureshi, M. (2018). The effect of perceived barriers on social entrepreneurship intention in Malaysian universities: The moderating role of education. *Management Science Letters*, *8*(5), 341–352. doi:10.5267/j.msl.2018.4.014

Shane, S., & Venkataraman, S. (2000). The promise of entrepreneurship as a field of research. *Academy of Management Review*, *25*(1), 217–226. doi:10.5465/amr.2000.2791611

Shi, L., Han, L., Yang, F., & Gao, L. (2019). The Evolution of Sustainable Development Theory: Types, Goals, and Research Prospect. *Sustainability*, *2019*(11), 7158. doi:10.3390u11247158

Shockley, G. E., & Frank, P. M. (2011). The functions of government in social entrepreneurship: Theory and preliminary evidence. *Regional Science Policy & Practice*, *3*(3), 181–198. doi:10.1111/j.1757-7802.2011.01036.x

Short, J. C., Moss, T. W., & Lumpkin, G. T. (2009). Research in social entrepreneurship: Past contributions and future opportunities. *Strategic Entrepreneurship Journal*, *3*(2), 161–194. doi:10.1002ej.69

Short, J., Ketchen, D. J. Jr, & Bergh, D. D. (Eds.). (2014). *Social entrepreneurship and research methods*. Emerald Group Publishing. doi:10.1108/S1479-838720149

Silajdžić, I., Kurtagić, S., & Vučijak, B. (2015). Green entrepreneurship in transition economies: A case study of Bosnia and Herzegovina. *Journal of Cleaner Production*, *88*, 376–384. doi:10.1016/j.jclepro.2014.07.004

Singh, E. H., Wangda, S., Khan, S., & Khan, S. A. (2020). Exploring the obstacles for start-ups in Bhutan: From a prevented entrepreneurs perspective. *International Journal of Innovation, Creativity and Change, 4*.

Singh, A. K., & Ashraf, S. N. (2020). Association of entrepreneurship ecosystem with economic growth in selected countries: An empirical exploration. *Journal of Entrepreneurship. Business Economics (Cleveland, Ohio)*, *8*(2), 36–92.

Singh, A. K., Ashraf, S. N., & Arya, A. (2019b). Estimating factors affecting technical efficiency in Indian manufacturing sector. *Eurasian Journal of Business and Economics*, *12*(24), 65–86. doi:10.17015/ejbe.2019.024.04

Singh, A. K., & Issac, J. (2018). Impact of climatic and non-climatic factors on sustainable livelihood security in Gujarat state of India: A statistical exploration. *Agriculture and Food Sciences Research*, *5*(1), 30–46. doi:10.20448/journal.512.2018.51.30.46

Singh, A. K., Issac, J., & Narayanan, K. G. S. (2019a). Measurement of environmental sustainability index and its association with socio-economic indicators in Asian economies: An empirical investigation. *International Journal of Environment and Sustainable Development*, *18*(1), 57–100. doi:10.1504/IJESD.2019.098641

Singh, A. K., & Kumar, S. (2022a). Influence of climate change on agricultural Sustainability in India: A state-wise panel data analysis. *Asian Journal of Agriculture*, *6*(1), 15–27.

Singh, A. K., & Kumar, S. (2022b). Expert's perception on technology transfer and commercialisation, and intellectual property rights in India: Evidence from selected research organisations. *Journal of Management, Economics, and Industrial Organization*, *6*(1), 1–33. doi:10.31039/jomeino.2022.6.1.1

Singh, A. K., & Kumar, S. (2022c). Exploring the impact of sustainable and environmental sustainability development on social-economic, science and technological development in selected countries: A country-wise panel data analysis. *Society & Sustainability*, *4*(1), 55–83. doi:10.38157s.v4i1.405

Singh, A. K., Kumar, S., Ashraf, S. N., & Jyoti, B. (2022). Implications of farmer's adaptation strategies to climate change in agricultural sector of Gujarat: Evidence from farm level data. *Research on World Agricultural Economy*, *3*(1), 42–57. doi:10.36956/rwae.v3i1.498

Singh, A. K., & Singh, B. J. (2020). Implications of intellectual property protection, and science and technological development in the manufacturing sector in selected economies. *Journal of Advocacy. Research in Education*, *7*(1), 16–35.

Singh, A. K., Singh, B. J., Kumar, S., & Lenka, S. K. (2021). Assessment of global sustainable development, environmental Sustainability, economic development and social development index in selected economies. *International Journal of Sustainable Development and Planning*, *16*(1), 123–138. doi:10.18280/ijsdp.160113

Singh, A. K., Singh, B. J., & Negi, V. (2020). Does sustainable development have a causal relationship with environmental development? Evidence from a country-wise panel data analysis. *International Journal of Technology Management & Sustainable Development*, *19*(2), 147–171. doi:10.1386/tmsd_00020_1

Skordoulis, M., Kyriakopoulos, G., Ntanos, S., Galatsidas, S., Arabatzis, G., Chalikias, M., & Kalantonis, P. (2022). The mediating role of firm strategy in the relationship between green entrepreneurship, green innovation, and competitive advantage: The case of medium and large-sized firms in Greece. *Sustainability*, *14*(6), 1–18. doi:10.3390u14063286

Smith, A. (2007). Translating sustainabilities between green niches and socio-technical regimes. *Technology Analysis and Strategic Management*, *19*(4), 427–450. doi:10.1080/09537320701403334

Smith, A., Stirling, A., & Berkhout, F. (2005, December). A. Stirling, F. Berkhout (2005)The governance of sustainable socio-technical transitions. *Research Policy*, *34*(10), 1491–1510. doi:10.1016/j.respol.2005.07.005

Söderholm, P. (2020). The green economy transition: The challenges of technology change for sustainability. *Sustainable Earth*, *3*(6), 1–11. doi:10.118642055-020-00029-y

Soomro, B., Ghumro, I., & Shah, N. (2019). Green entrepreneurship inclination among the younger generation: An avenue towards a green economy. *Sustainable Development*, *28*(4), 585–594. doi:10.1002d.2010

Sovacool, B. K. (2009). Rejecting renewables: The socio-technical impediments to renewable electricity in the United States. *Energy Policy*, *37*(11), 4500–4513. doi:10.1016/j.enpol.2009.05.073

Sovacool, B. K. (2016). How long will it take? Conceptualizing the temporal dynamics of energy transitions. *Energy Research & Social Science*, *13*(March), 202–215. doi:10.1016/j.erss.2015.12.020

Spear, R. (2006). Social entrepreneurship: A different model? *International Journal of Social Economics*, *33*(5 & 6), 399–410. doi:10.1108/03068290610660670

Sridhara, S., Gopakkali, P., Manoj, K. N., Patil, K. K. R., Paramesh, V., Jha, P. K., & Prasad, P. V. V. (2022). Identification of sustainable development priorities for agricultural through sustainable livelihood security indicators for Karnataka, India. *Sustainability*, *14*(1831), 1-23.

Staggenborg, S., & Ogrodnik, C. (2015). New environmentalism and Transition Pittsburgh. *Environmental Politics*, *24*(5), 723–741. doi:10.1080/09644016.2015.1027059

Stöppler. (2022). *What Is the Definition of Organic Food?* MedicineNet. https://www.medicinenet.com/what_is_the_definition_of_organic_food/views.htm

Stories. (2016). *This Farm of the Future Uses No Soil and 95% Less Water*. Retrieved from https://www.youtube.com/watch?v=-_tvJtUHnmU

Studdard, N., Dawson, M., Burton, S.L., Leonard, B., and Quisenberry, W. (2017). *Nurturing Social Entrepreneurship and Building Social Entrepreneurial Self-Efficacy: Focusing on Primary and Secondary Schooling to Develop Future Social Entrepreneurs*. Information Resources Management Association. doi:10.4018/978-1-5225-1923-2.ch011

Sulphey, M., & Salim, A. (2021). Development of a tool to measure social entrepreneurial orientation. *Journal of Entrepreneurship in Emerging Economies*.

Sun, X. (2012). Review and prospect on the UN's efforts for sustainable development. *China Popul. Environ.*, *22*, 1–6.

Surie, G. (2017). Creating the innovation ecosystem for renewable energy via social entrepreneurship: Insights from India. *Technological Forecasting and Social Change*, *121*, 184–195. doi:10.1016/j.techfore.2017.03.006

Survekshan, S. (2020). Innovation and Best Practices. Report by Ministry of Housing and Urban Affairs, Government of India.

Syed, R. T., Singh, D., & Spicer, D. (2022). Entrepreneurial higher education institutions: Development of the research and future directions. *Higher Education Quarterly*, (January), 1–26. doi:10.1111/hequ.12379

Tahamtan, I., Safipour Afshar, A., & Ahamdzadeh, K. (2016). Factors affecting number of citations: A comprehensive review of the literature. *Scientometrics. Springer Netherlands*, *107*(3), 1195–1225. doi:10.100711192-016-1889-2

Tan, W., Williams, J., & Tan, T. (2005). Defining the 'Social' in 'Social Entrepreneurship': Altruism and Entrepreneurship. *The International Entrepreneurship and Management Journal*, *1*(3), 353–365. doi:10.100711365-005-2600-x

Tasnim, N., & Afzal, M. N. I. (2018). An empirical investigation of country level efficiency and national systems of entrepreneurship using data envelopment analysis (DEA) and the tobit model. *Journal of Global Entrepreneurship Research*, *8*(37), 1–17. doi:10.118640497-018-0138-y

Tate, W. L., & Bals, L. (2018). Achieving Shared Triple Bottom Line (TBL) Value Creation: Toward a Social Resource-Based View (SRBV) of the Firm. *Journal of Business Ethics. Springer Netherlands, 152*(3), 803–826. doi:10.100710551-016-3344-y

Tawiah, V., Zakari, A., & Adedoyin, F. F. (2021). Determinants of green growth in developed and developing countries. *Environmental Science and Pollution Research International, 28*(1), 39227–39242. doi:10.100711356-021-13429-0 PMID:33751350

Terjesen, S., Hessels, J., & Li, D. (2016). Comparative international entrepreneurship: A review and research agenda. *Journal of Management, 42*(1), 299–344. doi:10.1177/0149206313486259

The Economic Time News. (2021). *No new fossil fuel projects for net-zero 2050 goal: IEA.* https://economictimes.indiatimes.com/news/international/business/no-new-fossil-fuel-projects-for-net-zero-2050-goal-iea/articleshow/82730817.cms

The Guardian. (2014). *World largest vertical farm New Ark green revolution.* Retrieved from https://www.theguardian.com/environment/2016/aug/14/world-largest-vertical-farm-newark-green-revolution

The Guardian. (2015). *Arable land soil food security shortage.* Retrieved from https://www.theguardian.com/environment/2015/dec/02/arable-land-soil-food-securityshortage

The Sustainable Development Goals Report. (2019). *United Nations.* https://unstats.un.org/sdgs/report/2019/The-Sustainable-Development-Goals-Report-2019.pdf

The Water Project. (2017). https://thewaterproject.org/water-scarcity/water-scarcity-andagriculture

Thompson, E. R. (2009). Individual Entrepreneurial Intent: Construct Clarification and Development of an Internationally Reliable Metric. *Entrepreneurship Theory and Practice, 33*(3), 669–694. doi:10.1111/j.1540-6520.2009.00321.x

Tian, X. (2018). *A bibliometric analysis on trends and characters of carbon emissions from transport sector.* doi:10.1016/j.trd.2017.12.009

Times of Oman. (2019). Retrieved from https://timesofoman.com/article/1900951/Business/Food-consumption-in-Oman-to-grow-46-annually-until-2023

Tiseo, I. (2021). *Global plastic production 1950-2020.* https://www.statista.com/statistics/282732/global-production-of-plastics-since-1950/

Tiseo, I. (2022). *Plastic production forecast worldwide 2025-2050.* https://www.statista.com/statistics/664906/plastics-production-volume-forecast-worldwide/

Tiwari, P., Bhat, A. K., & Tikoria, J. (2017). Predictors of social entrepreneurial intention:an empirical study. *South Asian Journal of Business Studies, 6*(1), 53–79. doi:10.1108/SAJBS-04-2016-0032

Tiwari, P., Bhat, A. K., & Tikoria, J. (2022). Mediating role of prosocial motivation in predicting social entrepreneurial intentions. *Journal of Social Entrepreneurship, 13*(1), 118–141. doi:10.1080/19420676.2020.1755993

Tiwari, P., Bhatt, A. K., & Tikoria, J. (2017). An empirical analysis of the factors affecting social entrepreneurial intentions. *Journal of Global Entrepreneurship Research*, *7*(9), 1–25. doi:10.118640497-017-0067-1

Tracey, P., & Jarvis, O. (2007). Toward a theory of social venture franchising. *Entrepreneurship Theory and Practice*, *31*(5), 667–685. doi:10.1111/j.1540-6520.2007.00194.x

Tran, A. P., & Korflesch, H. V. (2016). A conceptual model of social entrepreneurial intention based on the social cognitive career theory. *Asia Pacific Journal of Innovation and Entrepreneurship*, *10*(1), 17–38. doi:10.1108/APJIE-12-2016-007

Tripathy, U. (2018). *A 21st Century Vision on Waste to Energy in India: A Win- Win Strategy for Energy Security and Swachh Bharat Mission (Clean India Mission)*. Background paper for Eighth Regional 3R Forum in Asia and the Pacific. United Nations Centre For Regional Development. Retrieved from https://www.uncrd.or.jp/content/documents/6717FINAL-Background%20 paper_Tripathy.pdf

Trzyna, T. C. (1995). *A Sustainable World: Defining and Measuring Sustainable Development*. Earthscan Publication, Ltd.

Tu, B., Bhowmik, R., Hasan, M. K., Asheq, A. A., Rahaman, M. A., & Chen, X. (2021). Graduate Students' Behavioral Intention towards Social Entrepreneurship: Role of Social Vision, Innovativeness, Social Proactiveness, and Risk Taking. *Sustainability*, *13*(11), 13–36. doi:10.3390u13116386

Tucker, R., & Croom, R. M. (2021). A xenophilic perspective of social entrepreneurship. *Journal of Business Venturing Insights, 15*.

Tunio, M. N., Chaudhry, I. S., Shaikh, S., Jariko, M. A., & Brahmi, M. (2021). Determinants of the sustainable entrepreneurial engagement of youth in developing country—An empirical evidence from pakistan. *Sustainability (Switzerland)*, *13*(14), 7764. Advance online publication. doi:10.3390u13147764

Tuzlukova, V., & Heckadon, P. (2020). Teaching social entrepreneurship through problem-based learning: Pedagogy and practice in the business english classroom. *Journal of Teaching English for Specific and Academic Purposes*, *8*(2), 71–82. doi:10.22190/JTESAP2002071T

Tyres, A. (2013). *Environment*. Retrieved from https://corporate.apollotyres.com/responsibility/environment/

Ullah, A., Pinglu, C., Ullah, S., & Hashmi, S. H. (2021). Nexus of regional integration, socioeconomic determinants and sustainable development in belt and road initiative countries. *PLoS One*, *16*(7), 1–29. doi:10.1371/journal.pone.0254298 PMID:34242342

UNDESA. (2016). *World Population Prospects: The 2016 Revision – Key Findings and Advance Tables*. United Nations Department of Economic and Social Affairs, Population Division.

UNEP. (2022). *The Transition to a Green Economy: Benefits, Challenges and Risks from a Sustainable Development Perspective.* https://www.unep.org/resources/report/transition-green-economy-benefits-challenges-and-risks-sustainable-development, https://wedocs.unep.org/bitstream/handle/20.500.11822/9310/-Transition%20to%20a%20green%20economy:%20benefits,%20challenges%20and%20risks%20from%20a%20sustainable%20development%20perspective-2012UN-DESA,%20UNCTAD%20Transition%20GE.pdf?sequence=3&amp%3BisAllowed=

UNGA. (2020). *Entrepreneurship for sustainable development Report of the Secretary-General, United Nations General Assembly A/75/257, 27 July 2020, Seventy-fifth session.* UNGA.

United Nations. (2012). *The Future we Want.* United Nations.

United Nations. (2015). *Transforming Our World: The 2030 Agenda for Sustainable Development.* United Nations.

Urban Land Institute. (2016). *The Changing World with David Rosenberg of AeroFarms.* Retrieved from https://www.youtube.com/watch?v=HLL3CEhlNz0

Urban, B., & Kujinga, L. (2017). The institutional environment and social entrepreneurship intentions. *International Journal of Entrepreneurial Behaviour & Research, 23*(4), 638–655. doi:10.1108/IJEBR-07-2016-0218

Urbano, D., Ferri, E., Alvarez, C., & Noguera, M. (2017). Social entrepreneurship and institutional conditions: An empirical analysis in Spain. In *Social entrepreneurship in non-profit and profit sectors* (pp. 53–64). Springer. doi:10.1007/978-3-319-50850-4_4

U-tantada. (2019). Green Market Economy and Emerging Market Environment: Sustainable Adaptive Complex Systems. *International Review of Research in Emerging Markets and the Global Economy, 5*(1). https://www.researchgate.net/publication/333561173_Green_Market_Economy_and_Emerging_Market_Environment_Sustainable_Adaptive_Complex_Systems

Van der Sluis, J., Van Praag, M., & Vijverberg, W. (2008). Education and entrepreneurship selection and performance: A review of the empirical literature. *Journal of Economic Surveys, 22*(5), 795–841. doi:10.1111/j.1467-6419.2008.00550.x

Van Dijk, G., Sergaki, P., & Baourakis, G. (2019). *The Cooperative Enterprise – Practical Evidence for a Theory of Cooperative Entrepreneurship.* Springer Nature Switzerland AG. doi:10.1007/978-3-030-16279-5

Van Praag, C. M., & Versloot, P. H. (2007). What is the value of entrepreneurship? A review of recent research. *Small Business Economics, 29*(4), 351–382. doi:10.100711187-007-9074-x

VanSandt, C. V., Sud, M., & Marme, C. (2009). Enabling the Original Intent: Catalysts for Social Entrepreneurship. *Journal of Business Ethics, 90*(S3), 419–428. doi:10.100710551-010-0419-z

Varghese, T. (2018). Social Entrepreneurship Realities: Do a Country Need Social Entrepreneurs or Innovative Social Entrepreneurs? *International Review of Management and Business Research, 7*(1), 186–190. doi:10.30543/7-1(2018)-17

Verduijn, K., Dey, P., Tedmanson, D., & Essers, C. (2014). Emancipation and/or oppression? Conceptualizing dimensions of criticality in entrepreneurship studies. *International Journal of Entrepreneurial Behaviour & Research, 20*(2), 98–107. doi:10.1108/IJEBR-02-2014-0031

Verma, M. (2020). Editorial: Digital Media and the Academic World. *Journal of Content, Community & Communication, 13*(1), 2.

Vidal, I. (2005). Social enterprise and social inclusion: Social enterprises in the sphere of work integration. *International Journal of Public Administration, 28*(9-10), 807–825. doi:10.1081/PAD-200067347

Volery, T., & Hackl, V. (2010). The promise of social franchising as a model to achieve social goals. In *Handbook of Research on Social Entrepreneurship*. Edward Elgar Publishing. doi:10.4337/9781849804684.00015

Voorhees, C. M., Brady, M. K., Calantone, R., & Ramirez, E. (2016). Discriminant Validity Testing in Marketing: An Analysis, Causes for Concern, and Proposed Remedies. *Journal of the Academy of Marketing Science, 44*(1), 119–134. doi:10.100711747-015-0455-4

Wagner, J., & Sternberg, R. (2004). Start-up activities, individual characteristics, and the regional milieu: Lessons for entrepreneurship support policies from German micro data. *The Annals of Regional Science, 38*(2), 219–240. doi:10.100700168-004-0193-x

Wanne, B. (2019). *Is exponential growth of solar PV the obvious conclusion?* https://www.iea.org/commentaries/is-exponential-growth-of-solar-pv-the-obvious-conclusion

Webber, K. L., & Burns, R. (2021). Increases in graduate student debt in the US: 2000 to 2016. *Research in Higher Education, 62*(5), 709–732. doi:10.100711162-020-09611-x

Weerawardena, J., McDonald, R. E., & Mort, G. S. (2010). Sustainability of nonprofit organizations: An empirical investigation. *Journal of World Business. Elsevier Inc., 45*(4), 346–356. doi:10.1016/j.jwb.2009.08.004

Weerawardena, J., & Mort, G. S. (2012). Competitive strategy in socially entrepreneurial nonprofit organizations: Innovation and differentiation. *Journal of Public Policy & Marketing, 31*(1), 91–101. doi:10.1509/jppm.11.034

Weick, K. E., & Sutcliffe, K. M. (2011). *Managing the Unexpected: Resilient Performance in an Age of Uncertainty* (Vol. 8). John Wiley and Sons.

Wennekers, S., van Stel, A., Carree, M., & Thurik, R. (2010). The relationship between entrepreneurship and economic development: Is it u-shaped? *Foundations and Trends in Entrepreneurship, 6*(3), 167–237. doi:10.1561/0300000023

Wernimont, P. F., & Fitzpatrick, S. (1972). The meaning of money. *The Journal of Applied Psychology, 56*(3), 218–226. doi:10.1037/h0033107

WHO. (2020). *Water, sanitation, hygiene, and waste management for the COVID-19 virus: Interim guidance*. World Health Organization. https://www.who.int/publications-detail/water-sanitation-hygiene-and-waste-management-for-covid-19

Wieben, E. (2017). *Save Food For A Better Climate, Converting the food loss and waste challenge into climate action*. Food and Agriculture Organization of the United Nations. https://www.fao.org/3/i8000e/i8000e.pdf

Wikipedia. (2017). Retrieved from https://en.wikipedia.org/wiki/World_population

World Bank. (2014). *Arable land (% of land area)*. Retrieved from https://data.worldbank.org/indicator/AG.LND.ARBL.ZS

World bank. (2019). *Oman Food Products Imports by country in US$ Thousand 2018*. Retrieved from https://wits.worldbank.org/CountryProfile/en/Country/OMN/Year/LTST/TradeFlow/Import/Partner/by-country/Product/16-24_FoodProd

World Commission on Environment and Development. (2018). Our Common Future. Oxford University Press.

Worldometers. (2017). Retrieved from https://www.worldometers.info/world-population/

Wu, J. (2014). What is sustainability science? *Ying Yong Sheng Tai Xue Bao*, *2014*(25), 1–11. PMID:24765835

Wung, L., & Huang, J. (2019). Effect of Entrepreneurial Self-Efficacy on the Entrepreneurial Intentions of Students at a University in Hainan Province in China: Taking Social Support as a Moderator. *International Journal of Learning. Teaching and Educational Research.*, *18*(9), 183–200. doi:10.26803/ijlter.18.9.10

WWF. (2017). Retrieved from https://www.worldwildlife.org/threats/water-scarcity

Yamini, R., Soloveva, D., & Peng, X. (2020). What inspires social entrepreneurship? The role of prosocial motivation, intrinsic motivation, and gender in forming social entrepreneurial intention. *Entrepreneurship Research Journal*.

Yi, G. (2020). From green entrepreneurial intentions to green entrepreneurial behavior: The role of university entrepreneurial support and external institutional support. *The International Entrepreneurship and Management Journal*, *17*(2), 963–979. doi:10.100711365-020-00649-y

Yin, C., Salmador, M. P., Li, D., & Lloria, M. B. (2022). Green entrepreneurship and SME performance: The moderating effect of firm age. *The International Entrepreneurship and Management Journal*, *18*(1), 255–275. doi:10.100711365-021-00757-3

Youn. (2017). *Visit the World's Only Carbon-Negative Country*. Retrieved from https://www.nationalgeographic.com/travel/destinations/asia/bhutan/carbon-negative-country-sustainability/

Zahraie, B., Everett, A. M., Walton, S., & Kirkwood, J. (2016). Environmental entrepreneurs facilitating change toward sustainability: A case study of the wine industry in New Zealand. *Small Enterp. Dev., 23*(1), 39–57. doi:10.1080/13215906.2016.1188717

Zahra, S. A., Gedajlovic, E., Neubaum, D. O., & Shulman, J. M. (2009). A typology of social entrepreneurs: Motives, search processes and ethical challenges. *Journal of Business Venturing, 24*(5), 519–532. doi:10.1016/j.jbusvent.2008.04.007

Zaki, I. M., & Rashid, N. H. (2016). Entrepreneurship impact on economic growth in emerging countries. *The Business and Management Review, 7*(2), 31–39.

Žalėnienė, I., & Pereira, P. (2021). Higher Education For Sustainability: A Global Perspective. *Geography and Sustainability, 2*(2), 99–106. doi:10.1016/j.geosus.2021.05.001

Zanakis, S. H., Renko, M., & Bullough, A. (2012). Nascent entrepreneurs and the transition to entrepreneurship: Why do people start new businesses? *Journal of Developmental Entrepreneurship, 17*(01), 1–25. doi:10.1142/S108494671250001X

Zeng, J., & Ren, J. (2022). How does green entrepreneurship affect environmental improvement? Empirical findings from 293 enterprises. *The International Entrepreneurship and Management Journal, 18*(1), 409–434. doi:10.100711365-021-00780-4

Zettel, L. A., & Garrett, R. P. (2021). Venture-level outcomes of juggling and struggling. *Journal of Business Venturing Insights, 15*, e00225. doi:10.1016/j.jbvi.2021.e00225

Zhang, C., & Lin, Y. (2012). Panel estimation for urbanisation, energy consumption and CO2 emissions: A regional analysis in China. *Energy Policy, 49*(1), 488–498. doi:10.1016/j.enpol.2012.06.048

Zhao, H., Seibert, S. E., & Hills, G. E. (2005). The Mediating Role of Self-Efficacy in the Development of Entrepreneurial Intentions. *The Journal of Applied Psychology, 90*(6), 1265–1272. doi:10.1037/0021-9010.90.6.1265 PMID:16316279

Zhao, M., Liu, J., & Chenglishu, D. (2021). Pursuing sustainable development through green entrepreneurship: An institutional perspective. *Business Strategy and the Environment, 30*(8), 4281–4296. doi:10.1002/bse.2869

Zhao, X., Shang, Y., & Song, M. (2020). Industrial structure distortion and urban ecological efficiency from the perspective of green entrepreneurial ecosystems. *Socio-Economic Planning Sciences, 72*, 100757. doi:10.1016/j.seps.2019.100757

Zhu, D. (2016). Sustainability science: An object-process-subject analytical framework. *China Popul. Environ., 2016*(26), 1–9.

About the Contributors

Hesham Magd has more than 25 years of combined experience in traditional and nontraditional higher education teaching, training, consultancy, community development, academic administration, curricula design, organizational change and development, distinguished research and scholarly writing, resulting in Honors, awards and recognition for academic excellence and outstanding achievement. Hesham is currently heavily involved in International accreditation and reshaping the aviation education in Oman and offer strategic direction on the direction of the sector In his previous appointments throughout the world in British, European, and American oriented Curriculum (Middle East, USA, and UK), he has been the driving force behind strategic institutional development during the time of profound change in the Higher Education in the Middle East. Hesham has broad knowledge of the UK, USA, Middle East University Systems, and Quality and accreditation systems (AACSB, AABI, OAAA, NCAAA).

Dharmendra Singh is working as a program head (Finance) at Modern College of Business and Science, Muscat (Oman). He possesses a rich professional experience of over 21 years in the field of finance. He holds a Ph.D. (Finance), professional certifications like Certified Financial Planner (CFP), and an associate diploma (life insurance). He has published several articles & research papers in various international and refereed journals listed in ABDC and CABS. His research area includes banking, corporate finance, and entrepreneurship.

Raihan Taqui Syed is a Doctoral Candidate at the School of Management, University of Bradford, UK. Also, he is the Founding Director – the Center for Entrepreneurship & Business Incubation (CEBI) and Program Head – Management, Faculty of Business and Science at Modern College of Business & Science (MCBS), Muscat, Oman.

David Spicer is an Associate Professor at School of Management, University of Bradford, UK. Also, he is the University Enterprise & Entrepreneurship Champion, and Director of Business & Community Engagement.

* * *

Said Khalfan Al Amri is Currently working as Lecturer, Gulf College (Cardiff Met University, UK) Muscat Oman. Worked as Lecturer, Waljat Colleges of Applied Sciences (WCAS), Muscat, Sultanate of Oman, since January 2010 till March 2021. The college was an International Study Centre of BIT Ranchi, MESRA, in Muscat.

Neelufer Aslam is Currently working as Assistant Professor, Gulf College (Cardiff Met University, UK) Muscat Oman. Worked as Assistant Professor, Waljat Colleges of Applied Sciences (WCAS), Muscat, Sultanate of Oman, since October 2007 till July 2020. The college was an International Study Centre of BIT Ranchi, MESRA, in Muscat.

Ujjal Bhuyan works as Assistant Professor, in the Department of Commerce, Jagannath Barooah College, Jorhat, Assam. The author's areas of interest are entrepreneurship and financial planning.

Tarana Afrin Chandel has received her M. Tech degree from UP Technical University, U.P. and B. Tech degree from Magadha University, Bihar in the year 2009 and 2002 respectively and has completed her Ph.D. from Integral University in the month of August 2022. Presently she is working as an Associate Professor in Integral University, Lucknow, U.P.

Ritesh Dwivedi has more than 17 years of working experience with various Development Agencies / Government Projects / Academic Institutions in different positions. He has rich working experience in the area of social entrepreneurship and rural management. He has administered and monitored the functioning of different Social development projects. He has more than 60 research papers / book chapters in his credit, published in refereed Social Science / Management Journals. He has coordinated many batches of TATA Motors Training program and DGR Sponsored ex-servicemen management training programs. He can be reached at https://www.linkedin.com/in/dr-ritesh-dwivedi-74626529/.

Rajashri Kadam is dedicated and passionate faculty working as an Associate Professor and heading a programme of MBA Dual Management at School of Management (PG), MIT World Peace University, and Pune. She has 20 years of experience in Academics and Industry. She has proved her skills as consultant and academic advisor. Her more than 15 research Papers are published in national and International Journals of repute.

Shad Ahmad Khan is a faculty member at the College of Business at the University of Buraimi and leads Professional Development.

Elmar Lins was a Research Assistant and Doctoral candidate at the Chair for Entrepreneurship and Finance at Heinrich Heine University Düsseldorf. His research interests are in the fields of funding criteria for new ventures and applying quantitative empirical methods to shed light on the behaviour of social entrepreneurship. He has gained professional experience as a creator of multiple ventures and assignments in multi-national companies.

Garima Malik is a doctoral scholar of Marketing at Xavier School of Management, XLRI Jamshedpur, India. She has more than eighteen years of academic experience. She is also associated with Amity Business School, Noida, India. Her area of research includes gamification, marketing analytics , customer engagement and customer relationship management. Her research papers are published in various leading journals such as International Journal of Bank Marketing, Tourism Analysis , Journal of Event Management , Information Technology & Tourism, International Journal of Healthcare Management, Journal of Global Marketing, Innovative Marketing, Pacific Asia Journal of the Association for Information Systems, Journal of Science and Technology Policy Management among others. She can be reached at r17002@astra.xlri.ac.in.

Kaneez Masoom is an Assistant Professor of Business Management at School Of Management, BBD University, Lucknow, India. Her research and publications address digital marketing and branding. She is currently working on a series of publications and conference presentations addressing digital marketing, entrepreneurship, brands and consumer behaviour. She is pursuing PhD from Khwaja Moinuddin Chishti language university, Lucknow, India.

Anna Michels was a researcher at Faculty of Human Science at University of Cologne and is currently working as a federal lecturer. Her research interests are in the fields of federal government policy, inequalities, and social disparities from a multi-cultural perspective.

Meenal Pendse is working as an Area head for marketing and Assistant Professor at School of Management (PG) MIT World Peace University, Pune (Only Private University in India with 1st rank in Maharashtra, 26th Rank in India and 426 Rank in world, Under UI Green Metric World in 2021). Her research interests are in Consumer Behavior, Service Quality Management and Marketing Strategy. Dr. Meenal has a Ph.d in Management from R.T.M Nagpur University and M. B. A (Marketing) and B.C.S from University of Pune. With a strong background and diverse skill sets, She is confident in the creative ideas and successful solutions.

Madhuri Shete has three degrees to her credit namely – B.Sc. (statistics), M.B.A. (Marketing) and Ph.D. (Marketing). She is the second topper in B.Sc. (Statistics) at college level. She has an enriched experience of more than 18 years including 5 years' corporate experience and 13 years teaching experience. Her area of expertise includes marketing management, marketing research and research methodology. She has a valuable experience in teaching, research, administration and quality enhancement.

Shweta Shirolkar is an Assistant Professor at Dr Vishwanath Karad MIT World Peace University Pune, India. Her area of interest is Marketing research, Business Research, Research Methodology. She completed her MBA in Marketing and currently pursuing her Ph.D. from Symbiosis International (Deemed University). She has 4.5 years of industry experience in a Research Agency and academic experience of 7.5 years. She has attended and presented papers at various national/international conferences. She has also published Research papers in Journals with ISBN-ISSN. She has also published a Case study on family-owned businesses in Strategic Management Category at et cases listed as their product.

Balvinder Shukla is the Vice-Chancellor of Amity University Uttar Pradesh (AUUP) and Professor of Entrepreneurship with Master's Degree in Technology from Indian Institute of Technology (I.I.T) Kharagpur, PhD in from Queens University Belfast, United Kingdom (U.K). She has 35 years of professional experience in organisations like Shimnit Group, Interra Software, IIHT Systems and Amity Group of Institutions. She has also presented many papers and has organised over 150 seminars, conferences and management development programs. Her Specialty includes Strategic Management, Resource-based strategy, Business Restructuring, Automation, Entrepreneurship, Technology and Innovation Practices. She has recently co-authored a book 'The role of business incubators in the economic growth of India'.

Seema Varshney is Currently working as Assistant Professor, Gulf College(Cardiff Met University, UK) Muscat Oman. Worked as Assistant Professor, Waljat Colleges of Applied Sciences (WCAS), Muscat, Sultanate of Oman, since January 2007 till May 2019. The college was an International Study Centre of BIT Ranchi, MESRA, in Muscat.

Index

M

O

P

R

S

T

V

W

Ensure Quality Research is Introduced to the Academic Community

Become an Evaluator for IGI Global Authored Book Projects

The overall success of an authored book project is dependent on quality and timely manuscript evaluations.

Applications and Inquiries may be sent to:
development@igi-global.com

Applicants must have a doctorate (or equivalent degree) as well as publishing, research, and reviewing experience. Authored Book Evaluators are appointed for one-year terms and are expected to complete at least three evaluations per term. Upon successful completion of this term, evaluators can be considered for an additional term.

If you have a colleague that may be interested in this opportunity, we encourage you to share this information with them.

www.ingramcontent.com/pod-product-compliance
Lightning Source LLC
LaVergne TN
LVHW061540290926
849162LV00004B/863